Visiting the Fallen:
Arras Memorials

Visiting the Fallen: Arras Memorials

Peter Hughes

Pen & Sword
MILITARY

First published in Great Britain in 2015 by
PEN & SWORD MILITARY
An imprint of
Pen & Sword Books Ltd
47 Church Street
Barnsley
South Yorkshire
S70 2AS

Copyright © Peter Hughes, 2015

ISBN 978-1-47382-557-4

Typeset by Concept, Huddersfield, West Yorkshire, HD4 5JL.
Printed and bound in England by CPI Group (UK) Ltd, Croydon CR0 4YY.

Pen & Sword Books Ltd incorporates the imprints of Pen & Sword Archaeology, Atlas, Aviation, Battleground, Discovery, Family History, History, Maritime, Military, Naval, Politics, Railways, Select, Social History, Transport, True Crime, and Claymore Press, Frontline Books, Leo Cooper, Praetorian Press, Remember When, Seaforth Publishing and Wharncliffe.

For a complete list of Pen & Sword titles please contact
PEN & SWORD BOOKS LIMITED
47 Church Street, Barnsley, South Yorkshire, S70 2AS, England
E-mail: enquiries@pen-and-sword.co.uk
Website: www.pen-and-sword.co.uk

Dedication

To Camden – a place of magic and inspiration

Contents

List of Plates

A stonemason at work.

Early days at the Imperial War Graves Commission.

Renovation work on the Vimy Memorial, 1975.

Front elevation of the Canadian Memorial, Vimy Ridge.

Aerial view of the Canadian Memorial, Vimy Ridge, 26 July 1936.

Commemorating the fallen today – Canadian Memorial, Vimy Ridge.

Arras Memorial shortly after completion. The Flying Services Memorial is clearly visible through the archway of the main entrance.

Early evening in late March 2014 – Arras Memorial with Faubourg d'Amiens Cemetery in the foreground.

Arras Memorial and Flying Services Memorial in the early evening sunshine, March 2014.

A family tribute left in March 2014.

Trophies of war – Manfred von Richthofen's collection of identification numbers taken from some of the aircraft of his victims.

Flying Services Memorial – the names of men from the Commonwealth who fell in France and Flanders with the RFC, RNAS and RAF during the war and who have no known grave.

The Vis-en-Artois Memorial, Haucourt, designed by architect John Reginald Truelove.

Detail of the reliefs that adorn the Vis-en-Artois Memorial.

The Vis-en-Artois Memorial – a majestic tribute to almost 10,000 men whose names are inscribed on its walls.

The Vis-en-Artois Memorial. In the late afternoon sunshine the columns of the memorial cast their shadows across the panels containing the names of the fallen.

Acknowledgements

I would like to express my sincere thanks to the following people for their help during various stages of this work.

To Ian Small at the CWGC office in Maidenhead, who had to contend with my frequent requests for photographic material despite having to prepare for the 70th anniversaries of D-Day and Arnhem, as well as the start of the 1914–1918 centenary commemorations. With each request, Ian trawled the CWGC archives producing whatever was available and was never less than helpful.

To Parveen Sodhi at the Imperial War Museum, London, for her courtesy and help regarding the licensing of several of the photographs used to illustrate these books.

To the team at Pen & Sword Books, but especially to Design Manager, Roni Wilkinson, for his support and guidance in the months prior to my submission of the work and for his help in procuring some of the photographs used to illustrate it. Also to Matt Jones who oversaw the production, to Jon Wilkinson who did an amazing job designing the book's cover, and to my editor, Irene Moore, for her guidance and encouragement throughout the final stages.

To Ronelda Peters, part of the team at the Canadian National Memorial, Vimy, for her help regarding matters pertaining to the memorial itself. To Nelly Poignnonnec, Communication and Public Relations Officer at the CWGC in Beaurains, France, for putting aside the time to answer all my questions regarding the work of the Commission and for introducing me to many of the staff and craftsmen at Beaurains who somehow manage to cope with the extraordinary demands placed on the organization from around the world. To Isabelle Pilarowski at the Office de Tourisme, Arras, who shares my own desire to raise the profile of Arras and its battlefields as a key destination on the Western Front – we may yet succeed.

To Barrie Duncan, Assistant Museums Officer, Leisure & Culture, South Lanarkshire Council, who was ever ready to delve into long-forgotten editions of *The Covenanter* and provide information from all corners of the regimental archive. Similarly, thanks go to Sandy Leishman at the Highland Fusiliers HQ, Sauchiehall Street, Glasgow, who was extremely helpful on matters relating to the Highland Light Infantry and the Royal Scots Fusiliers in the Great War. He and Barrie were not the only keepers of regimental archives who gave up their time to answer questions, but both were especially helpful.

To the staff at the reading rooms of the British Library, the National Archives at Kew, the Guildhall Library in the City, and the Imperial War Museum, London, for their courtesy and service during the research phase of this project.

To author David Kent-Lemon, for his kind advice and support as I took my first steps towards having the work published and who was responsible for introducing me to Pen & Sword.

For many entirely different reasons, I should also like to extend recognition and thanks to the following: Hugh Harvey, friend and colleague for many years, who helped iron out some of the last remaining pieces of research required to complete this book. He has toured the Western Front with me since 1993, as have the following: Dave Beck, Jim Wilcox, Sam Oliver, Alan Oliver, Andy Cook, Douglas Mackenzie, Gareth Berry, not forgetting Dennis Harvey and Frank Wilcox, whose company we dearly miss. To Garry Reilly, Phil Hughes, Iain Petrie, Darren Bone, and countless other ex-colleagues from Camden who have been particularly supportive since I retired in July 2010, and who throughout the four years it took to complete this project provided encouragement along the way. A special mention goes to Danielle Louise Mackinnon, another friend and former colleague from Camden, who always believed in my ability to write and who encouraged me to do so, as did Jane Chiarello and Simon Turner. To all those other wonderful friends, whose kind invitations to lunch, etc. I sometimes had to decline and who never once complained. Finally, to Peter Gilhooley, who first introduced me to the Western Front Association in 1981. I made my first trip to the battlefields of France and Belgium with Peter in September that year and continued to tour with him for many years after that. His extensive knowledge and infectious enthusiasm fuelled my early interest in the Great War, an interest that has ultimately led to my writing these three books. If it were not for that initial spark, I might never have been inspired to write them.

This work is also dedicated to the memory of Dave Pilling who one night went out beyond the wire never to return.

Peter Hughes

Introduction

Like Ypres, Arras was briefly occupied by the Germans in the very early days of the war, but the French soon drove them out. For the remainder of 1914, and throughout 1915, French soldiers held a line just east of the town. In March 1916 the sector was handed over to the British who extended their line southwards from La Bassée. Thereafter, Arras remained in British hands. It was only in the final two months of the war, when the fighting drifted eastwards away from the town, that Arras could finally breathe a sigh of relief. It never quite suffered the destruction that Ypres did, though it was frequently subjected to heavy shelling, and in many places its streets and buildings were very badly damaged. It was a town battered and bruised, but essentially still intact. Like Ypres, it had always been a front line town, and for two and a half years it served as 'home' to countless British and Commonwealth soldiers. Both towns shared, and still share, a great deal in common.

Today, Arras receives far fewer visitors to its battlefields than either Ypres or the Somme. I would venture even further and say that, in comparison with the other two, it has been seriously neglected, the one notable exception being the Memorial Park at Vimy Ridge. Here, the tunnels, shell holes, craters, concrete trench reconstructions, and the crowning magnificence that is the Canadian National Memorial, provide sufficient visual stimulus to attract large visitor numbers. Sadly, for many, this is where their visit to the Arras battlefield begins and ends. I sincerely hope that the three books in this series help to change all that.

Prior to the publication of *Cheerful Sacrifice* by Jonathan Nicholls in 1990 it was difficult to find any account of the series of military operations, fought between April and May 1917, known collectively as the Battle of Arras. More recently, and assisted by Jeremy Banning and the Imperial War Museum, Peter Barton produced another fine publication, one of a series of books based on panoramas, 'then' and 'now', in many ways similar in style to the ones written by John Giles in his *Then and Now* series where original photographs were juxtaposed with their modern day equivalents. For several years, before either of these titles appeared, *Prelude to Victory* by Brigadier General Edward Louis Spears was on my bookshelf, along with the indispensable first volume of the *Official History* for 1917, but sadly, that was about it; Arras was truly neglected as a subject.

As for accounts of the 1918 fighting around Arras, these were, and still are, virtually non-existent; similarly with 1916. Leaving aside Norm Christie's short history, *The Canadians at Arras, August–September 1918*, which forms part of his *For King and Empire* series, the only published sources, and not always readily to hand, were individual unit histories, the five volumes of the *Official History* for 1918, together with a handful of Canadian memoirs. With all this in mind, I would like to think that my three books on Arras manage to fill in some of the gaps regarding this neglected part of the Western Front, notwithstanding my slightly unusual approach to the subject. Hopefully, they will complement what little already exists, at least from a British and Commonwealth perspective, and I really hope that people find them a useful addition. Incidentally, any of the above-mentioned works are well worth reading before considering a visit to Arras and its battlefields.

However, unlike these other books, the works that make up *Visiting the Fallen* are not an account of any particular battle that took place around Arras, nor are they a chronological narrative of any of the events that took place there; there is no conventional storyline. So, what exactly are they?

Perhaps the best way is to describe it as a kind of *Who's Who*, though, strictly speaking, that should read: 'Who was Who', since all the 'protagonists' are dead, buried now in one of the many CWGC cemeteries that dot the landscape in and around Arras, or else commemorated nearby on one of the four memorials to the missing. The books are principally concerned with the men who fought and fell around Arras, including, in many cases, the circumstances in which they died; they are, I suppose, simply an expression of remembrance.

Although the work is now divided into three parts: *Arras – North*, *Arras – South*, and *Arras – Memorials*, it was conceived, researched, and originally written as a single project lasting four years, in one continuous 'flow of the pen', as it were. The books are not really guidebooks in any conventional sense of the term.

In the first two books I have tried to outline briefly the nature of each cemetery in terms of size, character, and composition, before taking the visitor through the various plots and rows of graves, halting at many of the headstones where I then talk about the individuals buried there. Similarly, this third volume covering the memorials highlights many of the individuals commemorated at each of the four sites. The books only become 'guidebooks' once the visitor is inside the cemetery itself or standing in front of the memorial.

Each book has also been written with the curious reader in mind. At times, the detail may amount to more than the average visitor requires, but I would much rather leave it to the reader to decide which bits are relevant and which are not. Every headstone and every name on a memorial represents a unique human life, and therefore a unique story. Not all of these stories can be told, but many can, and that is really what the books are about. Although none of the three books provides a chronological narrative of the fighting, I do think that, collectively, they serve to illustrate quite well many aspects of life, and indeed death, on the Western Front. That, at least, was the intention when I wrote them, and partly the inspiration behind them.

In an age of satellite navigation and the internet, reaching any of the cemeteries or memorials should be an easy enough task. The list of CWGC cemeteries and memorials can now be downloaded onto a satellite navigation system and the organization's website now includes the GPS co-ordinates for each site. For anyone not relying on modern technology, I would suggest the 1:100,000 maps produced by the *Institut Géographique National* (IGN). Unfortunately, two of these maps are required: No. 101 'Lille – Boulogne-sur-Mer', and No. 103 'Amiens – Arras'. Investing in both will also come in very handy when visiting other parts of the Western Front. Personally, I would be inclined to run with both systems whenever possible. The Michelin 1:200,000 series, with the CWGC cemeteries and memorials overlaid and indexed, provide a useful pointer, but again two maps, No. 51 and No. 52, are required, and the scale is just a little too small for my liking.

With regard to maps, I know that many people will wonder why I have not included any within the body of my work. This would have been difficult to achieve with any clarity, not least because the actions described are extremely diverse, both in terms of chronology and location. I had to consult well over 200 maps during the course of my research. To condense all the topographical information into a handful of maps would have been virtually impossible, as well as potentially confusing. My own IGN maps, the Blue 1:25,000 series, are entirely overwritten in pencil showing redoubts, trenches, etc. Such detail and scale is essential when walking and describing the battlefields, but perhaps less important in a work whose subject happens to be mainly people. For the really committed visitor, the 1:25,000 series are the ones to go for, though several of them will be required on account of the larger scale.

On a personal note, I have been visiting the battlefields of the Western Front for over thirty years and have been a member of the Western Front Association since 1981. From the very first visit, I have always carried a notebook with me. Anything of interest ends up in the notebook; sometimes a note regarding an individual soldier, or maybe a particular group of headstones; sometimes recurring dates, or perhaps the predominance of a particular regiment in a cemetery; in fact, just about anything unusual or interesting that might be worth pursuing once back home in England with time to research. Very often curiosity pays off, sometimes spectacularly. This has always been my way when visiting the cemeteries and memorials on the Western Front and, at least in part, this is how these three books came to be written. I hope they encourage people to delve a little deeper and to be even more curious when next visiting the battlefields.

Finally, the original title for this work was *Withered Leaves on the Plains of France*. The words are taken from four lines of a poem by Edward Richard Buxton Shanks. While he and others from the Artists' Rifles were drilling in London's Russell Square, in the heart of Bloomsbury, he noticed the autumn leaves swirling on the ground, conscious of the fact that they would soon begin to moulder before turning to mud, and eventually dust. Within that image he saw a clear reflection of his own mortality, and that of his comrades, soon to leave for France and the trenches.

During my former working life I came to know Russell Square very well. Its lawns, flower beds, and the same trees that once stirred Shanks's imagination, formed a pleasant and familiar backdrop; not a place of quiet, but still a place where one could think. Over a period of time, seated outside the café there, I first conceived the idea of writing this work, though only as a single book, never imagining it would emerge as a three volume text. It was there too that I decided to use Shanks's metaphor in the title of the book. For the next four years, as the work took shape, it existed only under its original title until it was eventually changed to *Visiting the Fallen* at the suggestion of my publisher. So much for good intentions and poetic licence! However, let me say at this point that I very quickly warmed to the new title, liking it not least for its simplicity and direct appeal. I still, however, think of the 'Fallen', referred to in the title, as all those 'Withered Leaves'. A hundred years on, it remains a powerful and compelling image.

Arras – Memorials

This volume covers the Arras Memorial and the Flying Services Memorial, both of which share the same site next to the Citadelle in the Faubourg d'Amiens. It also covers the Canadian National Memorial at Vimy Ridge and the Vis-en-Artois Memorial. Together, the four memorials commemorate over 56,000 soldiers of the Great War whose remains have never been found or identified. All four are easy to find and are located on or close to main roads running in and out of Arras, or else on the ring road around the town. I have included the exact location of each in the text.

Although the four memorials have been grouped together for the purpose of this third volume, I appreciate that they are unlikely to be visited in isolation. Most people are likely to visit them in conjunction with a number of cemeteries according to inclination and the time they have available. Unfortunately, the hope of including all four in the previous two volumes – *Arras North* and *Arras South* – was always likely to prove impracticable given the size of those two works already. This book is therefore a companion volume to the other two.

Previous publications that have included memorials to the missing have tended to focus on fairly narrow criteria, often limiting their scope to VC winners, soldiers executed for military offences, a handful of officers, usually of senior rank, along with, perhaps, a few other fairly obvious inclusions. All of those common themes are covered here, but the dedication of an entire volume to the subject gave me the luxury of casting my net much wider and, whilst my choices are necessarily subjective, my aim was always to introduce as much variety and breadth as possible. I would like to think there are as many unsung heroes in the book as there are gallantry award holders, which is something I believe to be one of the distinguishing features of this project as a whole. At any rate, I hope the reader finds the mix both interesting and varied, and occasionally even surprising.

In the case of the Arras Memorial, and also the Vis-en-Artois Memorial, I have followed the regimental running order as it unfurls across each edifice from left to right. This method will prevent the visitor having to wander constantly back and forth in search of individual entries. Not only does it work, it also saves valuable time, and therefore makes perfectly good sense. Having used it many times during the past, it is my preferred method for conducting guided visits to these sites. I have also included guidance on how to tackle the Canadian Memorial at Vimy Ridge, which has its own particular sequence, though in the case of the Flying Services Memorial, this is very compact and easy to deal with regardless of how the visitor approaches it.

I know from experience that many people soon find themselves overwhelmed by the sheer torrent of names on memorials such as these. Within a very short space of time the brain can become de-sensitized, at which point it will simply switch off, often prompting the visitor to make an early exit. This is hardly surprising. Individual names can easily become lost among the crowded panels. Siegfried Sassoon put it rather well when he referred to them as 'these intolerably nameless names', a view with which many others would no doubt agree, although hopefully this volume will go some way towards countering that reaction. I would like to think that people will find plenty here to satisfy their curiosity, and I hope that when they next visit any of these four memorials they are tempted to remain a little while longer. Exploring the lives and stories behind these names should feel a little bit like browsing the shelves of a good bookshop. That, at least, was what I had in mind when I wrote it.

Finally, I should perhaps offer readers some explanation regarding the quotations that appear at the start of each chapter of this book. In the case of *Arras North* and *Arras South* I was able to indulge myself a little with regard to the chapter titles. I have my editor to thank for that. It was she who suggested coming up with a short title for each rather than playing safe and simply numbering them. I was very happy to accept the challenge, and so decided to give it some serious thought. As luck would have it, I happened to be in Aldeburgh at the time. After long walks on the beach and an hour or two in the convivial atmosphere of the White Hart, I felt sufficiently inspired to come up with a list of titles which, despite their quirkiness, seemed to work. Both editor and publisher seemed happy with them, I liked them, and so that was how we went to print.

However, for *Arras Memorials* I wanted to take a slightly different approach. Another possibility began to emerge as I remembered something I had once said while standing with a group of people in a field in France:

> *'We go to gain a little patch of ground*
> *That hath in it no profit but the name.'*

The words, spoken by an anonymous army captain, come from *Hamlet* and were written by William Shakespeare to describe the Battle of Fromelles some 300 years before it actually took place. At least, that was how I prefaced my talk as I went on to describe the events that took place on 19 July 1916 in the very fields where my group and I were standing. Factually, of course, my assertion was ridiculous; Shakespeare was no clairvoyant, but he did have a certain way with words. It was then that the thought occurred to me that he might perhaps like to introduce each of the four chapters in *Arras Memorials*. Well, why not?

Although I have taken the liberty of using all four quotations outside their original context, I still think the words have a particular resonance when used in connection with each of the four memorials. Each memorial makes its own powerful statement, but that impact is often quite difficult to put into words. Most people, myself included, would probably settle for some tired old cliché, which is why, in the end, I decided to turn to someone who had something to say about almost everything and who, moreover, could say it far better than most. If anyone out there knows a better way to sum up the Battle of Fromelles it would be really interesting to hear from them provided, of course, they can do so with the same economy – remember – just eighteen words.

'*What men of name . . .*', which introduces the Arras Memorial, brings with it the idea of the roll call, though when Richmond uses it after the Battle of Bosworth his enquiry concerns only those of noble birth who have fallen rather the common soldier. As for the fate of the common soldier, we have to turn to that arch-cynic, Sir John Falstaff, who disparagingly refers to his men as: '*Food for powder, food for powder, they'll fill a pit as well as better.*' Such sentiments, thankfully, no longer hold sway and my borrowing from Shakespeare is entirely ironic, and deliberately so. To my mind, the decision to commemorate the common soldier alongside his officers on an equal footing regardless of wealth, politics or social standing, is one of the most enduring legacies of the Great War; it is, perhaps, even its greatest legacy.

'*Once in my days I'll be a madcap*' are words spoken by the young Prince Hal in *Henry IV, Part 1*. Throughout the works of William Shakespeare references to aviation are in very short supply, for quite obvious reasons. All kinds of men volunteered for this fledgling arm of warfare, and although not all of them were youthful 'madcaps', there were quite a few of those characters around. Fighting on land and sea was nothing new, but war in the air was a completely different matter and often attracted the more 'adventurous' type. If you ask me, there was always something slightly 'madcap' when it came to fighting in the air, and if anyone embodied the youthful spirit of Prince Hal, and indeed the Royal Flying Corps, it was men like Sidney Edward Cowan. By the time he was killed in action at the ripe old age of 19, Cowan had been awarded not only the Military Cross, but also two bars to go with it, all of them for gallantry. There were, of course, many more like him, men whose courage often bordered on recklessness, whose sinews and nerves were frequently pushed towards breaking point as they risked all, each and every day, in an environment even more strange and unforgiving than the one inhabited by their army and navy comrades.

Among the many fine sculptures on the Canadian National Memorial at Vimy Ridge is the moving figure that represents 'Mother Canada' mourning her dead sons. '*Make dust our paper, and with rainy eyes write sorrow on the bosom of the earth*', are words spoken by Richard II. Though the context may be different, the words seem to reflect perfectly that powerful sense of national grief expressed so eloquently through Allward's portrayal of motherhood and perpetual sorrow. Anyone familiar with that particular sculpture will immediately get the connection.

The Vis-en-Artois Memorial commemorates the dead from many battlefields across Picardy and Artois, from Amiens through to the Armistice. How, then, do we try to sum up that series of encounters with the enemy, that final hard slog to victory when each day, after four long years of war, was essentially a means to an end? Battles still have to be won, even against an enemy close to defeat, and nobody gets to go home until the task has been achieved. '*We are but warriors for the working day*' strikes me as particularly apt, suggesting, as it does, the sense of weariness and resignation that many soldiers would have felt as the Allies edged ever closer to victory. For me, it captures not only that modest, yet heroic sense of duty, but also the commitment and determination to see the job through.

This, then, is the final book in the trilogy that is *Visiting the Fallen*. I have no idea how any of it will be received, but I do know that it has been an enormous pleasure to write. I hope others find equal pleasure in reading it and that all three books prove to be of some practical use. Whatever the reason for your trip, I hope these books help you to get more out of it.

Peter Hughes

Chapter One

'What men of name ...'
The Arras Memorial

The Arras Memorial, designed by architect Sir Edwin Lutyens, with sculptures by Sir William Reid Dick, was unveiled by Lord Trenchard, Marshal of the Royal Air Force, on 31 July 1932. The CWGC register points out that the dedication ceremony scheduled for 15 May was postponed owing to the death of the French President, Joseph Athanase Gaston Paul Doumer, following the successful attempt on his life in Paris on 6 May. He was assassinated by Paul Gorguloff, a Russian émigré suffering from mental illness, whilst attending a book fair. Doumer, who had lost five sons during the war, died in hospital the next day.

The memorial carries the names of almost 35,000 British, South African and New Zealand soldiers who fell in and around Arras during the Great War between spring 1916 and 7 August 1918 and who have no known grave. The CWGC register points out that it does not include soldiers who fell in similar circumstances at Cambrai; they are commemorated on the memorial at Louverval on the main Bapaume–Cambrai road. Members of the Australian Imperial Force and the Canadian Expeditionary Force who have no known grave, and who fell around Arras, are commemorated on the Australian Memorial at Villers-Bretonneux and the Canadian Memorial at Vimy Ridge respectively.

The memorial itself is quietly impressive and is located on the west side of the town on the ring road, the Boulevard Charles de Gaulle. It also sits next to the Citadelle, an equally impressive fortification and garrison, built by the military architect, Vauban, during the latter part of the seventeenth century.

I accept that many people will visit the memorial with a specific purpose in mind, perhaps to remember a relative whose name is inscribed on it, or maybe in connection with a particular regiment or battalion. However, there are many individuals commemorated on it whose stories may also be of interest and I hope that every visitor will take just a little more time to search out some of the names that I have opted to highlight. The way I have chosen to approach the memorial is to start at the north end and work from left to right. In this way, the visitor will avoid constantly having to move to and fro from one part of the memorial to the other, which soon becomes very tiresome and is best avoided.

The names are collated and recorded in the usual way for British memorials of this nature, in other words, by regimental order. Within that framework the names appear in descending order: firstly by rank, and secondly by alphabetical order within each rank. On a very practical note, it is often best to visit the memorial during the morning or early afternoon, particularly if the day is bright and sunny. Broadly speaking, the panels containing the names are west facing, and although some are partially shaded by the columns along the northern colonnade, the names can sometimes be difficult to read in very bright sunlight.

There are eleven holders of the VC commemorated here, and even one MBE, along with nineteen men with the DSO, eighty-seven with the DCM, 137 with the MC and 542 with the MM. Several of the above have bars to their original award. There are also six holders of the MSM, the Meritorious Service Medal, and one holder of the Territorial Decoration, the TD. The highest rank is that of lieutenant colonel, and there are eleven commemorated here, followed by twenty-seven majors, and so on.

Some regiments have no men listed here, but several have over 700, such as the Duke of Wellington's (West Riding) Regiment, the East Yorkshire Regiment, the Essex Regiment, the Machine Gun Corps (Infantry), the Gordon High-landers and the Royal Scots. A few regiments even have over 1,000 names inscribed, for example, the Middlesex Regiment, the West Yorkshire Regiment, the Northumberland Fusiliers, and finally, the Royal Fusiliers with 1,411.

The Royal Marine Light Infantry

Captain George GIBBINS, 2nd Battalion, Royal Marine Light Infantry, was killed in action near Havrincourt on 23 March 1918, aged 35. He had been soldiering for sixteen years and had seen action at Antwerp in 1914, and again at Gallipoli the following year, before returning to the Western Front. He was killed in action when the battalion came under heavy artillery and machine-gun fire. His battalion commander, Lieutenant Colonel Farquarson MC, was also badly wounded that day and was evacuated back to Dernancourt where he died the next day. He is buried at Dernancourt Communal Cemetery Extension.

Second Lieutenant Edward Wilmer COLLIER MC, 2nd Battalion, Royal Marine Light Infantry, was killed in action on 22 March 1918. I can find no trace of his MC in any of the gazettes. The Royal Naval casualty roll also makes no reference to his MC. Another officer from his battalion, Second Lieutenant Stanley Newson WITTING, was killed in action with him and is commemorated here on the memorial.

Serjeant Alfred Bert BARFOOT, 2nd Battalion, Royal Marine Light Infantry, was killed in action on 28 April 1917, aged 29. He is another soldier whose military career had taken him to some unusual locations in pursuit of British interests. Between 1908 and 1909 he took part in the Somaliland Expedition, which was followed immediately by service in the Persian Gulf between 1909 and 1914.

Private Gilbert LEWIS, 2nd Battalion, Royal Marine Light Infantry, was killed in action on 28 April 1917. The CWGC register notes that he was a former chorister at York Minster and an organist and chorister at St Luke's Church in York.

The Royal Naval Volunteer Reserve

Lieutenant Charles Percy ASBURY, Hood Battalion, Royal Naval Volunteer Reserve, was killed in action near Gavrelle on 23 April 1917, aged 22. He had previously served in Gallipoli.

Lieutenant Frank Oliver FORRESTER MC, Hawke Battalion, Royal Naval Volunteer Reserve, was killed in action on 25 March 1918. His MC was gazetted on 26 January 1917 and was awarded for conspicuous gallantry in action after he led a party of twenty men into an enemy trench with great gallantry, capturing 129 prisoners in a fine display of coolness and courage.

Sub Lieutenant Donald Frank BAILEY, Hood Battalion, Royal Naval Volunteer Reserve, was killed in action on 23 April 1917, aged 23. In August 1914 he went to France with Lady Dudley's Hospital, but from April 1915 until his death he served in the Hood Battalion, Royal Naval Volunteer Reserve. The Australian Voluntary Hospital was proposed and set up by Lady Rachel Dudley, wife of the 2nd Earl of Dudley. It arrived in France at the end of August 1914, but within days was forced to move from Le Havre to Saint-Nazaire as the German advance continued through France and Belgium. However, by 6 September it had begun to treat casualties from the early fighting and eventually moved to Wimereux, where it remained as an independent unit until it became part of No. 32 Stationary Hospital in 1916. At the beginning it was staffed by Australian doctors and nurses who had been working in Britain and had volunteered their services in support of the war effort. Lady Dudley was awarded the CBE for her services during the war, but unfortunately drowned in Ireland whilst bathing in the sea in 1920.

Sub Lieutenant John Francis St Clair BARTON, Hood Battalion, Royal Naval Volunteer Reserve, was killed in action on 13 March 1918, although the precise circumstances of his death remain obscure. He was one of very few casualties sustained by his division during the early part of March, but the divisional history acknowledges that he was one of several fine officers who fell during this period. The day prior to his death the Germans had put down a heavy bombardment on the Flesquières salient using gas shells. The division's frontage there was liberally dowsed with mustard gas, which was not in itself fatal, but did cause severe blistering and could lead to internal bleeding, particularly if residue settled on the lining of the respiratory system. In those cases the patient would invariably suffer severe breathing difficulties and die, often in agony. (Addenda Panel)

Petty Officer James INGLIS, Drake Battalion, Royal Naval Volunteer Reserve, was killed in action on 25 March 1918, aged 20. The Royal Naval casualty roll shows his unit as 190 Brigade, Light Trench Mortar Battery, although he was attached to the Drake Battalion when he died. He also held the *Croix de Guerre* (Belgium) which was gazetted posthumously on 14 September 1918. His brother, Serjeant Thomas Inglis, 12th Durham Light Infantry, was killed in action on 10 October 1916, aged 33, and is commemorated on the Thiepval Memorial.

Able Seaman John George HESLOP, 'A' Company, Hood Battalion, Royal Naval Volunteer Reserve, was killed in action on 24 March 1918, aged 29. His brother, Private William Andrew Heslop, was killed in action on 9 November 1915, aged 20, serving with the 1/7th Durham Light Infantry. He is buried at Houplines Communal Cemetery Extension. The brothers came from South Shields.

The Household Battalion

Captain Cecil Herbert BODINGTON, Household Battalion, was killed in action on 11 April 1917, aged 37. The CWGC record omits one of his first names – 'Wyndham'. He was educated at Charterhouse School, then at King's School, Canterbury, where he played rugby, but especially excelled at cricket. He later went on to play first class cricket for Hampshire. He continued his education at Peterhouse College, Cambridge, after which he went to India, working as a private tutor. He then returned to England where he carried on teaching, but in November 1914 he obtained a commission in the Royal Horse Guards, and in September 1916 he was transferred to the Household Battalion. He was killed by machine-gun fire whilst supporting the ill-fated attack on Roeux and Greenland Hill by the 1st Royal Irish Fusiliers and the 2nd Seaforth Highlanders on 11 April 1917.

Lieutenant Humphrey Herbert Orlando BRIDGEMAN, Household Battalion, was killed in action on 11 May 1917, aged 26. He had previously served in German South-West Africa and was the son of Brigadier General the Honourable Francis Charles Bridgeman, who had been a colonel in the Scots Guards and also the MP for Bolton between 1885 and 1895. Humphrey's grandfather was Orlando George Charles Bridgeman, 3rd Earl of Radford.

Second Lieutenant D'Urban John TYRWHITT-DRAKE, Household Battalion, was killed in action on 3 May 1917, aged 21. His parents were from South Africa, which is where he had his first experiences as a soldier. The CWGC register notes that he had taken part in the Rebellion, presumably a reference to the Boer, or Maritz, Rebellion in 1914, as well as the campaign in German South-West Africa. The family's ancestral home was a large house on the edge of Amersham in Buckinghamshire, known as 'Shardeloes'.

Another member of the family, Captain Thomas Victor Tyrwhitt-Drake, was killed in action on 29 January 1917 serving with the 1st Rifle Brigade. He is buried at Fins New British Cemetery, Sorel-le-Grand. He was killed when an enemy shell landed next to him.

Thomas was educated at Harrow, followed by the Royal Military College, Sandhurst, and was gazetted to the 5th Rifle Brigade in late November 1915, although he did not go to France until July the following year. One of the many tributes paid to him after his death came from a fellow officer who recalled that he had once played a key part in driving back an enemy attack by hurling bombs passed to him by his men.

The CWGC records also show a member of the family who died whilst serving with Australian forces on 3 December 1945. Captain John Tyrwhitt-Drake, who lived in Australia with his wife, is buried in Springvale War Cemetery, Melbourne.

The Cavalry

There are 117 entries on the memorial relating to cavalrymen. The Essex Yeomanry has the highest number of casualties recorded here with twenty-eight names, followed by the 10th (Prince of Wales's Own Royal) Hussars with twenty-five, then the 3rd (Prince of Wales's Own) Dragoon Guards with twenty. All three regiments were, of course, significantly involved in the events surrounding the capture of Monchy-le-Preux on 11 April 1917 and the area just to the south of the village near the Arras–Cambrai road. The other yeomanry regiment likely to be of interest is the Northamptonshire Yeomanry, which has seven casualties recorded on the memorial. Its capture of the river crossings at Fampoux on the opening day of the Battle of Arras was a small, but very important tactical success that demonstrated how, in certain circumstances, the flexibility and mobility of cavalry units could still prove useful on the battlefield. The Machine Gun Corps (Cavalry) also has thirteen entries here.

Captain Francis Charles LACAITA MC, 17th Lancers (Duke of Cambridge's Own), was killed in action on 3 April 1918, aged 30. He was seconded to his brigade's machine-gun company in February 1916. His MC was awarded for conspicuous gallantry in action after he had made a reconnaissance of a position and then brought his machine gun into action in time to cover the infantry's advance, setting a fine example of courage and coolness throughout the entire operation. The award was gazetted on 3 March 1917.

His father, Charles Carmichael Lacaita, was a respected botanist and had once served as the MP for Dundee. Sir James Lacaita KCMG, Francis's grandfather, was born in Italy, but came to Britain following the restoration of Bourbon rule, initially settling in Edinburgh. He continued to be involved in Anglo-Italian politics throughout his life and was professor of Italian at Queen's University, New York, for three years during the mid-1850s. In academic circles he was acknowledged as something of an authority on Dante.

Second Lieutenant Norman Otto Frederick GUNTHER MC, Royal East Kent (Duke of Connaught's Own) Yeomanry, attached 6th East Kent Regiment (The Buffs), was killed in action on 12 July 1917, aged 19. His battalion was occupying a series of trenches and posts east of Monchy-le-Preux following an unsuccessful raid on some German posts. He was killed defending a position there when it came under counter-attack.

He had been commissioned in the regiment in September 1915. His MC was gazetted on 20 July 1917 and was awarded for conspicuous gallantry and devotion to duty, leading his platoon forward under heavy machine-gun fire in support of a company that was in danger of being overwhelmed by enemy counter-attacks. He was eventually compelled to withdraw from his isolated position after an heroic defence of it and successfully fought his way back with one officer and eight other survivors.

His brother, Lieutenant Charles Emil Gunther, 2nd Life Guards, attached Guards Machine Gun Regiment, was also killed during the war and fell on 24 September 1918, aged 28. He is buried at Chapelle British Cemetery, Holnon. When the war broke out Charles returned home from Argentina to enlist and Norman left Eton to do likewise. Although their parents were descended from German families, neither boy was in any doubt about his decision to fight for the British Empire. Their father, Charles Eugene Gunther, was a banker, but was also the man behind the creation and marketing of the 'Oxo' cube.

Lieutenant Colonel Oliver Cyril Spencer WATSON VC DSO, Middlesex Hussars, commanding the 2/5th King's Own (Yorkshire Light Infantry), was killed in action on 28 March 1918, aged 41. He was educated at St Paul's School, then at the Royal Military College, Sandhurst, before serving with the 2nd Yorkshire Regiment in India. He took part in the Tirah Campaign, on the North-West Frontier, where he was wounded, and he also served in China during the Boxer Rebellion. He retired in 1904, but remained on the reserve of regular officers, and in 1909 he joined the 1st County of London Yeomanry. In the Great War he initially served at Gallipoli, but then returned to England to become second-in-command of the 2/5th King's Own (Yorkshire Light Infantry). He went to France with the battalion in 1917 and was wounded at Bullecourt on 3 May 1917.

His DSO, gazetted on 26 July 1917, was awarded for conspicuous gallantry, reorganizing men from several units, inspiring them by his own example of coolness, and confidently leading them forward in a second attack during which he was severely wounded. His VC was won near Rossignol Wood on 28 March 1918. As the Germans continued to apply pressure at that location, a counter-attack was made, initially halting the enemy's advance. However, his battalion's position consisted only of two improvised strongpoints and, realizing that immediate action was required, he led his small reserve of men in a further counter-attack. During that attack he organized bombing parties and led several assaults under intense fire. Finally, outnumbered, he ordered his men to retire, though he remained behind in a communication trench to cover their withdrawal. It was here that he was eventually killed. The citation concludes by stating that his counter-attack had been delivered at a critical moment and that his actions and self-sacrifice had undoubtedly saved that part of the line.

Private Frank Ellis BUNTING, Essex Yeomanry, was killed in action on 11 April 1917, aged 32. His parents, Isaac and Annie, are shown in the CWGC register as residing in Colchester and Vancouver, but he was born in Japan. He had been living there before the war and had to return to England from Japan in order to enlist. Vancouver was where his parents settled after the war, but they had spent most of their married life with their four children in Yokohama, Japan, where the family business was the growing and exporting of Japanese lilies. The business,

William Bunting & Sons, had been started in Colchester by Frank's grand-father, William, and had since earned a world-wide reputation for its bulbs, some of which were sent back to adorn the public spaces of Colchester, including Castle Park.

Squadron Serjeant Major William C. HOWARD DCM, Essex Yeomanry, was killed in action on 11 April 1917. He won his DCM for his gallant conduct as a serjeant on 13 May 1915 near Ypres following a successful counter-attack. After the attack, and although entirely isolated, he held on to his position with thirty men until after dark when he was ordered to withdraw.

The Royal Field Artillery
Major Frank William DUST MC, Royal Field Artillery, was killed in action on 23 April 1917, aged 27. His MC was gazetted on 11 December 1916 and was awarded for conspicuous gallantry in action after he had commanded and handled his battery with great courage and ability during operations, later retrieving two guns from front line trenches under most trying conditions. Before the war he had been a solicitor in Sheffield. He was killed in action near Lens.

Major Noel William FREEMAN MC, 68th Battery, 14 Brigade, Royal Field Artillery, was killed in action on 21 March 1918, aged 33. His MC was gazetted on 3 June 1918 in the King's Birthday Honours List. He was one of eight children, six of whom were boys, two of whom fell during the war. He attended Charterhouse School and University College, Oxford, before becoming a barrister.

His brother, Major Russell Herbert Freeman MC, who was killed in action on 21 July 1918 serving with the Royal Air Force, was also awarded the *Croix de Guerre* (France). Russell, who had previously served with the Worcestershire Regiment, is buried at Raperie British Cemetery, Villemontoire. Another brother, Max, finished his military career as a lieutenant colonel. However, it was another one of Noel's brothers, Wilfrid Rhodes Freeman GCB DSO MC, and three times mentioned in despatches, who went even further by becoming an Air Chief Marshal in the Royal Air Force. Wilfrid had initially served in the Manchester Regiment before he transferred to the Royal Flying Corps. In 1936, as Air Member for Research and Development, he was responsible for choosing the type of aircraft with which to equip the Royal Air Force as the prospect of another war with Germany began to loom ever closer. As such, he played a leading role in the emergence and development of the Hurricane, the Spitfire, the Mosquito, the Lancaster and the Halifax. In 1940 his department took on the responsibility for aircraft production. He was created a baronet in 1945.

Captain John Douglas BROOKSMITH MC, 47 Brigade, Royal Field Artillery, was killed in action on 21 March 1918. His MC was won as a lieutenant and was awarded for conspicuous gallantry during operations in which, on two occasions, he carried out difficult and dangerous reconnaissance patrols under heavy shell fire, sending back reports of an excellent standard. The award was gazetted on 20 October 1916.

Lieutenant O'Moore Charles CREAGH, 'C' Battery, 108 Army Brigade, Royal Field Artillery, was killed in action on 23 March 1918, aged 21. He was educated at Cheltenham College before going on to the Royal Military Academy, Woolwich. He was commissioned in the Royal Field Artillery in February 1915 and went to France two months later in April. He was wounded in the head whilst serving with the 67th Trench Mortar Battery and spent seven months in England recovering before he returned to the front in July 1916. He was killed in action near the village of Feuillaucourt, north of Mont Saint-Quentin, just outside Péronne. His distinguished service and gallantry in the field were recognized posthumously when he was mentioned in despatches on 21 May 1918.

He was the son of Charles Vandeleur Creagh CMG, of County Clare, who had previously served as Governor of British North Borneo. O'Moore's brother, James Vandeleur Creagh, was awarded the DSO in 1918 whilst serving as a commander in the Royal Navy and went on to become rear admiral.

He was also the nephew of Sir O'Moore Creagh VC GCB GCSI (1848–1923), co-author of *The Distinguished Service Order 1886–1923*, who had won his VC as a captain between 12 and 22 April 1879. It was awarded for outstanding leadership and determination after he had taken a detachment of around 150 men to the village of Kam Dakka on the Kabul River in order to defend it from a threatened incursion by Mohmand tribesmen. When the village was attacked by a force of around 1,500, the villagers joined forces with the attacking Mohmands, forcing Creagh to retire to the cemetery. Using the position as a redoubt, he made a stand there, repelling several attacks at the point of the bayonet until a relief force arrived. The enemy forces were then driven back across the river.

In addition to the VC, he also held the Order of the Rising Sun (Japan) and served as Secretary of the Military Department at the India Office between 1907 and 1909, then as commander-in-chief in India between 1909 and 1914. He also held the rank of Knight of Grace of the Order of St John of Jerusalem. Through his mother's side of the family he was related to General Sir Thomas Picton, the most senior British officer killed at the Battle of Waterloo.

Lieutenant James Henry VAN DER BURGH, 6 (London) Brigade, Royal Field Artillery, was killed in action on 21 May 1916, aged 23. His parents lived at No. 8, Kensington Palace Gardens, London, which was then, as it is now, a very fashionable part of London. His father was a knight of the Netherlands and a prominent businessman and philanthropist with interests in the art world.

Serjeant Charles DUFFUS MM and Bar, 88 Brigade, Royal Field Artillery, was killed in action on 21 March 1918, aged 27.

Serjeant William WALLACE DCM, 'A' Battery, 250 Brigade, Royal Field Artillery, was killed in action on 23 April 1917, aged 25. He had formerly served with the Northumbrian Field Artillery. His DCM was gazetted on 25 November

1916 and was awarded for conspicuous gallantry in action after extinguishing a fire in an ammunition store and removing ammunition at great personal risk, thereby saving many lives.

Gunner Archibald BARCLAY DCM MM, 41st Battery, 42 Brigade, Royal Field Artillery, was killed in action on 9 October 1917, aged 22. His DCM was gazetted on 13 February 1917 and was awarded for conspicuous gallantry in action after he repeatedly went out alone and mended the telephone lines under intense fire. On one occasion he repaired the line in seventeen places, and later brought a wounded man in to safety.

The Royal Garrison Artillery

Major Thomas Wedderspoon ALEXANDER, Royal Garrison Artillery, attached 'B' Battery, 255 Brigade, Royal Field Artillery, was killed in action on 21 March 1918, aged 34, and had previously been mentioned in despatches. Before the war he had been a solicitor on Rothesay, where he had also served as Deputy Clerk of the Peace and Sheriff Clerk of Buteshire.

Major Eustace Charles De NEUFVILLE DSO, 262nd Siege Battery, Royal Garrison Artillery, was killed in action near Vaulx Vraucourt on 21 March 1918. He also held the *Croix de Guerre* (Belgium). He was educated at Charterhouse School and New College, Oxford. Before the war he had embarked on a legal career and was a pupil at the Middle Temple before being called to the Bar. His DSO was gazetted in the New Year's Honours List on 1 January 1918.

Major Owen WAKEFORD MC, 76th Siege Battery, Royal Garrison Artillery, died of wounds on 21 March 1918. I can find no trace of his MC in any of the gazettes, though it is acknowledged in *Officers Died in the Great War*. His name appears in the *London Gazette* on 20 September 1917 with reference to performing the role of acting major, but there is no mention of the MC or any other decoration.

Gunner Archibald Frederick SMITH, 99th Siege Battery, Royal Garrison Artillery, was killed in action on the opening day of the Battle of Arras, 9 April 1917. His late father had also served as a battery serjeant major in the Royal Garrison Artillery.

The Royal Engineers

Major Austin Hanbury BROWN DSO MC, 2nd Field Company, Royal Engineers, was killed in action on 27 March 1918, aged 31. He was the son of Sir Robert Hanbury Brown KCMG and Lady Brown of Newlands, Crawley Down, Sussex. He was born in Cairo where his father worked on irrigation projects with the Royal Engineers between 1884 and 1903. Austin followed in his father's footsteps and spent some time in India, also working on projects involving water supply, before taking up a commission in the Royal Engineers in 1906.

At the outbreak of war Austin was back in Egypt, but was sent to France soon afterwards, on 5 November 1914, with the 2nd Field Company, Royal Engineers. His MC was gazetted on 14 January 1916. His DSO, gazetted on 4 February 1918, was awarded for conspicuous gallantry and devotion to duty whilst in charge of track construction prior to operations. The citation notes that his example and determination had ensured that the work was completed on time in spite of heavy shell fire, adding that his skilful organization had also enabled casualties to be kept to a relatively small number.

He married in January 1918, but was killed near Rosières during the German March Offensive. He was also mentioned in despatches on four occasions.

Brevet Major Malcolm Roy WINGATE DSO MC, 459th Field Company, Royal Engineers, was killed in action near Lagnicourt on 21 March 1918, aged 24. He was the second son of General Sir Reginald Wingate GCB GCVO GBE KCMG DSO DCL, 1st Baronet, who served as Sirdar of the Egyptian Army and Governor General of the Sudan between 1899 and 1916, and also as High Commissioner of Egypt between January 1917 and October 1919. In 1916 Sir Reginald was the General Officer Commanding the Hedjaz Operations during the Arab Revolt in which T.E. Lawrence played no small part.

His son, Malcolm, was commissioned in the Royal Engineers in April 1913 and went to France on 14 August 1914 where he took part in the Retreat from Mons, as well as actions on the Marne and the Aisne, and also at the First Battle of Ypres, serving with the 26th Field Company, Royal Engineers. In February and March the following year he was mentioned in despatches, and his MC was also gazetted in February that year. His DSO followed soon after that and was gazetted on 10 March 1915 in recognition of his conspicuous gallantry on numerous occasions under dangerous conditions, but especially at Givenchy on 27 January 1915 after leading a small party and blowing in the head of an enemy sap at a location known as the White House.

In April 1915 he was appointed staff captain to the engineer-in-chief at GHQ in France, where he remained until early 1917 when he asked to return to operational duties with a field company. By this time his services had also been recognized by the award of the *Croix de Guerre* with Palms (France), gazetted on 12 December 1916. He was again mentioned in despatches in May and December 1917, and was appointed brevet major on 1 January 1918. His death occurred whilst in command of the 459th Field Company, leading his men to forward positions during an enemy attack.

Captain John Benbow FABER MC, 1/3rd London Field Company, Royal Engineers, was killed in action on 18 September 1916. His MC was gazetted on 3 June 1916 in the King's Birthday Honours List.

Captain Percy Neil WHITEHEAD MC, 174th Tunnelling Company, Royal Engineers, was killed in action on 21 March 1918, aged 29. According to the war diary, he and another officer were working with fifteen other men when the enemy broke through their position on the morning of 21 March. He was shot through the head as he and Second Lieutenant R.A. Macdonald, together with the others, tried to hold the gap in the line. WHITEHEAD had already seen action in German South-West Africa as a trooper with the South African Light Horse before serving on the Western Front and had been wounded at Fricourt in 1916. Before the war he had studied at Clare College, Cambridge, where he represented his college at football and cricket. I can find no trace of his MC in any of the gazettes, though it is acknowledged in *Officers Died in the Great War* and in the roll of honour for Clare College.

Captain Raymond Burke WILLIAMS MC, 176th Tunnelling Company, Royal Engineers, was killed in action on 19 September 1916, aged 29. His MC was won as a second lieutenant and was awarded for conspicuous gallantry at Givenchy on 25 August 1915 whilst in charge of a mining operation. After the mine had been blown in, he immediately went down into the gallery to evacuate it on account of the concentration of gas fumes. Once there, he carried out the rescue of several men until he himself was overcome by the fumes, at which point he had to be dragged out. As soon as he had recovered, he went halfway down in order to direct further rescue attempts. The citation also notes that he had been in charge of mines in the Givenchy area since early July 1915 and had consistently shown the greatest coolness during difficult operations that called for the rapid charging and detonation of mines in very close proximity to the enemy's counter-mines. The award was gazetted on 2 October 1915.

Second Lieutenant Louis Charles Bowden MACKINNON, 518th Field Company, Royal Engineers, is recorded as having died on 23 March 1918, aged 30. On 21 March he had gone forward to blow up bridges in order to check the enemy's advance, but he and his men were surrounded. He may well have died of wounds two days later as a prisoner of war. He had also been a member of University of London OTC.

Second Lieutenant Alec SEARLE, 202nd Field Company, Royal Engineers, was killed in action on 23 April 1917, aged 26. In civilian life he had been an engineer and was an Associate Member of the Institute of Civil Engineers.

Company Serjeant Major Jacob BROOKS MM, 467th Field Company, Royal Engineers, was killed in action on 21 March 1918, aged 31, near the village of Écoust. He was killed by shell fire during the intense bombardment that preceded the German Offensive that day when the entire front of the 59th (2nd North Midland) Division collapsed. His body was never recovered.

He was a police officer in Derby before the war and had also served in Ireland with the Royal Engineers before going to France in February 1917. He saw action at Ypres later that year and was awarded the MM for bravery in the field in connection with his work during the fighting around the Menin Road and Polygon Wood in September. His MM was gazetted on 28 January 1918. His police background and associated skills no doubt provided the foundation for his promotion from sapper to company serjeant major.

Company Serjeant Major Alfred Bailey SWALLOW, 470th Field Company, Royal Engineers, was killed in action on 21 March 1918, aged 37. He held the Long Service and Good Conduct Medal and had served in India where he also received the Delhi Durbar Medal. This medal was issued to around a quarter of those serving in India in 1911 to mark the Coronation of King George V. His field company also formed part of the 59th (2nd North Midland) Division.

Corporal Paul Alfred BENCE MM, 95th Field Company, Royal Engineers, was killed in action on 6 May 1917. His unit formed part of the 7th Division. Before the war he moved from Bath to the Rhondda where he worked in the coal mines. His MM was awarded in connection with his work during the Battle of the Somme in 1916. He was working near Bullecourt when he was killed by a shell.

Second Corporal Robert SUTHERLAND, 'J' Special Company, Royal Engineers, was killed in action on 22 March 1918, aged 28. He was academically gifted and had gained a Master's degree in Mathematics in 1912, followed by a Bachelor of Science degree from Aberdeen University in 1915. He then spent a brief period teaching science at Inverurie Academy before joining the Royal Engineers in 1916. His science background made him an ideal candidate for one of the sixteen engineer companies formed after the Battle of Loos when the original four specialist gas companies were expanded. The original four companies were formed in July and August 1915 in response to the German use of chlorine gas in April that year. He was also a keen pianist, and whenever he was out of the line he would take every possible opportunity to play.

Pioneer George William ASHBY, 3rd Field Survey Company, Royal Engineers, was killed in action on 28 March 1917. Field Survey Companies specialized in carrying out topographical surveys, especially with regard to mapping, but they also worked closely with the artillery on matters such as observation and sound ranging.

The Grenadier Guards
According to the CWGC register, Lieutenant Colonel Percy Archer CLIVE DSO, 1st Grenadier Guards, was killed in action on 4 April 1918, aged 35, commanding the 1/5th Lancashire Fusiliers. However, the regimental histories of the Grenadier Guards and the Lancashire Fusiliers both show his death occurring on 5 April. He was killed during a counter-attack on the village of Bucquoy. On hearing that Captain W.G. Sutton, 1/8th Lancashire Fusiliers, had been wounded, Lieutenant Colonel CLIVE made his way over to ascertain the situation on his colleague's frontage, taking stretcher-bearers with him to attend to Sutton. Unfortunately, CLIVE was killed soon afterwards. He was twice mentioned in despatches and had been awarded the *Légion d'Honneur* and the *Croix de Guerre* (France).

His mother was the youngest daughter of the 7th Earl of Denbigh. He was educated at Eton and Sandhurst, and served as MP for South Herefordshire from 1908 until his death. Destined for a military career, he entered the Grenadier Guards in 1891 and served with the regiment in West Africa, taking part in the expedition to Annan. In 1899 he accompanied the regiment to South Africa where he served until 1901. He rejoined the colours on 5 August 1914 and by November that year he was with his old regiment in the trenches.

His *Légion d'Honneur* was presented to him in April 1915 by General Joffre. The trenches to the right of the Grenadiers' position were held by the French and a section had recently been captured by the Germans. A French party had been sent over to recover them, but no news had been received as to whether any of the party had managed to reoccupy them. The French proposed sending a reconnaissance party out to try to clear up this uncertainty and asked permission for the party to leave via trenches occupied by the 1st Grenadier Guards. This was a sensible precaution, as the Germans opposite the French section were likely to be on heightened alert.

Captain CLIVE volunteered to lead the French patrol and took with him Major Foulkes of the Royal Engineers. When they entered the enemy's trenches they found them to be unoccupied, although a dug-out contained equipment and two burning candles, indicating that it its occupants were probably not far away. The garrison was soon located in a connecting trench, and when CLIVE and the others were challenged, it became very clear that the only occupants were Germans. He and Major Foulkes managed to regain their own lines under a blaze of rifle fire, and were able to bring back good first-hand intelligence regarding the enemy's trench system. He was also mentioned in Sir John French's despatch that same month.

On 6 August 1915 he was wounded in the head whilst leading a working party at Givenchy. When two mines were exploded very close by, the debris completely buried Second Lieutenant Crookshank and the blast knocked CLIVE off his feet, injuring him. However, when assistance arrived, he still had the presence of mind to indicate where he believed Crookshank to be. Thanks entirely to his intervention, Crookshank was dug out relatively unscathed, but his own injuries were serious enough for him to be invalided home.

In May the following year he was promoted to lieutenant colonel and joined the 7th East Yorkshire Regiment as its commanding officer. Later that year, on 3 November 1916, he was again seriously wounded near Le Transloy, this time suffering a fractured thigh and a wound to the shoulder. He was sent home to recuperate, and whilst there he served briefly with the Southern Army at Brentwood, Essex, before returning to the front. He was again mentioned in despatches on 7 November 1917. He then took command of the 1/5th Lancashire Fusiliers on the last day of March 1918, but was killed just a few days later.

He was awarded the *Croix de Guerre* (France), which was gazetted posthumously on 10 October 1918. Curiously, there is no reference to the award of his DSO in *The Distinguished Service Order 1886–1923*, nor is it mentioned anywhere in the three volume regimental history of the Grenadier Guards or the two volume history of the Lancashire Fusiliers. A service of remembrance was held on 5 February 1919 at St Paul's Cathedral to commemorate all officers and men of the Brigade of Guards who fell during the war. His name is included in the roll of honour attached to the order of service, but the DSO does not appear against his name. However, the award is acknowledged in the *House of Commons Book of Remembrance 1914–1918* and in *Officers Died in the Great War*.

He had two sons and three daughters. His elder son, Major Mersey George Dallas Clive, was killed in action serving with the Grenadier Guards in North Africa in May 1943, whilst his second son, Lewis Clive, died in 1938 serving with the International Brigade in the Spanish Civil War. Mersey is buried in Medjez-el-Bab War Cemetery in Tunisia. Lewis has no known grave, but is commemorated on a memorial not far from where he fell during the Battle of Ebro in 1938. He was also an accomplished rower and had won a gold medal in the coxless pairs with Hugh Edwards at the summer Olympics in 1932. He had proposed marriage to Mary Farmar, better known as the author Mary Wesley, who portrayed him as 'Oliver' in her book, *The Camomile Lawn*, which was later adapted for television.

Serjeant Arthur SPOWAGE DCM, 2nd Grenadier Guards, was killed in action on 30 March 1918, aged 27. He was killed in a dug-out when a shell scored a direct hit on it. His DCM was gazetted on 28 March, just two days before his death. The citation records that he took charge of his platoon and led it forward with great determination and under heavy fire after its commanding officer had been wounded early in the attack. He also captured several machine guns, killing the gun teams. Realizing that the flank of the battalion was in the air, he then took his platoon across to fill the gap, consolidating the position under heavy fire and in doing so saved a critical situation from developing. In civilian life he had served as a police officer in Nottinghamshire.

Lance Serjeant Fred CRUNDWELL, 2nd Grenadier Guards, was killed in action on 27 March 1918. His brother, Private George Crundwell, also served with the 2nd Grenadier Guards and was killed in action near Ginchy on 25 September 1916, aged 21. He is buried in the Guards' Cemetery, Lesboeufs.

Private Alec DABELL, 3rd Grenadier Guards, was just 17 years old when he was killed in action on 27 March 1918. He came from Nottingham and had enlisted in 1914 when he was well under the age for joining the army.

The Coldstream Guards
Captain Quincy Shaw GREENE, 3rd Coldstream Guards, was killed in action on 28 March 1918, aged 26. He was an American by birth, but had joined the regiment in March 1915. He was killed by a sniper near the Ayette–Bucquoy Road and was a friend of fellow officer, Carlos Paton Blacker, otherwise often known as 'C.P. Blacker'. Blacker's memoirs were published in 2000 under the title *Have You Forgotten Yet?* GREENE is mentioned several times in the

narrative and was described by the author as '*an irrepressible talker*'. He was not the only American to serve with the Coldstream Guards. Lieutenant Dillwyn Parrish Starr, who is commemorated in the Guards' Cemetery, Lesboeufs, served with the 2nd Battalion and was killed on 15 September 1916.

Lieutenant Rupert Rochfort Molière TABUTEAU, 3rd Coldstream Guards, was killed in action on 28 March 1918, aged 29. His parents, who lived on the Isle of Wight, had several children. One of his sisters, Madeline, served as a nurse during the war. His brother, Reginald Molière Tabuteau, became a lieutenant commander in the Royal Navy and was awarded an OBE on 1 January 1919 for services between 1916 and the end of the war. Prior to that, Reginald had served as Deputy Governor of Parkhurst Prison between 1913 and 1916. We know that Rupert was a former pupil of Haileybury School in Hertfordshire and that he had sailed for Singapore in 1910. He was gazetted from the Special Reserve as a second lieutenant in May 1916 and was killed in action near the road running between Ayette and Bucquoy.

Lieutenant Walter Hugh WHETSTONE, 3rd Coldstream Guards, was killed in action on 28 March 1918, aged 20. His mother became Lady Hiley and lived at Berkeley House, Hay Hill, in London's Mayfair. He was educated at Harrow and the Royal Military College, Sandhurst. He was accepted for New College, Oxford, but never took up his place. He was also killed between Ayette and Bucquoy in the same defensive action in which GREENE and TABUTEAU died.

The Scots Guards
The CWGC records show twenty-nine names from this regiment. All the soldiers listed are NCOs or privates and there is one gallantry award holder amongst them: Serjeant Peter SMART MM, 2nd Scots Guards, who died on 20 May 1918. The majority of those commemorated are from the 2nd Battalion.

The Irish Guards
There are thirty-seven entries for this regiment, including one officer, Second Lieutenant Ernest Hamilton FALLOWS, who was killed in action on 25 March 1918. There are just two gallantry award holders: Sergeant Patrick DONOHOE MM, and Lance Corporal Edward DOONEY MM, both killed in action on 30 March 1918 whilst serving with the 1st Battalion. The men commemorated here are from both battalions of the regiment.

The Welsh Guards
There are just eighteen men listed, including two officers and one gallantry award holder.

Second Lieutenant Evan James DAVIES, 1st Welsh Guards, was killed in action on 28 March 1918 while repelling an enemy attack. Although a pending attack by the enemy was dispersed by our artillery, the Welsh Guards were driven off the high ground north of Boiry-Becquerelle and it was here that DAVIES was killed. The Germans had been massing in Boyelles for their attack against positions held by the 3rd Guards Brigade and had subjected the British lines to a bombardment for over four hours. That attack never materialized, thanks to some fine work by the Royal Field Artillery.

Second Lieutenant Cyril Duncan WHITEHOUSE, 1st Welsh Guards, was killed in action on 26 May 1918, aged 21. He had previously served with the Staffordshire Yeomanry and the Household Battalion and had only been with the 1st Welsh Guards since 13 March 1918. He was reported missing in action after going out on a reconnaissance patrol with eleven of his men. Having entered the enemy's positions, they soon ran into opposition and a fight then occurred at very close quarters. Only four of the eleven managed to escape and even they had to fight to extricate themselves from a difficult situation. The survivors were able to bring back five of those wounded, but Second Lieutenant WHITEHOUSE and two others had to be left behind. The Germans were seen to drag some bodies away from the scene of the fighting, obviously for identification purposes, but the men were already believed to have been killed.

Private Thomas GRIFFITHS MM, 1st Welsh Guards, was killed in action on 10 March 1918. His MM was won in 1917 during the fighting at Ypres. The line held by the battalion consisted merely of shell holes and the threat of enemy counter-attacks was constant. Despite being wounded, GRIFFITHS and two other men remained on duty, although this meant squatting in wet, muddy conditions until relieved. He was killed the following year during a raid on enemy trenches. Efforts to bring in the wounded after the raid were successful, but the bodies of Private GRIFFITHS and Private Lovell EVERSON were unable to be located, although it was already known that they had been killed. Private EVERSON is also commemorated on the memorial.

The Guards Machine Gun Regiment

There is just one soldier commemorated from this regiment: Private Thomas EMMS, 4th Battalion, who was killed on 4 April 1918.

The Royal Scots (Lothian Regiment)

Lieutenant Colonel William GEMMILL DSO, 8th Royal Scots, was killed in action on 25 March 1918, aged 40. He came from East Lothian. In 1899 he joined the Lothians and Berwickshire Yeomanry and served with it in South Africa between 1899 and 1901. In April 1904 he joined the Royal Scots and by 1910 he had risen to the rank of captain. He went to France in November 1914 as second-in-command of the 8th Battalion with the temporary rank of major and on 19 May 1915 he was given the temporary rank of lieutenant colonel. His DSO was gazetted a month later, on 23 June 1915, for distinguished service in the field. He was twice mentioned in despatches, once on 31 May 1915 and again on 1 January 1916.

Occasionally, there is a difference of opinion between regiments in respect of awards, especially awards of the VC where the recipient happens to be attached to another regiment at the time of winning the award. It was in such circumstances, in June 1915, that GEMMILL put pen to paper regarding the award of the VC to Lance Corporal William Angus. Angus was one of 120 men who were posted from the 8th Highland Light Infantry to the 8th Royal Scots for the duration of the war. Based on that fact, GEMMILL claimed that Angus's award should have been included in the list of honours awarded to the Royal Scots rather than the Highland Light Infantry. In some ways he had a point, especially as the 8th Highland Light Infantry was never deployed on overseas service during the war. The 120 men had been posted to the 8th Royal Scots at the end of October 1914 in order to bring it up to establishment before it went over to France. It was GEMMILL who had compiled the account of Angus's deed together with the recommendation that led to the award. It is not hard to see why he felt aggrieved.

GEMMILL had tremendous strength of character and presence and between 21 and 25 March 1918 he demonstrated remarkable leadership time and time again. As a pioneer battalion, the 8th Royal Scots had mostly wielded picks and shovels, but over those four days they showed that under his leadership they were tactically very capable too. On 21 March, just outside Labucquière, he skilfully moved two companies into shell holes rather than the cover offered by a sunken road. His judgement was later proved correct when the German artillery used the sunken road as a marker and poured shells into it. A few days later, from his HQ in a dug-out along the Bancourt–Bapaume road, he exposed himself to danger, rallying remnants of 153 Brigade as they retired and leading them back to their previous positions. He was killed in action on 25 March whilst fearlessly encouraging and directing the men of 'C' Company as they poured fire into the advancing enemy.

Captain James William BROWN MC, 11th Royal Scots, was killed in action on 21 March 1917. He fell during a daring daylight reconnaissance carried out that afternoon near Arras to try to find out whether or not the enemy's positions were strongly held. There was a suspicion that the Germans might be about to carry out a withdrawal and intelligence was required in order to clarify the situation. The reconnaissance was carried out in force and it soon became very apparent that the Germans were still there in some strength and had no intentions of retiring. BROWN and three other officers were killed in the operation.

His MC was awarded for conspicuous gallantry in action. When his battalion was checked in front of uncut wire, he and Second Lieutenant Winchester had rallied the men and led them to the enemy's second line. Later, these two officers organized and carried out a bombing attack that resulted in the capture of sixty-three prisoners. His award was gazetted on 25 September 1916. Coincidentally, both he and Second Lieutenant Winchester had been wounded soon after the battalion had taken over trenches near Festubert in July 1915.

Captain George Thomas McGILL MC, 2nd Royal Scots, was killed in action near Monchy-le-Preux on 3 May 1917, aged 34. He had previously served as colour serjeant with the Royal Scots and was gazetted as a second lieutenant in the regiment on 1 May 1915. He had also performed fine work at Serre during the Battle of the Ancre in November 1916. His MC was gazetted on 25 January 1917 in connection with those operations and was awarded for conspicuous gallantry in action. When one advance had broken down, he reorganized a firing line and led it forward in a second attempt to get through very thick wire. Later he established and held a line within fifty yards of the enemy's trenches.

Captain Gavin Lang PAGAN, 15th Royal Scots (1st Edinburgh Battalion), was killed in action on 23 April 1917 near Roeux. Before the war he had studied at Glasgow University, graduating with a Bachelor of Divinity degree, then a Master's degree. He followed his father by becoming a minister in the Church of Scotland. His father was a Moderator of the General Assembly.

Captain Ernest Gilbert TURNER DSO, 11th Royal Scots, was killed in action on 12 April 1917 when 27 Brigade and the South African Brigade belonging to the 9th (Scottish) Division attacked German positions around Greenland Hill. The attack took place at 5.00pm and was carried out without adequate or effective artillery support. The assembly positions for the attack were the old German trenches that had been captured on the opening day of the Battle of Arras on the rising ground north of Fampoux. The new German defences, which were situated about 1,000 yards further east, were hardly touched by the British barrage. As the 11th and 12th Battalions, Royal Scots, swept down the exposed slopes of the Point du Jour Ridge they were met by machine-gun fire, high explosive and shrapnel shells.

Captain TURNER's DSO was won at Ovillers on 10 July 1916 and was gazetted on 26 September that year. It was awarded for his gallantry during a combined bombing operation with another platoon. Between them they cut off and captured sixty-three prisoners. Two days later, he again did fine and gallant work during an attack, and afterwards returned under close machine-gun fire and rescued several wounded men.

Lieutenant Robert Thorburn ADAMSON, 4th Royal Scots, attached 13th Battalion, was killed in action on 23 April 1917, aged 23, when his battalion attacked south of the River Scarpe astride the Arras–Cambrai road on the opening day of what became known as the Second Battle of the Scarpe. Prior to the war he had gained a Master's degree from Edinburgh University.

Lieutenant William Robert Brown CASEBY MC, Royal Scots, attached 1st Lancashire Fusiliers, had previously served in Egypt and also at Gallipoli. His MC was won whilst serving with the 1st Lancashire Fusiliers and was awarded for his actions on 1 July 1916 when he was heavily involved in his battalion's unsuccessful attempt to reach the German trenches in front of Beaumont Hamel. CASEBY had arrived in the sunken lane opposite Hawthorn Redoubt with about sixty men after the initial assault by 'B' and 'D' companies had broken down. The remnants of 'A' and 'C' companies were gathered up by CASEBY who then led around seventy-five men in a further attempt to reach the German front line near the northern end of the village. He, along with three other officers and around ten other men, managed to reach the scattered shell holes in front of the German trenches, but were pinned down there by heavy fire. The rest of his party had either been killed or were lying wounded in the open ground behind him. Despite the hopelessness of the situation, CASEBY and his party did all they could throughout the day to keep up flanking fire towards Hawthorn Redoubt. That night CASEBY managed to crawl back to the sunken lane with three fellow officers and about twenty other ranks.

He was killed by a shell near Monchy-le-Preux on 25 April 1917 along with his commanding officer, Lieutenant Colonel Magniac, who is buried at Beaurains Road Cemetery.

Lieutenant James Brown KINCAID, 13th Royal Scots, was killed in action on 23 April 1917, aged 27. His brother, Second Lieutenant John Brown Kincaid, 1st Royal Scots Fusiliers, fell ten days later on 3 May. Before the war James had studied at Edinburgh University where he gained his Master's degree. He and his brother came from Berwick.

Second Lieutenant Robert Stephen BARCLAY, 3rd Royal Scots, attached 16th Battalion, was killed in action on 21 March 1918, aged 49. He was originally reported as missing in action whilst defending the line near Croisilles. Prior to the war he had studied Divinity, initially at St Andrew's University, then at Aberdeen University. It was while he was studying at Aberdeen that he became a member of its OTC. He began his career as a church minister, but eventually decided to enlist in December 1915. He was commissioned in July 1916 and went to France in 1917.

Second Lieutenant Laurence CRONEEN, 6th Royal Scots, attached 15th Battalion, is one of five second lieutenants from or attached to that battalion who are listed on the memorial and who were killed in action on 28 April 1917 near Roeux. The others are: William Sinclair MACKENZIE, 4th Royal Scots, attached 15th Battalion, Second Lieutenant Donald MUNRO, and Second Lieutenant Allan Clark WILSON. Second Lieutenant Frederick WESTWATER, 3rd Royal Scots, is shown attached to the 11th Royal Scots in the CWGC register, although he is listed in the regimental history as having been killed in action with the other four.

Second Lieutenant Gilbert Vere Faithfull DAVIES, 13th Royal Scots, is one of six officers from the battalion commemorated on the memorial who were killed in action south of Monchy-le-Preux on 23 April 1917. He was educated at Dulwich College and is a great uncle of the singer, songwriter and actress, Marianne Faithfull.

Second Lieutenant Robert GELLATLY, 13th Royal Scots, was killed on 23 April 1917, aged 31, although initially he was reported as missing in action. His late father had been Solicitor General of the Supreme Court in Jamaica. The remaining four officer casualties on the memorial who were killed with the 13th Royal Scots on 23 April 1917 are: Second Lieutenant Kenneth Gilbert MAC-LACHLAN, 8th Royal Scots, attached 13th Battalion; Second Lieutenant Robert MUNGALL, 7th Royal Scots, attached 13th Battalion; Second Lieutenant James Francis SCOTT, 3rd Royal Scots, attached 13th Battalion; and Second Lieutenant Charles Hoyle SMITH, 9th Royal Scots, attached 13th Battalion.

Second Lieutenant Cecil Goodall ROSS MC, 3rd Battalion, Royal Scots, attached 45th Trench Mortar Battery, was killed in action near Monchy-le-Preux on 23 April 1917, aged 20. He was educated at Loretto School in Musselburgh where he excelled at rugby, football and shooting, and where he was also head boy. He gained a place at Trinity College, Oxford, but on leaving school he chose instead to accept a commission. His MC was gazetted on 18 July 1917 and was awarded for conspicuous gallantry and devotion to duty. The citation goes on to state that he had commanded his battery with the greatest skill and determination and that his co-operation with the infantry and total disregard for his own personal safety contributed greatly to the success of the advance.

Second Lieutenant Munro Briggs SCOTT, 12th Royal Scots, was killed in action on 12 April 1917. He is one of thirty-seven men whose names are listed on the roll of honour at the Royal Botanic Gardens, Kew. Some of the men were working at Kew when they joined up, but others returned home from assignments and projects abroad in order to enlist. SCOTT was working at Kew as a botanist and herbarium assistant when he enlisted.

Second Lieutenant John Walcot STEWART MC, 16th Royal Scots, was killed in action on 21 March 1918, aged 33. He was a Writer to the Signet in Edinburgh, a private society of lawyers peculiar to the legal system in Scotland. His MC was awarded for conspicuous gallantry after volunteering to go out to within thirty yards of the enemy wire to bring in a wounded man. Two days later he volunteered to go out again to examine the condition of some wire and was badly wounded, but managed to crawl back in. The award was gazetted on 3 April 1916.

Second Lieutenant John Clarkson TREDGOLD MC, 3rd Royal Scots, attached 11th Battalion, was killed in action on 12 April 1917, aged 21. TREDGOLD's body was never recovered. Eight other officers from the 11th Royal Scots were wounded that day and casualties amongst the other ranks amounted to 150. The 12th Royal Scots also suffered a total of around 250 casualties. Neither battalion returned to the line until the beginning of May that year.

TREDGOLD's MC was gazetted on 30 May 1917 and was awarded for conspicuous gallantry and devotion to duty whilst carrying out a dangerous reconnaissance. He returned from it with valuable information and later on he rescued several wounded men under heavy fire. His family came from Rhodesia where his father was Attorney General. One of his brothers, Sir Robert Clarkson Tredgold, served as Minister of Defence in Rhodesia during the Second World War and later went on to hold a number of political and legal posts there.

Company Serjeant Major John Laidlaw RENWICK MC MM, 9th Royal Scots, was killed in action on 23 April 1917, aged 23, when his battalion attacked towards Roeux and the Chemical Works. His MC was gazetted on 20 July 1917 and was awarded for conspicuous gallantry and devotion to duty, commanding his company with great courage and initiative, capturing and consolidating his objectives, and capturing several prisoners. His MM was gazetted on 24 January 1917 and was awarded for bravery in the field whilst serving as a sergeant. He was a friend of Bill Hay and their story is movingly told in Jonathan Nicholls's book, *Cheerful Sacrifice*. RENWICK had helped to deal with some difficult pockets of Germans in and around a trench known as 'Poser Weg' on the opening day of the Battle of Arras. He and two signallers entered an enemy dug-out and 'terrified' twelve Germans into giving themselves up, three of whom were officers. 'Poser Weg' was eventually cleared. This is the same incident referred to in the citation for his MC.

Serjeant John SIMPSON DCM, 11th Royal Scots, was killed in action on 6 June 1917, aged 27. His DCM was gazetted on 11 March 1916 and was awarded for conspicuous gallantry and good work whilst leading his platoon under heavy fire during an attack on a trench and later on when he had to defend the position.

Corporal David BOWMAN, 16th Royal Scots, was 28 years old when he was killed in action on 10 April 1917. His brother, William, was also killed during the war, although a search of the CWGC records provides no clear match for him. The brothers came from Dunfermline in Fife.

Private Henry Moncrieff MACFARLANE, 13th Royal Scots, was killed in action on 11 April 1917. His father, David Macfarlane, had been the curator of the National Gallery in Edinburgh.

Private George McAVOY DCM, 12th Royal Scots, was killed in action on 9 April 1917. His DCM was won whilst serving with the 13th Battalion and was gazetted on 16 November 1915. It was awarded for conspicuous gallantry at Loos on 26 September 1915 where he displayed great courage throughout the engagement and rescued a wounded officer of the East Yorkshire Regiment on Hill 70 under heavy fire.

The Queen's (Royal West Surrey Regiment)
Captain Theodore Victor CHAPMAN MC, 2nd Queen's (Royal West Surrey Regiment), was 19 years old when he was killed in action on 12 May 1917 near Bullecourt. His MC was gazetted on 14 January 1916. His brother, Gordon, was

killed on 9 March 1916 in Mesopotamia whilst serving with the 53rd Sikhs (Frontier Force), although at the time of his death he was attached to 28 Brigade, 7th (Indian) Division, as brigade major. He was 33 years old when he died and is buried at Amara War Cemetery in Iraq. He was twice mentioned in despatches. Another brother, Captain Percival Christian Chapman, 26th Jacob's Mountain Battery, Royal Field Artillery, was killed in action on 1 May 1915, aged 31. He is buried at Alexandria (Chatby) Military and War Memorial Cemetery.

Captain James Wilson HART MC and Bar, 10th Queen's (Royal West Surrey Regiment), was killed in action on 24 March 1918, aged 24. His MC was gazetted on 27 August 1917 and was awarded for conspicuous gallantry and devotion to duty, leading his company into the enemy's front line and afterwards taking part in the final assault that inflicted heavy losses on the enemy. He then consolidated the position and remained there until relieved by the unit in support. The bar was added the following year and was gazetted on 25 March 1918. It was awarded for conspicuous gallantry and devotion to duty after taking command of his battalion during an attack and reorganizing it under very heavy fire once it had reached its objective. He then held his position for four days under repeated bombardments and heavy counter-attacks, maintaining complete control over his whole front. Throughout the operations he showed great fearlessness and powers of command.

Captain Alfred Eric RYAN MC, 11th Queen's (Royal West Surrey Regiment), was killed in action on 23 March 1918, aged 20. His MC was gazetted on 3 March 1917 and was awarded for conspicuous gallantry in action after going out on several occasions to make a daring reconnaissance of the enemy's trenches prior to a raid, bringing back most valuable information and setting a fine example of courage and determination. He was killed somewhere near Beugny, a couple of miles north-east of Bapaume, and was one of seven officers from his battalion reported missing in action that day; a further five officers were wounded and two were killed outright.

Corporal Albert BUTCHER MM, 10th Queen's (Royal West Surrey Regiment), was killed in action on 26 March 1918. He was one of four brothers who served during the war. His MM was gazetted in September 1916 and is believed to have been awarded for his work on the Somme as a stretcher-bearer rescuing several wounded men whilst under fire near Ovillers.

Corporal Walter Frederick HUMPHREY DCM, 11th Queen's (Royal West Surrey Regiment), was killed in action on 23 March 1918, aged 24. His DCM was gazetted on 26 January 1918 and was awarded for conspicuous gallantry and devotion to duty. Having crept forward to a shell hole close to an enemy strong-point under heavy machine-gun and rifle fire, he was able to put two machine guns out of action, thereby saving the lives of many in his company who were at risk while consolidating their position.

The Buffs (East Kent Regiment)

Lieutenant Colonel Charles Walter BLACKALL, 3rd East Kent Regiment, commanding the 4th South Staffordshire Regiment, was killed in action on 24 March 1918, aged 42. He was twice mentioned in despatches and had also served in the South African War. Before the war he was a professional actor and had also written poetry, which he continued to do whilst at the front. He went to France in November 1914, initially serving with the 1st Royal Welsh Fusiliers. In 1915 a collection of his poetry was published by Bodley Head under the title, *Songs from the Trenches*. He again served with his old regiment, The Buffs, before going on to command a battalion of the Cheshire Regiment, then the 4th South Staffordshire Regiment.

His widow, who was an actress, was one of the many subscribers who supported the compilation of the *Historical Records of the Buffs, 1914–1919*. His father, Major Robert Blackall, lived in Folkestone, although the family also owned land in Ireland, including a country residence. Charles's grandfather, Colonel Samuel Blackall, had served as Governor of Sierra Leone and then as Governor of Queensland, Australia.

Lieutenant Sinclair Beatty JOHNSON, 3rd East Kent Regiment, attached 7th Battalion, was killed in action on 27 May 1917, aged 20. He had been studying at the University of Toronto, where his parents lived, and was a member of its OTC. He was also amongst the first draft from his OTC to enlist.

Lieutenant John Elston LANE, 'B' Company, 4th East Kent Regiment, attached 7th Battalion, was killed in action on 3 May 1917, aged 20. He was educated at the Masonic School, Bushey, Hertfordshire, and at Magdalene College, Cambridge.

Second Lieutenant Geoffrey William CHURCH MC, 7th East Kent Regiment, was killed in action on 3 May 1917 near Chérisy. He was educated at Uppingham School in Rutland before going on to University College, London, to study engineering. His father was a solicitor and had served as Principal Clerk to the Registrar of the Chancery Division. The family lived in comfortable circumstances in Hertfordshire.

Alhough initially recorded as wounded and missing in action, he was seen to fall after he was hit by shrapnel and almost certainly died that day from the resulting wounds. His MC was gazetted on 17 April 1917 and was awarded for conspicuous gallantry and devotion to duty whilst leading a patrol under heavy fire during which he obtained valuable information. Later, he greatly assisted his company in maintaining its direction and also did invaluable work suppressing very heavy enemy sniper fire.

Second Lieutenant Charles Arthur Stirling MATHIAS MC, 'D' Company, 7th East Kent Regiment, was killed in action on 3 May 1917, aged 26. His MC was gazetted on 19 April 1917 and was awarded for conspicuous gallantry and devotion to duty after he had taken out a patrol and brought back most valuable information. Later he established a post on the left flank of the battalion and held it in spite of heavy enemy fire.

Serjeant Albert Arthur SAGGERS, 6th East Kent Regiment, was killed in action on 3 May 1917, the same day that his brother, Private Alfred SAGGERS, 7th Queen's (Royal West Surrey Regiment) was also killed. Alfred has no known grave and is commemorated here on the Arras Memorial with his brother.

Lance Serjeant Arthur Henry Richard CHAPMAN DCM, 7th East Kent Regiment, was killed in action on 3 May 1917. His DCM was gazetted on 17 April, shortly before his death. It was awarded for conspicuous gallantry and devotion to duty in organizing a post on the left flank of his battalion and securing it against attack. On another occasion he went forward with his section and obtained valuable information.

The King's Own (Royal Lancaster Regiment)
The regiment has 340 of its men listed here, including ten officers, all of them lieutenants or second lieutenants. Most of the men are from either the 1st or 8th Battalion.

Lance Corporal Edward BAMBER MM, 8th King's Own (Royal Lancaster Regiment), was killed in action on 23 March 1918, aged 20.

Lance Corporal Richard HINDLE, 1st King's Own (Royal Lancaster Regiment), was mentioned in despatches on three occasions. He was killed in action on 15 June 1917, aged 21.

Private Joseph MOORE, 1st King's Own (Royal Lancaster Regiment), was killed in action on 10 April 1917, aged 21. The CWGC register notes that his father, John James Moore, also fell in action, but the records provide no exact match for him.

The Northumberland Fusiliers
Captain Walter Harry Corfield BUCKNALL, 2nd Northumberland Fusiliers, attached 1st Battalion, was killed in action on 3 May 1917, aged 20. He was educated at Repton, followed by the Royal Military College, Sandhurst, and was gazetted in December 1914. He had been wounded on two previous occasions.

Captain Edward LAWRENCE MC DCM, 10th Northumberland Fusiliers, attached 1st Battalion, was killed in action on 28 March 1918. The citation for his MC was gazetted on 20 October 1916. It was awarded for conspicuous gallantry in leading a successful raid against the enemy's trenches. Although he was wounded early in the operation, he remained in command and even assisted to remove the wounded under heavy fire. His DCM was gazetted on 3 June 1915 while he was serving with the 16th (The Queen's) Lancers. The citation is one of the shortest and simply states that it was awarded for gallantry and ability whilst commanding his troop before and after being wounded. He had served with the regiment since 1907 and was also mentioned in despatches with it in October 1914. He was gazetted in the field from serjeant to second lieutenant on 2 March 1916. His file at the National Archives contains a note stating that he had been awarded the *Médaille Militaire* on 4 April 1915. It also suggests that the raid for which he was awarded the MC occurred on 31 August 1916.

Captain Douglas Francis De Renzy MARTIN, 1st Northumberland Fusiliers, was killed in action on 13 April 1917, aged 19. He was the son of the late Lieutenant General Sir A. de Renzy Martin KCB. Douglas's brother, Lieutenant Colonel Edward Cuthbert de Renzy Martin, served with the King's Own (Yorkshire Light Infantry) during the war and won the DSO and MC. He was also awarded the CMG and is one of a small number of British recipients of the Order of Skanderbeg awarded by the Royal Family of Albania.

Captain Edward George PASSINGHAM MC, 1st Northumberland Fusiliers, was killed in action on 3 May 1917, aged 21. His MC was gazetted on 11 May 1917 and was awarded for conspicuous gallantry and devotion to duty leading a raiding party with great courage and determination through uncut wire, then entering the enemy's front line trenches where he personally shot three of the enemy.

Captain Albert Edward PHELAN MC, 1st Northumberland Fusiliers, was killed in action on 20 November 1917, aged 28. His MC was gazetted on 1 January 1917 in the New Year's Honours List.

Captain Leslie William Whitworth QUIN MC, 3rd Northumberland Fusiliers, attached 27th Battalion (Tyneside Irish), was killed in action on 24 April 1917, aged 23. His MC was gazetted on 25 November 1916 and was awarded for conspicuous gallantry in action after leading a raiding party with great courage and skill. He maintained his position in the enemy's trenches for one and a half hours, setting a fine example to his men.

Captain James Herbert Cecil SWINNEY MC, 7th Northumberland Fusiliers, was killed in action on 16 April 1917, aged 22. His MC was gazetted on 6 March 1917 and was awarded for conspicuous gallantry and devotion to duty. At great personal risk he rescued an officer whose clothing had been set on fire by a flare. Although severely burnt, he remained in command of his company.

Captain Ben WILMOT MC, 20th Northumberland Fusiliers (Tyneside Scottish), was killed in action near Greenland Hill on 6 June 1917, aged 21. This was a small operation aimed at straightening the line and forcing the Germans to either dig a new line along the crest of the hill, or abandon the crest and dig a new line on its reverse slope. The attack, which took place at 8.00pm on 5 June, was considered a success and several positions and trenches were captured. The Germans responded by launching several counter-attacks during the early hours of the following morning, but were beaten back. Some posts were temporarily lost during the early hours of 7 June, but these were later restored. His MC was gazetted on 27 November 1916 and was awarded for conspicuous gallantry in action in leading a daring raid on the enemy's trenches in which an estimated thirty to forty of the enemy were killed, two of whom he personally accounted for with his revolver.

Lieutenant Alexander James Bartlett BEGG MC, 22nd Northumberland Fusiliers (Tyneside Scottish), was killed in action on 21 March 1918, aged 21. He was educated at Darlington Grammar School, Christ's Hospital and Peterhouse College, Cambridge, and was from Usworth in County Durham. His MC was gazetted on 4 June 1917 in the King's Birthday Honours List. There is a big discrepancy over the date of death for this officer. The 34th Division's history is very specific, stating that he and two other officers, together with their machine-gun detachments, were seemingly cut off from the rest of the battalion during the German advance across the Lys. The date for this action is 11 April 1918 when his battalion was defending a position north of the Armentières–Nieppe road. The Roll of Honour for Christ's Hospital shows his date of death as 21 March 1918.

Lieutenant Robert DONALD MC, 'B' Company, 24th Northumberland Fusiliers (Tyneside Irish), was killed in action on 28 April 1917, aged 27. The citation for his MC was gazetted on 18 July 1917. It was awarded for conspicuous gallantry and devotion to duty whilst in command of bombing parties that he had organized. During the operation he took charge of small parties from different units and used their grenades to inflict severe casualties on the enemy.

Lieutenant Philip Gerard FINCH MC, 1st Northumberland Fusiliers, was killed in action on 28 March 1918, aged 20. His MC was gazetted on 5 July 1918 and was awarded for conspicuous gallantry and devotion to duty after successfully dislodging a party of the enemy that had been holding out in an advanced post. The post had been established following an enemy counter-attack, but during the following days and nights he persistently harassed the enemy with bombs and rifle grenades, eventually forcing them to abandon their position. The citation concludes that throughout the operation he showed great coolness and courage.

Lieutenant John JAMIESON DCM, 23rd Northumberland Fusiliers (Tyneside Scottish), was killed in action near Roeux on 29 April 1917, aged 40. His DCM was won while he was serving as a serjeant with the 6th Cameron Highlanders. It was gazetted on 13 February 1917 and was awarded for conspicuous gallantry in action. It notes that he rendered most valuable service by gathering men for digging and coolly and collectedly superintending the work under heavy fire. He was commissioned on 4 March 1917. Strangely, there is no reference to the award of the DCM on his file at the National Archives.

Second Lieutenant William Richmond CLEPHAN MC, 6th Northumberland Fusiliers, was killed in action on 7 July 1917. His MC was gazetted on 17 April 1917 and was awarded for conspicuous gallantry and devotion to duty in carrying out several dangerous reconnaissance patrols from which he obtained very valuable information. Later he led an offensive patrol during which he made a very gallant attempt to rush an enemy sap and was wounded whilst doing so.

Second Lieutenant Stanley Edmonds COLTON MC, 1st Northumberland Fusiliers, was killed in action on 28 March 1918, aged 19. His MC was gazetted on 18 February 1918 and the citation for it appeared exactly five months later on 18 July. It was awarded for conspicuous gallantry and devotion to duty during an attack by the enemy. He succeeded in leading a bombing patrol along the whole of the support trench, which was occupied by the enemy. Later he led bombing parties against enemy blocks, engaging them with determination and vigour. The following day he succeeded in clearing a trench for a distance of 400 yards and then established a strong bombing post. In doing so, he showed courage and leadership of the highest order.

Second Lieutenant Ernest Harington HAWES, 20th Northumberland Fusiliers (Tyneside Scottish), was killed in action on 5 June 1916. He was the son of the late Major General William Harington Hawes CB, Indian Army.

Serjeant George MARTIN DCM, 12th Northumberland Fusiliers, was killed in action on 31 March 1917. His DCM was gazetted on 9 July 1917 and was awarded in recognition of his conspicuous gallantry. The citation for it is non-specific, but acknowledges that he had commanded his platoon with the utmost gallantry and initiative and that he had shown remarkable decisiveness and pluck at all times when under hostile fire. It concludes that his personal example had always been of the greatest value to his men.

Corporal Horace BAKEWELL MM and Bar, 23rd Northumberland Fusiliers (Tyneside Scottish), was killed in action on 29 April 1917. His MM was gazetted on 21 September 1916 and the bar to it on 18 June 1917. (Addenda Panel)

Lance Corporal Charles Henry BEAULAH, 13th Northumberland Fusiliers, was killed in action on 2 April 1917, aged 20. His brother, Private George Carlill Beaulah, also served with the Northumberland Fusiliers, but with the 1/4th Battalion. He was killed on 15 September 1916, aged 23. He has no known grave and is commemorated on the Thiepval Memorial on the Somme.

Private Matthew ACRID, 27th Northumberland Fusiliers (Tyneside Irish), was killed in action on 9 April 1917. His brother Edwin also fell, although there is no trace of any other soldier of that surname listed in the CWGC records. There is also no trace of Private Matthew ACRID serving with either the 27th or the 24/27th Northumberland Fusiliers in *Soldiers Died in the Great War*.

Private Robert Edward ALLAN, who died on 23 March 1918, is shown incorrectly as serving with the 33rd Northumberland Fusiliers (Tyneside Scottish); his unit was the 23rd Battalion.

Private Thomas EDWARDS, 22nd Northumberland Fusiliers (Tyneside Scottish), was killed in action on 5 June 1917, aged 25. He and his wife lived at 49 Chevington Crescent, Red Row, Morpeth. His parents lived not far away at 80 Hedgehope Terrace, Chevington Drift, Morpeth. The Arras Memorial shows another private by the name of Thomas EDWARDS, 1/7th Northumberland Fusiliers, who was killed in action on 17 April 1917, aged 20. His parents lived at 43 Hedgehope Terrace, Chevington Drift, Morpeth. There may well be a family connection between the two men; perhaps they were cousins.

Private Andrew LOWE, 1/5th Northumberland Fusiliers, was killed in action on 19 April 1917, aged 27. According to the CWGC register, he was one of three brothers who fell in the Great War. The CWGC records provide no clues as to the identities of the other two.

The Royal Warwickshire Regiment
Major George Walker COX, 1st Royal Warwickshire Regiment, attached 1st Essex Regiment, was killed in action on 3 May 1917, aged 31. On that day, according to the regimental history, the battalion was in billets in the Grande Place at Arras. This would suggest that he was probably killed by shell fire.

Captain John Stanley HARROWING MC, 2nd Royal Warwickshire Regiment, formerly Army Service Corps, was killed in action on 4 May 1917, aged 27. He held a Master's degree from Cambridge University. His MC was gazetted on 25 November 1916 and was awarded for conspicuous gallantry in action, leading his company with great courage and determination, consolidating the newly-won position, repulsing an enemy counter-attack, and setting a fine example to his men. His father was Sir John Harrowing who served as High Sheriff of Yorkshire between 1928 and 1929. The family operated a number of steam ships from its base in Whitby.

Captain Edgar Ernest JENKINS MC, Royal Warwickshire Regiment, attached 1/5th Lancashire Fusiliers, was killed in action on 25 March 1918, aged 31. His MC was gazetted on 1 January 1918 in the New Year's Honours List.

Lieutenant Norman Augustus Manders RING, 3rd Royal Warwickshire Regiment, attached 2nd Battalion, was killed in action on 4 May 1917, aged 27. He returned home from Buenos Aires, where he had been working for the Alto Paraná Development Company, in order to enlist. According to the roll of honour of British companies in Argentina, he returned home in 1915 and was wounded at Neuve Chapelle in March the same year. His father served in the Royal Navy.

Lieutenant Ralph SHAW DSO, Royal Warwickshire Regiment, attached 11th Battalion, was killed in action on 28 April 1917, aged 20. His DSO was gazetted on 18 July that year and was awarded for conspicuous gallantry in action.

After all the senior officers in the brigade had become casualties, he assumed command of the whole of the brigade's line showing great courage and judgement under heavy fire as he set about consolidating the position.

Second Lieutenant Harold Ligonier TREADWAY, 15th Royal Warwickshire Regiment, was killed on 8/9 May 1917, aged 26. He had returned home from Venezuela in order to serve.

Lance Corporal Bert HOLMES DCM, 1st Royal Warwickshire Regiment, was killed in action on 20 November 1917. His DCM was awarded for conspicuous gallantry and devotion to duty. The citation notes that, as a company runner for over two years, he was in the majority of the actions in which the battalion took part. It goes on to add that he always proved himself most reliable, and on many occasions had taken messages through very heavy fire displaying singular devotion to duty. The award was gazetted on 17 April 1918.

Private Albert Henry ENGLAND, 14th Royal Warwickshire Regiment, was killed in action on 7 May 1917, aged 31. He was one of three brothers who fell during the war. The CWGC records offer no clues as to the identity of the other brothers.

Private James Arthur JEFFERIES, 1/6th Royal Warwickshire Regiment, was killed on 19 June 1917, aged 21. His two brothers, Ernest and George Henry JEFFRIES, also fell. Ernest, who served as a private with the 5th Oxfordshire & Buckinghamshire Light Infantry, was killed in action a few weeks earlier on 3 May 1917, aged 23, and is also commemorated here on the Arras Memorial. With regard to the other brother, George Henry, he is very likely Lance Corporal George Henry Jeffries who was killed in action serving with the 2/5th Gloucestershire Regiment on 22 August 1917. He too has no known grave and is commemorated on the Tyne Cot Memorial. The spelling of his surname happens to be slightly different.

Private Charles SHOCK, 1/6th Royal Warwickshire Regiment, was killed in action on 19 June 1917, aged 22. His brother, Private Harold Shock, was killed in action on 27 August 1916 whilst serving with the 1/8th Royal Warwickshire Regiment. Harold is commemorated on the Thiepval Memorial.

Private Alfred William SPARROW, 15th Royal Warwickshire Regiment, was killed in action on 9 May 1917, aged 28. His brother, Private Edward SPARROW, is also commemorated here on the Arras Memorial. He fell in action a couple of weeks earlier on 25 April 1917 when serving with the 6th Bedfordshire Regiment, aged 36. The CWGC register shows Edward serving with the 5th Battalion, but the 1/5th Battalion was part of the 54th (East Anglian) Division and only ever served in the Mediterranean and Egypt. The 2/5th battalion and the 3/5th Battalion served at home for the duration of the war.

The Royal Fusiliers (City of London Regiment)

Captain Kenneth Edwards HAWKINS MC, 'B' Company, 7th Royal Fusiliers, was killed in action on 21 March 1918, aged 24, not 22 March as shown in the CWGC records. His MC was gazetted on 1 January 1918 in the New Year's Honours List. He was educated at King's School, Canterbury. In August 1914 he enlisted with the 1/16th Battalion, London Regiment (Queen's Westminster Rifles) and went to France later that year. He was commissioned in the Royal Fusiliers in 1915. He was killed by shell fire when in command of 'B' Company on 21 March during the opening phase of the German Offensive. After a spirited defence, the battalion was forced to withdraw and it was around this time that he was killed.

Captain Maurice Lake HILDER MC, 5th Royal Fusiliers, attached 23rd Battalion, was killed in action on 3 May 1917. He was killed by a shell as his battalion made a counter-attack to regain Fresnoy Trench, which had been captured the previous day, but then lost. Although the position was again recaptured, it could not be held.

He had attended Lancing College where he excelled at cricket and football. When he left school he joined his father's firm of solicitors, but when war broke out he chose to enlist. He was soon commissioned in the Army Service Corps and went to Gallipoli in June 1915. Whilst there he became ill and was evacuated back to England. After recovering he joined the 5th Royal Fusiliers and was then posted to the 23rd Battalion in France in September 1916.

His MC was gazetted on 11 May 1917 and was awarded for conspicuous gallantry and devotion to duty, leading his company in a most gallant manner, capturing a strong enemy position, and setting a fine example of courage and good leadership. The events referred to in the citation occurred on 10 March 1917 when he was involved in the capture of a German position near Grevillers Trench, known as The Ladies Leg. *Military Operations, France and Belgium, 1917, Volume One* makes a brief, but very favourable comment on this limited objective operation and attributes its success to careful and detailed co-operation between the artillery and the infantry.

Captain Nelson Rayner NEATE, MC, 11th Royal Fusiliers, was killed in action on 3 May 1917, aged 20. A brief note in the regimental history refers to him in connection with his company's supporting role during an attack on Chérisy. Its task was to mop up behind the leading troops and bring up supplies. Whilst mopping up, NEATE and his men were counter-attacked and he was last seen leading them against the enemy, revolver in hand. His MC was gazetted on 26 May 1917 and was awarded for conspicuous gallantry and devotion to duty. The citation states that he had displayed great courage and initiative throughout the day in question and, although wounded, had refused to leave his company until he was convinced that the line was secure against counter-attack.

Captain Spencer THOMSON MC, 14th Royal Fusiliers, attached 2nd Battalion, was killed in action on 24 April 1917 near the Bois du Vert, east of Monchy-le-

Preux, aged 32. A solicitor in civilian life, he had attended Durham School, then Christ Church College, Oxford, where he obtained a Bachelor of Arts degree. His MC was gazetted on 4 June 1917 in the King's Birthday Honours List. He had previously served in Gallipoli and Egypt.

Second Lieutenant Charles Frederick BISHOP, 13th Royal Fusiliers, was killed in action on 4 April 1918, aged 34. He was a civil servant in Sudan before the war. In 1899 Sudan was placed under Egyptian administration, but with Britain as the guiding hand, effectively placing it under British control.

Second Lieutenant Richard Bernard BOYLE, 4th Royal Fusiliers, was killed in action on 13 April 1917, aged 19. He was the 7th Earl of Shannon. Whilst attacking towards Guémappe, his battalion came under a hostile barrage, and then, as it was approaching the spur to the north-west of the village, it came under heavy rifle and machine-gun fire from both flanks, but especially from the direction of Wancourt. It was while the battalion was crossing the spur under a hail of fire that most of the officers became casualties, including Second Lieutenant BOYLE.

Second Lieutenant Gerald James Hardwicke COWIE MC, 10th Royal Fusiliers, was killed in action on 23 April 1917, aged 23. Although the CWGC register makes no specific connection, it is obvious that his brother, Lionel Jack Hardwicke COWIE, 2nd Royal Fusiliers, was also killed the following day, aged 20. He has no known grave and is commemorated on the Arras Memorial with his brother. The family residence is shown as Calcutta, India.

Second Lieutenant Frederick Charles Blakeman DAWSON, 4th Royal Fusiliers, attached to the Honourable Artillery Company, was killed in action on 3 May 1917, aged 27. He joined the University and Public Schools Brigade (Royal Fusiliers) in August 1914 and received his commission in October 1915.

Company Serjeant Major Donald Arthur BENNETT, 24th Royal Fusiliers, was killed in action on 14 April 1917, aged 33. He was mentioned in despatches and had previously served in Togoland.

Corporal George JARRATT VC, 8th Royal Fusiliers, was killed in action on 3 May 1917 near Pelves. His VC was gazetted on 8 June 1917 and was awarded for most conspicuous bravery and devotion to duty. He, together with some other wounded men, had been taken prisoner and were under guard in a dug-out. Later that evening the enemy were driven back by our troops and the leading infantry began to bomb the nearby dug-outs, including the one occupied by JARRETT and the others. When a grenade landed in the dug-out, Corporal JARRETT put both feet on it and the subsequent explosion blew off both his legs. The wounded men were later removed safely by our troops, but JARRETT died before he could be evacuated. The citation concludes that his supreme act of self-sacrifice undoubtedly saved the lives of several of those wounded men.

Lance Corporal Percy LUTON, 1st Royal Fusiliers, formerly 11th Battalion, was killed in action on 24 April 1917, aged 29. According to the CWGC register, he had enlisted in September 1914 and was wounded on the Somme on 1 July, although he could not have been serving with the 1st Battalion that day. *Soldiers Died in the Great War* shows him serving with the 2nd Battalion, in which case he would have received his wounds near Hawthorn Ridge.

Private Harvey ADAM, 10th Royal Fusiliers, was killed in action on 10 April 1917, aged 34. He had a Bachelor of Arts degree (London) as well as a Bachelor of Science degree. He was also a Fellow of the Royal Economic Society.

Private Alfred Ernest CLARKE, 7th Royal Fusiliers, was killed in action on 5 April 1918, aged 21. He was from St Margaret's, Hertfordshire and, according to the CWGC register, was one of six sons who served during the war, four of whom fell in action. The CWGC records contain insufficient information to identify any of the brothers who died.

Private Cyril Henry DAVENPORT, 2/4th Royal Fusiliers, was killed in action on 16 June 1917, aged 18. He was the son of Sir Henry Edward Davenport JP and former Sheriff of the City of London. The family lived in Queensgate, South Kensington, London.

Private Frederick Robert HALL, 'B' Company, 11th Royal Fusiliers, was killed in action on 3 May 1917, aged 37. He was educated at Rugby School and was an only son.

Private Alfred Charles PRATT, 9th Royal Fusiliers, was 39 years old when he was killed in action on 3 May 1917. He had previously served in the South African War and on the North West Frontier in India.

Private Mossman WILSON, 9th Royal Fusiliers, formerly 7th Battalion, was killed in action on 23 April 1917, aged 27. His brother, Pioneer William Wilson, was killed in action a few days later, on 29 April, when serving with 'A' Special Company, Royal Engineers. He is buried in London Rifle Brigade Cemetery, Belgium. The brothers came from Shilbottle in Northumberland.

The King's (Liverpool Regiment)

Captain Ninian John BANNATYNE, 1st King's (Liverpool Regiment), was mortally wounded on 3 May 1917 whilst taking part in operations against Oppy Wood and the nearby villages of Oppy and Fresnoy. Although wounded early in the attack, he remained in command of a composite unit made up of two companies of his battalion until he lost consciousness and died. His uncle, Lieutenant Colonel William Stirling Bannatyne, had commanded the 1st King's (Liverpool Regiment) at the First Battle of Ypres and was killed there on 24 October 1914, aged 45. His body was originally buried and marked, but his grave was subsequently lost and he is now commemorated on the Menin Gate. Ninian's grandfather and great uncle had also served as colonels in the King's (Liverpool

Regiment). Had he survived, this young officer might well have continued that family tradition.

Captain Ernest Reginald LAST MC, 1st Battalion, King's (Liverpool Regiment), was killed in action on 24 March 1918. His MC was gazetted on 24 June 1916 and the citation for it appeared later that year on 27 July. It was awarded for conspicuous gallantry after organizing an assault on the enemy's trenches. He displayed great coolness and utter disregard of personal danger during the operation, which was carried out under a heavy hostile bombardment.

Captain Leslie MORRISON MC, 1st King's (Liverpool Regiment), attached 1/7th Lancashire Fusiliers, was killed in action on 25 March 1918. His MC was gazetted on 15 March 1916 and was awarded for conspicuous gallantry whilst in charge of a bombing section that had attacked and captured a new crater. After the enemy had driven our parties back in a counter-attack, he led his bombers forward again and recaptured the position. His brother, Stanley, also fell. Stanley Morrison was killed in action south-west of Ovillers on 9 July 1916 whilst serving as a second lieutenant with the 19th Lancashire Fusiliers.

Lieutenant Alan Ralph BODEY, 7th King's (Liverpool Regiment), was killed some time between 21 and 28 June 1916, aged 21. He was from the Sefton Park area of Liverpool and had been a student at Gonville and Caius College, Cambridge.

Second Lieutenant Reginald Stuart TARRAN MC, 1st King's (Liverpool Regiment), was killed in action on 24 March 1918. His MC was gazetted on 19 September 1917 and was awarded for conspicuous gallantry and devotion to duty. After a hostile raid had penetrated our front line, he and another officer led a counter-attack with such vigour that the enemy was outflanked and twelve of them were captured. He then promptly and successfully reorganized the support line. His father served as a captain in the Army Ordnance Corps during the war.

Second Lieutenant Harry Ben WILLIAMS MC, 5th King's (Liverpool Regiment), was killed in action on 3 May 1917, aged 23. His MC was gazetted on 18 July 1917 and was awarded for conspicuous gallantry and devotion to duty. The citation notes that he behaved with great gallantry during an advance, at one point crawling out into the open and shooting an enemy machine gunner. On reaching his objective, he collected some men together and consolidated the position under heavy fire from close range.

Lance Serjeant Charles J. HAYWARD DCM, 1st King's (Liverpool Regiment), was killed in action on 1 June 1916. His DCM was gazetted on 11 March 1916 and was awarded for conspicuous gallantry. After an attack on the enemy's trenches, it was deemed necessary to determine the enemy's strength in the part of the line he was still holding. Corporal HAYWARD led a patrol in broad daylight and under heavy artillery, machine-gun and rifle fire, almost to the enemy's lines, and brought back valuable information regarding the situation.

Private William ARMSTEAD MM, 4th King's (Liverpool Regiment), was killed in action on 23 April 1917. He had won his MM six months earlier in unusual circumstances whilst serving with the 1st Battalion. He and several other men had been wounded and captured on 13 November 1916 during the Battle of the Ancre. ARMSTEAD had been wounded in the thigh. For some reason, none of the prisoners was taken back behind the lines; instead, they were kept in a German dug-out where they appear to have been well cared for. Some days later, during a bombardment, the prisoners were left inadequately supervised, where-upon ARMSTEAD and Lance Corporal George Herbert Wright, 13th Essex Regiment, took advantage of the situation by venturing out of the dug-out where ARMSTEAD killed three Germans using some stick grenades they had found nearby. However, their attempt to escape had to be abandoned when some more Germans began to approach.

The next day, 24 November, he and Wright eventually decided to make a break for it. Wright went first, but was shot thought the head. ARMSTEAD then spent several hours crawling back to our lines. When he returned home he gave an account of his extraordinary eleven days in captivity to his local newspaper, the *Oldham Chronicle*. Lance Corporal Wright is now buried at Puchevillers British Cemetery behind the old Somme battlefield. ARMSTEAD was killed whilst supporting a bombing attack by men of the 4th Suffolk Regiment in the Hindenburg Support Line.

Private William Ewart SIMS, 18th King's (Liverpool Regiment), was killed in action on 23 April 1917, aged 27. According to the CWGC register, he was a member of the OTC at Nottingham University and then went on to become a commercial artist.

The Norfolk Regiment

Captain John Eliot HANCOCK DSO, 9th Norfolk Regiment, was killed in action on 21 March 1918. His DSO was gazetted on 4 February 1918 and the citation for it appeared later that year, on 5 July. It was awarded for conspicuous gallantry whilst serving as a temporary lieutenant. When his company commander was seriously wounded, he took command of the left company during the attack. When it came under heavy machine-gun fire, he organized a frontal attack, whilst he and two NCOs rushed across the open from a flank, killing and wounding the enemy's gun teams and putting the guns out of action. He himself killed six men during the encounter. In the subsequent fighting he showed great initiative, clearing houses in a village and directing the line of advance.

Captain Maurice William Campbell SPROTT MC, 9th Norfolk Regiment, was killed in action on 21 March 1918. His MC was gazetted on 19 April 1917 and was awarded for conspicuous gallantry and devotion to duty during a raid on the enemy's trenches. Not only did he carry out the task allotted to him with conspicuous success, he also showed great pluck in getting the wounded back under heavy fire.

Lieutenant George Philip BURLTON MC, 1st Norfolk Regiment, was killed in action on 5 June 1916. His MC was gazetted on 22 January 1916 and was awarded for conspicuous gallantry on the night of 1 December 1915 near Mametz. After a German mine exploded, he went to the location to help. Regardless of the risk to his personal safety he volunteered to be lowered down the shaft and, through his personal endeavour and example, he was instrumental in saving the lives of several unconscious men. On 5 June 1916 he was killed by a shell near the Arras–Bailleuil road. Fellow officer, Lieutenant Leo EDWARDS, was with him at the time and was wounded by the blast, dying from his wounds three days later. He is also commemorated here on the Arras Memorial.

Lieutenant Cubitt Austen IRELAND MC, 6th Norfolk Regiment, attached 7th Battalion, was killed in action on 14 October 1917. His MC was gazetted on 26 July 1917 and was awarded for conspicuous gallantry and devotion to duty. The brief citation recounts that, although wounded, he led his men forward with the greatest gallantry and determination, and in doing so undoubtedly saved a critical situation.

Serjeant James Samuel JOHNSON DCM MM and Bar, 7th Norfolk Regiment, was killed in action on 14 October 1917. His DCM was gazetted on 26 January 1918 and was awarded for conspicuous gallantry and devotion to duty after the enemy had penetrated our front line and formed a bombing block on his flank. Twice he organized a bombing attack, even going forward himself over the open to reconnoitre the enemy's position. On his return he led the attack himself, continually making his way into the open to throw his bombs. Throughout the operation he showed an absolute disregard of danger, and by his fine piece of initiative and devotion to the task he set a splendid example to his men.

Private Hedley Stephen LUCAS, 8th Norfolk Regiment, was killed in action on 22 May 1917, aged 38. He had served with Paget's Horse in the South African campaign.

The Lincolnshire Regiment
Captain Arnold James RAHLES-RAHBULA, 8th Lincolnshire Regiment, was killed in action on 28 April 1917. His brother, Second Lieutenant Esmond Herbert Rahles-Rabulah, won the MC whilst serving with the Machine Gun Corps. It was awarded after he had held up the enemy with his guns until the last moment in order to cover infantry units as they were withdrawing. In doing so, and to avoid capture, he had to ford a river under rifle fire in order to extricate himself. Under his leadership his section was able to complete its withdrawal with very little loss.

Lieutenant Wyllard Fleetwood COCKS, 10th Lincolnshire Regiment, was mortally wounded on 9 April 1917, aged 25. He was shot in the groin as he was leading his men forward and bled to death after refusing help. He insisted on watching his men continue their advance and spent the last fifteen minutes of his life quietly propped up and smoking his pipe. A fellow officer, Second Lieutenant Lodge, came to his aid, but was also immediately hit by a bullet, strongly suggesting that both men had been shot by a sniper. This may well explain why COCKS declined further attempts to help him.

Second Lieutenant Harold Charles CHASE, 4th Lincolnshire Regiment, was killed in action on 8 June 1917, aged 24. He had originally enlisted in the Royal East Kent Yeomanry in October 1914 and had been in France since January 1917.

Second Lieutenant Harold Percival HENDIN MC, 10th Lincolnshire Regiment, was killed in action on 28 April 1917, aged 23. His MC was gazetted on 19 August 1916 and was awarded for conspicuous gallantry and determination during operations. With only four men, he bombed his way along the enemy's front and then, after collecting up men from other regiments, he established and held his position for twelve hours. He later withdrew his men to another position and held it for three days. This incident is referred to by Martin Middlebrook in his book, *The First Day on the Somme*. It was described by Major W.A. Vignoles, 10th Lincolnshire Regiment, who noted in his diaries that HENDIN was the only officer from the battalion to enter the enemy's trenches near La Boisselle on 1 July 1916. After the event, HENDIN commented modestly that it was just by luck that he had managed to get across no man's land, which it probably was, but he went on to add that it was also down to luck that he managed to hold on, which certainly was not the case.

Company Serjeant Major Wilfred Ernest HAMP DCM MM, 1/5th Lincolnshire Regiment, was killed in action on 26 June 1917, aged 32. HAMP was one of four men killed in a captured dug-out when a delayed action booby-trap exploded. His DCM was gazetted on 25 August 1917 and was awarded for conspicuous gallantry and devotion to duty after taking command of his company when his officers had been wounded. He showed the greatest initiative and energy in leading the men to their objective and overseeing their subsequent withdrawal. During that withdrawal he assisted a wounded officer and a badly wounded NCO back to our trenches. The citation concludes that his conduct during the operation was admirable and that he had set a splendid example to the men.

   In his book, *The First Day on the Somme*, Martin Middlebrook tells how a company of the 1/5th Lincolnshire Regiment had been detailed to go out that night to locate and relieve a group of Sherwood Foresters who were believed to be still out in the German lines and possibly cut off. When one platoon set off in the open, it happened to be facing the wrong way. HAMP intervened and corrected the error, but refused to move off with his party until more specific information was provided. An argument ensued with the officer in charge, but HAMP stood his ground and declined to set off without proper orders or directions. No action was taken against him despite being informed at the time that his actions could be interpreted as disobeying orders.

Private Horace BARNARD MM, 8th Lincolnshire Regiment, was killed in action on 28 April 1917. His brother, Rifleman Mark Barnard, was killed in action on 13 May 1915 when serving with the 1st Rifle Brigade and is commemorated on the Menin Gate at Ypres.

Private James Arthur DEAN, 8th Lincolnshire Regiment, was killed in action on 5 April 1918. His brother, Harry, was also killed during the war. The CWGC records offer at least two possible candidates for his brother, neither of whom can be identified conclusively.

The Devonshire Regiment
Captain Leonard Evelyn Leigh MATON MC, 1st Devonshire Regiment, was serving as a brigade major when he was killed in action on 9 May 1917, aged 34. He was twice mentioned in despatches. His MC was gazetted on 14 January 1917, although there appears to be no citation for it.

Lieutenant Brian Wilmot L'Estrange MALONE, 1st Devonshire Regiment, was killed in action on 23 April 1917, aged 20. He was educated at Rugby School and the Royal Military College, Sandhurst, and had served overseas since May 1915. His father, Major Cecil Richard Robyn Malone, had served with the Worcestershire Regiment and the family lived in Penzance in Cornwall.

Lieutenant William John PETERS MC, 1st Devonshire Regiment, was killed in action on 23 April 1917. His MC was gazetted on 24 June 1916 and the citation appeared a month later, on 27 July. It was awarded for his work with the 38th Trench Mortar Battery after he had kept his trench mortars in action during a very heavy bombardment, showing conspicuous gallantry and devotion to duty.

Second Lieutenant Oswald William HARDWCK, 1st Devonshire Regiment, was killed in action on 9 May 1917, aged 25. His brother, Private Gerald Leslie Hardwick, was killed in action near Courcelette on 26 September 1916, aged 28. He is commemorated on the Vimy Memorial. Gerald was living in Canada when war broke out and was a civil engineer by profession. He enlisted at Valcartier on 24 September 1914 and initially served as a trooper in the Fort Garry Horse. However, by the time he came to England in October that year as part of the First Canadian Contingent, he was serving with the 6th Battalion, Canadian Infantry. Two months later he reverted back to the cavalry and, nominally at least, he remained a cavalryman until his death, although he was killed on the Somme serving in a dismounted capacity. The CWGC register shows him serving with the Canadian Corps Cavalry Regiment.

Private Frederick William John KING, 8th Devonshire Regiment, was killed in action on 7 May 1917, aged 29. He lived with his wife in Upper Holloway, north London. According to the CWGC register, he was one of eight brothers who served during the Great War, five of whom fell. Unfortunately, the CWGC records offer no clues as to the identity of his brothers.

The Suffolk Regiment

Major Harold PRETTY MC, 4th Suffolk Regiment, was killed in action on 24 March 1918. His MC was gazetted on 1 January 1918 in the New Year's Honours List.

Captain Douglas William Arthur NICHOLLS MC, 7th Suffolk Regiment, was killed in action on 10 April 1917. His MC was gazetted on 28 August 1916 and was awarded for conspicuous gallantry in action. During an assault he showed great coolness under heavy machine-gun fire, correcting the direction of an assaulting wave by means of compass bearing after it had lost its way in the darkness. He was later wounded whilst rallying the men to lead them forward again.

Lieutenant John Percival Curtis ASHWORTH MC, 7th Suffolk Regiment, was killed in action on 28 April 1917 during the fighting that took place that day near Monchy-le-Preux. He had also been mentioned in despatches a few months earlier in January. His MC was awarded posthumously for gallantry in action. When his battalion was held up during its advance, he went forward and carried out a reconnaissance under very heavy fire and brought back valuable information. His brother, Rupert Henry William Ashworth, served with the New Zealand Expeditionary Force and, although both brothers were living in New Zealand before the war, John chose to return to England in order to enlist. Their grandfather was Colonel William Charles Chester-Master and their great grandfather was Sir William Curtis, 3rd Baronet.

Lieutenant Wilfred Rodenhurst HALL MC, 11th Suffolk Regiment, was killed in action sometime between 21 and 22 March 1918, aged 20. His MC was gazetted on 18 October 1917 and the citation for it appeared on 7 March 1918. It was awarded for conspicuous gallantry and devotion to duty after he had taken command of the company following heavy casualties, including his senior officers who were all wounded. He reorganized the company and rallied the men, encouraging them with a display of great courage and coolness.

Second Lieutenant Arthur PRYKE MC, 2nd Suffolk Regiment, was killed in action on 11 April 1917, aged 22. His MC was gazetted on 18 July 1917 and was awarded for conspicuous gallantry and devotion to duty after he showed great coolness and courage whilst serving as intelligence officer, particularly with regard to two reconnaissance patrols that he carried out around new positions under heavy fire of all kinds. On each occasion he returned with valuable information which he then reported once he had arrived back at Battalion HQ. On a later date, he carried out a reconnaissance under similar conditions, but was wounded as he was returning.

Serjeant James Henry BUTCHER DCM, 7th Suffolk Regiment, was killed in action on 28 April 1917. His DCM was awarded for conspicuous gallantry during operations after the men in charge of a machine gun had all become casualties.

The gun was within twenty yards of the enemy's trench, yet he succeeded in bringing it back under heavy machine-gun and rifle fire. The award was gazetted on 20 October 1916.

Corporal Bertie Phillip NICHOLS, 8th Suffolk Regiment, was killed in action on 19 May 1917, aged 22. His brother, Rifleman John William NICHOLS, had been killed in action two weeks earlier. John fell on 3 May whilst serving with the 9th Rifle Brigade, aged 20. John is also commemorated here with his brother on the memorial.

Lance Corporal Luke ALDOUS, 7th Suffolk Regiment, who was killed in action on 23 April 1917, aged 22, came from Bedfield, Framlingham, Suffolk. He may possibly be related to Lance Corporal William ALDOUS, 9th Suffolk Regiment, who was killed in action on 19 October 1917, aged 27, and who came from Little Green, Saxted, Framlingham, in Suffolk. There is also the possibility that he may be related to Lance Corporal Edward William ALDOUS, 1/6th North Stafford-shire Regiment, who was killed in action on 24 May 1917, aged 30. He came from Cretingham, Framlingham, in Suffolk. If the men were related to each other, all three are commemorated here on the memorial.

Prince Albert's (Somerset Light Infantry)
Lieutenant Colonel William WATSON, 1st Somerset Light Infantry, command-ing the 2/5th King's Own (Yorkshire Light Infantry), was killed in action by a shell on 3 May 1917, aged 36. He had only recently returned from hospital to resume command of his battalion and was killed going forward with other officers in an attempt to reorganize and rally his men during the early hours of 3 May during the attack on Bullecourt. The attack began at 3.45am in darkness which, combined with the smoke and dust created by the barrage, had reduced visibility to a matter of yards. Most of the troops who attacked that day lost direction and found it extremely difficult to locate their objectives. On the other hand the German machine gunners managed to inflict heavy casualties everywhere along the line, even though firing blindly into the same obscurity. WATSON's men succeeded in reaching the enemy's front line, but failed to penetrate beyond. After he was killed, a second attempt also failed to get beyond the scattered shell holes in front of the enemy's wire. All the officers killed or missing that day from the 2/5th King's Own (Yorkshire Light Infantry) are commemorated on the Arras Memorial.

Private George Edward RYMAN, 8th Somerset Light Infantry, was killed in action on 28 April 1917, aged 19. The CWGC register points out that his father and six brothers also served. CWGC records suggest that he was the only family member to be killed during the war.

The Prince of Wales's Own (West Yorkshire Regiment)
Major Guy Nelson STOCKDALE MC and Bar, West Yorkshire Regiment, attached 11th Essex Regiment, was killed in action on 21 March 1918. His MC was gazetted on 24 June 1916 and the citation for it appeared a month later on

27 July. It was awarded for conspicuous courage and ability whilst serving as a lieutenant with the regiment's 1st Battalion. The entry in the *London Gazette* cites the manner in which he had handled his company during an attack, successfully consolidating his position under heavy machine-gun and rifle fire. The citation concludes by stating that on all occasions he had proved to be a capable and brave leader. The bar to his MC was gazetted on 14 November 1916 and was awarded for conspicuous gallantry in action whilst leading a bombing attack with great gallantry and ability, materially assisting the success of the operation and setting a fine example to all. *Officers Died in the Great War* makes no reference to the bar.

Lieutenant Tom Elsworth ARMISTEAD MC, 2/6th West Yorkshire Regiment, was killed in action on 3 May 1917 near Bullecourt. He was commissioned in the West Yorkshire Regiment from Lancing College OTC in September 1914. His MC was gazetted in the New Year's Honours List on 1 January 1917. His brother, Major Richard Burnie Armistead MC, also served with the West Yorkshire Regiment, and survived the war. Unlike his brother's award, Richard's MC was awarded for gallantry after leading his company and capturing an important enemy strongpoint. Once the position was secure, he took up an advanced position under heavy shell fire in order to oversee its consolidation. Another brother, Captain James Henry Armistead, also served in the West York-shire Regiment and survived.

Lance Corporal George Myers KIRK, 12th West Yorkshire Regiment, was killed in action on 3 May 1917, aged 19. His father, Albert Kirk, also served as a lance corporal, but with the 2/7th West Yorkshire Regiment. He was killed in action on 26 February 1917 and is buried at Puchevillers British Cemetery.

Private Herbert BOLINGBROKE, 1st West Yorkshire Regiment, was killed in action on 21 March 1918, aged 25. He was awarded the *Croix de Guerre* (Belgium) in April 1918.

The East Yorkshire Regiment
Captain James Carlton ADDY MC, 10th East Yorkshire Regiment, was killed in action on 3 May 1917, aged 26, whilst commanding 'A' Company in an attack near Oppy Wood. He had previously served in Egypt. His MC was gazetted on 4 June 1917 in the King's Birthday Honours List. His brother, Roland, also served, but was more fortunate and managed to survive.

Captain Harold William BROOKE, 'B' Company, 7th East Yorkshire Regiment, died of wounds on 24 April 1917 after his battalion had carried out an attack on Bayonet and Rifle Trenches under heavy artillery, rifle and machine-gun fire. Unknown to Captain BROOKE and the others, the Germans had filled in part of the forward trench, which was Bayonet Trench, forcing the attackers to continue their assault on Rifle Trench over the top in full view of the defences that lay ahead. Another part of Bayonet Trench had also been blocked and the enemy had set up a machine gun nearby dedicated solely to its defence. It was here that

Captain BROOKE was mortally wounded whilst leading a bombing party against the blocked trench in an attempt to clear it.

Captain Ernest William REEVE MC, 11th East Yorkshire Regiment, was killed in action on 3 May 1917, aged 39, during the attack on Oppy Wood. He was originally reported as missing, but was later presumed to have been killed. He was commissioned in November 1914 and his MC was gazetted on 4 June 1917 in the King's Birthday Honours List.

Lieutenant Errol Seymour RERRIE MC, 3rd East Yorkshire Regiment, attached 7th Battalion, was killed in action on 12 May 1917. His MC was gazetted on 26 September 1916 and was awarded for conspicuous gallantry during operations in which he twice led most daring reconnaissance patrols, each time lying out on the enemy's parapet in order to obtain information. On the second occasion he shot two of the enemy with his revolver. Whilst trying to bring one of the bodies back for identification purposes, he was spotted by the enemy and was subjected to heavy rifle fire and bombs.

Second Lieutenant Harry Liddell BAMBRIDGE MC, 7th East Yorkshire Regiment, was killed in action on 31 March 1918. Before the war he was a bank cashier with the National Provincial Bank in Leeds and had also been a member of the OTC at Queen's University, Belfast. His MC was gazetted on 27 September 1917 and the citation followed on 9 January 1918. It was awarded for conspicuous gallantry and devotion to duty whilst leading a successful raid on enemy trenches. Although the enemy's wire remained uncut, he still led his platoon forward with great skill, initiative and gallantry. When the officers from another company had become casualties, he took command of their men as well as his own and withdrew in accordance with the initial plan.

Second Lieutenant Marcus Henry CLIFT, 11th East Yorkshire Regiment, was killed in action on 8 November 1917. He was one of three brothers who served, two of whom fell. Private Sydney Clift was killed in action on 5 August 1916 when serving with the 18th Battalion, Australian Infantry. He is buried at Serre Road Cemetery No. 2. The family lived in Hampstead, London.

Second Lieutenant John HARRISON VC MC, 11th East Yorkshire Regiment, was killed in action on 3 May 1917, aged 26. Before the war he was well known in the north of England as a rugby league player. He played for Hull and had been selected for the Great Britain side that was set to tour Australia in 1914, but the outbreak of war caused the tour to be cancelled.

His MC, gazetted on 17 April 1917, was awarded for conspicuous gallantry and devotion to duty, handling his platoon with great skill and courage. He succeeded in reaching his objective under the most trying conditions and captured a prisoner, setting a splendid example throughout the operation, which was carried out on 25 February 1917. On discovering that the Germans had withdrawn, HARRISON pushed on as far as the fourth German trench, but then returned, noting that it was in very poor condition. His patrol managed to penetrate further than any of those sent out on his flanks, but he was ordered to pull back to the third line of trenches in order to avoid being exposed. Accordingly, he withdrew with his men before nightfall.

His VC, which was gazetted on 14 June 1917, was awarded for conspicuous bravery and self-sacrifice whilst leading his company in an attack on Oppy Wood. The smoke and dust from our own barrage and that of the enemy's, made it difficult to determine whether the barrage had lifted from the enemy's front line. His initial attack was repulsed by heavy rifle and machine-gun fire, but he re-organized his men as best as he could while pinned down in no man's land before attacking the enemy's position again. When this second assault also failed, he assaulted the machine-gun position single-handed and was killed whilst silencing it with a bomb. His body was never recovered.

Second Lieutenant Benjamin HUTCHINSON MC, 11th East Yorkshire Regiment, was killed in action on 3 May 1917, aged 23. His MC was gazetted on 17 April 1917 and was awarded for conspicuous gallantry and devotion to duty after taking his platoon across no man's land with sixty boxes of bombs for use by another party that was carrying out a reconnaissance of the enemy's line. Later he laid out a guiding tape in the most trying of circumstances.

Serjeant Thomas JACKSON DCM, 7th East Yorkshire Regiment, was killed in action on 24 March 1918. Whilst serving as the battalion's signalling sergeant he frequently rendered valuable service by maintaining and restoring communications, often under heavy fire. His DCM was awarded for conspicuous gallantry and devotion to duty in carrying out these tasks on numerous occasions. His award was gazetted later that year on 21 October 1918.

Serjeant Ernest MARRITT DCM, 11th East Yorkshire Regiment, was killed in action on 8 November 1917. He was a native of Hull and died serving with the 11th East Yorkshire Regiment (2nd Hull Pals). His DCM was gazetted the following year on 17 April and was awarded for conspicuous gallantry and devotion to duty during an attack in which he commanded a Lewis gun section. He showed resource and courage during the operation and it was his decisive role and handling of the situation that led to the capture of two enemy strongpoints and a machine gun.

Private Frederick Allan KIRKWOOD 1/4th East Yorkshire Regiment, was killed in action on 23 April 1917, aged 22. His brother, Private Ernest William KIRKWOOD, 12th East Yorkshire Regiment (3rd Hull Pals), was killed two weeks later on 3 May. Neither has a known grave and both are now commemorated here on the Arras Memorial.

The Bedfordshire Regiment

Regimental Serjeant Major William Thomas THEOBALD MC, 4th Bedfordshire Regiment, was killed in action on 25 March 1918, aged 39. His battalion was heavily engaged in defensive actions that day, initially near High Wood, falling back later towards Thiepval as the Germans continued to press forward across the old Somme battlefield. His MC was gazetted on 1 January 1918 in the New Year's Honours List. He was also mentioned in despatches on 9 April 1917.

Company Serjeant Major Richard M. BRAND DCM MM, 7th Bedfordshire Regiment, was killed in action near Chérisy on 3 May 1917 when the battalion came under heavy machine-gun fire. Survivors of the attack occupied a series of shell holes in front of Fontaine Trench and Wood Trench, but they eventually withdrew to their original positions when it became clear that there was no longer any chance of success that day. His DCM, gazetted on 25 November 1916, was awarded for conspicuous gallantry in action. Having assumed command of his company, he led it with great courage and initiative, reorganizing it and consolidating the position that had been gained during the operation.

Serjeant Frank William BAYFORD MM, 7th Bedfordshire Regiment, was killed in action on 3 May 1917, aged 22. His MM was awarded for his actions and conduct between 26 and 30 September 1916 near Thiepval and the Schwaben Redoubt, where he was also wounded.

Serjeant William FALLA DCM, 1st Bedfordshire Regiment, was killed in action on 28 June 1917, aged 31. His DCM was gazetted on 17 December 1914 and was awarded for conspicuous gallantry as a private on 7 November 1914 when he led a charge on a trench occupied by twenty-one of the enemy. Reaching it first, he destroyed it, killing some of the occupants and capturing others. The action in question occurred after a German attack had broken through on the left flank of his battalion south of Hooge, near Ypres. The attack was repulsed and the line was successfully restored.

Corporal Frank BRADLEY MM, 1st Bedfordshire Regiment, was killed in action on 23 April 1917. His MM was gazetted on 9 December 1916, although there does not seem to be any mention of him or his award in the battalion's war diary. Two other men from his battalion, who were also awarded the MM in the same Gazette, are referred to by name in the diary entry for 17 December. Their ribbons were presented to them by General Horne, Commander of the First Army, in the theatre at Béthune. Why BRADLEY's name does not appear in the diary entry for that day is not at all clear, but it could be that he was away from his battalion at the time.

Private John Edward WADHAMS, 4th Bedfordshire Regiment, was killed in action on 27 March 1918, aged 27. His younger brother, Private Thomas Edward WADHAMS, is also commemorated on the memorial and was killed in action a week earlier on 21 March serving with the 6th Battalion, Machine Gun Corps.

The Leicestershire Regiment
Captain John Clive SPENCER, 11th Leicestershire Regiment, was killed in action on 21 March 1918, aged 33. He was the son of the late Honourable John and Mrs Spencer and worked as a civil engineer in India before the war.

Lieutenant Christopher Francis ATTER, 1st Leicestershire Regiment, was killed in action on 21 March 1918, aged 19. When he enlisted in the regiment's 5th Battalion in August 1914 he was just 15 years old. He had also been wounded during his service. His brother, Private James Edward Atter, was killed in action when serving with the 5th Leicestershire Regiment on 16 April 1916, also aged 19. He, like Christopher, had enlisted in August 1914 and he went to France in February 1915. He is buried at Écoivres Military Cemetery.

Serjeant William Henry Abba BARRETT DCM, 11th Leicestershire Regiment, was killed in action on 22 March 1918. His DCM was gazetted on 3 September 1918 and was awarded for conspicuous gallantry and devotion to duty during a hostile attack. When all the officers of his company had become casualties, he assumed command and, although wounded, he kept the company under perfect control until fresh officers were able to arrive and take it over. In spite of his wounds he refused to retire and did splendid work, not only by encouraging and cheering the men, but also by superintending the issue of rations and ammunition.

Serjeant Albert Edward MUNN DCM, 9th Leicestershire Regiment, was killed in action on 3 May 1917, aged 30. His DCM was gazetted on 3 March 1917 and was awarded for conspicuous gallantry in action after organizing a number of men, who had become detached from the rest of their unit, and then leading them forward to the third objective, thereby protecting the left flank of the battalion on his right. The entry in the *London Gazette* is not easy to locate on account of the spelling of his surname, which is shown as 'Mann'.

Serjeant Herbert SHAW, 8th Leicestershire Regiment, was killed in action on 3 May 1917, aged 23. The CWGC register shows his sister residing at No. 5, Captain Albert Ball VC Memorial Houses, Church Street, Linton, Nottingham.

Lance Serjeant Percy FEARIES DCM, 2/4th Leicestershire Regiment, was killed in action on 24 March 1918. His DCM was gazetted on 18 June 1917 and was awarded for conspicuous gallantry and devotion to duty, displaying great courage and ability whilst commanding a patrol under heavy fire. The citation concludes that at all times he had a set a fine example.

Lance Serjeant George THORNE DCM, 11th Leicestershire Regiment, was killed in action on 21 March 1918. His DCM was gazetted on 13 February 1917 and was awarded for conspicuous gallantry and devotion to duty whilst serving as a private. The citation states very briefly that he, in company with another man, constantly patrolled between the lines looking for wounded and brought back valuable information. There are no further details in the citation with regard to when or where this occurred.

Corporal Maurice Andrew COPP, 'B' Company, 2/4th Leicestershire Regiment, was killed in action on 22 March 1918. He was 21 years old when he was killed and was one of five brothers who served during the war.

Lance Corporal Edward Arthur KIRK, 9th Leicestershire Regiment, was killed in action on 3 May 1917, aged 27. His brother, Private George Thomas Kirk, had enlisted at the same time and had also served in the same battalion. George was killed in action on 25 September 1916. Edward's army number was 24057 and George's was 24060. George also has no known grave and is now commemorated on the Thiepval Memorial.

Lance Corporal Herbert George WILKINSON, 8th Leicestershire Regiment, was killed in action on 3 May 1917, aged 35. He had previously served with the Royal Fusiliers and the 20th Hussars and was also a veteran of the South African campaign.

Private Horace CARR, 1/4th Leicestershire Regiment, was killed in action on 22 April 1917. His brother, Serjeant Edgar Carr, was killed in action towards the end of the Battle of Loos, on 13 October 1915, aged 27, whilst serving in the same battalion as his brother. He also has no known grave and is commemorated on the Loos Memorial.

The Royal Irish Regiment
There are just four privates and one officer from this regiment recorded on the memorial. All four belong to the regiment's 2nd Battalion. As regards the officer, Second Lieutenant Peter Leo McGRANE was killed whilst attached to the 1st Battalion, Royal Inniskilling Fusiliers, part of the 29th Division. The four privates were killed in action between 20 and 22 November 1917 during operations connected to the capture of Tunnel Trench, whereas McGRANE was killed earlier in the year on 20 May. McGRANE's father was a Justice of the Peace in County Dublin and the family is shown in the CWGC register as residing at Knocklyon Castle, which was originally a defensive structure built in the fifteenth century. The castle was bought by the family in 1826.

Alexandra, Princess of Wales's Own (Yorkshire Regiment)
Captain David Philip HIRSCH VC, 4th Yorkshire Regiment, was killed in action on 23 April 1917, aged 20. His VC was gazetted on 14 June 1917 and was awarded for most conspicuous bravery and devotion to duty in an attack near Wancourt. Although already twice wounded and having arrived at the first objective, he returned over fire-swept slopes to ensure that a defensive flank was being established. The machine-gun fire was so intense that it was necessary for him to move continuously up and down the line encouraging his men to dig and hold the position. In the face of a counter-attack and machine-gun fire he continued to encourage his men by standing on the parapet and steadying them until he was killed. The citation notes that his conduct throughout was a magnificent example of the greatest devotion to duty. He had previously been mentioned in despatches.

Second Lieutenant Ernest Frederick BEAL VC, 13th Yorkshire Regiment, was killed in action on 22 March 1918, aged 35. He had attended Brighton Grammar

School before going on to work for his father, who was a shopkeeper selling stationery. In September 1914 at the age of 31, Ernest enlisted locally as a trooper with the 2/1st Sussex Yeomanry. He initially served in the Balkans, but in September 1917 he was commissioned in the Yorkshire Regiment, originally with the 3rd Battalion, but was then posted to the 13th Battalion.

His VC was gazetted on 4 June 1918 and was awarded for most conspicuous bravery and determined leadership at Saint-Léger on 22 and 23 March 1918 whilst commanding a company detailed to occupy a section of trench. Once there, he discovered that a gap of some 400 yards existed between the left flank of his company and the next unit, and that this gap was now strongly occupied by the enemy. The gap needed to be closed, but there were no more troops available to carry out this task. With a small party of less than a dozen men, BEAL led an attack on the enemy's position. When his party reached one of the German machine guns, he leapt forward, killing the crew with his revolver and capturing the gun. Continuing along the trench, he encountered and dealt with another machine gun in exactly the same manner. In total, he captured four machine guns and inflicted many casualties on the enemy. Later that evening, after a wounded man had been left in the open under heavy fire, he went out to him and carried him to safety on his back, despite the close proximity of an enemy machine gun and the extreme danger to himself. Unfortunately, the following morning, BEAL was killed by a random shell.

Regimental Serjeant Major Harold KEETLEY MC, 7th Yorkshire Regiment, was killed in action on 14 May 1917, aged 33. His MC was gazetted on 26 March 1917 and was awarded for conspicuous gallantry in action. He showed great courage and initiative during an attack in which he personally accounted for a number of the enemy. Later he materially assisted in repelling an enemy counter-attack.

The Lancashire Fusiliers
Major David Charles Edward French COMYN, 10th Lancashire Fusiliers, was killed in action on 12 May 1917, aged 41. He was a Fellow of the Royal Geographical Society and an Esquire of the Order of the Hospital of St John of Jerusalem. He had also served in the South African War. He came from County Galway in Ireland. He was killed during an unsuccessful attack to capture two enemy trenches south of Gavrelle. Once captured, the intention had been to establish a series of posts beyond both trenches. Casualties for the operation amounted to thirteen officers, including Major COMYN, and 226 other ranks.

With attention about to turn to the Battle of Messines Ridge and the Third Battle of Ypres, all operations on the Arras front around this time, and indeed elsewhere, were required to be carried out with regard to 'economy of infantry'. The casualties sustained by COMYN's battalion on 12 May seem strangely at odds with that directive, but there was also a considerable element of bad luck involved. Shortly before the operation took place, a German aircraft had dropped a series of lights parallel to the assembly position of the attackers. This was a very deliberate act, effectively marking the location from which the attack was to be made. It was a very skilful piece of flying on the part of the German airman, which enabled the enemy's artillery to open up with deadly accuracy on the assembled attackers before the operation could be aborted.

Lieutenant Guy Bayford BELL, 5th Lancashire Fusiliers, attached 35th Company, Machine Gun Corps, was killed in action on 28 April 1917, aged 42. He returned from Australia to enlist and had initially served with the 28th Battalion, London Regiment (Artists' Rifles).

Second Lieutenant Bentinck Aglionby BINGHAM, 3rd Lancashire Fusiliers, attached 10th Battalion, was killed in action on 12 May 1917, aged 27. He had completed his education at King's College, London, where he had studied Theology and had been a member of its OTC. His family was from County Mayo, Ireland, and was descended from John Bingham, 1st Baron Clanmorris of Newbrook.

Second Lieutenant Bernard Matthew CASSIDY VC, 2nd Lancashire Fusiliers, was killed in action near Fampoux on 28 March 1918, aged 26. Bernard and his brother, John, had both initially enlisted in the Lancashire Fusiliers, although John was subsequently posted to the 1st Battalion and Bernard to the 2nd Battalion.

Bernard's VC was gazetted on 30 April 1918 and was awarded for conspicuous bravery, self-sacrifice, and exceptional devotion to duty during an enemy attack. He was in command of the left company of his battalion at a time when the divisional front was in danger. However, prior to this, he was given orders to hold his position at all costs.

When the enemy came on in overwhelming numbers in an attempt to turn the flank, he continually rallied his men under a terrific bombardment. Under his personal leadership, the enemy was then turned out of the trench on several occasions. Later, when his company became surrounded, he continued to fight on, encouraging and exhorting his men until he was eventually killed. However, his efforts were not in vain because the enemy was held up, which undoubtedly averted a disaster on the left flank.

His brother, John, was also commissioned and was awarded the MC which was gazetted on 4 February 1918. It was awarded after his unit was held up by rifle and machine-gun fire during an advance. He rallied his men, withdrawing them skilfully and successfully whilst exposed to fire the whole time. He brought back all the wounded, and finally carried in a badly wounded officer himself. Whilst doing so, he was attacked by an enemy party, which he successfully fought off with his revolver.

Second Lieutenant Lewis Charles Bagot CHESTER, 15th Lancashire Fusiliers, was killed in action on 4 April 1918, aged 20, although the regimental history records that he was killed the following day during a night attack on German trenches about three-quarters of a mile south of Ayette. The German garrison, estimated at around 100, replied with heavy rifle and machine-gun fire. The men of 'D' Company managed to bomb their way along 200 yards of enemy trench, where they successfully established a block, but the Germans swiftly counter-attacked before the supporting platoon was able to reach the survivors of the original raiding party.

When he and two fellow officers, Second Lieutenant H.A. Davis and Lieutenant A.G. Edghill, received orders to withdraw, Davis, who had been responsible for setting up the block, refused to leave the position exposed until all his men had withdrawn. Similarly, Second Lieutenant CHESTER was the last of his party to retire but, unlike Davis, he was killed as he was making his way back. Second Lieutenants Edghill and Davis both received the MC for this exploit, but unfortunately, Second Lieutenant CHESTER did not. Sadly, Second Lieutenant Ashley Gay Edghill died of wounds ten days later on 15 April 1918. He is buried at Doullens Communal Cemetery Extension, No. 1.

Lewis's brother, Lieutenant Greville Arthur Bagot Chester, was killed in action on 13 October 1914, aged 23, whilst serving with the 1st North Staffordshire Regiment. He is buried at Outtersteene Communal Cemetery Extension, Bailleul. Another brother, Anthony James Bagot Chester, fought in both the First and Second World Wars and reached the rank of major in the Royal Artillery. He was awarded the MC in the King's Birthday Honours List on 5 June 1916. Anthony's son also won the MC during the Second World War when serving with the Coldstream Guards.

Second Lieutenant Eric William ROSE MC, 1/8th Lancashire Fusiliers, was killed in action on 5 April 1918. His MC was gazetted on 26 July 1918 and was awarded for conspicuous gallantry and devotion to duty in action. The citation notes that, although he was a very junior officer, he commanded his company with great courage and ability, and that his resolution whilst leading a counter-attack was worthy of the utmost praise.

Company Quartermaster Serjeant Robert SHAW DCM, 1/8th Lancashire Fusiliers, who had formerly served with the 2nd King's Own (Royal Lancaster Regiment), was killed in action on 5 April 1918, aged 26. The citation for his DCM, which was gazetted posthumously on 3 September 1918, notes that he had performed fine work throughout the retirement in March earlier that year. On one occasion when all the officers were out of action, he took command of his company, rallying the men and leading them forward to a new position, which he had already personally reconnoitred. The citation comments that his behaviour, which had been splendid throughout, had set a brilliant example to all. During fighting at Bucquoy, he volunteered to carry out a reconnaissance in an effort to try to link up with troops on the right of his battalion, but was never seen again.

Serjeant John HEYWOOD, 11th Lancashire Fusiliers, was killed in action on 26 April 1916, aged 43. He was an experienced soldier who had previously served in the Sudan and in the South African campaign.

Corporal John MACK DCM, 11th Lancashire Fusiliers, was killed in action on 23 March 1918. His DCM was gazetted on 16 August 1917 and was won during the attack and capture of an enemy position when he had shown the greatest courage and energy, frequently leading assaults and entering the enemy's trenches before our barrage had properly lifted from them. The citation concludes that his spirit and dash inspired all about him.

Private John Francis BISHOP, 1/8th Lancashire Fusiliers, was killed in action on 25 March 1918, aged 24. His brother, Private Reginald Charles Bishop, who was killed in action on 18 April 1918 whilst serving with the 15th Durham Light Infantry, is commemorated on the Tyne Cot Memorial.

The Royal Scots Fusiliers
Captain Cyril Martin HADDEN, 3rd Royal Scots Fusiliers, attached 1st Battalion, was killed in action on 28 March 1918, aged 37. He had also been wounded on three previous occasions. Before the war he had studied at Aberdeen University where he obtained a Master's degree.

Second Lieutenant Alexander RAMSAY MC, 1/4th Royal Scots Fusiliers, attached 1st Battalion, was killed in action on 28 March 1918. His MC was gazetted on 17 September 1917 and was awarded for conspicuous gallantry and devotion to duty during an enemy bombardment. With great promptness and courage he made his way to a heavily shelled trench where he attended to the wounded. By his timely aid and presence of mind, he undoubtedly saved several lives and was instrumental in getting the wounded bandaged and removed before further casualties from shell fire could occur. The citation notes that in doing so he set a fine example to all ranks.

Company Serjeant Major George Albert MACK, DCM, 2nd Royal Scots Fusiliers, was killed in action on 23 April 1917, aged 38. He had won his DCM as a lance corporal at Vailly in September 1914 whilst serving with the 1st Battalion. There, on three occasions, he carried wounded men from the trenches to safe cover, each time crossing a hundred yards of open ground under heavy fire. The award was gazetted on 1 May 1915.

The Cheshire Regiment
Major John Rushton MOORE MC, 3rd Cheshire Regiment, attached Machine Gun Corps, was killed in action between 21 and 23 March 1918. His MC was gazetted in the King's Birthday Honours List on 3 June 1916.

Serjeant William CUTHBERTSON DCM MM, 9th Cheshire Regiment, was killed in action on 14 March 1918. His DCM was awarded after he had volunteered to carry out a patrol in front of his company's position, returning with valuable information. Later that night he again went out on patrol; although badly hit, he managed to evade the enemy, crawling back to his own trenches with information that was urgently required. The citation notes that his courage and determination set a fine example to the rest of his company.

Private William Morbon POOLE, 5th Cheshire Regiment, was killed in action on 13 May 1917, aged 21. His brother, Private Arthur Poole, was killed serving with the 20th King's (Liverpool Regiment) on 30 July 1916, aged 26. He also has no known grave and is commemorated on the Thiepval Memorial.

The Royal Welsh Fusiliers

Lieutenant Colonel Albert John Stanley JAMES DSO MC, 10th Royal Welsh Fusiliers, commanding the 8th King's Own (Royal Lancaster Regiment), was killed in action near Guémappe on 28 March 1918. His DSO was gazetted on 3 June 1918 in the King's Birthday Honours List. He was killed by a shell whilst personally reorganizing his own battalion and small detachments of at least two others after his flanks had come under threat following the retirement of units either side of it. Colonel JAMES landed in France with the 10th Royal Welsh Fusiliers on 27 September 1915 and remained with the battalion until the British Army was forced to reorganize in February 1918. Following that restructuring, he briefly took over the 8th Entrenching Battalion before he assumed command of the 8th King's Own (Royal Lancaster Regiment). His DSO was awarded for services in the field rather than for any specific act of gallantry. His MC was gazetted on 1 January 1917 in the New Year's Honours List and was also awarded for services in the field.

Company Serjeant Major William WHITBREAD DCM MM, 1st Royal Welsh Fusiliers, was killed in action on 14 May 1917. His DCM was gazetted on 25 November 1916 and was won as an acting company serjeant major. It was awarded for conspicuous gallantry in action after leading several bombing attacks with great courage and skill, capturing 100 yards of the enemy's trenches. Later he led three rushes to extend his gains in the face of intense fire.

Serjeant Thomas HUGHES DCM MM, 2nd Royal Welsh Fusiliers, was killed in action on 23 April 1917 near Tunnel Trench. His DCM was won as an acting corporal and was awarded for conspicuous gallantry whilst conducting night patrols, particularly on the night of 27/28 March 1915 when he was wounded. The award was gazetted on 30 June 1915 and his exploit is described in some detail in J.C. Dunn's excellent work, *The War the Infantry Knew 1914–1919*. He went out on 28 March as part of a small party to bomb an enemy post. He and the officer in charge had been out previously to reconnoitre the position and had almost been trodden on by a German patrol. Although they managed to bomb the post, HUGHES was wounded in the leg, as was the officer with him.

Corporal George William HOOD DCM, 1st Royal Welsh Fusiliers, was killed in action on 15 May 1917, aged 19. He chose to serve under the name of 'John BURTON', which is how he is listed in *Soldiers Died in the Great War*, although the war memorial in Crewe shows him as 'Hood'. His DCM was gazetted on

18 July 1917 under the name of J. BURTON and was awarded for conspicuous gallantry and devotion to duty while performing the role of acting corporal. The citation records that he rendered most valuable assistance by taking a section of bombers to the aid of the battalion on his flank. Although surrounded at one point, he fought his way out with just five men.

Private Eden Thomas BAYLISS, 1st Royal Welsh Fusiliers, was killed in action on 4 May 1917, aged 26. His brother, Private Frederick William Bayliss, who had originally served with the Devonshire Regiment, was killed on 2 October 1917, after having transferred to the 155th Company, Labour Corps. He is buried at Coxyde Military Cemetery.

Private Daniel DAVIES DCM, 9th Royal Welsh Fusiliers, was killed in action on 22 March 1918, aged 27. His DCM was awarded for conspicuous gallantry and devotion to duty as a stretcher-bearer during an attack. He continually attended to the wounded under rifle and shell fire, and on one occasion he left the trench under heavy fire to rescue a badly wounded man who was lying out in the open. The citation concludes that he set a splendid example of courage and devotion to duty. His award was gazetted on 26 January 1918.

The South Wales Borderers
Serjeant Albert WHITE VC, 2nd South Wales Borderers, was killed in action on 19 May 1917, aged 23. His death occurred during an attack north-west of Monchy-le-Preux near Bit Lane and Devil's Trench. As soon as the British barrage opened up, the German machine guns also began firing. After two officers were shot, it seemed as though the battalion's attack might break down completely. It was at this point that Serjeant WHITE tried to retrieve the situation. After identifying one of the enemy machine guns responsible for holding up the advance of his company, he unhesitatingly and with total disregard for his own personal safety dashed towards the gun in a bid to capture it. Firstly, he disposed of the small party of Germans covering the position, shooting three and bayoneting the fourth, but just as he was about to tackle the gun and its crew he was hit. He fell within a few yards of the gun, his body riddled with bullets, having willingly sacrificed his own life in an attempt to secure the success of the operation and the safety of his comrades. The attack did, in fact, break down and the sixty-one survivors eventually made their way back to our lines, half of them wounded. However, WHITE and fifty-one other ranks still lay out on the battle-field, most of them dead, others wounded and still under fire. The citation for his VC was gazetted on 27 June 1917 and it was awarded for conspicuous bravery and devotion to duty.

Lance Corporal George Alfred FIELD, 1st South Wales Borderers, was killed in action on 20 February 1916, aged 18. He was killed near Loos during an assault on two craters, known locally as Harrison's Crater and Hart's Crater. His father,

Arthur S. Field, had served as a major in the Oxfordshire & Buckinghamshire Light Infantry.

The King's Own Scottish Borderers

Captain Samuel FARISH, 1st King's Own Scottish Borderers, was killed in action near Monchy-le-Preux on 24 April 1917, aged 21. He enlisted in August 1914. He had been wounded twice; once on 8 December 1915 at Tartali in Serbia during defensive operations against Bulgarian forces around Crête Simonet, and again at Ypres on 21 August 1916. However, he could not have been serving with the King's Own Scottish Borderers in December 1915, as none of the regiment's battalions ever served in Macedonia. The 10th (Irish) Division was involved in the operations at Tartali, so presumably he would have been serving with one of its battalions when he was wounded.

Captain Sidney McGOWAN MC, 5th King's Own Scottish Borderers, was killed in action on 25 May 1917. He had originally served with the Lanarkshire Yeomanry, but was commissioned in the 2/5th King's Own Scottish Borderers in September 1915. Although he is shown serving with this regiment in the CWGC register, he was not with any of its battalions at the time of his death. He joined the 1/6th South Staffordshire Regiment in July 1916, just after it had been involved in the failed attack at Gommecourt, and went on to win his MC with the battalion on the night of 2/3 October 1916 near Berles-au-Bois. His MC was gazetted on 20 October 1916, soon after the event, and was awarded for conspicuous gallantry during a raid. The citation states that his contribution to the operation played a significant part in its success. It notes that he had handled his section of the raiding party with great skill and determination. He was subsequently transferred to the 1/6th North Staffordshire Regiment and was killed in action during an attack on a trench known as Nash Alley, near Liévin.

Captain Thomas Mayne REID MC, 9th King's Own Scottish Borderers, attached 6th Battalion, was killed in action near Greenland Hill on 3 May 1917, aged 31. His MC was gazetted on 3 March 1917 and was awarded for conspicuous gallantry in connection with a raid. Prior to the raid, he carried out several valuable patrols and during the raid itself he showed marked courage, successfully firing two Bangalore torpedoes. The raid took place on 11 January that year and resulted in the capture of three prisoners at a cost of one man killed and one other wounded.

Second Lieutenant Ninian Parker LAIRD DCM, 3rd King's Own Scottish Borderers, attached 7/8th Battalion, was killed in action on 28 March 1918, aged 39. He had enlisted in August 1914 and had previously served as a staff serjeant with the 2nd London Sanitary Corps, part of the Territorial Force. His DCM was awarded whilst serving as a staff serjeant in the Royal Army Medical Corps and was gazetted on 22 September 1916. According to the citation, he had set a fine example whilst in charge of stretcher-bearers during operations in which all the wounded were collected, despite heavy shell and machine-gun fire.

Second Lieutenant Percy John WILDMAN-LUSHINGTON, 3rd King's Own Scottish Borderers, attached 6th Battalion, fell in action near Greenland Hill on 3 May 1917, aged 28. His brother, Gilbert Vernon Wildman-Lushington, was killed in a flying accident near Eastchurch in December 1913 whilst serving with the Naval Wing of the Royal Flying Corps. He broke his neck when a landing went wrong during a flight with Captain Henry Fawcett, who was piloting the aircraft. He is buried in Christ Church Cemetery, Portsdown Hill, Hampshire. Fawcett survived the crash, but was killed in action on 29 December 1918 when serving with the Royal Marine Light Infantry during the Russian Campaign. He is buried at Murmansk New British Cemetery. Their late father had served as a captain in the King's Own Scottish Borderers. Gilbert's claim to fame was that he once gave flying instruction to Winston Churchill in a dual-control aircraft.

Company Serjeant Major Thomas PRENTICE MC, 1st King's Own Scottish Borderers, was killed in action on 16 April 1917, aged 32. His MC was gazetted on 22 September 1916 and was awarded for conspicuous gallantry earlier in the year opposite Beaumont Hamel on 1 July. When all his officers had become casualties, he took command of the company and held his ground with great determination until ordered to withdraw. The citation ends by stating that from the very start of the campaign he had done fine work.

Private John CURRIE, 'D' Company, 6th King's Own Scottish Borderers, was killed in action on 3 May 1917, aged 35. Before the war he had taught Art at the Academy and Technical College in Galashiels and had also gained a diploma from the renowned Glasgow School of Art.

The Cameronians (Scottish Rifles)

Captain Charles Mortimer Austin GUNN, 5th Cameronians, was killed in action on 20 May 1917, aged 21. He was educated at Glasgow High School, then at Glasgow University, where he became a member of its OTC. He had intended to pursue a career in business, but when war broke out he decided to enlist, accepting a commission in the 11th Cameronians in November 1914. He was wounded at Mametz in October 1916. The entry in the CWGC register is quite unusual in so far as it comments on the manner of his death, noting that he was killed whilst working a machine gun that had jammed during an early morning attack at Fontaine-lès-Croisilles.

His brother, Private Thomas Stanley Gunn, also attended Glasgow University and was intending to pursue a career in accountancy. When war broke out he joined the 9th (Glasgow Highlanders) Highland Light Infantry, but was killed near Givenchy on 26 February 1915, aged 24. His unit had carried out a raid there a week earlier, to which the Germans responded by frequently shelling the battalion's trenches. Thomas is buried at Gorre British and Indian Cemetery.

Lieutenant Douglas Ambrose SEATH, 2nd Cameronians, attached 10th Battalion, was killed by a shell on 24 April 1917 whilst supervising his men as they were digging trenches near some captured positions. He was wounded on two previous occasions during his service, one of which was at Martinpuich on 15 September 1916. According to his commanding officer, Lieutenant SEATH had sent back a message shortly before his death stating that he had captured the trench and was digging in. He also added that he had sent sixty prisoners back and concluded his message with the words: '*Scotland for Ever!*'

The entry in the CWGC register shows him attached to the 6th Border Regiment, but this is not the case. Quite apart from the above account, the 6th Border Regiment was not involved in the Second Battle of the Scarpe, although it was in the general vicinity of Arras as part of the 11th (Northern) Division. Lieutenant SEATH had, however, previously served with the 28th Battalion, London Regiment (Artists' Rifles), and had enlisted on the day that war was declared. His father had served as a captain in the artillery.

Captain James Wallace KENNEDY, 4th Cameronians, attached 1st Battalion, was killed in action on 27 May 1917, aged 22. Although he was an only son, his parents also had three daughters and the family lived in Edinburgh in moderate but comfortable circumstances. James attended George Watson's College between 1902 and 1911 where he became a keen member of the college's scout troop and OTC. After leaving school he followed his father into banking and began his career at the Leith branch of the Bank of Scotland. Around this time he also became a member of the Royal Scots Cadet Corps where he became a serjeant. When the war broke out his experience and background made him an ideal candidate for a commission, but he was subsequently gazetted in the Cameronians rather than the Royal Scots. He went to France in March 1916 and he was later mentioned in despatches. He was killed during operations to capture part of the Hindenburg Support Trench. Although the support line was reached and held throughout 27 May, the 1st Cameronians and the 2nd Royal Welsh Fusiliers found themselves back in their original positions by 8.00am the following day. After all their efforts, the objective had proved untenable.

Second Lieutenant John Dormer CLARK, 6th Cameronians, attached 1st Battalion, was killed in action on 27 May 1917, aged 21. His brother, Captain Allan La Barte Clark, Royal Army Medical Corps, was killed in action in Salonika on 18 September 1918, aged 27, whilst attached to the 12th Cheshire Regiment. He is commemorated on the Doiran Memorial in northern Greece. Their father, John Clark, served as Chief Constable of Hamilton in Lanarkshire between 1919 and 1922.

Second Lieutenant Alexander McEwan FISHER, 'C' Company, 10th Cameronians, was killed in action on 24 April 1917, aged 26. He fell somewhere between Cavalry Farm and the River Cojeul. The battalion's assembly trenches were heavily shelled about twenty minutes before the attack, which took place at

4.00pm. When the advance started it was met by heavy machine-gun fire from the direction of Cavalry Farm. 'A' and 'C' Companies managed to get within 200 yards of the farm before the attack broke down. Before the war FISHER had been a junior partner in a firm of solicitors in Wishaw, near Motherwell.

Second Lieutenant Alexander Tudhope GRAY, 6th Cameronians, attached 10th Battalion, was killed in action on 21 April 1917, aged 35. Regimental sources show his death occurring on 22 April 1917 whilst carrying out a reconnaissance. He initially served in Egypt as a private with the Army Service Corps, but was commissioned in the Cameronians towards the end of 1916. The CWGC register notes that his father had served as a major and that the family was from Carluke in Lanarkshire.

Second Lieutenant Stewart Lindsay Leighton NEWLANDS, 7th Cameronians, attached 1st Battalion, was killed in action on 27 May 1917. His brother, Private George Rennie Newlands, 5th Cameron Highlanders, died of wounds on 16 April 1917, aged 20. He is buried at Étaples Military Cemetery. The brothers came from the Crosshill area of Glasgow.

Second Lieutenant Thomas Armin OPPÉ, 4th Cameronians, attached 1st Battalion, was killed in action on 20 May 1917, aged 36. His brother, Lieutenant Henry Sigismund Oppé, was killed in action on 6 November 1915 at Gallipoli. Although gazetted to the 11th Yorkshire Regiment, Henry was actually killed whilst serving with the 6th Battalion after he and other men had been drafted in during October to replace losses. Just three weeks after arriving on the peninsula he was shot dead by a sniper. He was 35 years old when he died and is buried in Hill 10 Cemetery. The family came from Pamber Heath, near Basingstoke in Hampshire.

Second Lieutenant Alexander Stewart PRATT, 12th Cameronians, attached 10th Battalion, was killed in action on 24 March 1917 during a raid. His position for the raid was at the front of the first column of men from 'B' Company. Accompanied by five other men, he made his way as far as the enemy's support line without encountering any opposition other than wire. Eventually he reached a block where the communication trench intersected the support trench. Here he found two German sentries bearing rifles. PRATT shot both of them, but as he was scaling the block he was struck and killed by a grenade thrown from a distance of about fifteen yards. This was the furthest point reached by his party during the raid. When the attackers withdrew they were unable to recover his body.

Second Lieutenant Frank Arthur RAYNES MC, 3rd Cameronians, attached 17th Royal Scots, was killed in action on 27 March 1918, aged 26. His MC was gazetted on 9 January 1918 and was awarded for conspicuous gallantry and devotion to duty under very difficult circumstances when the garrison of a farm was surprised by an enemy raiding party in thick fog and the sentry groups were being bombed out of their positions. Although attacked from three sides, he showed admirable presence of mind and disregard of danger. With the assistance of other officers and NCOs, he collected the scattered sentries and reformed the line. He then led them forward across the open and recaptured the original position.

Second Lieutenant William Marshall STEWART, 8th Cameronians, attached 10th Battalion, was killed in action on 24 March 1917, aged 27. He fell whilst taking part in a raid and was one of a number of men killed or wounded by British shells when they fell short at the start of the operation. Arrangements had been made for the artillery and trench mortar barrage to fall on the enemy's front line for five minutes in order to allow the two companies to cross no man's land and reach the enemy's wire. However, a sudden drop in air temperature caused the gun barrels to contract slightly, but sufficient to create friction and drag on the shells as they left the barrels, consequently reducing their range by just a fraction. STEWART was within twenty-five yards of the German front line when he was killed.

His brother, Surgeon Thomas Louis Grenet Stewart, died of wounds whilst serving as a Sanitary Medical Officer with 1st Royal Naval Brigade HQ attached to the Hospital Ship *Ascania*. His death occurred on 4 June 1915 at the Third Battle of Krithia during the Gallipoli Campaign. He had studied Medicine at the University of Glasgow and came from the Barrhead area of the city. He was 27 years old when he died and is buried at East Mudros Military Cemetery.

Second Lieutenant Frederick Whitecross TURNER, 4th Cameronians, attached 10th Battalion, was killed in action near Feuchy on 9 April 1917, aged 23. He enlisted in October 1914 and was gazetted in September 1915. He came from the Hillhead area of Glasgow. The battalion came under heavy enemy shell fire as it advanced. TURNER was killed whilst attempting to carry the advance through the barrage towards the Brown Line, which was the objective. By 4.00pm the 10th Battalion and the 7/8th King's Own Scottish Borderers had captured this important position. The battalion war diary records that TURNER was one of two officers killed that day along with twenty other ranks, although a further two officers and 112 other ranks were wounded. The 15th (Scottish) Division was the only division to capture the Brown Line, south of the River Scarpe, on the opening day of the Battle of Arras.

Serjeant John ERSKINE VC, 5/6th Cameronians, was killed in action on 14 April 1917, aged 23. His VC was awarded for most conspicuous bravery at Givenchy on 22 June 1916 as an acting serjeant. When the near lip of a crater was being consolidated after the explosion of a large enemy mine, ERSKINE rushed out under continuous fire and, with utter disregard for his own safety, rescued two wounded men. It was initially believed that the officer in charge of his party was dead, but later, seeing the officer show signs of movement, ERSKINE ran out and bandaged his head. Despite being repeatedly fired on, he remained with the officer for a good hour or so while the rest of his party dug a shallow trench towards them. He then assisted in bringing in the officer, shielding him with his own body to lessen the chance of his being hit again. Unfortunately the officer, Second Lieutenant David James Stevenson, died from his wounds the same day and is buried at Gorre British and Indian Cemetery. The award was gazetted on 5 August 1917. At the time of his death he was an acting company serjeant major.

The Royal Inniskilling Fusiliers

Lieutenant Gerald Hans Hendrick AYLMER, 'B' Company, 2nd Royal Inniskilling Fusiliers, attached 1st Battalion, was killed in action on 16 April 1917. He was from County Kildare and was the youngest of four children born to Hans Hendrick Hendrick-Aylmer, barrister-at-law, and a graduate of Trinity College, Dublin. The family was well-established and well-connected, with a lineage going back to at least the fifteenth century. Other records often show Gerald's surname as Hendrick-Aylmer, which I believe is the correct version. His two nephews were killed in action during the Second World War. Lance Corporal Cecil Penrose was killed in action on 14 March 1942 and is commemorated on the Alamein Memorial in Egypt; Lieutenant Guy Trevenan Penrose was killed in action serving with the Royal Artillery on 15 November 1942 and is buried at Tabarka Ras Rajel War Cemetery in Tunisia. Their father was Brigadier John Penrose MC, Royal Artillery.

Lieutenant Malcolm Wilfred Forester HALL, 5th Royal Inniskilling Fusiliers, attached 1st Battalion, was killed in action on 20 May 1917, aged 29. He had been wounded at Gallipoli. He was the son of the late Colonel Henry Adair HALL, who served with the 52nd (Oxfordshire) Regiment of Light Infantry, which in 1881 amalgamated with the 43rd (Monmouthshire) Regiment of Foot to become the Oxfordshire & Buckinghamshire Light Infantry.

The Gloucestershire Regiment

Captain Wilfrid Wharton PARR MC, 12th Gloucestershire Regiment, was killed in action on 8 May 1917, aged 44. He was commissioned in the Gloucestershire Regiment in April 1915 and his MC was gazetted in the New Year's Honours List in 1917. After the village of Fresnoy was captured by Canadian troops on 4 May, the 5th Division took over the newly won positions. On 8 May, using a fresh division, the Germans launched a counter-attack to retake the village and it was during this struggle that Captain PARR was killed whilst trying to restore the line. He was initially reported as missing in action, but one account insists that he was last seen fighting at close quarters, armed only with an entrenching tool. His brother, Lieutenant Hugh Wharton Myddleton Parr, was killed in action serving with the 1/5th South Staffordshire Regiment on 5 May 1915, aged 35. He is buried at Saint-Quentin Cabaret Military Cemetery.

Captain Joseph Herbert WRIGHT MC, 8th Gloucestershire Regiment, was killed in action on 25 March 1918, aged 33. His MC was also gazetted in the New Year's Honours List in January 1917. Before the war he had studied in London where he graduated with a Bachelor of Science degree. He then went on to teach

Science at a school in Gloucestershire. When the war broke out, he initially joined the Gloucestershire Hussars, but in November 1914 he was commissioned in the 8th Gloucestershire Regiment. He then went overseas as part of the 19th (Western) Division and saw action on the Somme, where he was wounded on 3 July in the fierce fighting that took place around the village of La Boisselle. He was wounded for a second time during the capture of Messines Ridge in June 1917 and was eventually killed in action the following year whilst fighting a rearguard action near Vélu Wood.

Second Lieutenant Cyril Austin OLDS DCM, 3rd Gloucestershire Regiment, attached 1st Battalion, was killed in action by shell fire near Loos on 16 April 1916, aged 21. His DCM was won as a private whilst serving in the Royal Army Medical Corps and was awarded for the gallant manner in which he carried out his duties under heavy shell fire. His award was gazetted on 1 April 1915.

Private Bertram Douglas BROOMFIELD, 8th Gloucestershire Regiment, is shown as having died between 21 and 28 March 1918. Such an extended period is fairly unusual with regard to the Great War, although it is seen far more frequently in relation to May 1940. Nevertheless there are other cases, especially in March 1918, where the exact date of death remains uncertain. This merely reflects the confusion, and sometimes the isolation, in which units and detachments fought as they retreated during the German advances in March.

Private Alfred Gordon SMITH, 12th Gloucestershire Regiment, was killed in action on 8 May 1917, aged 20. His father, James Smith, had served as a squadron serjeant major in the Pembroke Yeomanry.

The Worcestershire Regiment
Lieutenant Colonel Alfred Caldier LADD, 14th Worcestershire Regiment, was killed in action on 25 March 1918. He had previously served in the South African War and had also been awarded the *Croix de Guerre* (Belgium). He served throughout the war with the 14th Battalion and rose from second lieutenant to become its adjutant, then second-in-command, and finally its commanding officer early in 1918. His battalion was the pioneer battalion attached to the 63rd (Royal Naval) Division. On 25 March it fought a rearguard action near the village of Courcelette with the 1st Battalion Royal Marine Light Infantry on its left. Later in the day the Royal Marines withdrew, leaving the 14th Worcestershire Regiment to cover their retirement. Lieutenant Colonel LADD was badly wounded during this phase of the fighting and was sent back on a stretcher. However, he died from his wounds later that day in German captivity after the stretcher-bearers lost their way and were captured.

Captain James Robert BLAKE, 8th Worcestershire Regiment, attached 14th Battalion, was also killed in action on 25 March 1918, aged 24. He was twice mentioned in despatches and was wounded on 3 February 1917 just north of the River Ancre whilst following up an attack on enemy trenches by the 63rd (Royal

Naval) Division. When BLAKE and others from 'D' Company went forward to consolidate the captured trenches they became involved in the fighting that was still taking place there. BLAKE was one of three officers and eighteen men from his company who became casualties before the position could be entrenched satisfactorily. He was declared missing in action near Courcelette during the same fighting in which his commanding officer was wounded and captured. He is remembered back home by a stained glass window in Worcester Cathedral.

Captain Eric Alexander Ogilvie DURLACHER MC, 5th Worcestershire Regiment, attached 2nd Battalion, was killed in action on 20 May 1917. He was wounded whilst leading his company forward in a local attack on a section of the Hindenburg Line between Croisilles and Fontaine-lès-Croisilles. He refused to break off in order to have his wounds dressed and was shot dead later that day. His MC was gazetted on 17 April 1917 and was awarded for conspicuous gallantry and devotion to duty during a raid on the enemy's trenches on the night of 27/28 February 1917 when he displayed great courage and initiative and carried out the task allotted to him with conspicuous success. The raid took place near Cléry on the Somme and was directed against a small salient in the German lines. Sixteen prisoners were captured and the number of enemy dead was estimated at around fifty after some fierce fighting at close quarters. The raiders sustained around sixty casualties, which also bears testimony to the severity of the fighting, although the majority of these were wounded and returned to our own lines.

Captain Archibald Edward OSBORNE, 5th East Kent Regiment (The Buffs), attached 10th Worcestershire Regiment, was killed in action on the evening of 21 March 1918 in a counter-attack on the village of Doignies. The attack, delivered by his battalion and the 8th Gloucestershire Regiment, was supported by tanks; however, all of them broke down or were soon put out of action. The 8th Gloucestershire Regiment managed to enter the village, but was unable to hold it and was forced to retire. The 10th Worcestershire Regiment was involved in bitter fighting around the sunken road between Doignies and Beaumetz-lès-Cambrai, which was almost certainly where OSBORNE fell. He was gazetted initially from the Honourable Artillery Company, but also served with the 7th Loyal North Lancashire Regiment. He was awarded the *Croix de Guerre* with Palm (France) and had been mentioned in despatches.

Second Lieutenant Frederick Carlton James BRAKE, 10th Worcestershire Regiment, was killed in action on 21 March 1918, aged 24. He initially served at the 5th Canadian General Hospital as a private in the Canadian Army Medical Corps, but he also went on to serve in Salonika. He was the son of a career soldier and veteran of the South African campaign, Major Timothy Francis Brake, Royal Army Medical Corps. Frederick was born in the garrison town of Aldershot, but at some stage he moved to British Columbia where he worked as a bank clerk before enlisting in June 1915.

Second Lieutenant Geoffrey Douglas Lothian NICHOLSON, 4th Worcestershire Regiment, was killed in action on the morning of 23 April 1917, aged 19. He fell as his battalion was attacking towards Infantry Hill, just east of Monchy-le-Preux. The battalion began to take casualties from enemy shelling as soon as it left the trenches, but still managed to push on to the summit of the hill where it began to consolidate. Throughout the day casualties continued to mount, mainly from shelling, but the battalion was able to hold on without support until the afternoon when one company of the 16th Middlesex Regiment managed to get through. Later, a German counter-attack retook a small copse on the southern slopes of the hill, forcing the battalion's right flank to fall back. A consolidated line west of the copse was eventually handed over during the early hours of the 24th, but the remainder of the men on the left-hand side of the hill were forced to hold on to their position until the following night. He was the only son of Major General Cecil Lothian Nicholson CMG, commander of the 34th Division from 1916 to 1919 and eight times mentioned in despatches.

Serjeant Bertram SALT DCM, 10th Worcestershire Regiment, fell in action on 21 March 1918. His DCM was won during a daylight raid on an enemy position when he led his men through a heavy hostile barrage and up to the enemy's wire. Before he got through the wire he killed three of the enemy. He then entered the German trench with his men, bombed the dug-outs and obtained identifications. After the raiding party had withdrawn, he went back into no man's land on two occasions and, in spite of intense machine-gun fire, brought in two of his wounded comrades. The citation concludes that his example, initiative and utter disregard for danger had a splendid effect on his men. The award was gazetted on 4 March 1918.

Private Leonard John BROWN, 3rd Worcestershire Regiment, was killed in action on 28 April 1916, aged 21. His brother, Lance Corporal Herbert Leslie Brown, was killed in action the following year on 9 October 1917 whilst serving with the 6th York & Lancaster Regiment near Ypres. He is commemorated on the Tyne Cot Memorial.

Private James CLEWLEY MM, 10th Worcestershire Regiment, was killed in action on 25 March 1918 near Loupart Wood, south of Grévillers, as his battalion conducted a fighting retreat, withdrawing by alternate companies. His MM was gazetted on 1 September 1916.

Private Harry COLLINS, 3rd Worcestershire Regiment, was killed in action on 28 April 1916, aged 21. His brothers, Frederick and Thomas Henry, were also killed in action. The CWGC records do not assist in the identification of either brother.

Private Frederick SMITH, 14th Worcestershire Regiment, was killed in action on 21 March 1918, aged 19. His elder brother, Private Joseph Henry Smith, was killed in action the following day, aged 24, serving with the 2nd Yorkshire Regiment. He is commemorated on the Pozières Memorial.

Private William ANDREWS MM, 'C' Company, 2/7th Worcestershire Regiment, was killed in action on 24 October 1917. He was a member of a raiding party that assaulted the enemy's trenches east of the Chemical Works that day. The raid was successful in so much as the necessary identifications were made and an enemy machine gun was damaged. However, several men were wounded, some of whom were later rescued, but five were found to be still missing. One of the missing men was Private ANDREWS.

The East Lancashire Regiment

Second Lieutenant Basil Arthur HORSFALL VC, 11th East Lancashire Regiment, was killed in action on 27 March 1918, aged 30. His VC was gazetted on 22 May 1918 and was awarded for most conspicuous bravery and devotion to duty. On 27 March during a German attack he was in command of the centre platoon. When his three forward sections were driven back, he reorganized the remainder of his men and, despite having been wounded in the head, he led a counter-attack and successfully recovered his platoon's original positions. When he became aware that two of the three officers in his company had been killed and the other wounded, he refused to have his own wounds dressed in spite of their severity. His platoon was later withdrawn owing to heavy shell fire, but once the shelling stopped, he immediately led another counter-attack, recovering the ground that had been lost. He and his men were again ordered to withdraw when the line came under renewed pressure, but he was the last to leave and was killed in action soon afterwards whilst carrying out the retirement. His death occurred somewhere between Ablainzevelle and Moyenneville.

He was born in Ceylon and, after completing his education in England, he returned there where he worked for a while in rubber planting before joining the Civil Service in Colombo.

Serjeant Joseph BATTY MM and Bar, 2nd East Lancashire Regiment, was killed in action on 17 February 1918. Both awards were gazetted within weeks of each other, the MM on 16 November 1916 and the bar on 6 January 1917. He is shown on the Addenda Panel.

Private William ASPDEN, 8th East Lancashire Regiment, was killed in action on 21 May 1917, aged 25. Private Austin Segar ASPDEN and Private Albert ASPDEN, both of the 11th East Lancashire Regiment, were killed in action on 27 March 1918, and are both shown on the Addenda Panel of the memorial. I have no information to suggest the three men were related, but there is a possibility that they could have been, especially as Austin and Albert came from parts of Lancashire very close to each other. The CWGC register provides no additional details in relation to William's family or his address in England.

Private George Alfred ASPIN, 11th East Lancashire Regiment, was killed in action on 1 July 1917. Private Harry ASPIN, 11th East Lancashire Regiment, was killed in action on 21 March 1918 and Corporal Thomas ASPIN, 11th East Lancashire Regiment, was killed in action on 28 June 1917. All three men were residents of Blackburn and, although I have been unable to establish any link between them, there is a fair possibility that they were related.

The East Surrey Regiment

Captain William BLACKMAN DCM, 1st East Surrey Regiment, was killed in action near Fresnoy on 8 May 1917, aged 29. He had enlisted in 1906 and had served in India between 1908 and the outbreak of war. He was gazetted as a second lieutenant in December 1915. His DCM was won whilst serving with the regiment's 2nd Battalion and was gazetted on 30 June 1915. The citation notes that over a period of time, including most recently at Hill 60, he had consistently shown gallant conduct as an NCO, setting a fine example by consistently performing acts of self-sacrifice and devotion to duty under fire, such as bringing in wounded men. The circumstances of his death and the events of 8 May 1917 are worth noting.

Following the successful capture of Fresnoy by Canadian troops a few days earlier, the new line formed a small salient around the eastern and southern parts of the village. Captain BLACKMAN and 'B' Company occupied the northern end of the battalion's front, whilst the 12th Gloucestershire Regiment extended the line northwards from the track linking Fresnoy to Bontemps. When the Germans counter-attacked in the early hours of 8 May 1917, they managed to breach the line between the two battalions in a short, but fierce encounter.

BLACKMAN had sent one of his officers and a small party of men to clarify the situation, but they were captured as they were returning, and so BLACK-MAN was initially unaware of the extent of the breach, or even that a counter-attack by the 12th Gloucestershire Regiment had temporarily restored the situation there. When the Germans renewed their attack in strength around 4.00am the right and centre companies of the 1st East Surrey Regiment were able to repel them, and were helped in this task by significantly better light.

Meanwhile, Captain BLACKMAN was now the only surviving officer on the left of the battalion's front and, with his company severely depleted, his men were unable to prevent the Germans from forcing their way along both sides of the Fresnoy–Bontemps track. Within a short space of time the Germans managed to work their way around the left flank and to the rear of what remained of 'B' Company, which now found itself surrounded on three sides. It was here that BLACKMAN fell in hand to hand fighting that lasted over an hour. The German advance was temporarily checked by oblique fire from 'A' Company to the right, but by this time the men of 'B' Company were already dead or were wounded and had been captured.

Captain BLACKMAN is one of 105 officers and men of the 1st East Surrey Regiment commemorated on the Arras Memorial, all of whom were killed in action at Fresnoy on 8 May 1917. For a very small action lasting around four hours the total battalion casualties came to 120 killed, 54 wounded and 321 missing in action, including those who were captured. Some of those who died that day are listed below.

Second Lieutenant Stanley Michael GASHION, 1st East Surrey Regiment, was killed in action at around 6.00am on 8 May whilst carrying out a reconnaissance near Fresnoy Wood.

Second Lieutenant Edward Thomas MOBBS, 1st East Surrey Regiment, was one of BLACKMAN's officers. He was 21 years old and was killed during the initial assault on 'B' Company's position. MOBBS was in charge of two platoons on the extreme left of the company's front where it joined the line held by the 12th Gloucestershire Regiment. It was news of his death that prompted BLACK-MAN to send Second Lieutenant Windebank and a small party of men to clarify the situation. Windebank was about to return with an update regarding the counter-attack by the 12th Gloucestershire Regiment when he and his men were captured.

Second Lieutenant Oliver Arthur STRONG, 1st East Surrey Regiment, was killed in action trying to deny the Germans access to an old communication trench. This trench ran at right angles to the original line held by 'A' Company. If the enemy could gain access to this trench they would be able to get in behind the rest of the battalion and cut it off. STRONG's company commander was aware of this and needed time to withdraw his men into the trench to defend it. Second Lieutenant STRONG was asked to cover the withdrawal by defending the point of access to the trench and was given half of No. 2 Platoon with which to carry out this difficult, but vitally important, task. Unfortunately, STRONG was unable to hold out for very long and fell soon after receiving his orders.

Private Alfred Arthur BAILEY was also part of 'B' Company. After the Germans had been beaten back by fire from 'A' Company, they left machine-gun detachments in shell holes close to the East Surrey's trenches. BAILEY was killed as he dashed forward single-handed in an attempt to bomb one of these guns. He was just 19 years old.

Private Alfred William BRADEN, 1st East Surrey Regiment, was also killed in action on 8 May 1917 when he and ten other men became trapped in a dug-out used as a company HQ. The party, under the command of Second Lieutenant Sutton, refused to surrender and defended the position for six and a half hours under a hail of bombs. The Germans then threw burning brushwood into the entrances of the dug-out in an attempt to kill the defenders or force their surrender. Fortunately, some British shells began to land close to the dug-out forcing the enemy to withdraw. Second Lieutenant Sutton then managed to break out with the seven survivors and led them to the comparative safety of some trenches occupied by the 12th Gloucestershire Regiment. Private BRADEN is known to have been killed during this epic struggle, but two other men who failed to make it back with Second Lieutenant Sutton were reported as missing in action. One of the men, Company Serjeant Major Wilkins, was later captured in the dug-out, but survived the war. Private Henry Skinner, however, is still recorded as missing in action, presumed dead, but is not commemorated here on the memorial. His only memorial at present is the CWGC database and he is one of 176 casualties of the Great War commemorated in this manner.

Private Sydney ELLIOT, 1st East Surrey Regiment, was killed in action on 8 May 1917, aged 32. The CWGC register briefly alludes to the above narrative by pointing out that he died after his company was surrounded by the enemy. The register also mentions that he had been a scenic artist before the war.

Captain Thomas Shirley KING, 4th East Surrey Regiment, attached 7th Battalion, was killed in action on 3 May 1917, aged 35. He was educated at the Oratory School, Birmingham, and Exeter College, Oxford. He had already served with the 4th East Surrey Regiment during the South African War, after which he went on to hold an appointment in the Colonial Civil Service in Brunei. He then returned from British North Borneo in 1915 to rejoin his old battalion.

Lance Serjeant Alexander (Sandy) TURNBULL, 8th East Surrey Regiment, was killed in action on 3 May 1917, aged 33. Before the war he was a professional footballer and had played for both Manchester City and Manchester United. However, his footballing career was not without controversy. His first brush with the football authorities came after Manchester City was found guilty of irregularities concerning payments to its players, all of whom were suspended. The ban was eventually lifted at the end of 1906, but by 1 January 1907 he was playing for Manchester United, scoring twenty-seven goals in twenty-five games. He was a member of the Manchester United team that won the league in 1908. The following year he scored the only goal in the FA Cup Final when United beat Bristol City. He was banned yet again following allegations of match fixing and played his last game in 1915 against Sheffield United. The ban was lifted posthumously.

The Duke of Cornwall's Light Infantry
Lance Corporal Thomas Richard QUARTERMAN, 1st Duke of Cornwall's Light Infantry, was killed in action on 23 April 1917, aged 19. His elder brother, Private John Arthur QUARTERMAN, was killed a few weeks later on 20 May, aged 28, serving with 167th Company, Machine Gun Corps. Both brothers are now commemorated here on the memorial.

The Duke of Wellington's (West Riding Regiment)
Captain Kenneth Edward CUNNINGHAM, 2nd Duke of Wellington's Regiment, was killed in action on 3 May 1917, aged 32. His brother, Captain Charles Clement Francis Cunningham, fell whilst serving with the 2nd Argyll & Sutherland Highlanders when the battalion sustained heavy casualties at High Wood. He was wounded there and died on 19 August 1916, aged 33. He is buried in Dernancourt Communal Cemetery.

Second Lieutenant Albert Edward TAYLOR DCM, 2nd Duke of Wellington's Regiment, was killed in action on 9 April 1917, aged 26. His DCM was gazetted on 19 November 1914 and was won as a company serjeant major with the battalion. It was awarded for conspicuous gallantry and skill having taken command of his company on 8 November near Ypres after all the officers had been killed or wounded. He succeeded in retaking some trenches and brought his men out of action once the operation was concluded.

Private Albert Victor SMITH, 2/6th Duke of Wellington's Regiment, was killed in action on 3 May 1917, aged 22. His brother, Private Arthur Herbert SMITH, is also commemorated on the Arras Memorial. He was killed in action on 30 March 1918 whilst serving with the 2/4th York & Lancaster Regiment.

The Border Regiment

Captain Arthur Plater NASMITH DSO, 7th Border Regiment, was killed in action near Monchy-le-Preux on 23 April 1917. His DSO was gazetted on 10 January 1917 and was awarded for conspicuous gallantry in action, displaying great courage and initiative, organizing and leading a successful attack, and setting a splendid example throughout the operation. The attack referred to in the citation took place at Zenith Trench near Le Transloy on 2 November 1916.

NASMITH was a pupil at Marlborough College where he excelled at rugby. He then went to work with his father at the Stock Exchange and became a member in 1904. When war broke out he joined the Inns of Court OTC and from there he was commissioned in the Border Regiment. He served on the Western Front from the middle of 1915 until his death.

Two of NASMITH's brothers also served during the war. Captain Martin Eric Nasmith VC KCB KCMG, Royal Navy, won his VC in 1915 as a lieutenant commander in charge of HM Submarine *E.11* during the Gallipoli Campaign. He also served in the Second World War. The other brother, Major Reginald Nasmith DSO MC, served with the Highland Light Infantry and the Machine Gun Corps in Mesopotamia. His MC was gazetted on 17 January 1917 and the DSO on 25 November 1918.

Second Lieutenant Frank ANDREW, 7th Border Regiment, was killed in action on 23 April 1917 and had previously been mentioned in despatches. He was 20 years old when he died. He was originally reported as missing in action and was probably killed by shell fire.

Second Lieutenant Ernest Henry BELCHAMBER, 'D' Company, 7th Border Regiment, was killed in action on 23 April 1917, aged 22. Before the war he worked for the Irrawaddy Flotilla Company in Burma and returned home in February 1915 in order to enlist and serve his country. The Irrawaddy Flotilla Company was a large passenger ferry and cargo operation owned by a Scottish business group based in Glasgow. At its peak it ran 600 steam ships, but when the Japanese invaded Burma in the Second World War the entire fleet was scuttled to prevent it falling into enemy hands.

Second Lieutenant Ernest George DOWDELL MC, 3rd Border Regiment, attached 8th Battalion, was killed in action on 22 March 1918. His MC was gazetted on 17 April 1917 and was awarded for conspicuous gallantry and devotion to duty after passing through a very heavy enemy barrage on two occasions and obtaining most valuable information. He was wounded whilst carrying out these actions.

Regimental Serjeant Major Frank Le Boutilier ALLBEURY DCM MM, 1st Border Regiment, was killed in action on 23 April 1917 when two heavy shells fell on the battalion's HQ, one of which killed him, as well as a serjeant, two men from the battalion's scouting section and a signaller. The battalion's adjutant, Lieutenant Cullis, was also wounded in the explosion. The other shell hit the roof of the dug-out, burying the commanding officer and other members of his staff. ALLBEURY's DCM was gazetted on 12 March 1917 and was awarded for conspicuous gallantry in action whilst serving as a serjeant. The citation is very brief and merely states that he had entered an enemy trench where he captured twelve prisoners, setting a splendid example of courage and devotion to duty.

Serjeant John Alfred SHORT, 7th Border Regiment, was killed in action on 19 April 1917. He held the *Médaille Militaire* (France).

Lance Serjeant Arthur Reginald CAIN MM, 'C' Company, 1st Border Regiment, was killed in action on 23 April 1917. He had previously served in Gallipoli with the battalion, which was part of the 29th Division.

Private Henry George CRITTELL, 'D' Company, 7th Border Regiment, was killed in action on 19 November 1917, aged 22. His brother, Private William John Manuel Crittell, was killed in action on 1 July 1916 during the opening day of the Battle of the Somme whilst serving with the 7th Queen's (Royal West Surrey Regiment). He is commemorated on the Thiepval Memorial.

The Royal Sussex Regiment
Second Lieutenant Albert CARTER DCM, attached to the 9th Royal Sussex Regiment, was killed in action on 12 April 1917, aged 27. *Officers Died in the Great War* makes no reference to his DCM, although it was gazetted on 1 January 1917. The citation for it appeared on 13 February that year and states that it was awarded for conspicuous gallantry and devotion to duty whilst dressing a wounded officer in the open under intense fire. It was won while he was serving as a serjeant with the 1st Royal Fusiliers and goes on to say that he had performed consistently good work throughout.

His file at the National Archives contains a touching note from his niece in Canada who wrote to the War Office some years later under the mistaken belief that her uncle had been awarded the VC. Her information was based on a newspaper cutting which the family had since lost. In her letter she goes on to say that the children at his former school in Bethnal Green had been given a half day's holiday in remembrance of him and that the newspaper article had also contained a testimony from one of his teachers who had paid for his first pair of trousers, as his mother had been unable to afford them. He initially joined the army in 1903 but deserted soon after enlisting, although he subsequently returned. During the Great War he was gazetted as a second lieutenant for services in the field.

Company Serjeant Major Frederick BARNARD DCM, 9th Royal Sussex Regiment, is shown as having been killed in action between 12 and 13 April 1917, aged 23. His death occurred when his battalion carried out an attack on 12 April with the 2nd Leinster Regiment against German positions around the Bois en Hache on the eastern edge of Vimy Ridge. His DCM was awarded for conspicuous gallantry and devotion to duty, guiding reinforcements through heavy fire at a critical time when they were most urgently needed, setting a fine example to all. His brother, Mark, fell on 13 May 1915, aged 24, serving as a rifleman with the 1st Rifle Brigade. He has no known grave and is commemorated on the Menin Gate.

Serjeant Alfred William BEALE MM, 7th Royal Sussex Regiment, was killed in action on 9 April 1917. Although the battalion history makes no specific mention of how he won his gallantry award, which was gazetted on 14 September 1916, it does state that he was one of fourteen NCOs and men who received the MM in connection with the fighting at the Hohenzollern Craters at the beginning of March that year.

Serjeant Bertie Charles BRAGG DCM MM, 9th Royal Sussex Regiment, was killed in action on 17 July 1917. His DCM was gazetted on 20 October 1916 and was awarded for conspicuous gallantry during operations. The citation states that when the enemy counter-attacked our newly captured position he did fine work with his machine gun. Then, after his gun had been put out of action, he took some bombs and went forward to help the bombers. His example greatly encouraged the men around him and the enemy's attack was repulsed.

Private Robert BOTTOMS, 9th Royal Sussex Regiment, was killed in action on 13 April 1917, aged 26. His brother, Private Thomas Bottoms MM, was killed on 1 July 1916 when serving with the 109th Company, Machine Gun Corps. He is commemorated on the Thiepval Memorial.

The Hampshire Regiment

Lieutenant George William BAXTER, 13th Hampshire Regiment, attached 2nd Battalion, was killed in action on 14 April 1917 when two companies from the 2nd Hampshire Regiment came up in support of the now-celebrated action by Lieutenant Colonel James Forbes-Robertson VC DSO and Bar MC of the Newfoundland Regiment with seven of his own men and a private from the 1st Essex Regiment just east of Monchy-le-Preux. Forbes-Robertson and his group were later joined by one of his orderly room staff, Corporal J. Hillier, and for four hours this gallant little band managed to hold off an enemy counter-attack until the men of the Hampshire Regiment arrived at around 2.45pm. During that time they were all that stood between the enemy and Monchy-le-Preux.

Second Lieutenant Eric Archdall REID, 1st Hampshire Regiment, was killed in action on 29 March 1918, aged 19. His father, Sir Archibald Reid CMG KBE, was an eminent radiologist. Soon after the outbreak of the war Sir Archibald was appointed to oversee all matters relating to X-ray work for the British and Dominion Forces at home and abroad. Sir Archibald Reid died in 1924.

Company Serjeant Major George Edward HARBOURNE, 14th Hampshire Regiment, was killed in action on 22 March 1918, aged 33, whilst attached to the 17th Entrenching Battalion. He had served in the army for eighteen years before his death.

Company Serjeant Major Geoffrey William LUND DCM, 2nd Hampshire Regiment, was killed in action on 21 April 1917, aged 30. He won his DCM in action after taking command of his company when all the officers had been wounded. He then showed conspicuous courage and ability in organizing his company's defences. The award was gazetted on 11 December 1916.

Serjeant William SHELLEY, 1st Hampshire Regiment, was killed in action on 28 March 1918, aged 38. He held the Long Service and Good Conduct Medal and had served for twenty years in the ranks, including service during the South African campaign.

Private Walter BARTRUP, 2nd Hampshire Regiment, was killed in action on 14 April 1917, exactly two weeks before his brother, Private Albert BARTRUP, who was killed on 28 April 1917 whilst serving with the 10th Royal Dublin Fusiliers. Albert is also commemorated here on the Arras Memorial. Walter fell during the struggle that took place in the fields just east of Monchy-le-Preux when two companies of the 2nd Hampshire Regiment managed to link up with and relieve Lieutenant Colonel Forbes-Robertson's gallant little band of men, thereby halting a German counter-attack aimed at recapturing the village.

The South Staffordshire Regiment
Lieutenant Colonel John (Jack) STUART WORTLEY, 2/6th South Staffordshire Regiment, was killed in action on 21 March 1918. As a pupil at Eton, he earned himself a reputation for practical jokes rather than academic or sporting prowess, so at the age of 17 his parents decided to curtail his formal education in favour of an apprenticeship in the Merchant Navy, a move that seemed to suit the young Jack. The story goes that he once found himself penniless in Sydney where he knew only two people, the Governor and a barman; of course Jack chose to work for two weeks as an assistant bar-tender.

In the South African War he initially served with the Hertfordshire Yeomanry, but later obtained a commission in the Scottish Horse and was twice mentioned in despatches during the campaign. For a short while he even worked in the Criminal Investigation Department in Johannesburg. However, soldiering at home held little appeal for him, so after a brief spell with the Cameronians he arranged for a secondment to the Northern Nigeria Regiment as its Transport

Officer. After this latest adventure, he transferred to the 11th Sudanese Regiment and in 1910 he received the Order of the Medjidie after taking part in a campaign against local insurgents.

When he finally returned home, he was placed on the reserve of officers where he remained until war was declared. In September 1914 he was given command of the 21st Royal Fusiliers (4th Public Schools Battalion) and in November the following year he took the battalion to France. However, in April 1916 the battalion was recalled to England, where it was disbanded to provide men for officer training and subsequent commissions. He returned home with it, but was then appointed as second-in command of the 2/5th South Staffordshire Regiment. By February 1917 he was back in France with his new battalion, but subsequently transferred to the 2/6th South Staffordshire Regiment and saw action later that year at Bourlon Wood near Cambrai.

On 21 March 1918, after a fierce bombardment that heralded the start of the German Offensive, the 2/6th South Staffordshire Regiment and the rest of the 59th (2nd North Midland) Division were simply overwhelmed as their section of front collapsed under sheer weight of numbers. He was killed in action that morning around 9.00am and his body was never found. The author, John Buchan, paid great tribute to him in his work, *These for Remembrance*, commenting that, as a born sailor, it was perhaps fitting that his body was never recovered for burial which in some ways made it rather like a burial at sea.

Captain John Maxwell EDGAR, 4th South Staffordshire Regiment, was killed in action on 22 March 1918, aged 30. He was a schoolmaster before the war and held a Master's degree from Edinburgh University. He had also been a member of the OTC during his time at Sheffield University and was gazetted in March 1915.

Second Lieutenant John Stanley GOODWIN, 1st South Staffordshire Regiment, attached 22nd Manchester Regiment, was killed in action on 28 March 1917, aged 24. Having enlisted in the Royal Army Medical Corps in January 1915, he went on to serve with the Royal Engineers before being gazetted in January 1916.

Second Lieutenant Horace JOHNSON, 5th South Staffordshire Regiment, was killed in action on 28 April 1917, aged 26. He was educated at Bridge Trust Grammar School, Handsworth, in Birmingham, and went on to gain a Bachelor of Arts degree at Birmingham University before teaching English and Music at a school in Newton Abbot in Devon.

Second Lieutenant James MILLER DCM, 2nd South Staffordshire Regiment, was killed in action on 25 March 1918. His DCM was won whilst serving as a company serjeant major in the 1st Dorsetshire Regiment. It was gazetted on 11 March 1916 and was awarded for conspicuous gallantry throughout the campaign, although the citation mentions one occasion when he went out and brought in a wounded man in full view of the enemy's trenches. It continues by stating that he was conspicuous during attacks for his coolness in rallying the men and bringing up reinforcements.

Serjeant Alfred CLEVELEY MM, 1st South Staffordshire Regiment, was killed in action on 12 May 1917. Prior to the war he had worked as a butler.

Lance Corporal Ernest Louis Eric BROSINOVICH, 8th South Staffordshire Regiment, was 17 years old when he was killed in action on 16 May 1917. The family address is shown as the Rue Richer, Paris. Why and how he came to enlist in the regiment remains obscure and there is no reference to him in *Soldiers Died in the Great War*. The question remains as to why he chose the British Army over that of the French.

Lance Corporal William George Arthur EATWELL DCM, 2/6th South Staffordshire Regiment, was killed in action on 21 March 1918, aged 20. His DCM was awarded for his conspicuous display of gallantry and devotion to duty whilst acting as a runner. He succeeded in taking messages to and from the line under heavy enemy barrages at a time of grave difficulties when this was the only effective means of maintaining contact between the companies of his battalion. His work was described as excellent. The award was gazetted on 21 October 1918.

Lance Corporal John Edward McDONALD, 1st South Staffordshire Regiment, formerly Royal Army Ordnance Corps, was killed in action on 14 May 1917, aged 28. His brother, Lance Corporal William George McDonald, was killed in action on 28 September 1915, aged 26, serving with the 2nd East Kent Regiment (The Buffs). He is commemorated on the Loos Memorial.

The Dorsetshire Regiment

Private Eric Marshall LARNDER, 6th Dorsetshire Regiment, was killed in action on 23 April 1917, aged 24. The CWGC register points out that he was the son of Colonel Eugene William Larnder, Royal Army Veterinary Corps but, more interestingly, it notes that he had been gazetted in the British West Indies Regiment in 1913, only to resign his commission in 1916. He then came to England where he enlisted as an ordinary soldier.

Private John William O'BRIEN, 6th Dorsetshire Regiment, was killed in action on 25 March 1918, aged 22. His father had been killed in Gallipoli in 1915. The CWGC records are inconclusive with regard to identifying John's father.

The overwhelming majority of the regiment's men listed on the memorial were killed whilst serving with the 6th Battalion, which was part of the 17th (Northern) Division. After the opening day of the Battle of Arras, this division became heavily involved in the fighting just south of the River Scarpe near Monchy-le-Preux.

The Prince of Wales's Volunteers (South Lancashire Regiment)

There are just seven officers and men from this regiment listed on the memorial. Few of its battalions spent much time on the Arras battlefields and only the 11th Battalion was present on 9 April 1917 in its role as pioneers to the 30th Division. However, none of its men are commemorated here. The few men listed are from the 2nd Battalion, the 8th Battalion, and the 1/5th Battalion, and there is also one former member of the 7th Battalion who was killed serving with the 6th Entrenching Battalion.

The Welsh Regiment

Corporal William John HEATH DCM, 9th Welsh Regiment, was killed in action on 23 March 1918, aged 26. His DCM was awarded for conspicuous gallantry and devotion to duty during an enemy attack. During a night reconnaissance patrol he made a careful assessment of the situation before dealing effectively with a number of enemy posts and taking several prisoners. The citation also notes that throughout the operation he showed great gallantry and initiative. The award was gazetted on 3 September 1918.

Private George Ernest HUMPHRIES, 9th Welsh Regiment, was killed in action on 23 March 1918, aged 35. The CWGC register shows that his wife and parents lived in Shropshire and that he had worked as a chauffeur-gardener. His parents are shown residing at Tickwood Lodge, Much Wenlock. This was part of Tickwood Hall, a large country residence that would have employed a number of staff, such as gardeners and chauffeurs.

The Black Watch (Royal Highlanders)

Captain John George ANDERSON MC, Royal Army Medical Corps, attached 1/6th Black Watch, was killed in action on 21 March 1918, aged 38. He was from County Down. His MC was gazetted on 2 January 1918 as part of the New Year's Honours List and he had also been mentioned in despatches. According to the regimental history, it appears that he was killed somewhere near Lagnicourt after the battalion decided to pull back to the Beaumetz–Morchies Line and failed to inform him of the withdrawal.

Captain William Alexander CARSWELL MC, 10th Black Watch, attached 7th Battalion, died of wounds on 21 March 1918, aged 24. His brother, Captain John Dingwall Carswell, was seriously wounded near Bernafay Wood on 11 July 1916 whilst serving with the regiment's 8th Battalion. He died three days later and is commemorated on the Thiepval Memorial. Another brother, Private Archibald Carswell, served with the 2nd Dragoons (Royal Scots Greys) and died at home on 27 January 1915. He is buried in Kilmichael Parish Churchyard. Their father, Major Archibald Carswell, had also served with the Black Watch. I can find no trace of William's MC in any of the gazettes. The award is shown against his name in *Officers Died in the Great War*, but the regimental history makes no reference to it. He spent most of the war in Salonika with the

10th Battalion and was wounded there in January 1917. Later that year he was hospitalized.

Captain John S. STRANG MC, 9th Black Watch, was killed in action on 28 March 1918. *Officers Died in the Great War* makes no reference to his MC and I can find no trace of it in any of the gazettes. The regimental history complicates matters by referring in the narrative to the award of a bar to his MC, but in Appendix I, which is the record of officers' service, it refers only to the award of the MC, noting that it was gazetted on 4 October 1917, with no mention of any bar. The same records show that he was wounded in August 1916, and again in August the following year. He only returned to the battalion on 16 February 1918 after recovering from his wounds.

Captain Norman Robertson TAYLOR MC, 5th Black Watch, attached 8th Battalion, was killed in action on 3 May 1917, aged 28. His MC was gazetted on 12 January 1917 and was awarded for conspicuous gallantry in action. The citation records that although he had initially been in the support line, he came up to the firing line where he organized the defence of the left flank. Later, he organized and led bombing attacks with great courage and determination.

Second Lieutenant James Robert Hay McINTOSH DCM, 7th Black Watch, was killed in action on 23 March 1918, aged 25. His DCM was gazetted on 27 July 1916 and was won as a serjeant whilst serving in the same battalion. It was awarded for conspicuous gallantry and devotion to duty. Although severely wounded, he continued to advance and bayoneted three of the enemy. He then accompanied one of his officers, Lieutenant Herd, to search for missing bombers. He eventually fainted as a result of his injuries whilst returning to his own lines and had to be carried in.

Company Serjeant Major Hugh Drummond STRACHAN DCM, 9th Black Watch, was killed in action on 9 April 1917. His DCM, won as a serjeant with the 2nd Battalion, was awarded for conspicuous gallantry leading his platoon after the officer commanding it had been killed. He charged several times ahead of his bombers, bayoneting several of the enemy. The award was gazetted on 30 March 1916.

Private William BROWN MM and Bar, 7th Black Watch, was killed in action on 21 March 1918, aged 21. The regimental history records that he died of wounds on 31 March 1918.

Private Hugh M. DICKSON, 'B' Company, 8th Black Watch, was killed in action on 3 May 1917, aged 24. His role in the battalion was as a signaller. His brother, Private William M. DICKSON, was killed in action with the 9th Black Watch on 30 March 1918, aged 19. He is also commemorated here on the memorial with his brother.

Private James McGREGOR DCM, 6th Black Watch, was killed in action on 23 January 1918, aged 28. His DCM, gazetted on 5 August 1915, was won whilst serving with the 1st Black Watch. It was awarded for conspicuous gallantry and devotion to duty on 9 May 1915 at Rue du Bois. Whilst lying on the German parapet firing, Private McGregor saw a bomb thrown into a shell hole some distance behind him. Knowing that an officer and two men were wounded and sheltering in the shell hole, he ran back, picked up the bomb and hurled it away before it exploded, thereby undoubtedly saving their lives.

The Oxfordshire & Buckinghamshire Light Infantry

Second Lieutenant John Legge BULMER, 'A' Company, 4th Oxfordshire & Buckinghamshire Light Infantry, attached 5th Battalion, was killed in action on 3 May 1917, aged 22. He was educated at Marlborough College and went on to study at Merton College, Oxford, where he was Postmaster between 1913 and 1915.

At the time of researching this book it is believed that the remains of a body found in a garden in Beaurains may be that of Second Lieutenant BULMER, although at present there are three other possible candidates: Lieutenant Stanley ASHMAN, Second Lieutenant Charles Croke HARPER and Second Lieutenant William Charles HAYNES. All three fell on 3 May 1917 and were serving with the 5th Battalion at the time of their deaths. There is a chance that one of the four names will be removed from the memorial in due course.

Private Alfred WHETSTONE, 2nd Oxfordshire & Buckinghamshire Light Infantry, was killed in action on 28 April 1917, aged 23. His brother, Frank, was killed the following year on 21 March 1918, aged 21, serving with the Machine Gun Corps. Frank also has no known grave and is commemorated on the Pozières Memorial on the Somme.

The Essex Regiment

Captain Reginald Davies HICKSON MC, 9th Essex Regiment, died of wounds on 30 April 1917, aged 29. His MC was gazetted on 11 May 1917 and was awarded for conspicuous gallantry and devotion to duty. With great coolness and total disregard for danger he went forward under very heavy fire and personally supervised the withdrawal of his advanced parties at a most critical time.

Captain John Herbert Victor WILLMOTT MC, 3rd Essex Regiment, attached 2nd Battalion, was killed in action on 28 March 1918. His MC was gazetted on 6 April 1918 and was awarded for conspicuous gallantry and devotion to duty, re-organizing his company, and men of other units, when an attack was held up. He then gained touch with the battalion on his right under the most trying conditions. The citation concludes by stating that throughout the entire operation he was an example of cheerfulness and determination.

Second Lieutenant Cyril Herbert FLINN, 1st Essex Regiment, was killed in action on 14 April 1917, aged 20. The CWGC register tells us that he was Prize

Cadet in the Sandhurst Entrance Exam. He had also been awarded a Bachelor of Science degree from University College, London.

Second Lieutenant William Brown PATERSON MC, 3rd Essex Regiment, attached 13th Battalion, was killed in action on 28 April 1917, aged 26. His MC was gazetted on 13 February 1917 and was awarded for conspicuous gallantry in action. The citation notes that he went forward under very heavy fire to find out the situation and brought back most valuable information. He then performed excellent work, holding the position until relieved.

Second Lieutenant Frank Wesley PETERS MC, 1st Essex Regiment, attached 9th Battalion, was killed in action on 18 July 1917, aged 23. He was born in Canada and had enlisted in the 2nd Canadian Mounted Rifles in December 1914. He then served with the Canadian Expeditionary Force until May 1917 when he obtained a commission in the Essex Regiment. He was killed in fighting near Monchy-le-Preux during one of the many local attacks that took place just east of the village. In defending his position, he was wounded three times before being killed. By sad coincidence, his MC was gazetted on the day he died and was awarded for conspicuous gallantry, devotion to duty, dash and initiative. The citation refers to a particular occasion when three of his men were wounded; he went forward under machine-gun fire and brought all three men back to cover.

Serjeant Bertie Charles BRAGG DCM MM, 9th Essex Regiment, was killed in action on 17 July 1917. His DCM was gazetted on 20 October 1916 and was awarded for conspicuous gallantry during operations. When the enemy counter-attacked a newly captured position, he did fine work with his machine gun. After his gun was hit, he took some bombs and went forward to help the bombers. His example greatly encouraged the men around him and the enemy's attack was repulsed.

Lance Corporal Frederick CARDY MM, 11th Essex Regiment, was 22 years old when he was killed in action on 21 March 1918. His brother, Private Arthur Cardy, was killed in action with the regiment's 2nd Battalion on 1 July 1916, the opening day of the Battle of the Somme. He is buried at Serre Road Cemetery No. 2.

Private Edward Baker BODMAN, 1st Essex Regiment, was killed in action on 14 April 1917, aged 26. He had previously served for seven years in India. The regiment's 1st Battalion was in Mauritius when war broke out.

The Sherwood Foresters (Nottinghamshire & Derbyshire Regiment)
Major Charles Reginald Chenevix TRENCH, 2/5th Sherwood Foresters, was killed in action on 21 March 1918, aged 30. He was wounded twice that day near the village of Noreuil and was later stretchered back to a dug-out where he died. He was mentioned in despatches in connection with his actions on 21 March after his battalion had made a gallant attempt to stem the German Offensive. He was

educated at Charterhouse School and went on to take his degree at Merton College, Oxford. He then joined the Inns of Court OTC before obtaining his commission in the 2/5th Sherwood Foresters. He was in Ireland during the Easter uprising in 1916, so that he and his battalion only arrived in France at the start of 1917.

His father, Herbert Francis Chevenix Trench, lived at Sandhurst in Surrey where he was a clergyman. Charles's grandfather, the Most Reverend and Right Honourable Richard Chevenix Trench, had been Dean of Westminster, Archbishop of Dublin, a Member of the Privy Council, a poet, and had still found time to father fourteen children.

Captain Kenneth Norman BION MC, 1st Sherwood Foresters, attached 2nd Battalion, had been mentioned in despatches on two occasions and was killed on 21 March 1918. He and his battalion were withdrawing over open ground when they were strafed by an enemy aircraft. He received a bullet wound to the head and died almost immediately. His MC was gazetted on 14 January 1916. On 5 July that year he was wounded somewhere between La Boisselle and Ovillers. His parents came from Western Australia.

Captain Albert Light Moody DICKINS MC, 7th Sherwood Foresters, was killed in action on 21 March 1918, aged 21. His MC was gazetted on 27 October 1917 and the citation for it appeared on 18 March 1918. It was awarded for conspicuous gallantry and devotion to duty as a lieutenant whilst commanding a patrol. He and his men came across four of the enemy, two of whom they killed, but the other two made off. Whilst returning from their patrol, they came across an enemy party of about twenty. DICKINS ordered his men to charge them, which they did. During the fight they killed one of the enemy, wounded two more and drove off the remainder.

Captain Alfred Bibbington WALLIS, 6th Sherwood Foresters, was killed in action on 21 March 1918, aged 26. He was educated at Giggleswick School in Yorkshire, followed by St John's College, Oxford, where he graduated with a Bachelor of Arts degree.

Lieutenant Edward HOPKINSON MC, 8th Sherwood Foresters, was killed in action on 23 April 1917. His MC was gazetted on 26 May 1917 and was awarded for conspicuous gallantry and devotion to duty when in command of a reconnaissance patrol. He inflicted many casualties on the enemy and successfully repulsed all counter-attacks on his position. The citation also states that he had done fine work on many previous occasions.

Second Lieutenant William Peter DUFF MC, 8th Sherwood Foresters, was killed in action on 23 April 1917, aged 21. His MC was gazetted on 14 November 1916 and was awarded for conspicuous gallantry in action. He showed great courage and determination in bombing enemy dug-outs and then carried back a wounded man. The citation concludes by stating that on previous occasions he had also shown conspicuous courage.

Company Serjeant Major William WHITEHEAD DCM MM, 2/7th Sherwood Foresters, was killed in action on 21 March 1918. His DCM was awarded for conspicuous gallantry and devotion to duty during operations. During a period of four days' continuous fighting he set a magnificent example of courage and fortitude to the NCOs and men of his company. On one occasion he volunteered to carry an urgent message to the front line through a very heavy barrage. The award was gazetted on 21 October 1918. His MM was gazetted on 19 February 1917.

Lance Corporal G.W. BOORER, 2/7th Sherwood Foresters, was killed in action on 21 March 1918. His son, George Henry Boorer, who served as a driver with the Army Service Corps during the Second World War, died on 10 May 1943. He is buried in Woolwich Cemetery near to where his family lived. It is unusual for *Soldiers Died in the Great War* not to show soldiers' first names, but his entry, like the CWGC register, only refers to him by his initials. The entry in the CWGC register regarding his son refers to him only by his initials.

Lance Corporal John JOHNSON, 2/6th Sherwood Foresters, was killed in action on 21 March 1918, aged 24. The CWGC register notes that he was wounded on four previous occasions.

Private Charles F. CHILTON, 2/6 Sherwood Foresters, was killed in action on 21 March 1918, aged 19. His son, Charles Chilton, whom he never saw, went on to have a successful career with the BBC. In the early Sixties he wrote and presented a series of radio programmes entitled *The Long, Long Trail*, which told the story of the war through the popular songs of the day. The programmes were a tribute to his father but they also led to the stage hit *Oh What a Lovely War* which Charles produced in 1963.

Private George HODGKINSON, 2nd Sherwood Foresters, was killed in action on 21 March 1918, aged 20. His brother, Private Joseph Hodgkinson, also fell in action whilst serving with the 1st Cheshire Regiment on 4 September 1916, aged 21. Joseph's body was never recovered and he is now commemorated on the Thiepval Memorial.

Private Albert Oliver NICHOLLS, 2/6th Sherwood Foresters, was killed in action on 21 March 1918. His brother, Private Arthur Vernon Nicholls, was killed on the Somme serving with the regiment's 1st Battalion on 7 July 1916, aged 26. He too has no known grave and is commemorated on the Thiepval Memorial.

Private Harold SMITH, 10th Sherwood Foresters, was killed in action on 9 July 1917, aged 20. His elder brother, Private Cyril Smith, was killed on 28 May 1915, aged 26, serving in the Chatham Battalion, Royal Marine Light Infantry, at Gallipoli. He is commemorated on the Helles Memorial.

The Loyal North Lancashire Regiment
Captain Edward Maurice GREGSON, 4th Loyal North Lancashire Regiment, was killed in action on 28 June 1916, aged 26. He was a member of the North of

England Institute of Mining Engineers and an associate of the Surveyor's Institute. It is surprising that the army did not appear to make use of his professional skills when there was ample scope for men of his knowledge and experience. Of course, there may have been other reasons why he preferred to serve in the infantry.

Captain William Howard PROCTOR DSO, 10th Loyal North Lancashire Regiment, was killed in action on 23 April 1917, aged 23. His DSO was gazetted on 26 September 1916 whilst serving as a second lieutenant. It was awarded for conspicuous gallantry in action supporting a bombing attack on a strongly held trench. When the attack was checked, he joined in at once with great determination carrying the whole attack forward. Although wounded through the jaw by a bullet, he led his men on until exhausted through loss of blood.

Lieutenant Richard Basil Brandram JONES VC, 8th Loyal North Lancashire Regiment, was killed in action near Broadmarsh Crater at Vimy Ridge on 21 May 1916, aged 19. His VC was gazetted on 5 August 1916 and was awarded for most conspicuous bravery. He and his platoon were holding a recently captured crater when around 7.30pm the enemy fired a mine forty yards to his right. At the same time the German artillery put down a heavy barrage, isolating him and his platoon, before the enemy's infantry attacked in overwhelming numbers. Lieutenant JONES kept his men together, steadying them by his fine example. As the enemy advanced on his position he shot fifteen of them, counting them aloud as he did so in order to cheer and encourage his men. When he ran out of ammunition, he was about to throw a bomb when he was shot through the head and killed. The citation notes that his splendid example and courage had so inspired his men that when they too had run out of ammunition and bombs they threw stones and ammunition boxes at the enemy until only nine were left. Only then were these remaining men forced to retire.

Second Lieutenant Edwin IBBOTSON MC, 10th Loyal North Lancashire Regiment, was killed in action on 11 April 1917, aged 20. The day before his death his battalion had moved up to what had previously been the German second line where it established itself in a series of shell holes. The next day, with the help of a tank, the battalion attacked a trench that was situated on its exposed flank running from the Cambrai road towards Guémappe. He was killed in action during that attack. His brother, Second Lieutenant Robert IBBOTSON, 5th Essex Regiment, attached 13th Battalion, was killed in action on 28 November 1917, aged 27. He is also commemorated on the memorial with his brother. Their parents came from Southport in Lancashire, but both men are recorded as having enlisted in Canada in 1914. Edwin served with the 2nd Canadian Mounted Rifles before transferring to the Loyal North Lancashire Regiment.

Company Serjeant Major John William HALLIDAY DCM MM, 10th Loyal North Lancashire Regiment, was killed in action on 22 March 1918. His DCM was gazetted on 18 July 1917 and was awarded for conspicuous gallantry and devotion to duty during an attack. When all the officers had become casualties, he led two companies forward with great skill and courage.

The Northamptonshire Regiment
Private George BURCHNELL, 'D' Company, 6th Northamptonshire Regiment, was killed in action on 3 May 1917, aged 19. His brother, Private Harold Robert Burchnell, was killed in action near Festubert on 9 May 1915, serving with the regiment's 2nd Battalion. He is commemorated on the Ploegsteert Memorial.

Princess Charlotte of Wales's (Royal Berkshire Regiment)
Second Lieutenant Basil LYONS, 5th Royal Berkshire Regiment, was killed in action on 19 July 1917, aged 30. He was one of thirteen men from the battalion who were killed in action that day in a local operation near Long Trench, just east of Monchy-le-Preux. Twelve of them, including Second Lieutenant LYONS, are commemorated here on the memorial. He had previously served for nine years in India with the 1st (King's) Dragoon Guards. His brother, Rifleman Alfred Stanley Lyons, was killed in action on 25 September 1916, aged 27, serving with the 1/9th Battalion, London Regiment (Queen Victoria's Rifles). He is commemorated on the Thiepval Memorial.

Second Lieutenant Arthur MAYBURY DCM, 1st Royal Berkshire Regiment, attached 5th Battalion, was killed in action on 19 July 1917. His DCM was gazetted on 11 March 1916 and was won whilst serving with the regiment's 2nd Battalion. It was awarded for consistent good work since his battalion's arrival at the front. The citation notes that he had been cool and reliable under all circumstances.

Corporal Henry Robert CHAPMAN DCM, 5th Royal Berkshire Regiment, was killed in action on 19 July 1917. His DCM was gazetted on 11 May 1917 and was awarded for conspicuous gallantry and devotion to duty. Having collected six men, he charged an enemy bombing party, killing nine of them. He showed great courage and initiative throughout. His award was won whilst he was serving as a lance corporal.

Private Harry SMITH, 1st Royal Berkshire Regiment, was killed in action on 3 May 1917, aged 39. He was the eldest of nine brothers who served during the Great War, three of whom fell. One of his brothers, Private Arthur Smith, 3rd Wiltshire Regiment, died at home on 11 March 1916, aged 21. He is buried at Ramsbury (Holy Cross) Churchyard. There are two other 'Smiths' on the war memorial there: G. Smith and L. Smith. One of them is likely to be the remaining brother, although the local roll of honour provides no clues as to which of the two it might be.

The Queen's Own (Royal West Kent Regiment)
Second Lieutenant Horatio Geoffrey Cornwallis MANN MC, 6th Queen's Own (Royal West Kent Regiment), was killed in action on 17 July 1917. His MC was

gazetted on 1 January 1917 in the New Year's Honours List. His battalion was part of the 12th (Eastern) Division and spent a good deal of 1917 in trenches near Monchy-le-Preux. On 17 July his battalion was involved in one of the many local attacks that took place in this area during the summer and autumn of 1917. When his men arrived at the German trenches they believed them to be unoccupied, but the enemy was lying prone in them. When they were discovered, a brief fight broke out in which the men of the 6th Queen's Own had to resort to picks and shovels, having already slung their rifles over their shoulders believing the trench to be clear. It is likely that Second Lieutenant MANN was killed sometime after this when he and his men were trying to hold on to Long Trench.

Second Lieutenant Maurice John Lea WALKER, 6th Queen's Own (Royal West Kent Regiment), was killed in action near Monchy-le-Preux on 3 May 1917, aged 24. He was educated at Uppingham School and Pembroke College, Cambridge. His battalion was deployed during the evening to try to clear up part of 37 Brigade's front, but it came up against heavy fire from a position around Devil's Trench, which was still occupied by the Germans. Earlier in the day, men of the 6th East Kent Regiment (The Buffs) had been cut off by the enemy's garrison in Devil's Trench, but later fought their way back through the position, although only two officers and eight other ranks out of the original forty returned safely.

Serjeant Lewis William HOWARD MM, 10th Queen's Own (Royal West Kent Regiment), was killed in action on 23 March 1918, aged 37. He had previously served with the 1st Grenadier Guards in the South African campaign.

Private Archie ACOTT, 10th Queen's Own (Royal West Kent Regiment), was killed in action on 23 March 1918, aged 24. He was the youngest of three brothers who served during the Great War, but he is the only 'Acott' listed on the Wrotham war memorial in Kent. It would appear that he may have been the only one out of the three to have been killed, although I have been unable to confirm this.

Private Reginald ALLCORN, 10th Queen's Own (Royal West Kent Regiment), was killed in action on 23 March 1918, aged 21. His brother, Private Thomas Louis Allcorn, was killed in action on 30 July 1916, aged 23, serving with the 1st Queen's Own (Royal West Kent Regiment). Thomas is commemorated on the Thiepval Memorial.

The King's Own (Yorkshire Light Infantry)
Second Lieutenant Herbert William HAYWARD, 6th King's Own (Yorkshire Light Infantry), was killed in action on 23 July 1916, aged 35. He was mentioned in despatches and had served in the South African War with the 2nd Scots Guards.

Second Lieutenant Martin Oliver WALSH MBE (Military), 2/4th King's Own (Yorkshire Light Infantry), was killed in action on 3 May 1917, aged 23. WALSH is one of just eight holders of the MBE buried or commemorated on the Western Front as a result of the 1914–1918 conflict, though he is the only one with no known grave. One of the eight is buried in Belgium at White House Cemetery and the other seven are to be found here in France. His MBE was gazetted on 4 June 1918 in the King's Birthday Honours List. The very short citation accompanying the entry merely states that it was awarded for an act of gallantry performed not in the presence of the enemy. The regimental history makes no specific reference to the incident that led to the award, which I find strange, to say the least.

Serjeant Fred ROBERTS DCM, 5th King's Own (Yorkshire Light Infantry), was killed in action on 27 March 1918, aged 22. His DCM was gazetted on 28 March 1918 and was awarded for conspicuous gallantry and devotion to duty when his platoon was held up by an enemy strongpoint garrisoned by twenty-five men and a machine gun. The advance had gone ahead without support from tanks, which left his platoon to deal with the position without any assistance. He and two men made their way around it and bombed it from the rear. In doing so, they were able to cut off the retreat of the garrison, which was subsequently accounted for. He was responsible for killing and capturing a large number of the enemy and, although wounded, he remained with his platoon after the assault.

Corporal Garnet Edward WOOLSEY, 2/4th King's Own (Yorkshire Light Infantry), was killed in action on 28 March 1918, aged 21. Although the surname is spelt differently, his first name tends to suggest that the family may have chosen it out of admiration for Field Marshal Sir Garnet Wolseley (1833–1913) a notable Victorian military commander. Similarly, Corporal WOOLSEY's father was christened William Cardinal Woolsey, presumably after Cardinal Thomas Wolsey (sometimes spelt Woolsey), who became Lord Chancellor under Henry VIII. The family lived near Boston in Lincolnshire. The naming of children after well-known historical or national figures was once far more common than it is nowadays.

Corporal Walter WRAY, 9th King's Own (Yorkshire Light Infantry), was killed in action on 25 April 1917, aged 28. His brother, Private Matthew Wray, was killed in action on 28 August 1918 serving with the 10th West Yorkshire Regiment. He has no known grave and is commemorated on the Vis-en-Artois Memorial.

Private Herbert James BOAM DCM, 2/5th King's Own (Yorkshire Light Infantry), was killed in action on 27 March 1918. His DCM was awarded for conspicuous gallantry and devotion to duty when an enemy machine gun began to inflict heavy casualties on his company. On his own initiative, he rushed the position single-handed and put the gun out of action, thereby saving many further casualties and enabling the advance to continue.

The King's (Shropshire Light Infantry)

Captain George Frederick JONES MC, 7th King's (Shropshire Light Infantry), was killed in action on 28 March 1918. His MC was gazetted on 6 April 1918 and was awarded for conspicuous gallantry and devotion to duty when he assumed command of his company during an attack after the officer in charge had been killed. He showed most skilful leadership in capturing a number of enemy posts and, when troops on his left flank fell back, he and his men held their position against a determined counter-attack.

Second Lieutenant Victor George URSELL, 8th King's (Shropshire Light Infantry), attached 7th Battalion, was killed in action on 3 May 1917 during his battalion's advance in support of the 2nd Royal Scots' attack around the Bois du Vert. Machine-gun fire from Infantry Hill was responsible for checking the attackers who by 8.00am were forced to break off their advance and dig in. According to the CWGC register, his body was found seventeen days later deep within former enemy lines. He was buried out on the battlefield, but his grave was subsequently lost as a result of shell fire and further fighting. He had served as an intelligence and liaison officer in Salonika. Before the war he had studied Mathematics at Balliol College, Oxford, where he gained a first class Honours degree.

Private John BRITTAIN, 1st King's (Shropshire Light Infantry), had previously served in the South African campaign with the King's Own (Royal Lancaster Regiment). He was 36 years old when he was killed on 21 March 1918.

Private Thomas BURGESS, 5th King's (Shropshire Light Infantry), was killed in action on 12 October 1916, aged 26. Although the CWGC register makes no reference to his brother, Private John A. BURGESS was killed in action the following year on 28 April 1917, aged 28, serving with the 1st King's (Liverpool Regiment). It is obvious from the address of both men that they were brothers. John is also commemorated here with his brother.

Private Harvey BUTTERWORTH, 7th King's (Shropshire Light Infantry), was killed in action on 28 March 1918, aged 21. His brother, Fred, was killed in action with the 10th Lancashire Fusiliers on 7 July 1916, aged 26. Another brother, James Robert Butterworth, was killed in action on 3 September 1916, aged 22, serving with the 20th Manchester Regiment. Both were privates and neither has an identified grave. Both are now commemorated on the memorial at Thiepval.

Private Leonard CARTWRIGHT MM, 1st King's (Shropshire Light Infantry), was killed in action on 21 March 1918, aged 20. His MM was one of several gallantry awards conferred after the battalion had organized and carried out two raids on German trenches near Hulluch on 1 and 4 June 1917. The initial raid was the longer and more successful of the two and resulted in the destruction of several machine-gun posts. The battalion reported heavy casualties inflicted on the local garrison at a cost of one officer and three men killed and a further two officers and eleven other ranks wounded. Although no prisoners were taken, identifications were made before the raiders withdrew. The affair on 4 June was not as successful and lasted only ten minutes. Whether CARTWRIGHT took part in one or both of these operations is not stated, but his contribution was clearly recognized and rewarded.

Private James Edward COOPER MM, 5th King's (Shropshire Light Infantry), was killed in action on 27 March 1918. The regimental history makes no specific reference to his award or how it was won.

The Duke of Cambridge's Own (Middlesex Regiment)
Captain Stanley READ MC, 17th Middlesex Regiment, was killed in action near Oppy Wood on 28 April 1917, aged 21. His MC was gazetted on 4 June 1917 in the King's Birthday Honours List.

Lieutenant Albert Luvian WADE, 17th Middlesex Regiment, attached Trench Mortar Battery, was also killed in action near Oppy on 28 April 1917. He was educated at Dulwich College and had been captain of the College XV between 1902 and 1904. He later played rugby for the London Scottish Club, as well as the Barbarians, and represented Scotland against England at Inverleith in 1908, a game that Scotland won. He was born in Glasgow and was 32 years old when he was killed.

Second Lieutenant Frank Stanley BONATHAN MC, 17th Middlesex Regiment, was killed in action on 28 April 1917, aged 23. His MC was gazetted on 27 November 1916 and was awarded for conspicuous gallantry in action as a serjeant major with the same regiment, rendering most valuable assistance in organizing a minor operation and controlling the trench whilst under intense fire.

Second Lieutenant Rupert Anthony GREEN, attached 23rd Middlesex Regiment, was killed in action on 25 March 1918, aged 34. He had previously served during the Rebellion in South-West Africa, as well as in East Africa and Italy.

Second Lieutenant Walter Daniel John TULL, 5th Middlesex Regiment, attached 23rd Battalion, formerly 17th Battalion, was killed in action on 25 March 1918, aged 29. His is one of the names most frequently recognized on the memorial; he is considered to be the first black soldier in the British Army to receive a commission.

He was also well known in his day as a professional footballer with Tottenham Hotspur and Northampton Town. The CWGC register also notes that he was a previous winner of the FA Amateur Cup whilst playing for Clapton Football Club. He and his brother had been orphaned, but he managed to achieve success through his sporting ability and had many other qualities besides. He was present during the fighting on the Somme, at Messines Ridge and at Third Ypres, but he also served in Italy towards the end of 1917 and into 1918 where he was mentioned in despatches for leading a party of men on a raid across the fast-flowing River Piave.

He was killed near Favreuil, just north of Bapaume, and was seen to fall by one of his men, Private Billingham, who made an attempt to rescue him, but was unable to do so. Within the Middlesex Regiment the 17th Battalion was also known as the 1st Football Battalion and the 23rd Battalion as the 2nd Football Battalion.

Serjeant Albert BROWN DCM, 11th Middlesex Regiment, was killed in action on 12 May 1917. His DCM was gazetted on 22 January 1916 and was awarded for conspicuous gallantry on the night of 20/21 October 1915 at the Quarries near Loos. After a superior number of the enemy had driven back a party of bombers of another regiment, Private BROWN, along with an officer and two other privates, bombed them back with great dash, and in doing so saved a critical situation.

Lance Corporal Leonard Alfred ATTWELL, 17th Middlesex Regiment, was killed in action on 28 April 1917, aged 25. His brother, Private Frederick Harold Attwell, fell in action on 26 May 1917 serving with the 26th Company, Labour Corps, although he had originally been in the Queen's (Royal West Surrey Regiment). He is buried at Saint-Pol Communal Cemetery Extension.

Lance Corporal John MULVEY, 13th Middlesex Regiment, was killed in action on 15 April 1917, aged 26. His father had been a sergeant in the Royal Irish Constabulary and he served for ten years in its mounted section.

Private Herbert G. BREMNER, 17th Middlesex Regiment, was killed in action on 28 April 1917. His brother, Private Robert Bremner, also fell whilst serving with the 9th Devonshire Regiment on 1 July 1916, aged 21. He was killed near Mametz and is commemorated on the Thiepval Memorial. The family was from Tottenham in north London. A surprising number of Londoners served with the 9th Devonshire Regiment.

Private Reginald Gordon DENTON, 17th Middlesex Regiment, was killed in action on 3 January 1918, aged 23. He enlisted in the 16th Middlesex Regiment (Public Schools Battalion), in January 1915 and was wounded on 10 January 1916. His father, Lieutenant Colonel William Denton, resigned his commission in the 7th King's (Liverpool Regiment) on 3 July 1914, a month before the outbreak of war. By December that year he was again commissioned in the King's (Liverpool Regiment) and appointed as major with the 7th Battalion.

Private Julian GOULD, 'D' Company, 16th Middlesex Regiment, was killed in action near Monchy-le-Preux on 31 May 1917, aged 25. The CWGC register includes the note: '*A Good Artist*', and refers to a memorial booklet with prints that was published in 1917. GOULD was indeed a promising young artist who studied at the Municipal School of Art in Leicester. He then went to Paris in order to sketch. His father, Frederick James Gould, was a teacher, author, socialist and secularist. He and his father were certainly no apologists when it came to war, but Julian was finally persuaded to enlist after the sinking of the SS *Lusitania* in May 1915. His sense of moral outrage over the incident was enough to persuade him that he now had a duty to take up arms against Germany, although he still shared his father's strong socialist views.

He fought on the Somme in 1916, but he also found time behind the lines to sketch French rural life. He wrote letters home describing the countryside, complaining mildly that '*pencil travels inelegantly in numbed hands*'. After his death in 1917, his father produced a booklet, *Memorial Notice of Julian Gould*, containing images of his son as a child, some of his early art work, and some of the drawings he had made in France, together with some of his son's letters and letters of condolence following his death. His father, who had sung in St George's Chapel, Windsor, presented Princess Beatrice with a personal copy of the work. With some reluctance, his father eventually came round to understanding his son's reasons for going to war, comforted in part by the moral argument that had guided his son's decision to fight.

Private Walter John LARKIN, 'A' Company, 19th Middlesex Regiment, was killed in action on 26 March 1918 and had previously served in Italy. His brother, Private Frederick Edward Larkin, was killed in action on 1 July 1916 near Gommecourt, aged 21, serving with 'C' Company, 14th Battalion, London Regiment (London Scottish). He is commemorated on the Thiepval Memorial.

Private James RAMSAY, 4th Middlesex Regiment, was killed in action on 28 April 1917, aged 33. He served under the name of James Ramsey FREW and had returned to England from Santiago in Chile in December 1914 in order to enlist. The CWGC register shows his parents living in Santiago where there was a small, ex-patriot community, mainly comprising professional or commercial people. He was killed in action between Fampoux and Greenland Hill.

Private William Henry TOWNSEND, 1/7th Middlesex Regiment, was killed in action on 2 May 1917, aged 33. He had served for nine years in India and had also taken part in the South African campaign.

The King's Royal Rifle Corps
Major Frank Maxwell KING, King's Royal Rifle Corps, attached 9th Loyal North Lancashire Regiment, was killed in action on 22 March 1918.

Captain Laurence Drury CHIDSON MC, 13th King's Royal Rifle Corps, was killed in action on 23 April 1917, aged 22. When his company came up against enemy machine-gun fire to the right of its position, he and his bombers attempted to bomb their way along a trench in order to deal with it. As they approached the position they met opposition and CHIDSON was killed in the ensuing fight. His battalion had already reached its final objective, which was the Plouvain–Gavrelle road, but the units on either flank had been delayed leaving CHIDSON and his men to try to deal with the machine gun, which was enfilading their position. Several of his men were killed with him, as was Second Lieutenant Francis Edgar MACKENZIE who is also commemorated here with CHIDSON.

Captain Edward Maurice GONNER MC, 16th King's Royal Rifle Corps, was killed in action on 23 April 1917. His MC was gazetted on 4 June 1917 in the King's Birthday Honours List. He was killed during his battalion's attack on the Hindenburg Line. He was known to have been wounded in the attack and was initially recorded as wounded, but missing in action. He was commanding 'B' Company at the time of his death and was one of nine officers from the battalion who became casualties that day, six of whom were wounded. The attack had started badly when the tanks failed to arrive on time; by 2.30pm the supply of bombs had run out and the attack then broke down completely. The 98th Brigade had also been held up, which had then left the battalion's left flank unprotected.

Captain James Rockcliffe SMITH MC, 16th King's Royal Rifle Corps, was killed in action near Fontaine-lès-Croisilles on 20 May 1917, aged 34. He was commissioned in September 1914 and served in France and Flanders from November the following year until his death. He was killed in action near Bullecourt whilst leading his company in an attack on enemy positions. His MC was gazetted on 1 January 1917 and was awarded to him in recognition of his role during the battalion's attack at High Wood in July 1916 where he was wounded. The 16th Battalion was otherwise known as the Church Lads' Brigade.

Captain Erwin Wentworth WEBSTER, 13th King's Royal Rifle Corps, was killed in action on 9 April 1917, aged 37. He had studied for his degree at Oxford and was later elected as a Tutor and Fellow of Wadham College, Oxford. He had also studied at the British School in Athens and was a well-respected classical scholar, whose works included a translation of Aristotle's *Meteorologica*.

He was commissioned in the 13th King's Royal Rifle Corps in November 1914 on the same day that another Oxford man and classical scholar, Guy Dickins, was commissioned in the battalion. They had met at the British School in Athens and knew each other as friends. Dickins, who was a Fellow at St John's College, Oxford, lectured on classical history and archaeology. He died on 17 July 1916 from wounds received four days earlier when a shell burst next to him as he was attending to a wounded man near Pozières. Captain Dickins is now buried in Saint-Pierre Cemetery, Amiens.

WEBSTER's late father had been an Anglican minister in the Basses Pyrénées in the south of France. He too was a respected scholar and had written extensively on Basque history and culture. He had also studied at Oxford, at Lincoln College, and died in 1907 leaving most of his work to the Bodleian Library.

According to the CWGC register, Lieutenant Charles Scroop EGERTON-GREEN, 2nd King's Royal Rifle Corps, was killed in action on 1 July 1916, aged 20. *The King's Royal Rifle Corps Chronicle 1916* refers to his death on the night of 30 June when the battalion carried out an offensive operation at the Triangle near Loos. He had joined the 5th Battalion from Eton before transferring to the 2nd Battalion in October 1915. His eldest brother, Captain John William Egerton-Green, 1st Rifle Brigade, died of wounds on 9 October 1917, aged 25. He is buried at Boulogne Eastern Cemetery.

Second Lieutenant Alfred George BULL DCM, 5th King's Royal Rifle Corps, attached 8th Battalion, was killed in action on 6 August 1918, aged 27. His DCM was gazetted on 9 July 1917 and was awarded for conspicuous gallantry and devotion to duty whilst serving as a company serjeant major. The citation makes it clear that the award was not for any single act, but was given in recognition of his consistent performance and good work over a period of time, noting that at all times he had set a splendid example to his men.

Second Lieutenant Thomas Marwood HEXT, 1st King's Royal Rifle Corps, was killed in action on 28 April 1917, aged 19, by shell fire near Oppy. His father was Lieutenant Colonel Francis Marwood Hext of the Devonshire Regiment, who also served as High Sheriff of Devon in 1933. HEXT was educated at Eton, then at Trinity College, Cambridge, before entering Sandhurst. He was gazetted in the King's Royal Rifle Corps in October 1916 and served with the 1st Battalion from December that year.

Second Lieutenant Harold Douglas WEST, 1st King's Royal Rifle Corps, was serving as adjutant of the battalion when he was killed in action on 25 March 1918, aged 35. He left the battalion HQ around 7.00am to clarify some orders issued by the brigade, but was not seen again. Two hours later, orders were received for the battalion to fall back towards Eaucourt l'Abbaye on the old Somme battlefield.

Serjeant William Lawrence WESTLEY, 9th King's Royal Rifle Corps, was killed in action on 27 June 1916, aged 32. His father had served as a colour serjeant with the Somerset Light Infantry.

Lance Corporal Arthur Leonard HUGHES, 18th King's Royal Rifle Corps, was killed in action on 28 March 1918, aged 25. His brother, Corporal Frank Hughes, also fell. He was killed in action on 11 April 1917 whilst serving with the 2nd East Yorkshire Regiment, aged 28, and is commemorated on the Doiran Memorial in Northern Greece.

Lance Corporal John Edgar REES, 2nd King's Royal Rifle Corps, was killed in action near Loos on 1 July 1916, aged 41. His father, Captain James Rees, had served in the South African War and in German South-West Africa with the 1st Rhodesian Regiment.

Rifleman Arthur ALLCHURCH, 2nd King's Royal Rifle Corps, was killed in action on 1 July 1916, aged 24. He was one of twenty-four men reported missing after an unsuccessful and costly raid on German positions near the Double Crassier, Loos. Thirty-six other ranks were killed and 167 were wounded in the operation. Officer casualties amounted to five killed and six wounded. The CWGC register mentions that he '*came with the contingent from Hong Kong*'. I could find no reference elsewhere to this 'contingent'. The 3rd and 4th Battalions were in India when the war broke out, but not in Hong Kong.

Rifleman Harold Frank BROOKS MM, 6th King's Royal Rifle Corps, was 19 years old when he was killed in action on 20 May 1917. The 6th Battalion moved to Sheerness shortly after mobilization and remained in that area of England throughout the war as part of the Thames and Medway Garrison; it never actually went overseas and he was obviously killed whilst serving with one of the other battalions. His MM was gazetted on 9 July 1917. *The King's Royal Rifle Corps Chronicle 1917* notes only that the MM was awarded in 1917.

The Duke of Edinburgh's (Wiltshire Regiment)

The 191 members of the Wiltshire Regiment are from the 1st Battalion, 2nd Battalion or the 6th Battalion. The majority of them are 1918 casualties; 113 of the 136 listed as having fallen that year did so on 23/24 March, including the one officer. All forty-nine who fell in 1917 were killed in action in April during the Battle of Arras and all belonged to the 2nd Battalion. The remaining six fell in May 1916, five of whom served with the 1st Battalion.

There is just one officer among them: Captain Sidney Frederic TERRY, who was killed in action on 24 March 1918. Unfortunately, the CWGC register omits the fact that he was posthumously awarded the MC. The award was gazetted on 3 June 1918 in the King's Birthday Honours List. The roll of honour for St Olave's School in Orpington also shows the award next to his name, although his middle name is recorded as 'Frederick', as it is in the gazette. I have since notified the CWGC regarding the omission.

Among the other ranks are five men who were awarded the MM. Private Ernest William MISSEN MM, 2nd Wiltshire Regiment, was killed in action on the opening day of the Battle of Arras His was the earliest of the five to be awarded when it was gazetted on 21 September 1916.

Private Alexander Beville MILLS MM, 1st Wiltshire Regiment, was presumed to have been killed in action on 24 March 1918, aged 36. Unusually, there is a citation recommending his award in the 25th Division's History. It records that on the night of 18 July 1917 he was in the line at Railway Wood, east of Ypres, under a heavy enemy bombardment. At the time he was occupying a Lewis gun post and was twice blown off his feet and buried when shells landed near him. On both occasions he managed to extricate himself and, although other members of his team were wounded by the blasts, he continued to work the gun, setting a magnificent example to those around him.

The Manchester Regiment

Captain Charles Frederick DUGUID DSO MC, 22nd Manchester Regiment, was killed in action on 13 May 1917, aged 24. His MC was gazetted on 3 March 1917 and was awarded for his splendid example and conspicuous gallantry in action. After capturing a position, he reorganized his company under very heavy fire and, despite difficult conditions, he consolidated and held the captured trench. His DSO was gazetted on 11 May 1917 and was also awarded for conspicuous gallantry and devotion to duty after he made his way through uncut enemy wire with twenty men from his company and then set up a strongpoint in a small length of enemy trench where he remained for thirty-six hours, holding off several enemy counter-attacks.

Captain Noel Brendan GILL, 18th Manchester Regiment, was just 20 years old when he was killed in action on 23 April 1917 near Chérisy. The CWGC register notes that he had been a member of the OTC at the Royal College of Surgeons in Ireland and that he was gazetted in the summer of 1915. His brother, Owen, also served in the Great War, but survived and returned home to the family's farm in County Tipperary. As well as farming, their father, Robert Paul Gill, was a local architect and engineer. The boys' uncle was the Irish politician, Thomas Patrick Gill, MP for South Louth and a supporter of the Irish Nationalist politician, Charles Stewart Parnell, whom Asquith referred to as one of the three or four greatest men of the nineteenth century.

Lieutenant Frank Wright ROBINSON MC, 14th Manchester Regiment, attached 22nd Battalion, was killed in action on 13 May 1917, aged 22. His MC was gazetted on 26 May 1917 and was awarded for conspicuous gallantry and devotion to duty after he organized and led an attack on an enemy strongpoint, capturing it, together with twenty-two prisoners, and setting a splendid example to his men.

Private Frederick James BAYTON, 19th Manchester Regiment, was killed in action on 23 April 1917, aged 19. Two of his brothers also died during the war. The eldest, Able Seaman Harry Lewis Bayton, died serving in the Royal Navy on HMS *Opal* on 12 January 1918, aged 24. The destroyer was out on patrol with two other Royal Navy vessels looking for German warships laying mines off the Scottish coast. The *Opal* and the *Narborough* were ordered back to Scapa Flow when a heavy storm blew in. Both ships ran aground off the coast of Orkney. There were no survivors from HMS *Narborough* and only one from HMS *Opal*.

The other brother, Private Belcher Bayton, was killed on 1 July 1916 with the 8th Royal Sussex Regiment, the pioneer battalion to the 18th (Eastern) Division. Harry is commemorated on the Portsmouth Naval Memorial and Belcher is buried at Dive Copse British Cemetery, Sailly-le-Sec.

Private James GREEN, 18th Manchester Regiment, was killed in action on 23 April 1917, aged 21. His father, also James Green, was a former honorary regimental quartermaster serjeant with the Duke of Lancaster's Own Yeomanry.

The Prince of Wales's (North Staffordshire Regiment)

Lieutenant Robert Basil Cautley AKED MC, 2/5th North Staffordshire Regiment, was killed in action on 21 March 1918, aged 20. He was commissioned in the North Staffordshire Regiment from the OTC at Charterhouse School in October 1915. His MC was gazetted on 18 February 1918, followed by the citation five months later on 18 July. It was awarded for conspicuous gallantry and devotion to duty after a night raid in which a fellow officer was wounded. AKED carried him for 400 yards back to our lines. Later, he made three more journeys across no man's land, as far as the enemy's trenches, searching for and bringing in other wounded men, ceasing only when the enemy re-occupied the position. His was a splendid example of courage and self-sacrifice.

Serjeant Leslie Stuart LIDDLE, 1/6th North Staffordshire Regiment, was killed in action on 24 May 1917, aged 23. His brother, Lance Corporal Sidney Herbert LIDDLE, was killed in action on 1 May 1917, aged 24, serving with the 24th Royal Fusiliers. He is also commemorated here on the memorial.

The York & Lancaster Regiment

Lieutenant Colonel Theodore EARDLEY-WILMOT DSO, York & Lancaster Regiment, attached 12th Suffolk Regiment, was 38 years old when he died of wounds on 22 March 1918. A career soldier, he was gazetted as a second lieutenant in the East Surrey Regiment and served for seven years in the Indian Army between 1901 and 1908. He was severely wounded at the Second Battle of Ypres in 1915 and only returned to the front in 1916. His DSO was gazetted on 1 January 1917 for service in the field and he had also been mentioned in despatches.

Theodore and his wife had two children, a son and daughter. His son, Major Anthony Revell Eardley-Wilmot, was killed on 11 August 1944 with the 3rd Irish Guards and is buried at Tilly-sur-Seulles War Cemetery in Normandy.

Theodore's brother, Edward Gwynne Eardley-Wilmot MA, served with the 7th Royal Welsh Fusiliers during the war. He was described as a brilliant scholar and was an assistant master at Harrow prior to his enlistment. He survived the war and went on to become a barrister.

Other members of the family also served during the war. Lieutenant Frederick Eardley-Wilmot, Princess Patricia's Canadian Light Infantry, is buried at Voormezeele Enclosure No. 3 in Belgium. He was mortally wounded in the chest by a sniper whilst in the company of his battalion commander shortly after bringing up machine guns to the front line. He was the only son of Colonel Arthur Eardley-Wilmot CMG, Royal Horse Artillery, and was 20 years old when he died on 19 March 1915.

Lieutenant Commander Trevor Eardley-Wilmot DSO, who survived the war, was related to Frederick through their great-grandfather, Sir John Eardley-Wilmot, 1st Baronet, who was lieutenant governor of Tasmania.

Captain John Vere Eardley-Wilmot was killed in action on 15 August 1944 serving with the 21st Armoured Regiment. He is buried at Bretteville-sur-Laize

Canadian War Cemetery in Normandy. His father had served with the Canadian Engineers during the Great War.

Second Lieutenant John Marmaduke STROTHER MC, 3rd York & Lancaster Regiment, attached 10th Battalion, was killed in action on 28 April 1917, aged 24. His MC was gazetted on 3 March 1917 and was awarded for conspicuous gallantry in action. The citation states that, although he had been wounded, he carried out a dangerous reconnaissance and remained on duty until his battalion was relieved, setting a fine example throughout.

Second Lieutenant Douglas Henry WELLS MC, 5th York and Lancaster Regiment, was killed in action on 3 May 1917. His MC was gazetted on 28 April 1917, a few days before his death. It was awarded for conspicuous gallantry and devotion to duty whilst in command of a difficult reconnaissance patrol from which he returned with most valuable information. The citation goes on to add that he later rendered invaluable service when commanding a company.

Serjeant Charles ATKINSON, 2nd York and Lancaster Regiment, was killed on 21 March 1918, aged 40. He held the Long Service and Good Conduct Medal. His battalion belonged to the 6th Division, which was holding part of the front near Quéant on the day he was killed.

Serjeant Briscoe BAYNES DCM, 10th York & Lancaster Regiment, was killed in action on 23 April 1917. His DCM was awarded for conspicuous gallantry and initiative shown on several occasions. The citation refers specifically to a time when he kept his men working steadily whilst under hostile bombing, and also to another occasion when he cleared a wrecked post whilst under fire from a sniper. His award was gazetted on 21 June 1916. His father owned the music hall act known as the 'Al Fresco' troupe in the West End.

Private John Henry BEVERLEY, 2nd York & Lancaster Regiment, was killed in action on 21 March 1918, aged 20. He had been awarded a Royal Humane Society Certificate and came from the Rotherham area of South Yorkshire.

Private Alfred BULLIVANT, 12th York & Lancaster Regiment, was killed in action on 12 May 1917, aged 19. His brother, Private George Bullivant, fell whilst serving with the 7th Duke of Cornwall's Light Infantry on 7 August 1917, aged 24. He is commemorated on the Menin Gate at Ypres.

The Durham Light Infantry
Lieutenant William Gladstone WYLIE MC and Bar, 9th Durham Light Infantry, was killed in action on 28 March 1918, aged 22. His MC was gazetted on 20 July 1917 and was awarded for conspicuous gallantry and devotion to duty leading his platoon against an enemy machine gun with great skill and determination. Although severely wounded, he never ceased to encourage his men and refused to leave his post until dusk.

The bar to his MC was gazetted on 21 January 1918 and the citation for it appeared a few months later on 25 April. It was awarded for conspicuous gallantry and devotion to duty whilst in command of a party of 200 men carrying ammunition to the front line. On arrival there was no dump and no guide, but he succeeded in delivering his stores. The task was carried out under intense shell fire, which caused numerous casualties amongst his party. Throughout the operation, which lasted all of twenty-seven and a half hours, he set a fine example of good leadership.

Second Lieutenant Geoffrey CATES, 10th Durham Light Infantry, attached 2nd Battalion, was killed in action on 21 March 1918, aged 24. His brother, Second Lieutenant George Cates, 2nd Rifle Brigade, won the VC on 9 March 1917 after he struck a grenade buried just below the surface whilst deepening a trench. When it started to burn, he placed his foot on it, whereupon his leg and lower body took the full impact of the explosion. In doing so he successfully saved the lives of several of his men while sacrificing his own. He is buried at Hem Farm, Hem-Monacu.

Another brother, Private William Frederick CATES, lost his life at sea and is commemorated on the Halifax Memorial. He died on 27 June 1918 whilst serving with the Canadian Army Medical Corps. He was aboard the Hospital Ship *Llandovery Castle* when it was sunk off the coast of Ireland by the German U-boat *U-86*.

Serjeant Isaac HARBRON, DCM, 18th Durham Light Infantry, was killed in action on 18 May 1917. His DCM was gazetted posthumously on 18 July 1917. It was awarded for conspicuous gallantry and devotion to duty when leading his platoon three times during an assault, on each occasion reorganizing the men under cover, whilst he remained exposed to close enemy fire. His platoon achieved its objective, largely owing to the moral effect of his gallant leadership and extraordinary coolness under every form of fire. Two weeks earlier on 3 May, his battalion had been involved in an epic series of assaults to recapture the site of the ruined windmill at Gavrelle, eventually managing to secure it against heavy opposition and at some cost. The memorial carries the names of thirty-nine men from his battalion who fell in action on 3 May 1917, most, if not all, from 'C' Company.

The Highland Light Infantry
Lieutenant Colonel Spencer ACKLOM DSO & Bar MC, Highland Light Infantry, was killed in action on 21 March 1918 whilst commanding the 22nd Northumberland Fusiliers (Tyneside Scottish). He was educated at St Paul's, School in London, then at the Royal Military College, Sandhurst, before embarking on a military career. His father, also Lieutenant Colonel Spencer Acklom, had taken a similar path subsequently serving with the Connaught Rangers. His son was gazetted in the Highland Light Infantry in 1902 and by 1913 had risen to become adjutant of the 1st Battalion. He went to France with the Highland Light Infantry and remained with the regiment until his transfer to the

22nd Northumberland Fusiliers in May 1916. His MC, gazetted on 14 January 1916, was awarded for gallantry at Richebourg in 1915.

He was with the 22nd Northumberland Fusiliers at La Boiselle on 1 July 1916, successfully leading a party into the German third line trenches where they secured a position, albeit a precarious one. That position lay about 100 yards north of the large new crater, now known as Lochnagar Crater. He and his party beat off no fewer than six enemy counter-attacks that day and from his base there others were able to make several attempts to bomb their way up a communication trench leading to the village itself. Overnight and throughout the following day, he maintained command and control of this vital foothold where he was reinforced by men of the 9th Cheshire Regiment with three machine guns.

The message he sent back to Brigade HQ late on the evening of 2 July was extremely positive and stated that his party, now consisting of five officers and 155 men, was in good spirits with plenty of food and water and had set up two Stokes mortars. The final part of the message read: '*Position Secure*'. His outstanding leadership at La Boiselle earned him the DSO, which was gazetted on 1 January 1917 in the New Year's Honours List. There is absolutely no doubt that his actions during those first two days enabled further progress to be made on 3 July.

He went on to lead the 22nd Northumberland Fusiliers throughout 1917, including at the Battle of Arras, but he was killed in action on 21 March 1918, the opening day of the German Offensive. Throughout that difficult day he remained at his battalion HQ, which was situated in a trench known as Bunhill Row, about 1,000 yards north of the village of Écoust and tucked into the railway embankment that lies south of the road running between Croisilles and Bullecourt. Although his front trenches had been obliterated, he continued to hold his position in anticipation of a promised counter-attack by the 40th Division on his right flank. By remaining there, ACKLOM and what was left of his battalion would be able to cover the left flank of this attack. Unfortunately, the counter-attack never materialised and his HQ became cut off. Around 5.00pm he was killed whilst trying to lead his staff out of the hopeless position in which they now found themselves.

For his actions that day he was posthumously awarded a bar to his DSO, which was gazetted on 3 June 1918. His conduct and leadership throughout the war had earmarked him for command of a brigade, but that achievement was cut short by his death.

Captain Hugh Thomas BOSHELL, 4th Highland Light Infantry, attached 10th/11th Battalion, was killed in action on 22 March 1918, aged 22. He was the son of Major Francis Sydney Boshell DSO MC, 1st Royal Berkshire Regiment. His father's DSO was awarded in 1919 for services during the war and his MC was gazetted in the New Year's Honours List 1918. The family came from Wokingham in Berkshire.

Captain Walter McFarlane COULTER MC, 6th Highland Light Infantry, attached 9th Battalion (Glasgow Highlanders), was killed in action on 20 May

1917. He was one of eighty officers and men from his battalion who were killed in action between 20 and 21 May 1917, but only a few have ever been found and identified. He was killed somewhere between the first and second German trench lines during the early stages of an attack carried out by 33rd Division on part of the Hindenburg Line.

He had joined the battalion as a private in August 1914 and went to France with it in 1915. He was wounded in the arm during the battalion's first taste of action on 16 May 1915 at the Battle of Festubert. He was subsequently commissioned and rejoined the battalion in September 1916. His MC was awarded for his part in a successful trench raid that took place near Bouchavesnes on the night of 7 February 1917. The award was gazetted on 26 March 1917. His father had been the Commissioner of Police in the British Virgin Islands.

Second Lieutenant James Henderson CAMPBELL MC, 4th Highland Light Infantry, attached 10th Battalion, was killed in action on 24 April 1917, aged 23. His MC was gazetted on 18 July 1917 and was awarded for conspicuous gallantry and devotion to duty, commanding his company with great dash and skill. When the advance was temporarily held up, he carried out a flank attack that enabled the main line of advance to proceed. The citation adds that he showed great gallantry and coolness under heavy shell and machine-gun fire.

Second Lieutenant Daniel SHERIDAN MC DCM, 2nd Highland Light Infantry, was killed in action on 24 March 1918, aged 29. He was shown missing in action on 24 March 1918, the date on which his death is now presumed to have occurred. His DCM was won serving as a company serjeant major and was gazetted on 14 November 1916 for conspicuous gallantry. After the battalion had reached its final objective, he went out alone to reconnoitre the new position. He entered a dug-out where he captured a machine gun and a solitary German and when he had finished there he made his prisoner carry the gun back to our lines.

His MC was gazetted posthumously on 23 July 1918 and was awarded after he took command of two platoons and led them to cover a gap of around 600 yards between two brigades as the enemy was advancing towards it. He achieved this in spite of heavy rifle and machine-gun fire from an enemy force vastly superior to his. Despite being wounded on his way to the position, which he had been ordered to hold for as long as possible, he continued to encourage and lead his men forward, maintaining heavy and accurate return fire on the enemy. In doing so he enabled the right section of the brigade next to him to withdraw whilst he and his men covered its flank. Out of the two platoons that he led forward, only four men survived. His body was never found and it was presumed that he was one of those killed, but his gallant and courageous leadership prevented a very serious situation from becoming critical. His division's losses might easily have been greater had it not been for his gallant action. He also held the Bronze Medal for Military Valour (Italy).

Company Serjeant Major Angus BRUCE DCM, 14th Highland Light Infantry, was killed in action on 27 March 1918, aged 37. He was a former pipe-major in the 1st Scots Guards. His parents came from Uig on the Isle of Skye, but before the war he had lived in Windsor with his wife. The citation for his DCM, gazetted on 11 March 1916, shows him serving with the 12th Battalion. It was awarded for conspicuous gallantry and ability after all his officers had been put out of action in an attack on the enemy's front trench. He then assumed command and handled his men with the greatest ability, setting a fine example of devotion to duty throughout the entire action.

Lance Corporal Alexander McGECHAEN, 9th Highland Light Infantry, was killed in action on 20 May 1917, aged 40. The CWGC register points out that he had served in the army for twenty-one years.

Private J. FOX, 2nd Highland Light Infantry, was executed on 12 May 1916. His case was a rare one: that of striking a superior officer. He was on parade during a kit inspection when he was criticised for the state of his rifle and boots. Not only did FOX verbally abuse the officer, but he made the mistake of threatening the officer with his rifle. He was swiftly disarmed by one of the NCOs and then placed under arrest. Although FOX put forward the mitigating circumstances of drink and family problems, his defence was dismissed and he was found guilty as charged. Sadly, he is not included in *Soldiers Died in the Great War*.

Seaforth Highlanders (Ross-Shire Buffs, The Duke of Albany's)

Major Charles Ernest JOHNSTON DSO TD, 6th Seaforth Highlanders, was reported missing in action after he was wounded on 23 March 1918, aged 43. In 1914 he had been the battalion's recruiting officer in Morayshire and only went to France in 1917 when he was appointed as second-in-command of the 6th Seaforth Highlanders.

His DSO citation, which is quite a lengthy one, was gazetted on 2 December 1918. On 21 to 22 March 1918, during operations east of Bapaume, he was in command of his battalion in the Beaumetz–Morchies line, south-east of the village of Beaumetz-lès-Cambrai. Although subjected to a heavy artillery and machine-gun barrage, he moved about regardless of the danger to himself, supervising his defensive positions and encouraging his men to make a firm stand to the last. When the enemy broke through on the left of his battalion, he showed great skill and daring by organizing a defensive flank on the Cambrai road, which prevented the enemy entering Beaumetz. When the battalion received orders to retire to a new line behind Beaumetz-lès-Cambrai on 23 March, he personally organized and supervised the withdrawal before setting up a new defensive position for his battalion.

Throughout this period he showed not only the greatest devotion to duty, but also remarkable organizational skills and consummate bravery whilst under immense pressure. It was largely owing to his splendid example that the battalion put up such an excellent defence and inflicted such heavy casualties on the enemy. His citation points out that the stand made by the 51st (Highland) Division on the Bapaume–Cambrai road owed a great deal to his actions and powers of leadership and did much to save the situation on that part of the field. He continued to command his battalion on 23 March until he was eventually wounded. Owing to the proximity of the enemy, it proved impossible to bring him back behind our lines. It is presumed that he died later that day. He was also twice mentioned in despatches.

Captain Ian MACKENZIE MC, 5th Seaforth Highlanders, was killed in action on 21 March 1918, aged 24. He was educated at Fettes College, Edinburgh, and Balliol College, Oxford, where he is mentioned on both rolls of honour. However, despite searching several variations of his surname and first name, I can find no trace of his MC in any of the gazettes. The MC is shown next to his name in *Officers Died in the Great War*, however the spelling of his surname is different to that shown in the CWGC register. There is, however, a citation relating to the award of the MC to a Lieutenant John MACKENZIE, Seaforth Highlanders, who is shown as acting captain. It is included in the same *Edinburgh Gazette* as the citation for Second Lieutenant David Dandie CAIRNIE's MC, who served with MACKENZIE in the 5th Battalion. I have a very strong suspicion that 'Ian' and 'John' MACKENZIE are one and the same man. If my suspicions are correct, his MC was awarded for conspicuous gallantry and devotion to duty when in command of his company in a most critical situation. He moved about freely and in the open, organizing and controlling his men under heavy fire. In doing so, he captured all of his objectives.

Lieutenant George Monro MacBEY MC, 6th Seaforth Highlanders, was killed in action on 22 March 1918, aged 20. His MC was gazetted on 10 January 1917 and was awarded for conspicuous gallantry in action at Beaumont Hamel in November 1916. Although severely wounded, he remained on duty, collecting men and directing operations. Throughout the operation he set a splendid example, not least by personally capturing fifty prisoners. He was killed fighting near the Bapaume–Cambrai road.

Lieutenant Rowland REES MC, 6th Seaforth Highlanders, was killed in action on 25 March 1918, aged 35. His MC was gazetted on 26 July 1917 and was awarded for conspicuous gallantry and devotion to duty. Whilst carrying out a reconnaissance he found some troops carrying out an attack but without any leading officer. He took command of them and directed their fire to good effect. He then returned to his own battalion and was able to give an accurate account of the situation ahead.

Second Lieutenant David Dandie CAIRNIE MC, 5th Seaforth Highlanders, was killed in action on 21 March 1918, aged 31. Prior to the war he worked as a chemist. His MC, gazetted on 4 February 1918, was awarded in recognition of his splendid courage and resource at Cambrai in November 1917 when advancing up an enemy trench at the head of his men. Seeing a machine gun in action, he dashed thirty yards to it, shot its crew and captured the gun. The citation appeared in the *Edinburgh Gazette* on 8 July 1918. One of his sons, John Bruce

Cairnie, also served with the Seaforth Highlanders from 1914 until his transfer to the King's African Rifles in 1917. Unlike his father, he survived the war and left behind an excellent diary which is well worth searching out.

Second Lieutenant Andrew Bremner SINCLAIR, 5th Seaforth Highlanders, attached 8th Battalion, was killed in action on 10 December 1917, aged 23. His brother, William Baikie Sinclair, died whilst serving with the Royal Navy and is commemorated on the Chatham Naval Memorial. He was aboard HMS *Princess Irene* when it blew up after striking a mine off Shearness on 27 May 1915. Only one member of the crew survived; all the others went down with the ship. William had been awarded the Messina Medal for his part in the relief work carried out by the Royal Navy following the earthquake that destroyed much of Messina in Sicily in 1908.

Serjeant Thomas DICKSON, 8th Seaforth Highlanders, had previously served with the 1st Battalion. He was an experienced soldier who had taken part in several campaigns, including the Chitral Expedition, the Sudan and the South African War. He was 42 years old when he was killed in action on 12 April 1918.

Serjeant Alexander EDWARDS VC, 6th Seaforth Highlanders, was killed in action on 24 March 1918. His VC was won at Ypres on 31 July 1917, the opening day of the Third Battle of Ypres. It was awarded for most conspicuous bravery, leading a detachment forward against a machine gun, killing its team and capturing the gun. Later, when an enemy sniper was causing casualties, he went out, stalked him and killed him, despite being badly wounded in the arm. By that time the company had only one officer remaining. Realizing that the success of the operation depended on the capture of the furthest objective, he led the men to that objective, subsequently showing great skill in its consolidation and carrying out a daring reconnaissance. He sustained two more wounds the following day in a display of coolness that imbued his men with a fine fighting spirit. Throughout the entire operation he showed a complete disregard for his personal safety.

Lance Corporal John BARRON, 2nd Seaforth Highlanders, was killed in action on 12 April 1917, aged 23. His brother, Private Duncan Barron, was killed in action on 21 March 1918 serving with the 6th Cameron Highlanders. He is buried at Monchy-le-Preux British Cemetery. He was the son of James and Isabelle Barron of Ord Distillery, Muir of Ord, Ross-shire.

The whisky industry ran up against many difficulties between 1914 and 1918. Lloyd George did everything he could to cut consumption, particularly amongst the British workforce, including raising excise duty. Grain was also in short supply and, while many small, independent distilleries suffered, Distillers Company Limited found that it could still make money, firstly by selling its yeast, which was vital for bread production, and also by producing industrial alcohol. It is estimated that fifty million gallons of proof alcohol went to the munitions industry for the manufacture of propellant. A number of small distilleries were snapped up by the bigger players as they looked to strengthen their portfolios. In

1924 the Muir of Ord distillery was acquired by Dewar's. For anyone not familiar with Glen Ord Single Malt Whisky, it makes for a good restorative after a day touring the battlefields.

Lance Corporal John H. MacDONALD, 5th Seaforth Highlanders, and Private William MacDONALD, 4th Seaforth Highlanders, were brothers who were killed in action on the same day, 21 March 1918. Their late father, William MacDonald, had been a pipe major who had composed several pieces for the instrument.

Private Albert (Harry) GAYLOR, 6th Seaforth Highlanders, was killed in action by shrapnel on 21 March 1918. He was one of six brothers, five of whom served in the Great War. He had originally enlisted in April 1914 under his real name, 'Harry', but was medically discharged on Christmas Day the same year. However, he was determined to re-enlist and in April 1915 he joined the 6th Seaforth Highlanders, but under the assumed first name of Albert. He was wounded three times during his three years at the front and fought at Loos, the Somme, Ypres and Cambrai. On one occasion he was briefly buried alive, but prompt action by colleagues saved his life. During the rescue he was injured in the back when he was struck by a pick-axe used by one of the rescue party.

The Gordon Highlanders
Major Thomas MacWHIRTER MC, 9th Gordon Highlanders, was killed in action on 27 April 1917, aged 30. His MC was gazetted on 17 January 1916, although I can find no trace of any citation. His brother, Serjeant William Tait MacWhirter, died as a result of illness during the Gallipoli Campaign on 16 November 1915, aged 19, whilst serving with the 1st Light Horse Field Ambulance, Australian Army Medical Corps. He is commemorated on the Lone Pine Memorial. The CWGC register shows a small variation in the spelling of his surname.

Captain Archibald Randall DAVIDSON, 1st Gordon Highlanders, was killed in action on 14 June 1917, aged 21. His father, Major George Harry Davidson DSO, had served with the Royal Scots between 1887 and 1910 and as adjutant between 1894 and 1898. He saw action in Zululand and also took part in the South African War, receiving the DSO in September 1901 for services during operations in Cape Colony. Although he had two daughters, Archibald was his only son.

Lieutenant Tom Calto Pirie CAMPBELL MC, 4th Gordon Highlanders, attached 1st Battalion, was killed in action on 28 March 1918, aged 24. His MC was gazetted on 18 July 1917 and shows his middle name as 'Catto'. It was awarded for conspicuous gallantry and devotion to duty whilst working as intelligence officer for his battalion. The citation records that he had performed most valuable work and had shown an utter disregard for his personal safety when obtaining information of great value under heavy fire.

Lieutenant Patrick Edward DOVE, 1st Gordon Highlanders, was killed in action on 14 June 1917, aged 19. His parents were the late Sir Patrick Dove KC and Lady Loetitia Rose. I have not been able to establish any direct link, but Lieutenant DOVE may well be related to the Scottish socio-political theorist, Patrick Edward Dove, best-known for his work, *The Theory of Human Progression*.

Second Lieutenant Robert Donald HIGH, 4th Gordon Highlanders, was killed in action on 22 March 1918, aged 37. He took an Arts degree at Aberdeen University before going on to a teaching career. He was an assistant master at Moffat Academy before being appointed headmaster of Ladykirk Public School in Berwickshire where he and his wife lived. He enlisted in the 4th Gordon Highlanders at the start of 1916 and was commissioned the following year. It is believed that he fell in action somewhere just south of the Bapaume–Cambrai road.

Second Lieutenant John LITTLE DCM, 8th Gordon Highlanders, died of wounds on 24 April 1917, aged 28. His DCM was won whilst serving as a serjeant with the 7th Cameron Highlanders and was gazetted on 1 January 1917. It was awarded for conspicuous gallantry and devotion to duty after he took charge of two platoons and kept up a continuous supply of bombs to the front line. It adds that on another occasion he displayed great courage and skill in handling a working party under fire. The citation appeared on 13 February 1917. He was commissioned in February, a couple of months before he died. Prior to the war he had been a teacher.

Second Lieutenant Christopher SANDERSON DSO, 1st Gordon Highlanders, was killed in action on 18 June 1917. He had previously distinguished himself as a serjeant and went on to win his DSO shortly after receiving his commission. It was won during an operation to recapture the Bluff on 2 March 1916 following its loss a few weeks earlier on 14 February. Things had gone well for two of the battalions involved, namely the 2nd Suffolk Regiment and the 8th King's Own (Royal Lancaster Regiment), but some of the Gordon Highlanders had become held up on the left of the attack by a machine gun that had already caused a number of casualties. Realizing this, Sanderson led a group of bombers forward and put the gun out of action. During the assault he personally threw bombs, silencing two groups of enemy bombers and incurring minor injuries whilst doing so. Later, two enemy bombers appeared to the rear of his position, at which point he went out into the open and shot both of them. The operational report states that the capture of the enemy trench was largely due to his gallantry and leadership and adds that he was immediately recommended for an award. His DSO was gazetted a few weeks later on 30 March. He was wounded and gassed later that year. During his military service he was also awarded two foreign decorations, the Military Cross (France) and the Order of St George (Russia).

Second Lieutenant James William SMITH, 7th Gordon Highlanders, was killed in action on 21 March 1918, aged 23. The CWGC register also refers to his father who lost his life at sea when his boat was torpedoed. The ship was the SS *Perth*, a cargo ship, and James's father was Able Seaman Andrew Anthony Smith who served with the Mercantile Marine. The ship was sunk off the east coast, near Harwich, on 1 April 1916, with the loss of six lives. The date of death for Able Seaman Smith is shown in the CWGC register as 2 April. Both father and son are commemorated on the Whiteness and Weisdale War Memorial on Shetland.

Second Lieutenant Alexander Vivian STEWART, 4th Gordon Highlanders, was killed in action on 23 April 1917, aged 21. He was a medical student at Edinburgh University before the war and enlisted in August 1914.

Second Lieutenant William Henry SUTHERLAND MC, 4th Gordon Highlanders, was killed in action on 23 March 1918. His MC was gazetted on 26 November 1917 and its citation on 6 April 1918. It was awarded for conspicuous gallantry and devotion to duty when leading an attack on an enemy strongpoint, capturing it with great dash and determination. Later, when the position was in danger of being surrounded, he showed great initiative and skill in reorganizing the line, setting up and consolidating a good defensive position to the rear.

Serjeant William James MARTIN DCM, 8/10th Gordon Highlanders, was killed in action on 21 March 1918, aged 21. His DCM was gazetted on 26 January 1918 and was awarded for conspicuous gallantry and devotion to duty. The citation states that during an advance he displayed the greatest courage and determination, locating hostile machine guns and handling his platoon so skilfully that the emplacements were rushed with a minimum of casualties. At one point, when the crew of a gun was knocked out by shell fire close to his position, he dashed forward under heavy machine-gun fire, carried away the gun and brought it into action, inspiring his own platoon and all around him by his coolness and fearless bearing.

Serjeant Archibald Stuart SINCLAIR, 'B' Company, 7th Gordon Highlanders, was killed in action on 22 April 1917, aged 39. The CWGC register also notes that his father, James Sinclair, had previously held the same rank.

Corporal Alexander DAVIDSON DCM, 4th Gordon Highlanders, was killed in action on 25 March 1918, aged 22. His DCM was gazetted on 6 February 1918 and was awarded for conspicuous gallantry and devotion to duty after attacking and capturing an enemy post of eight men single-handed. An unforeseen consequence of his prompt and courageous action was that an enemy machine gun, positioned so as to defend the post, was also abandoned.

Corporal Robert RICHARDSON DCM, 6th Gordon Highlanders, fell in action on 23 March 1918, aged 28. His DCM was gazetted on 10 January 1917 and was awarded for conspicuous gallantry in action, having displayed great courage and determination during a bombing attack against the enemy. The citation adds that his actions materially contributed to the success of the operation. It was won while he was serving as a lance corporal.

Lance Corporal William BRODIE, 2nd Gordon Highlanders, was killed in action on 7 May 1917, aged 20. His brother, James, also fell. The CWGC records offer no assistance in identifying James.

Lance Corporal John R. LAWRENCE DCM, 5th Gordon Highlanders, was killed in action on 9 April 1917. His DCM was gazetted a week later on 17 April 1917 and was won whilst serving as an acting lance corporal. It was awarded for conspicuous gallantry and devotion to duty during a raid on the enemy's trenches. The citation notes that he had set a splendid example throughout the raid and was the last man of his section to leave the enemy's trench. During the raid he killed an enemy machine gunner and destroyed his gun.

Lance Corporal Harry YOUNG DCM, 7th Gordon Highlanders, was killed in action on 26 March 1918. His award was gazetted on 26 January 1918 and was awarded for conspicuous gallantry and devotion to duty after he had gone forward with the greatest determination and silenced an enemy machine gun, capturing a team of seven men. By his gallant and fearless action he enabled his company to take the position without serious loss.

Private Alexander J. ADAMS, 6th Gordon Highlanders, was killed in action on 16 May 1917, aged just 17.

Private William ALANACH, 6th Gordon Highlanders, was killed in action on 21 March 1918. His father, John, worked at the Balmenach distillery in Cromdale, Morayshire. At its best, Balmenach is a very fine dram, but the distillery was closed during the war and remained so for a while afterwards. It has since had a chequered history and during the Second World War its buildings were requisitioned as a billet for men of the Royal Corps of Signals.

The distillery was originally established by the great grandfather of Sir Robert Bruce Lockhart. Sir Robert served as a diplomat in Russia during the Great War and was once accused of plotting to assassinate Lenin. He was imprisoned in the Kremlin until he was exchanged for Maxim Maximovich Litvinoff, a Russian diplomat. He also went on to work in Czechoslovakia and during the Second World War he became liaison officer to the Czech government-in-exile and was appointed Director General of Political Warfare by Sir Winston Churchill. He also worked for Lord Beaverbrook between the wars.

Sir Robert knew Balmenach well and wrote affectionately about it in his book, *Scotch*. He describes how, on rainy days, an empty malt barn would become an indoor cricket pitch for playing tip and run; and how with shilling rods and a tin of worms, the local youngsters would fish the nearby burn for trout. This was the world in which Private William ALANACH grew up, a world that he left behind forever when he marched away to war.

Private John Arthur BURNESS, 7th Gordon Highlanders, was 19 years old when he was killed in action on 23 April 1917, aged 19. The CWGC register notes that his father, A.W. Burness, had formerly served as a regimental serjeant major in the Gordon Highlanders. He served with the Gordon Highlanders during the South African campaign.

Private Alexander George SUTHERLAND, 4th Gordon Highlanders, was killed in action on 23 April 1917, aged 31. He was a graduate of both Aberdeen and Cambridge Universities and had previously served under the Crown Agents for the Colonies in Southern Nigeria. He came from Buckie, Banffshire. The Crown Agency was an administrative body that assisted in running the overseas territories of the Empire, mainly with regard to finance, trade and commercial matters

The Queen's Own (Cameron Highlanders)
Captain James Bannerman LORIMER, 'C' Company, 5th Cameron Highlanders, attached 8th Rifle Brigade, was killed in action on 3 May 1917, aged 37. His late father was John Campbell Lorimer KC, Sheriff of the Counties of Aberdeen, Kincardine and Banff. He enlisted in August 1914 and was gazetted in December that year. A collection of his letters written between 1914 and his death are now deposited at the National Library of Scotland. Most were written from the front and offer a valuable insight into the life of a battalion officer. As far as I know, the collection has never been published.

Second Lieutenant Alexander Robert MACDONALD MC, 7th Cameron Highlanders, was killed in action on 28 March 1918, aged 47. His MC was gazetted on 22 April 1918 and was awarded for conspicuous gallantry and devotion to duty whilst in command of a raiding party. Finding loose wire across a gap in the enemy's wire, he cleared it with assistance from one of his NCOs and led his party into the enemy's trench. He then successfully dealt with the enemy in the trench and when some of them tried to escape, he pursued them, killing one and capturing three. He then withdrew the whole of his party successfully, having set them a fine example of coolness and courage throughout the entire operation.

Second Lieutenant James MILLER MC, 6th Cameron Highlanders, was killed in action on 11 March 1918, aged 28. His MC was gazetted on 26 September 1917 and the citation for it appeared on 9 January 1918. It was awarded for conspicuous gallantry and devotion to duty after he organized and led a raid against an enemy machine-gun position. During the assault he showed the greatest coolness and personal courage, leading his party across ground that he had been unable to reconnoitre beforehand. He personally captured the machine gun and a prisoner, but shot the remainder of the crew as they retired. It was largely owing to his skilful leadership that the enterprise was carried out with very few casualties.

Corporal Gilbert McKIE DCM, 7th Cameron Highlanders, was killed in action on 24 March 1918, aged 22. His DCM was gazetted on 21 October 1918 and was awarded for conspicuous gallantry and devotion to duty. The citation records that his work had been magnificent, especially on one occasion when he distinguished himself through the skilful handling of his guns during a critical situation. It adds that he had taken part in every raid carried out by the battalion and had always shown the same qualities of coolness and initiative in trying circumstances.

Private Frank William Sydney KEIGWIN, 5th Cameron Highlanders, was killed in action on 3 May 1917, aged 19. The CWGC register notes that he had been a journalist, but does not give any further information.

Private Alexander William MACDONALD, 7th Cameron Highlanders, was killed in action on 28 March 1918, aged 32. The CWGC register notes that he had been wounded on four previous occasions.

Private William SCOLLAY, 6th Cameron Highlanders, who had formerly served with the Lovat Scouts, was killed in action on 28 March 1918, aged 19. His elder brother, Lance Corporal John Scollay, served with the 4th Gordon Highlanders, but died of wounds on 21 May 1917, aged 21. He is buried at Aubigny Communal Cemetery Extension. Another member of the Scollay family, possibly a cousin, was killed at sea on 16 April 1918 when the armed merchant ship, SS *Ladoga*, was sunk by a German U-boat in the Irish Sea with the loss of twenty-nine lives. Peter David Scollay, who served with the Mercantile Marine, is commemorated on the Tower Hill Memorial in London and came from East Yell in Shetland. William and John lived in Scalloway, which is on Mainland, Shetland, south of Yell.

The Royal Irish Rifles
There are just thirty-one men of the Royal Irish Rifles recorded on the memorial and all of them are riflemen or NCOs. Almost half are from the period between April and May 1916, the majority of whom were killed or died of wounds on 17 May whilst serving with the 2nd Battalion. A further fourteen fell during the first week of the German Offensive in March 1918. Those who fell in 1916 were part of the 25th Division, whereas those who died in 1918 were with the 36th (Ulster) Division.

Princess Victoria's (Royal Irish Fusiliers)
Captain John Kirk BOAL, 3rd Royal Irish Fusiliers, attached 1st Battalion, was killed in action near Roeux on 3 May 1917, aged 20. He was one of five officers from his battalion killed that day; a further six were wounded and the total casualties for other ranks came to 126. Like many of the battalions that were still involved in the fighting around Arras in early May, the 1st Royal Irish Fusiliers had already taken part in several actions and was becoming tired and depleted.

After the fighting on 3 May the battalion was left with just six officers and 236 other ranks still fit for duty.

Private Edward BRADY DCM, 1st Royal Irish Fusiliers, died of wounds on 12 April 1917. His DCM was gazetted on 9 July 1917 and was awarded for conspicuous gallantry and devotion to duty as a runner carrying messages under heavy fire.

Private Robert McCLINTOCK, 1st Royal Irish Fusiliers, was killed in action on 11 April 1917, aged 19. His brother, Rifleman David McClintock, was killed in action at the Battle of Le Cateau on 26 August 1914 when serving with the 2nd Royal Irish Rifles, aged 28. He is commemorated on the memorial at La Ferté-Sous-Jouarre.

The Connaught Rangers
There are just three men from this regiment commemorated on the memorial. All three were killed in action during the attack on Tunnel Trench on 20 November 1917 and all three are from the 6th Battalion.

Princess Louise's (Argyll & Sutherland Highlanders)
Captain William Dawson MUNRO MC, 8th Argyll & Sutherland Highlanders, was killed in action on 16 May 1917. His MC was gazetted on 10 January 1917 and was awarded for conspicuous gallantry in action. Accompanied by just one other officer and a handful of men, he captured an enemy battalion commander and forty-five other prisoners. Later he supervised the consolidation of the position, setting a splendid example to his men. In addition to the prisoners, large quantities of ammunition and provisions were also captured. This act of gallantry occurred on 13 November 1916 during the capture of Beaumont Hamel by the 51st (Highland) Division. Captain MUNRO was also awarded the *Croix de Guerre* (France), which was gazetted on 1 May 1917.

The other officer referred to in the citation is Second Lieutenant George Eric Edwards DSO, 6th Seaforth Highlanders. EDWARDS, who subsequently was also promoted to captain, was killed in action at Cambrai on 20 November 1917. He is now buried at Orival Wood Cemetery, Flesquières. Edwards and his small party arrived outside a large dug-out where he negotiated the surrender of all those inside. Unaware of how small his party was, the Germans agreed, but before Edwards could arrange for their orderly exit and surrender, an enemy party arrived on the scene armed with bombs. A brief fight took place during which Edwards and his men were overwhelmed. He and the survivors of his party were then taken prisoner and marched off to another dug-out, which happened to be a battalion HQ.

A short while later it became apparent that British troops were now in Beaumont Hamel in greater numbers and Edwards was again able to persuade his captors that it would be in their best interests to surrender. The German battalion commander took only a short time to consider the situation before agreeing to surrender to Edwards and his men. Owing to the depleted numbers in his party, Edwards was obliged to hand over his prisoners to men of the 63rd (Royal Naval) Division who happened to be nearby, including those from the dug-out whose surrender he had negotiated earlier. According to the divisional history, Edwards was responsible for the capture of between 300–400 prisoners.

Second Lieutenant George BEATTIE MC, 11th Argyll & Sutherland Highlanders, was killed in action on 23 April 1917. His MC was gazetted on 26 September 1916 and was awarded for conspicuous gallantry during operations. The citation notes that he and Lieutenant William Irvine had crawled from a shell hole for a distance of 150 yards and, despite being frequently under fire, they succeeded in bringing back a wounded officer on a waterproof sheet from within fifty yards of the enemy's trench. Irvine also received the MC and went on to survive the war.

Second Lieutenant Frederick HAYWORTH, 7th Argyll & Sutherland Highlanders, attached 14th Battalion, London Regiment (London Scottish), was killed in action on 12 May 1917, three weeks after his brother, Harry, had been killed on the same battlefield serving in the same battalion. The brothers were from Ayr and had both studied at Glasgow University. Frederick, the elder of the two, was 24 years old when he died. Before the war he worked as a bank clerk with the Royal Bank of Scotland in Glasgow. His brother, Second Lieutenant Harry Asher Hayworth, is buried at Arras in the Faubourg d'Amiens Cemetery and was 21 years old when he died on 15 April.

Second Lieutenant Robert LYON, 5th Argyll & Sutherland Highlanders, attached 8th Battalion, was killed in action on 17 March 1917, aged 51. His father had been a church minister in Perth, Scotland, and he was a graduate of St Andrew's University. He had previously served in Matabeleland and also in the South African War. He was in Africa in 1914 when the war broke out, but returned home to enlist.

Serjeant James FERGUSON DCM, 11th Argyll & Sutherland Highlanders, was killed in action on 9 April 1917, aged 30. His DCM was awarded as a corporal for conspicuous gallantry in action after twice leading a party of bombers and clearing the enemy from their position. The citation goes on to state that he set a splendid example of coolness and initiative throughout the operation, which he also carried out with great courage and determination. The award was gazetted on 14 November 1916.

Lance Corporal Allan James REID, 1/7th Argyll & Sutherland Highlanders, was killed in action on 23 April 1917, aged 20. His parents lived at No. 76A, Dunnikier Road, Kirkcaldy in Fife. Very close neighbours also lost a son later that year. Air Mechanic Thomas Cousin Robertson, 52 Squadron, Royal Flying Corps, was killed in action on 21 October 1917, aged 36; his parents lived at

No. 80, Dunnikier Road. Robertson happens to be commemorated on the Flying Services Memorial here at Arras. Both men would probably have known each other before going their separate ways during the war. It seems entirely appropriate that they are now both reunited, at least at the same location, if not on the same memorial.

Private John Stuart GRANT, 2nd Argyll & Sutherland Highlanders, was killed in action on 24 April 1917; he came from Grantown-on-Spey. He was working in Edinburgh as a tailor before the war and joined the 6th Seaforth Highlanders in October 1916. Although subsequently discharged through poor health, he remained determined to do his duty and eventually re-enlisted in the Argyll & Sutherland Highlanders. His brother, Private Andrew Thomas Bain Grant, 6th Seaforth Highlanders, was killed in action on 15 June 1915 and is commemorated on the memorial at Le Touret. Andrew had also been a tailor in Edinburgh before the war and had joined the Territorial Army when he was just 16 years old. He had only been at the front for six weeks when he was killed. Their other brother, Harry, was severely wounded, but survived the war.

Private Donald Louttit MOWAT, 5th Seaforth Highlanders, was killed in action on 22 March 1918. He enlisted in 1914 and took part in fighting on the Somme in 1916, including the Battle of the Ancre in November. He also saw considerable action throughout 1917 when he fought at the Battle of Arras, the Third Battle of Ypres and at Cambrai, but he fell in action during the early days of the German March Offensive. His brother, Robert George Reid Mowat, who served with the 7th Argyll & Sutherland Highlanders, was more fortunate and survived the war.

The Prince of Wales's Leinster Regiment (Royal Canadians)
There are just thirty-four men from this regiment listed on the memorial and all of them are privates or NCOs. Thirty-two of them belong to the 2nd Battalion and were killed in action on 12 April 1917 during the attack on the Bois en Hache at the northern end of Vimy Ridge.

The Royal Munster Fusiliers
Lieutenant Colonel Henry Mark TUITE, Royal Munster Fusiliers, commanding the 26th Royal Fusiliers, was killed in action on 24 March 1918, aged 34. TUITE was wounded after remaining behind in command of a small rearguard in order to cover the rest of his battalion as it retired. An attempt was made to carry him back, but with the Germans closing in on his small detachment, TUITE ordered those with him to leave him and make their way back. It was later presumed that he died from his wounds that day and that he was buried by the Germans. His grave was clearly never found. His father served in the Indian Army and retired with the rank of colonel.

Lieutenant Eustace Roland WHITBY MC, 1st Royal Munster Fusiliers, was killed in action during the attack on Tunnel Trench on 20 November 1917, aged

28. His MC was gazetted on 28 September 1916 and was awarded for conspicuous gallantry in action. When all the officers in his company became casualties, he took command of it and, although wounded, endeavoured to gain more ground until he became unconscious.

The Royal Dublin Fusiliers

Serjeant William J. O'KEEFFE, 1st Royal Dublin Fusiliers, was killed on 16 April 1917, aged 30. Prior to joining the army, he served as a constable in the Royal Irish Constabulary. His late father, Patrick, also served in the Royal Irish Constabulary as a sergeant.

Corporal William JENNINGS, 1st Royal Dublin Fusiliers, was killed in action on 24 September 1917, aged 21. His brother, Joseph, also fell. The CWGC records provide no obvious match for Joseph, though he may be Private Joseph Jennings, 10th Royal Dublin Fusiliers, who died in Ireland on 16 August 1917.

Private Albert BARTRUP, 10th Royal Dublin Fusiliers, was killed in action on 28 April 1917, aged 37. His brother, Private Walter BARTRUP, had been killed a fortnight earlier with the 2nd Hampshire Regiment and is also commemorated here on the memorial. Their father, Joseph, lived in Canning Town, London. Later that year he was to lose yet another son; Rifleman Alfred Bartrup, 16th Rifle Brigade, was killed in action on 5 August 1917 near Ypres fighting with the 39th Division. Like his two brothers, he also has no known grave and is commemorated on the Menin Gate at Ypres.

Private Stephen BYRNE, 1st Royal Dublin Fusiliers, was executed by firing squad on 28 October 1917 after going absent from his unit. When it came to his trial he offered the explanation that he had felt unwell and had not had any leave. These were familiar complaints shared by many soldiers, particularly on the Western Front, which is probably why they were easily dismissed as mitigation and, although there appear to have been no other aggravating factors in his case, he was not offered any second chance. He had enlisted under the alias of 'Monaghan'.

The Rifle Brigade (The Prince Consort's Own)

Second Lieutenant Malcolm Hutchinson HOUSE, 8th Rifle Brigade, was killed in action on 3 May 1917, aged 19. The family home was in Malvern, Worcestershire. His father was a master at Malvern College, although Malcolm was actually educated at Rugby School where he was captain of the cricket XI and played for the rugby XV. He was also elected a Scholar of Corpus Christi College, Oxford, in 1915, but he chose to serve instead.

Lance Serjeant Thomas JACKSON DCM, 1st Rifle Brigade, was killed in action on 4 May 1917, aged 25. His DCM was gazetted on 11 December 1916 and was won as an acting corporal. It was awarded for conspicuous gallantry in action. He went forward with another man on two separate occasions to carry out a reconnaissance. On one occasion they killed two of the enemy and destroyed a machine gun. Later they killed four of the enemy and used one of the enemy's machine guns to good effect.

Lance Corporal Michael McMORROW DCM, 9th Rifle Brigade, was killed in action on 3 May 1917, aged 25. His DCM was gazetted on 14 November 1916 and was awarded for conspicuous gallantry and initiative. After his corporal had been killed, Private McMORROW took command of his gun team and worked the gun with the greatest bravery and judgement. On two occasions he returned under heavy machine-gun fire to bring up ammunition for it.

Rifleman John William NICHOLS, 9th Rifle Brigade, was killed in action on 3 May 1917, aged 20. His brother, Corporal Bertie Phillip NICHOLS, was killed in action a couple of weeks later on 19 May serving with the 8th Suffolk Regiment. Both are commemorated here on the Arras Memorial.

The Honourable Artillery Company (Infantry)
Second Lieutenant Aubrey Moore BECK, 2nd Battalion, Honourable Artillery Company, was killed on 15 May 1917. He had only been with his battalion for a week before he was killed in trenches opposite Bullecourt.

Second Lieutenant Ernest William Frost HAMMOND MC, 2nd Battalion, Honourable Artillery Company, was killed in action when his battalion was involved in the attack on Bullecourt on 3 May 1917. He had joined the regiment in 1911, but initially served with the 1st Battalion between September 1914 and October 1915 during which time he was wounded. The occasion on which he was wounded was also the same action in which he won his MC for conspicuous gallantry and devotion to duty during a bomb fight near Sanctuary Wood on 30 September 1915. Although he was severely wounded in the right side during the afternoon and unable to use his right arm, he remained at the front using only his left arm until after nightfall when his wound forced him to retire. The award was gazetted on 2 November 1915. When he returned to the front in October 1916 he was posted to the 2nd Battalion.

Private Ernest Walter MORRIS, 2nd Battalion, Honourable Artillery Company, was killed in action near Bullecourt on 3 May 1917, aged 28. He was better known as the music hall entertainer 'Barclay Morris'.

The Monmouthshire Regiment
There are forty-four men from the Monmouthshire Regiment recorded on the memorial, mainly from the regiment's 1st Battalion. Just over half of these men were killed in 1918 during the first three weeks of April. There are just two officers: Second Lieutenant Ronald William THOMPSON, 1st Monmouthshire Regiment and Second Lieutenant Albert KING, 2nd Battalion.

Second Lieutenant Albert KING had enlisted on New Year's Eve 1914 and obtained his commission in October 1916. He was killed in action near Monchy-le-Preux on 31 May 1917. His death occurred at night whilst taking a platoon from another company to join his own men on a working party. He was killed by an enemy shell along with a sergeant from the other platoon. Both men were buried on the battlefield, but their graves have since been lost. The sergeant killed with Second Lieutenant KING was Sergeant William George HOPKINS. He is also one of the forty-four Monmouthshire men commemorated here on the memorial.

Second Lieutenant Ronald William THOMPSON, 1st Monmouthshire Regiment, was killed in action on 11 April 1918, aged 24. His death occurred at the Battle of Estaires during the German Offensive on the Lys.

The London Regiment

Captain John Reginald HOUGHTON MC, 1st (City of London) Battalion, London Regiment (Royal Fusiliers), was killed in action on 21 March 1918. His MC was gazetted on 3 June 1918 in the King's Birthday Honours List.

Serjeant William George COX DCM, 1st (City of London) Battalion, London Regiment (Royal Fusiliers), was killed in action on 9 April 1917. His DCM was gazetted on 4 June 1917 and the citation for it appeared a month later on 9 July. The citation is rather vague and merely states that it was awarded for great initiative and gallantry during operations and that he had rendered most valuable service at critical periods.

Private Percy George PREECE, 2/2nd (City of London) Battalion, London Regiment (Royal Fusiliers), was 24 years old when he was killed in action on 15 June 1917. He was one of three brothers killed in the war. Private Edward Charles Preece was killed in action on 10 August 1917, aged 24, serving with the 7th Queen's (Royal West Surrey Regiment) and is commemorated on the Menin Gate at Ypres. The other brother, Private Horace Frank Preece, was killed in action on 10 April 1917, aged 25, serving with the 15th Durham Light Infantry, although he had previously served with the King's Royal Rifle Corps. He is buried in Cojeul British Cemetery, Saint-Martin-sur-Cojeul.

Private Albert Ernest BEST, 2/3rd (City of London) Battalion, London Regiment (Royal Fusiliers), was killed in action on 15 June 1917. His brother, Private Frederick Arthur BEST, also served in the same battalion and was killed in action on the same day. Both men are commemorated here on the Arras Memorial. The family lived in the St John's Wood area of London.

Captain John Stewart CALDER MC and Bar, 1/5th (City of London) Battalion, London Regiment (London Rifle Brigade), was killed in action on 28 March 1918. His MC was gazetted on 18 January 1918 and its citation appeared on 25 April after his death. It was awarded for conspicuous gallantry, devotion to duty and the capable manner in which he handled his company in an attack. Having reached his objective, he gathered together men from several other units and organized the consolidation of the newly won position. As a consequence of his prompt action, two bombing attacks were easily repulsed. The citation concludes by stating that throughout the entire operation his cheerfulness and courage inspired all ranks.

The bar to his MC was gazetted soon afterwards, on 22 June 1918, and was awarded for a similar display of conspicuous gallantry and devotion to duty whilst in charge of a raiding party on the enemy's trenches. Seeing that the leading wave was held up in the enemy's wire, he immediately ran forward and fired from point blank range at some of the enemy who were bombing the men closest to the wire. Realizing that the main raiding party would not be able to penetrate the wire, he conducted a cool and methodical withdrawal. As the withdrawal was taking place, he remained behind to supervise the evacuation of every wounded case. The raid took place on 16 March 1918 near Gavrelle.

Prior to the war he worked as a schoolmaster after gaining a Bachelor of Science degree whilst studying in London. His brother, Colin Stewart Calder, served as a private in the 14th Battalion, London Regiment (London Scottish), and was killed in action on 9 April 1917, the opening day of the Battle of Arras. He is now buried in London Cemetery, Neuville-Vitasse.

Serjeant James GRATION DCM, 5th (City of London) Battalion, London Regiment (London Rifle Brigade) was killed in action on 24 March 1918, aged 27, whilst posted to the 1st Battalion Artists' Rifles. He had won his DCM at Ypres on 31 October 1917 during an operation in which 'D' Company was tasked with taking a pillbox that was believed to house several snipers. The conditions were atrocious and the mud made the going extremely slow. As they approached the pillbox the Germans opened up with rifles and machine-gun fire. The officer commanding the assault party was mortally wounded, as were several other men. Sergeant GRATION and a few others managed to reach the objective where they bayoneted some of the occupants. The garrison had already been reinforced from enemy positions in nearby shell holes and it soon became obvious to GRATION and his party that they would not be able to hold their current position against any counter-attack. Accordingly, and very wisely, they withdrew.

Lance Serjeant Thomas DAVIES MM, 1/5th (City of London) Battalion, London Regiment (London Rifle Brigade), formerly 7th Middlesex Regiment, was just 18 years old when he was killed in action on 28 March 1918. His death occurred near Gavrelle.

Lance Serjeant James HOUSTON MM, 1/5th (City of London) Battalion, London Regiment (London Rifle Brigade), was also killed in action near Gavrelle, on 28 March 1918, aged 33.

Rifleman Walter Raymond CHAPMAN, 'A' Company, 2/5th (City of London) Battalion, London Regiment (London Rifle Brigade), was killed in action on 18 May 1917, aged 21. He was the youngest of three brothers who fell during the war. Private George Frederick Chapman was killed on 6 October 1916, aged 30, whilst serving with the 1/22nd Battalion, London Regiment. He is buried in Caterpillar Valley Cemetery on the Somme. The other brother, Private Archibald Gordon Chapman, is buried at Wimereux Communal Cemetery. He died of wounds on 29 August 1916, aged 31, and was serving with the 10th Royal Fusiliers at the time of his death.

Rifleman Alfred Daniel JOHN, 2/5th (City of London) Battalion, London Regiment (London Rifle Brigade), was killed in action on 18 June 1917, aged 23. He had returned home from Shanghai in order to enlist.

Rifleman Noel L. William PARRY, 5th (City of London) Battalion, London Regiment (London Rifle Brigade), was killed in action on 21 March 1918, aged 19. His brother, Lieutenant Henry Maysmore Parry, had been killed in action ten days earlier on 11 March whilst serving with the 2/10th Middlesex Regiment in Palestine. He is buried in Jerusalem War Cemetery and had previously served with the 1/14th Battalion, London Regiment (London Scottish) in 1914. He could well have been a survivor of the fighting at Messines Ridge when the London Scottish was called upon to support the line held by the Cavalry Corps.

Rifleman Sidney George TRIM, 2/5th (City of London) Battalion, London Regiment (London Rifle Brigade), was killed in action on 26 May 1917, aged 21. His brother, Rifleman Leonard John Trim, was killed serving with the London Rifle Brigade a week earlier on 17 May, aged 19. He is buried at HAC Cemetery, Écoust-Saint-Mein.

Lance Corporal Huse Lindsay Phillips WILTSHIRE, 2/6th (City of London) Battalion, London Regiment (Rifles), was killed in action near Bullecourt on 21 May 1917. He was one of five brothers who served during the Great War, but appears to have been the only one to lose his life in the conflict. He was formerly a constable in the Royal Irish Constabulary.

Serjeant Charles Ernest CLARK MM, 8th Battalion (City of London), London Regiment (Post Office Rifles), was serving with the 1/17th (County of London) Battalion, London Regiment (Poplar and Stepney Rifles), when he was killed in action on 22 March 1918. His MM was gazetted on 13 March 1918 shortly before he was killed. He was born in Maldon, Essex, but enlisted in Hackney.

Corporal Benjamin MAUND, 'B' Company 1/8th (City of London) Battalion, London Regiment (Post Office Rifles), was killed in action on 21 May 1916, aged 21. The CWGC register notes that he was a sorter in the foreign section of the GPO in London. He was killed in action near Zouave Valley when the Germans carried out an attack that day against a section of trenches on that part of Vimy Ridge. Although the objectives were limited, the preceding artillery barrage was heavy and the infantry attack that followed was fierce and incisive.

A stonemason at work. (*CWGC, Goodland Collection*)

Early days at the Imperial War Graves Commission. The Arras area headquarters after the Armistice. (*IWM Collection*)

This photograph was taken in 1975 during renovation work. Crates of new stone have arrived on site. Today's battle on Vimy Ridge is against the elements. The work being carried out in the photograph took place less than forty years after the memorial was inaugurated. (*CWGC*)

The Canadian Memorial on Vimy Ridge, designed by architect and sculptor, Walter Seymour Allward who claimed that the inspiration for the design came to him in a dream. Today the visitors' centre at Vimy Ridge tells the story of how Allward's vision became a reality. (*CWGC, Leslie Thompson Collection*)

Aerial view of the Canadian Memorial, Vimy Ridge, during the inauguration ceremony, which took place on 26 July 1936. It is estimated that around 100,000 people attended the ceremony, including over 6,000 Canadian veterans and widows. *(Peter Taylor Collection)*

Commemorating the fallen today – the Canadian Memorial on Vimy Ridge. This photograph was taken in the late afternoon of 9 April 2007 at the dedication of the restored memorial by Queen Elizabeth II on the ninetieth anniversary of the capture of Vimy Ridge. *(CWGC)*

The Arras Memorial shortly after construction. The Flying Services Memorial can be seen through the main entrance archway. Both memorials were unveiled by Lord Trenchard, Marshal of the Royal Air Force, on 31 July 1932. (*CWGC*)

Early evening in late March 2014. The Arras Memorial with the Faubourg d'Amiens Cemetery in the foreground. (*J.P. Hughes Collection*)

The Arras Memorial and Flying Services Memorial in the early evening sunshine, March 2014. (J.P. Hughes Collection)

A family tribute March 2014. This superb portrait of Private 31017 Arthur Lane, 1st East Surrey Regiment, was left by his family during a recent visit. Arthur was killed in action during his battalion's gallant stand at Fresnoy on 8 May 1917. He and many of his comrades are now commemorated on the Arras Memorial. (J.P. Hughes Collection)

Trophies of war. Manfred von Richthofen's collection of identification numbers taken from some of the aircraft of his victims – a very personal and somewhat macabre memorial to men of the Royal Flying Corps and the Royal Naval Air Service. (see Appendix for a list of victims)
(*Peter Taylor Collection*)

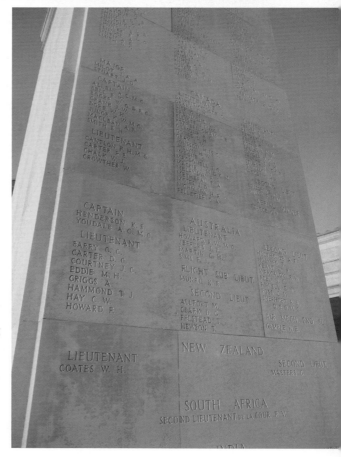

Flying Services Memorial, Arras. This panel shows the names of men from the Commonwealth who fell on the Western Front whilst serving with the Royal Flying Corps, Royal Naval Air Service, or Royal Air Force during the Great War and who have no known grave.
(*J.P. Hughes Collection*)

The Vis-en-Artois Memorial, Haucourt, about eight miles east-south-east of Arras. The memorial was designed by the architect J.R. Truelove to form the rear wall of Vis-en-Artois British Cemetery. Its superbly detailed neoclassical reliefs and sculptures were designed by Ernest Gillick. Of the four memorials to the missing to be found on the Arras battlefield, this is the least visited.
(J.P. Hughes Collection)

One of the reliefs that adorn the Vis-en-Artois Memorial. This example shows the wonderful attention to detail achieved by Ernest Gillick in his sculpture. His work provides a powerful, yet very dignified, expression of remembrance.
(J.P. Hughes Collection)

The Vis-en-Artois Memorial. The neoclassical style is evident from this photograph. It is a majestic tribute to almost 10,000 men whose names are inscribed on its walls. (*J.P. Hughes Collection*)

The Vis-en-Artois Memorial. In the late afternoon sunshine the columns of the memorial cast their shadows across the panels bearing the names of the fallen. The photograph was taken on 1 April 2014 during a research visit. (*J.P. Hughes Collection*)

Piper Simon CAMPBELL, 14th (County of London) Battalion, London Regiment (London Scottish), was killed in action on 13 May 1917, aged 19. He came from South Uist. Although the battalion was a London unit, the London Scottish was very much a mirror image of the Scottish regiments north of the border. It had its own unique tartan, known as 'Elcho' tartan after its first commanding officer, Lord Elcho. The cloth itself was a grey weave, often referred to as 'Hodden Grey'.

Captain Hobart Brooks FARQUHAR, 15th (County of London) Battalion, London Regiment (Prince of Wales's Own Civil Service Rifles), was killed in action on 22 May 1916, aged 41. He had previously taken part in the Matabele Campaign and had also served in the South African War with Thorneycroft's Mounted Infantry. He was the son of the late Admiral Sir Arthur Farquhar KCB, who retired in 1916, and was one of thirteen children, eight of whom were boys. Their grandfather, also Sir Arthur Farquhar, had served in the Royal Navy during the French Revolutionary Wars and the Napoleonic Wars, attaining the rank of rear admiral.

When the Germans launched their attack on the British trenches in front of Zouave Valley in late May 1916, FARQUHAR's company was called upon to deliver a counter-attack with the help of some men of the 8th Battalion, London Regiment (Post Office Rifles). There was also the promise of support on the right from the 6th and 7th Battalions of the London Regiment (City of London Rifles) and on the left from the 18th Battalion, London Regiment (London Irish Rifles). At 2.00am on 22 May, with no time to reconnoitre the ground and no opportunity to co-ordinate the attack with the supporting units on either side, 'B' Company went forward. The Germans, however, had already wired the captured British front line trenches and the men of the Civil Service Rifles were forced to occupy scattered shell holes in front of their objective under heavy fire. Without any supporting barrage to assist his men in their attempt to recapture the trenches, FARQUHAR took the decision to withdraw his men, with 'C' Company forming a defensive flank. Soon after making those arrangements, he was killed.

Amongst the men killed with Captain FAQUHAR that day were Lieutenant Bernard 'Bobby' SCOTT, aged 20, Company Serjeant Major Frank 'Kaffir' HOWETT, Serjeant Trevor Phillips CHICK, and Lance Serjeant Archibald John ANDREWS, who was also affectionately known as 'Long' or 'Driver' ANDREWS. Their bodies were never recovered and all four men are now commemorated on the memorial with their company commander.

Later that day, some men from 'C' Company went out in broad daylight in a bid to rescue the wounded, many of whom were lying out in shell holes in the hot sun. CHICK was one of those who crawled out to assist a man from the Post Office Rifles. As he was on his way back, he was shot just above the heart and died about ten minutes later. CHICK's brother, Private Gerald Henry Chick, had been killed in action on 1 November 1914 serving with the 14th Battalion,

London Regiment (London Scottish) near Messines Ridge. He is commemorated on the Menin Gate.

Company Serjeant Major Roland Hanwell 'Bulldog' Harris also went out to try to find his best pal, 'Kaffir' HOWETT, and although he failed to find him, he managed to bring in several wounded men before daylight under artillery and machine-gun fire. He was awarded the MC for his actions that day and was later commissioned within the regiment. Unfortunately, he was killed in action on 27 December 1917 with the 2nd Battalion in Palestine. After leading a counter-attack under heavy shell fire, he and seven or eight others became cut off and were surrounded, but he managed to bayonet three of the enemy before he fell. He is buried in Jerusalem War Cemetery. 'Bulldog' was a formidable character and had managed to forge a good understanding with his friend 'Kaffir' HOWETT, who was something of a kindred spirit. Together, both men formed part of the foundation on which the battalion was built.

The Territorial Army was very much under-appreciated in 1914, but many of its battalions fought extremely well when under good leadership. There was often a great camaraderie and sense of pride amongst the men and the 1/15th Battalion is a fine example of what 'part-time' soldiering could achieve.

Private John Stuart Russell STEVENS, 15th (County of London) Battalion, London Regiment (Prince of Wales's Own Civil Service Rifles), was killed in action on 9 February 1916, aged 20. The battalion had not yet moved down to the Vimy sector and was occupying trenches near Loos when he was killed. His father was the Reverend John Stevens DD D.Litt Hon.CF and the family lived at Bowes Park in north London. The 'CF' is a common abbreviation and suggests that the Reverend Stevens was, or had been a Chaplain to the Forces.

Second Lieutenant Stanley Charles YEATES, 'B' Company, 1/16th (County of London) Battalion, London Regiment (Queen's Westminster Rifles), was killed in action on 14 April 1917, aged 24. The CWGC register states that he returned from Brazil in 1914 in order to enlist. He served with the Artists' Rifles OTC prior to obtaining his commission in July 1916.

Serjeant Albert E. CLARK MM, 1/16th (County of London) Battalion, London Regiment (Queen's Westminster Rifles), was killed in action on 28 March 1918. His MM was won just south of Gommecourt on 1 July 1916 at Etch Trench when he and two other men tried to bomb their way towards a strong supporting redoubt, known as the Quadrilateral. However, the opposition there proved too strong and they were soon forced back.

Captain Kenneth D'Aguilar HOUSTON, 1/18th (County of London) Battalion, London Regiment (London Irish Rifles) was killed in action on 24 March 1918, aged 37. He had played rugby for London Irish and was vice-president of the club between 1913 and 1914. He worked as a legal clerk before the war and served with the Inns of Court OTC before receiving his commission. His late father,

Sir Arthur Houston LLD KC, was a well known and distinguished member of the legal profession.

Serjeant Frederick JONES DCM, 1/18th (County of London) Battalion, London Regiment (London Irish Rifles), was killed in action on 15 March 1916. His DCM was gazetted on 14 January 1916. The citation followed on 11 March and records that it was awarded for conspicuous gallantry. When the signal officer had been killed, he took command of the signallers and established communications by wire at great personal risk. He was constantly in the open repairing the wires under heavy fire.

Rifleman James Herbert PARKER, 1/18th (County of London) Battalion, London Regiment (London Irish Rifles), was killed in action on 21 March 1918, aged 19. He was one of three brothers who fell during the Great War. Serjeant Arthur Edward Parker, 8th Somerset Light Infantry, was the first to die. He was killed in action near Fricourt on 1 July 1916, aged 26. He is commemorated on the Thiepval Memorial. Fitter Thomas Henry James Parker, 'A' Battery, 174 Brigade, Royal Field Artillery, was killed in action on 9 April 1918, aged 33. He is buried at Abbeville Communal Cemetery Extension.

Second Lieutenant Thomas Reginald DAWSON, 19th (County of London) Battalion, London Regiment (St Pancras Rifles), was killed in action on 4 February 1916. He was educated at Westminster School and won an Exhibition to Christ Church College, Oxford. That was in July 1914, but with war looming he decided to serve his country and obtained a commission in the 19th Battalion, London Regiment, in October that year. There is a very odd entry on the Christ Church College roll of honour claiming that he died at home in the Empire Hospital, Vincent Square, Westminster, from wounds received at Loos on 25 September 1915. If that were the case, it is difficult to see how his name appears on the Arras Memorial to the Missing. His father was a prosperous tea merchant and the family lived in very comfortable circumstances in Beckenham, Kent.

Second Lieutenant Albert John EVANS, 19th (County of London) Battalion, London Regiment (St Pancras Rifles), attached 2/2nd (City of London) Battalion (Royal Fusiliers), was killed in action on 15 June 1917, aged 30. He was wounded on the opening day of the Battle of Loos, 25 September 1915, whilst serving with the 19th Battalion, and was killed in action with the 2/2nd Battalion near Bullecourt as part of the 58th (2/1st London) Division. The battalion suffered heavy casualties during the fighting there; two officers and twenty-one other ranks were killed, but another five officers and 156 other ranks were wounded and a further ten officers and 207 other ranks were recorded as missing. According to the CWGC register, his father was a superintendent in the Metropolitan Police Force.

Lance Serjeant Frank Wotton EASTLAKE DCM, 1/21st (County of London) Battalion, London Regiment (First Surrey Rifles), was killed in action on 23 May

1916, aged 25. His DCM was awarded whilst serving as a lance corporal in the battalion. It was awarded for conspicuous gallantry after he had spent six hours in an exposed position on the parapet of a captured enemy trench, throwing bombs to prevent a counter-attack by the enemy. Before the war he worked as an assistant librarian at Holborn Public Library.

Rifleman Frederick Albert BAKER, 1/21st (County of London) Battalion, London Regiment (First Surrey Rifles), was just 16 years old when he was killed in action on 23 May 1916. He was from Old Ford, Bow, in the East End of London.

Second Lieutenant Dudley BLOFELD MC, 1/22nd (County of London) Battalion, London Regiment (The Queen's), was killed in action on 8 October 1916. His MC was gazetted on 19 August that year and was awarded for conspicuous gallantry during a raid when he was the first man to enter the enemy's trenches. He personally bombed many of the dug-outs before getting all of his men back to the British lines, including the wounded.

Major Thomas Charles HARGREAVES DSO, 23rd (County of London) Battalion, London Regiment, was killed in action on 23 March 1918. His DSO was gazetted on 14 November 1916 and was awarded for conspicuous gallantry in action at Starfish Trench, near Flers, where he had led the advance with skill and determination after the attack had been held up by machine-gun fire. Later, he set a fine personal example when beating off a counter-attack on an exposed flank. He was also wounded during these operations.

Lieutenant Henry Spencer EWEN MC, 1/23rd (County of London) Battalion, London Regiment, was killed in action near Aveluy Wood on 5 April 1918, aged 29. His MC was gazetted on 18 February 1918 and the citation appeared on 18 July that year. It was awarded for conspicuous gallantry and devotion to duty organizing and supervising the construction of a communication trench under heavy shell fire. Though he was twice badly shaken by exploding shells, he showed great courage and disregard for danger. When casualties were caused amongst the men, he encouraged the rest by his splendid example.

Private Clifford COUSINS DCM, 1/23rd (County of London) Battalion, London Regiment, was killed in action on 9 December 1917, aged 18. Despite his youth, COUSINS had shown conspicuous gallantry and devotion to duty during a raid. On hearing that some of the enemy in a dug-out were giving trouble, he immediately ran over to the action. On arrival he was wounded in the face, neck and shoulder when one of the enemy threw a bomb at him. He rushed the party with his rifle, bayoneting the first man and shooting another, at which point the rest surrendered. When he and his comrades eventually withdrew, he brought back an enemy machine gun. The award was posthumously gazetted on 4 March 1918. He had previously served with the Middlesex Regiment.

On the same day that the battalion lost Private Clifford COUSINS DCM, it also lost another man who held the same award: Lance Serjeant John St Vincent JERVIS-HUNTER DCM, who was a member of 'D' Company. He won his DCM during an attack on enemy trenches during which he carried out a daring reconnaissance, returning with valuable information. The citation goes on to state that he displayed extraordinary energy, encouraging his men, and remained cheerful throughout the operation. His award was gazetted on 16 August 1917. The 'Jervis' part of his surname can be traced back to Admiral Sir John Jervis, 1st Viscount and Earl of St Vincent whose victory at the Battle of Cape St Vincent earned him the title.

Private Oliver John SPRINGETT, 1/23rd (County of London) Battalion, London Regiment, was killed in action on 23 March 1918, aged 27. His brother, Rifleman William SPRINGETT, also aged 27, was killed in action on 23 April 1917 serving with the 13th Rifle Brigade. The boys came from Southwark and their age suggests that they were probably twins. Both men are now commemorated here on the memorial.

Company Serjeant Major Albert J. BAXTER MC, 1/24th Battalion (County of London), London Regiment (The Queen's), was killed in action on 5 April 1918, aged 22. His MC was gazetted on 20 August 1917. It was awarded for conspicuous gallantry and devotion to duty after his company commander had become a casualty. He showed great ability and presence of mind, reorganizing the ammunition supply for his own company, as well as that of another, transferring it to forward points where it was urgently required. The citation adds that he worked unceasingly throughout the operation and freely exposed himself to danger, concluding that in twenty-seven months of active service he had consistently shown proof of his worth.

The Hertfordshire Regiment
Major Edward Hildred Hanbury CARLILE, Hertfordshire Yeomanry, attached to the Hertfordshire Regiment, was the only son of Colonel Sir Hildred Carlile, 1st Bart CBE and Lady Carlile of Ponsbourne Park. He had only been at the front for two months when he was killed in action on 22 March 1918, aged 37. Although his father held the rank of colonel in the King's Own (Yorkshire Light Infantry), it was merely an honorary title granted to him on account of his work with the Yeomanry and Volunteer movement. However, he did carry out work with the Red Cross during the war.

The Herefordshire Regiment
There are seven men listed on the memorial from this regiment; six of them privates, the other an officer. Lieutenant Edward Guy PRITCHETT was killed in action on 16 May 1918. Private Frederick Concert WEAVER was killed on 3 May 1917 and the others all fell in March the following year. All of these men would have been killed whilst serving with the King's (Shropshire Light Infantry).

The Northern Cyclist Battalion

Captain Frank Douglas BALFOUR MC, Northern Cyclist Battalion, attached 15th Battalion, London Regiment (Prince of Wales's Own Civil Service Rifles) was killed in action on 23 March 1918. His MC was gazetted on 22 April 1918 and was awarded for conspicuous gallantry and devotion to duty. He succeeded in holding his position, despite his left flank having been turned, after the enemy had captured the trenches to his immediate left. The citation concludes that his example of courage and leadership ensured that his men held their position under very difficult circumstances.

Lieutenant Pattison Reay RIDLEY MC, Northern Cyclist Battalion, was killed in action on 3 May 1917. He joined the Northern Cyclist Battalion in 1912, but eventually went overseas in July 1916 with the 2/5th Duke of Wellington's Regiment. His MC was awarded for his role in an attack on an enemy trench whilst in command of a party numbering around 150 officers and men. Despite having to cross 500 yards of unknown and difficult country by compass bearing, he successfully maintained direction and during the attack he shot one of the enemy and captured another. He then succeeded in consolidating the newly won position. He was initially reported missing in action on 3 May 1917 and was later presumed to have been killed that day.

The Machine Gun Corps (Infantry)

Major John Herbert OLIVER-THOMPSON, 40th Battalion, Machine Gun Corps, was killed in action on 21 March 1918, aged 22. He had previously been mentioned in despatches. The CWGC record incorrectly shows him as '40th Company'.

Captain Adrian Hubert GRAVES MC and Bar, 40th Battalion, Machine Gun Corps, was killed in action on 22 March 1918, aged 21. His MC was gazetted on 25 August 1916 while he was serving as a second lieutenant in the Machine Gun Corps. It was awarded for conspicuous gallantry in action after he brought his guns into action under heavy fire, repelling a sudden counter-attack at close quarters. The citation concludes by adding that on many other occasions he had shown great bravery during attacks.

The bar to his MC was awarded exactly one year later when it was gazetted on 25 August 1917. It was awarded for conspicuous gallantry and devotion to duty, this time commanding his guns with great ability during a critical situation. Realizing that his objective was untenable owing to heavy fire, he moved into the front line where he remained for forty-eight hours without relief. Although suffering two separate wounds, he displayed a fine example of cheerfulness and endurance.

Lieutenant George Vyvyan SPURWAY MC, 56th Battalion, Machine Gun Corps, was killed in action on 21 March 1918. His MC was gazetted on 20 July 1917 and was awarded for conspicuous gallantry and devotion to duty whilst supporting an infantry attack. For forty-eight hours he rendered valuable service to the infantry, reorganizing scattered men and securing the line against enemy counter-attacks with his fire. The citation notes that he and the men were exposed to heavy fire throughout the operation, but he inspired those around him by his energy and spirit.

He was one of five brothers, three of whom fell in action during the war. Second Lieutenant Richard Popham Spurway, 2nd Somerset Light Infantry, was killed in action on 13 August 1915 and is commemorated on the Helles Memorial in Turkey. Lieutenant Alexander Popham Spurway, HMS *Victory*, died from illness on 29 November 1915 and is commemorated on the Plymouth Naval Memorial. Another brother, Francis Edward Spurway, had also served with the Somerset Light Infantry during the war, but in 1928 he became an army chaplain. He also played first class cricket for Somerset.

Lieutenant George Kenneth STEINBERG MC, 34th Battalion, Machine Gun Corps, was killed in action on 22 March 1918, aged 25. His MC was gazetted on 17 December 1917. The citation, which appeared on 23 April 1918, notes that it was awarded for conspicuous gallantry and devotion to duty during an enemy barrage after one of his machine guns was blown up and all the NCOs had become casualties. He then collected the remaining guns and moved them forward to an advanced position where he personally supervised the action of each gun whilst under the heaviest of shell fire.

Second Lieutenant Charles Edward AMOS, 40th Battalion, Machine Gun Corps, had previously served in Gallipoli and Egypt and was killed in action on 22 March 1918, aged 22. On the face of it, his was just another death that occurred during the March Offensive, but it should be borne in mind that here was a soldier with a good deal of experience behind him whose presence on the battlefield would have made a significant contribution during those difficult days in March and who would have inspired others around him.

Second Lieutenant John Thomas KIRK MC, 15th Company, Machine Gun Corps, was killed in action on 28 March 1918. His MC was gazetted on 26 September 1917 and its citation appeared on 9 January 1918. It was awarded for conspicuous gallantry and devotion to duty when in charge of a section of machine guns. Having taken up a position, he held it with great determination, materially helping to break up a succession of counter-attacks by lying out in front of his gun positions and picking off the enemy with his rifle.

Second Lieutenant William Duncan TARBET, who was killed in action on 9 April 1917, aged 21, is shown serving with the 7th Seaforth Highlanders, but his death occurred whilst with the Machine Gun Corps.

Second Lieutenant Osmond Bartle WORDSWORTH, 21st Company, Machine Gun Corps, was killed in action on 2 April 1917, aged 29. He was educated at Winchester School, where he won prizes for Greek, before going on to Trinity

College, Cambridge, where he gained a First Class Tripos in 1909, followed by a First Class Tripos Part II the year after. After the award of his Master's degree in 1913 he became a master at Lancing College and also lectured at Selwyn College, Cambridge. He then spent a brief period teaching at Trinity College, Toronto, in 1914.

On 1 May 1915 he and his sister left New York aboard the SS *Lusitania*, his intention being to return to England so that he could enlist. When the ship was torpedoed and sunk off the coast of Ireland, he managed to survive in the water long enough to be rescued, despite the fact that he had given away his lifebelt to another passenger before the boat sank. He was, in fact, one of the last passengers to leave the sinking ship. His sister, Ruth Mary Wordsworth, also survived.

Once back in England, he was commissioned in the Oxfordshire & Buckinghamshire Light Infantry in June 1915, but then transferred to the 21st Company, Machine Gun Corps in April the following year. He was killed in action on 2 April 1917 as the 30th Division pressed home its attack on Hénin-sur-Cojeul during an operation with other divisions against a series of villages that formed a strong outpost line in front of the Hindenburg Line. He had left cover in order to speak with one of his teams as it was engaging the enemy and, whilst doing so, he was shot in the chest. He was subsequently buried at Hénin, but his grave was later lost. His father, the Reverend Christopher Wordsworth, was Chancellor of Salisbury Cathedral.

Second Lieutenant Alex James YATES DCM, 4th Company, Machine Gun Corps, was killed in action on 28 March 1918. His DCM was won as a lance corporal whilst serving with the 9th Battalion, London Regiment (Queen Victoria's Rifles). It was gazetted on 14 January 1916 and the citation for it appeared on 11 March 1916. It was awarded for conspicuous gallantry whilst rescuing wounded soldiers from brigade HQ which was on fire.

Serjeant Henry James RAY DCM, 11th Company, Machine Gun Corps, was killed in action on 24 June 1917, aged 25. His DCM was gazetted on 18 July 1917 and was awarded for conspicuous gallantry and devotion to duty. Despite casualties within his section, he assumed command of the remaining men and handled them with great skill and determination, setting a fine example under heavy shell fire throughout the whole time.

Corporal Arthur Osgood PORTER DCM, 51st Company, Machine Gun Corps, was killed in action on 23 March 1918, aged 19. His DCM was gazetted on 3 September 1918 and was awarded for conspicuous gallantry and devotion to duty when in charge of one of the machine guns in a strongpoint that had been formed after the enemy's advance had penetrated part of our line. He inflicted casualties of the heaviest description on the enemy, whose further progress he checked for some time, holding on to the post to the last and firing the gun himself when all the other members of the gun team had become casualties. His coolness and disregard for danger set a fine example to those men who had collected to man the strongpoint and upon whom it had a marked influence. The CWGC record shows his unit as the 51st 'Company', but that unit became part of the 17th Battalion, Machine Gun Corps at the end of February 1918. The 51st Battalion, Machine Gun Corps, came into existence on 19 February 1918.

Private Gordon Phillip PIPE DCM, 51st Company, Machine Gun Corps, was killed in action on 21 March 1918. His DCM was gazetted on 3 September 1918 and was awarded for conspicuous gallantry and devotion to duty after he had asked permission to remain behind in a strongpoint that had been formed when an enemy's advance had penetrated our line. He fought at the strongpoint for five hours, latterly firing one of the guns himself once the remainder of the gun's crew had become casualties. He remained at his post until ordered by his commanding officer to retire. The citation concludes that his gallant conduct was of the greatest value in delaying the enemy's advance. This was the same action in which Corporal PORTER won his DCM. As with Corporal PORTER, the same caveat applies with regard to his unit.

Private Edward SHERROTT, 2nd Battalion, Machine Gun Corps, was killed in action on 27 March 1918, aged 21. His brother, George, nominally with the 8th Norfolk Regiment, was killed in action near Ypres on 29 November 1917, aged 19, whilst attached to the 53rd Company, Machine Gun Corps. George had initially enlisted in the 21st Battalion, London Regiment (First Surrey Rifles) in May 1915. He is buried at Cement House Cemetery. The family came from Camberwell in south London.

The Tank Corps

Second Lieutenant Geoffrey ASKEW MC, 10th Battalion, Tank Corps, died of wounds on 25 March 1918, aged 22. His MC was gazetted on 2 December 1918 and was awarded for conspicuous gallantry and devotion to duty whilst serving as a tank engineer. After a long trek, when the battalion's tanks were again ordered into action, he went from tank to tank under heavy shell fire ensuring that they were all mechanically fit before starting off. In the case of one tank, he had to accompany it into action in order to complete repairs, and even manned one of the guns when it became involved in action, inflicting many casualties on the enemy. Later he went on foot across open ground to repair another tank and again helped to work the guns until it was put out of action. Undaunted, he and its crew abandoned it and joined the infantry with their machine guns. Although he was wounded during this last action, he behaved with splendid courage and determination throughout the operation.

The Labour Corps

Private George BALL, 198th Labour Company, Labour Corps, died on 23 March 1919, aged 33 (Addenda Panel). He is one of just seven men commemorated on the memorial who died in 1919.

The Army Service Corps

Company Quartermaster Serjeant Alfred William CHANDLER, 1st GHQ Reserve Motor Transport Company, Army Service Corps, was killed in action on 24 March 1918, aged 35. Military mechanized transport was becoming increasingly available and varied by 1918 and had already begun to play an important part in the logistics of warfare, particularly with regard to supply of materials up to the battlefield, though horse and mule transport was still widely used. In recognition of the corps' service during the war the Royal prefix was added in late 1918.

The Royal Army Medical Corps

Captain John George ANDERSON MC, Royal Army Medical Corps, was killed in action on 21 March 1918, aged 28. His MC was gazetted on 1 January 1917 in the New Year's Honours List. He had also been mentioned in despatches.

Captain Percy Herbert BURTON MRCS LRCP LSA (London Hospital), Royal Army Medical Corps, attached 2/4th (City of London) Battalion, London Regiment (Royal Fusiliers), was killed in action by a shell on 12 May 1917, aged 49. His battalion had just relieved Australian troops in the front line near Bullecourt when his death occurred.

Captain Douglas William HUNTER DSO, Royal Army Medical Corps, attached 10th West Yorkshire Regiment, was killed in action on 25 March 1918, aged 39. He had studied Medicine at the University of Glasgow, graduating there in 1901. Between then and the outbreak of war he worked in Bradford and at the Royal Albert Institute in Lancaster.

His DSO was gazetted on 25 August 1916 and was awarded for conspicuous gallantry at Fricourt between 1 July and 3 July at the start of the Battle of the Somme. During the fighting there he had laboured incessantly, tending and clearing the wounded in the front line trench, as well as in the open, whilst under very heavy fire. At a very critical time, when the battalion's casualties had been heavy, he reorganized and steadied his stretcher-bearers by his magnificent example and skilful control. Once the battalion had withdrawn, he continued to search the battlefield looking for wounded men, showing an absolute disregard for danger. The 10th West Yorkshire Regiment, to which he was attached, suffered the highest number of battalion casualties on the opening day of the Battle of the Somme, a total of 710. His citation is unusual in so far as the original one was later substituted in favour of a more detailed account that appeared in the *London Gazette* on 26 September 1916.

Captain Samuel Edward McCLATCHEY, Royal Army Medical Corps, attached 18th Welsh Regiment, was killed on 25 March 1918, aged 37. He was one of a number of medical personnel commissioned in early September 1914 with the temporary rank of lieutenant in the Royal Army Medical Corps. He was awarded the Order of St Sava 5th Class (Serbia) in May 1916. The battalion to which he was attached was part of the 40th Division and was carrying out a fighting retreat around Ervillers and Gomiécourt on the day he died. He originally came from Portadown, County Armagh.

Captain Thomas Ainsworth TOWNSEND MC and Bar, Royal Army Medical Corps, was killed in action on 24 March 1918. His MC was gazetted on 27 November 1916 and was awarded for conspicuous gallantry and devotion to duty. The citation records that he showed great courage and determination under heavy fire whilst rescuing several men who had been buried. The citation adds that he had also done very fine work on three previous occasions.

The bar to his DSO was gazetted on 22 July 1918 and was also awarded for conspicuous gallantry and devotion to duty. Although twice wounded, he refused to have his own wounds attended to, but carried on dressing the wounds of others under a continuous and heavy bombardment of explosive and gas shells. Not only did he attend to those from his own unit who had been wounded and gassed, he also tended wounded men from neighbouring battalions whose medical officers had become casualties, all of which he carried out under conditions of great difficulty. The citation concludes that his utter disregard for personal danger and splendid devotion to duty were a magnificent example to all.

The Army Chaplains' Department

The Reverend Alan Cecil JUDD MC, Chaplain 4th Class, attached 2/5th Sherwood Foresters, was killed in action on 21 March 1918, aged 31. He was educated at St Paul's School and Exeter College, Oxford. The battalion to which he was attached was part of the 59th (2nd North Midland) Division. By the end of the day's fighting on 21 March, around 650 men of all ranks from this battalion had either been killed or were unaccounted for. Many of them were captured, including the battalion's commanding officer, Lieutenant Colonel Gadd MC. JUDD's MC was gazetted on 17 December 1917 and was awarded for conspicuous gallantry and devotion to duty whilst attending to the wounded under shell fire. He went out searching shell holes for wounded men, assisting them to the dressing station, and in one case carrying a man on his back. The citation goes on to state that his cheerfulness had a splendid effect in the front line trenches which he continually visited. The citation was published on 23 April 1918.

General List (New Army)

Captain Daniel PIZA, General List, attached 64th Trench Mortar Battery, was privately educated and had travelled extensively from an early age. Later, he served with Brabant's Horse during the South African campaign, but continued to travel widely after that war, not only in Africa, but also in Central America, the Caribbean and Mexico. However, when war was declared he returned home to serve his country again. He was gazetted in the early part of 1916 and was killed in action just south of Hénin when in command of trench mortar batteries in 64 Brigade's sector on 9 April 1917, which was his forty-fourth birthday.

Captain Theodore Percival Cameron WILSON, General List, was attached to the 10th Sherwood Foresters when he was killed in action on 23 March 1918. WILSON was a minor poet whose work was rescued from obscurity by Field Marshal Wavell, who included WILSON's 'Magpies in Picardy' and some other verses in an anthology of war poetry. Some of WILSON's work had already been published, but had attracted little attention. Today his work is largely ignored and has drifted once more into the obscurity from which it was temporarily reprieved.

The New Zealand Engineers
There is just one member of the New Zealand Expeditionary Force recorded on the memorial. Serjeant Claude Searle POWNCEBY, New Zealand Engineers, was 39 years old when he was killed in action on 14 September 1916. Although the New Zealand Division was to go into action the following day on the Somme opposite Flers, its tunnelling companies and a number of its engineers were deployed in and around Arras. On the night of 14 September 1916 a group of eight New Zealand Engineers took part in an unsuccessful raid on the enemy's trenches. Their role was to blast a hole in the German wire, follow the main body of raiders from the 15th Cheshire Regiment into the enemy's lines and destroy a mine shaft. Serjeant POWNCEBY is believed to have been one of four men who managed to force their way through to the enemy's trenches before being killed.

Two weeks after the opening of the Battle of Arras a grave was found at Saint-Laurent-Blangy with an inscription in German to '*four brave Englishmen*'. One of the four was Lieutenant William Macliesh Durant, the officer in charge of the party of New Zealand Engineers during the raid. The inscription also referred to two NCOs and one other man. Durant's body was identified and he is now buried in Plot I, Row A, at Point du Jour Military Cemetery, Athies. The remaining three bodies were never conclusively identified, although Serjeant POWNCEBY was undoubtedly one of them. The German inscription is interesting in so far as it refers to the soldiers as 'Englishmen'.

The South African Regiment
There is a total of seventy-seven members of the South African Brigade commemorated on the memorial. Just over half are from the 4th Regiment, though all four regiments are represented.

Sergeant Septimus Heyns LEDGER, 2nd South African Regiment, was killed in action on 12 April 1917, aged 26. He had played international rugby for South Africa and took part in the 1912–1913 tour of Great Britain in which the Springboks beat all four home nations, as well as France. He joined his battalion in late July 1916 after the fighting at Delville Wood and was one of many men drafted in at that time to replace the heavy losses sustained during the middle of July. He was killed in action when the 9th (Scottish) Division, which included the South

African Brigade, carried out an unsuccessful attack between Fampoux and Greenland Hill.

Lance Corporal David McGilvray BAXTER, 'C' Company, 4th South African Regiment, was a veteran of several previous campaigns, including the Boer Rebellion in 1914, the campaign in German South West Africa, and early engagements in Egypt. He was killed on 1 February 1917, aged 30.

Chapter Two

'Once in my days I'll be a madcap'
The Flying Services Memorial, Arras

This memorial is set within the central open space just inside the main entrance to the much larger Arras Memorial that sits on the ring road on the western side of the town in the Faubourg d'Amiens district. It is easily accessible by car, but can also be reached on foot from the centre of town by a twenty minute walk. The column itself is a simple, yet very dignified memorial to the 991 men of the Royal Naval Air Service, Royal Flying Corps, Royal Air Force and Australian Flying Corps who lost their lives on the Western Front and who never had a grave or whose graves were lost during the war. The CWGC register points out that it includes those attached to flying units from other branches of the armed services, as well as those who had originally enlisted or who transferred in.

The architect, Sir Edwin Lutyens, designed both the Arras Memorial and the Flying Services Memorial and Sir William Reid Dick was responsible for the sculpture and reliefs.

There are two VC holders commemorated on the memorial, but there are many more people of interest on it, together with a wealth of stories. *Airmen Died in the Great War* shows twenty-eight flying casualties from the outbreak of war to the end of 1914 and three of them are commemorated here. Perhaps surprisingly, only four airmen from 1915 have no known resting place out of the 209 that fell during that year. Air casualties were far higher in 1917 than in 1916 and 1918 put together: 2,837 compared with 771 and 919, respectively. However, the proportion of those with unknown graves is disproportionately weighted towards 1918 rather than either of the other years. Consequently, there are 507 men on this memorial from the final year of the war compared with just 87 from 1916 and 388 from 1917.

The names appear on the memorial firstly by rank and then within each rank alphabetically. The side of the column directly facing the main road is the place to start. The Royal Flying Corps casualties are listed first, then those of the Royal Naval Air Service, followed by those of the Royal Air Force and those of other nations. The names on the addenda are to be found at the base of the panel containing the names of men of the Royal Naval Air Service.

In the case of this memorial I have decided not to cover each of the three air services separately. This is such a small memorial that it is just as easy to walk around it picking out the names by order of rank. This should not cause the visitor any inconvenience.

Major Lanoe George HAWKER VC DSO, 24 Squadron, Royal Flying Corps, had been a natural candidate for flying and had all the credentials. He was a keen mechanical engineer and joined the Royal Engineers as an officer cadet after leaving school. He became a qualified pilot before the outbreak of war, serving with the Royal Flying Corps before August 1914. He was posted to France in October that year. He won his DSO in 1915 for his role in bombing a German airship hangar at Gontrode in April that year. He showed great skill during that attack, offsetting the increased personal risk of bombing it from a height of just 200 feet by using the position of an unmanned German captive balloon to give him cover from fire as he approached and released his bombs. His DSO was gazetted on 8 May 1915.

His VC soon followed when in July 1915, while flying alone, he attacked three enemy aeroplanes one after the other, forcing one to disengage and driving another to the ground in a state of damage. The third one was also driven to the ground, crashing and killing its crew. HAWKER became the first British and Dominion ace and was consequently a well-known public figure.

However, on 23 November 1916 his luck ran out. He flew that day along with two others: John Oliver Andrews, who went on to reach the rank of Air Vice Marshal, and Robert Henry Magnus Spencer Saundby, who survived the war and retired in 1946, also as an Air Vice Marshal. Andrews had to return to base when his engine and fuel tank were hit. Saundby had to do likewise after a skirmish with enemy fighters. HAWKER had already decided to break off and head back to base, flying low, but he was pursued by Manfred von Richthofen, who fired off a burst hitting HAWKER in the head at an altitude of just 150 feet. HAWKER, who was probably killed immediately, crashed near Luisenhof Farm, a couple of miles south of Bapaume, just behind German lines. Though buried by a cross-roads in a marked grave, HAWKER's body was never found and remains lost to this day.

Major Edward MANNOCK VC DSO and two Bars MC and Bar, was killed in action on 26 July 1918, aged 31, whilst serving with 85 Squadron, Royal Air Force. He was shot down by machine-gun fire from German ground forces shortly after scoring his sixty-first victory. He was working in Turkey for a British telephone company when the war broke out and was interned for a while until he was repatriated owing to poor health. He recovered and was commissioned in the Royal Engineers, but then transferred to the Royal Flying Corps in August 1916.

He initially served with 40 Squadron, then 74 Squadron, Royal Flying Corps, before taking over 85 Squadron on 18 June 1918. Although some of his first victories occurred near Arras, the majority took place north of the La Bassée Canal. His VC was awarded for his outstanding performances between 17 June and 22 July 1918 during which time he scored eight victories in a splendid display of gallantry, fearlessness, skill and devotion to duty. These victories were achieved in the wake of a truly outstanding score of twenty victories in May 1918.

Major Richard RAYMOND-BARKER MC, 3 Squadron, Royal Air Force, was Manfred von Richthofen's seventy-ninth victory and the last airman to die at his hands. He returned from working overseas to serve as a private in the Middlesex Regiment, but was commissioned at the end of 1914 in the Northumberland Fusiliers. He then transferred to the Royal Flying Corps in August 1915 and began flying operationally in November the same year.

His MC was gazetted on 17 September 1917 and was awarded for his leadership of a fighting patrol that had attacked a large enemy formation and destroyed two of its aircraft. The citation includes the fact that he had also led a photographic reconnaissance flight, though under attack, returning successfully with images of the target area. It adds that he had assisted in the destruction of seven enemy aircraft, had always behaved with gallantry, and had flown with great skill on every occasion.

His death came on 20 April 1918 while commanding 3 Squadron when his flight was attacked near Hamel, south of the River Somme. He fell during the ensuing fight and his body was never found.

His elder brother, Lieutenant Henry Edward Raymond-Barker, had been a member of the Ceylon Planters' Rifle Corps and served with the Indian Army in Egypt and Mesopotamia. He survived the war, as did his younger brother, Lieutenant Aubrey Basil Raymond-Barker, though he was taken prisoner in the latter part of 1916 when his aircraft was shot down south of Arras.

Richthofen, who was killed in action on 21 April 1918, the day after bringing down Major RAYMOND-BARKER, scored his eightieth and final victory against Second Lieutenant David Greswolde Lewis during the same fight in which RAYMOND-BARKER was killed.

Major James Duff STUART, 43 Squadron, Royal Flying Corps, who had formerly served with the 1st Canadian Pioneer Battalion, died of wounds on 7 March 1917, aged 22. He was the son of Brigadier General James Duff STUART from Vancouver, Canada. His pilot, Lieutenant Stanley James PEPLER, formerly 51st Battalion, Canadian Expeditionary Force, died the previous day when their two-seater 1½ Strutter aircraft was brought down. PEPLER is also commemorated on this memorial. As with all Canadian airmen of the First World War who had previously served with Canadian army units, they are listed in CWGC records as serving with the Canadian Expeditionary Force rather than the Royal Flying Corps. There are forty-six on the memorial.

Captain Ralph Newton ADAMS MC, 23 Squadron, Royal Flying Corps, was killed in action on 10 October 1916, though his observer, Lieutenant H.G. Ogg, was unhurt and survived the war. ADAMS was an only son and was educated at Charterhouse School. Although originally gazetted in May 1914 to the 7th Royal Fusiliers, he went to the front in December that year where he joined the regiment's 4th Battalion. He was invalided home in February 1915; in August the same year he was gazetted to the Royal Flying Corps, returning to the front in March 1916. During his short flying career he won the MC the same month that he became a flight commander. His MC, gazetted on 27 July 1916, was awarded for an attack on six hostile aircraft over enemy lines and bringing one of them down in flames. Joined by another of our machines, they then drove off the remainder, causing another to fall out of control. The citation notes that he had also brought down an enemy aircraft on a previous occasion.

Captain Arthur Spencer ALLEN MC, 9 Squadron, Royal Flying Corps, had won his MC serving with the 18th Battalion, Canadian Infantry, before transferring to the Royal Flying Corps. The award was for conspicuous gallantry on several occasions, notably when he organized and led parties against an enemy post, dispersing them with bombs. He had also previously volunteered to go out and cut a gap in the enemy wire prior to a raid. He was originally posted as missing in action on 30 April 1917, aged 21. His pilot, Second Lieutenant D. McTavish, was taken prisoner.

Captain John Roy ALLEN DSC, 215 Squadron, Royal Air Force, was killed in action on 12 April 1918, aged 22. His DSC was awarded in recognition of services on the night of 11/12 July 1917, as was that of another member of his squadron, Flight Lieutenant Lancelot Giberne Sieveking, when both men had dropped bombs on enemy railway lines and ammunition dumps. The awards were gazetted on 28 August 1917. Sieveking survived the war, although he was shot down and captured later that year. He was an interesting character who began writing his first novel in his early teens, though it only appeared in print when he was in his mid-twenties. However, he also went on to enjoy a successful career with the BBC. His brother, Captain Valentine Edgar Sieveking DSC and Bar, was shot down and killed, aged 26, serving with 214 Squadron, Royal Air Force, on 18 May 1918. He is buried in Zeebrugge Churchyard. Another brother, Geoffrey Edward Sieveking, served during the war with the Machine Gun Corps and, like Lancelot, he also survived. Their mother, Isabel, was an active member of the suffragette movement.

Captain Hugh William Eames BARWELL MC, 18 Squadron, Royal Flying Corps, was killed in action on 25 March 1918, aged 25. He was initially commissioned in the infantry in October 1914 and it was with the Royal Warwickshire Regiment that he won his MC for conspicuous gallantry in action. The citation, which was gazetted on 3 March 1917, is rather vague and notes only that he had shown marked courage and initiative throughout and had materially assisted in keeping the battalion together under the most trying of circumstances.

Captain John Vincent ASPINALL, 11 Squadron, Royal Air Force, had previously served with the Worcestershire Regiment before transferring to 22 Squadron in 1916 flying FE2b aeroplanes. He became a flight commander with 11 Squadron in spring 1918. He was shot down on 15 May 1918 between Ovillers and Contalmaison, shortly after achieving his sixth victory near Mametz. His observer, who was also killed, is often referred to in many records as Second Lieutenant Paul Victor DE LA COUR. He is, however, listed in the CWGC register under his full name, Paul Victor DORNONVILLE DE LA COUR. He had previously served as a lieutenant with the Danish Cavalry, as had his father, and had also served during the South African War. He joined the Royal Flying Corps from the 4th South African Regiment.

There is an interesting postscript to this story. In 1923 ASPINALL's father attended Doullens Communal Cemetery Extension No. 2 with officials from the Imperial War Graves Commission and the mother of another airman, Captain Francis Leopold Mond. She had made extensive enquiries regarding the whereabouts of her son's body. His body and that of his observer, Lieutenant Edgar Meath Martyn, were known to have been retrieved from the wreckage of their aircraft after it came down near the River Somme. For some reason they were not buried nearby and their bodies were sent down river. From there they appear to have been buried without any authority and without any record being kept. Mond's mother was convinced that her son's body was buried in the cemetery at Doullens, and furthermore she was convinced that the man buried in the grave marked with ASPINALL's name was, in fact, her own son (Plot I.B.29). One can only imagine the scene that day in 1923 when the grave was exhumed and the body was found to be that of her son Francis, not ASPINALL. The grave next to his (Plot I.B.28), was also exhumed. It had been presumed that it was that of Lieutenant DE LA COUR, but the man buried there was Lieutenant Edgar Martyn.

Captain John Douglas BELL MC and Bar, 3 Squadron, Royal Air Force, was 24 when he died. He was born in South Africa and had served in German South-West Africa with the Transvaal Light Horse. He joined the Royal Flying Corps on 1 June 1916 and was posted to 27 Squadron in October that year. He was involved in several encounters with German fighters while carrying out daylight bombing raids and claimed three victories during his initial time in France.

He was subsequently posted back to England with 78 (Home Defence) Squadron where, on the night of 25/26 September 1917, he attacked a German Gotha south of Brentwood, Essex, engaging it for over a quarter of an hour. The Gotha came down in the North Sea, but was never counted as part of his victories. He became a flight commander with 3 Squadron in February 1918 and scored seventeen of his eventual twenty victories between March and his death on 27 May, a tally which earned him his MC and Bar. His MC was awarded for his exceptional leadership and skill when in command of a long distance bombing raid that destroyed a large ammunition dump and for carrying out a further difficult mission single-handed during which he succeeded in reaching his objective under extremely adverse weather conditions. The award was gazetted on 18 June 1917. The bar to his MC was gazetted on 13 May 1918 and was awarded for conspicuous gallantry in leading his formation, destroying three enemy aircraft and driving a further two out of control. The citation adds that it was entirely owing to his splendid skill and fearless leadership that his flight had reached a very high state of efficiency.

Captain William Otway BOGER DFC, 56 Squadron, Royal Air Force, trans-ferred to the Royal Flying Corps from Lord Strathcona's Horse, a Canadian cavalry regiment with which he served from August 1914 to September 1916. He initially flew as an observer with 11 Squadron and he was wounded on 23 December the same year. He subsequently trained as a pilot and then joined 56 Squadron, Royal Air Force, in late May 1918. He managed to score five victories and it was during this time that he was awarded the DFC before finally being shot down on 10 August 1918.

The award and citation for his DFC were gazetted on 2 November 1918. The citation bears testimony to his outstanding skill, leadership, resilience and courage and records that he had taken part in twenty-eight offensive patrols and twelve aerial combats to date. During those missions he had personally accounted for four enemy aircraft and had shown remarkable coolness and bravery. On one notable occasion he had spotted nine enemy scouts. Unable to reach their height, he led his four machines to a point just below the enemy formation in order to tempt them to attack. At first they declined to engage, so he repeated the man-oeuvre, at which point they broke off and attacked him and his flight. In doing so, one of the enemy machines was shot down out of control, after which it appears that the others lost their appetite to continue the fight. After reforming his patrol he met a further two enemy scouts and shot one of them down in flames.

Captain William Arthur BOND MC and Bar, 40 Squadron, Royal Flying Corps, had previously served with the King's Own (Yorkshire Light Infantry). He was 28 when he was killed in action on 22 July 1917 having taken over command of the squadron. Five victories were credited to him, but there are conflicting accounts of his death. His squadron claimed he was shot down by anti-aircraft fire, but German accounts claim that it was by fire from one of their airmen.

BOND had been instrumental in developing highly-skilled low level attacks, such as the one on 2 May 1917 in which he and five others took part. They had spent long hours in training, practising how best to use trees, houses and ground contours in order to screen them from ground fire. On 2 May they crossed the German lines at a height of just fifty feet and destroyed four enemy balloons in an audacious and remarkably well co-ordinated operation with our artillery. BOND arranged for our artillery to put down a heavy barrage on the German trenches near to where the balloons were located, leaving only a corridor through which he and his men flew with great skill to reach and destroy their targets. It was for this action that he won the bar to his MC, although the citation, which was gazetted on 16 August that year, also adds that on another occasion he had attacked an enemy machine from close range, bringing it down out of control, before engaging another which then stalled and fell sideways.

His MC, however, was won while serving with the 7th King's Own (Yorkshire Light Infantry) and was gazetted on 24 June 1916. While out on patrol, he and his men encountered an enemy party during which BOND and a fellow officer were wounded when bombs were exchanged. The enemy then retired, but opened up on that location with machine-gun fire. Despite being wounded, BOND and another man, Private Garnett, rescued the other officer, bringing him back across 200 yards of ground under heavy machine-gun fire.

The CWGC cemetery register tells us that in civilian life BOND was a sub-editor at the Paris *Daily Mail* and that he had previously served in Gallipoli having enlisted in September 1914.

One of the five men who flew with BOND during the balloon-busting exploit on 2 May 1917 was Second Lieutenant Lewis Laugharne Morgan MC who was shot down later that year and lost a leg. Undaunted, and fitted with an artificial limb, he rejoined in March 1918, but was killed in England serving as a flying instructor when his aircraft suffered engine problems on take-off and crashed into a railway embankment. He is now buried in Canterbury Cemetery, Kent.

Captain Norman Alexander BROWNING-PATTERSON, 60 Squadron, Royal Flying Corps, was killed in action on 21 July 1916 while leading a patrol over enemy lines. He went to the front in August 1914 with the original British Expeditionary Force and took part in the Retreat from Mons and subsequent battles for which he was mentioned in despatches by Sir John French. He transferred to the Royal Flying Corps as an observer in September 1915 and was gazetted as a flight commander on 3 July the following year.

Captain William Jameson CAIRNES, 74 Squadron, Royal Air Force, was an Irishman who served with 19 Squadron, Royal Flying Corps, during spring and summer 1917 after service at home. His unit suffered heavy casualties during that period, but he survived and was promoted flight commander. He scored three victories before returning to the Home Establishment as an instructor, but then returned to France early in 1918 as flight commander with the newly formed 74 Squadron, increasing his tally to five victories. On 1 June 1918 his machine was shot down, losing a wing as it descended, giving him little chance of survival. The fatal crash occurred near Estaires.

Captain William Fulton CLEGHORN DFC, 218 Squadron, Royal Air Force, was killed in action on 2 October 1918, aged 23. His observer, Lieutenant F.H. Stringer, survived and was taken prisoner. His DFC was gazetted on 3 August 1918 and records that he was a distinguished and gallant leader who to date had taken part in no fewer than fifty-nine bombing raids. In one of the more recent raids his formation was attacked by a large number of enemy aircraft, although it still succeeded in dropping sixty-eight bombs on its objective. In the fight that followed, three enemy aircraft were destroyed and five others were brought down out of control.

Captain Carleton Main CLEMENT MC, 22 Squadron, Royal Flying Corps, was killed in action on 19 August 1917, aged 21. He attended Toronto University and initially enlisted as a private with the 47th Battalion, Canadian Infantry, before receiving his commission in March 1916 and transferring to the Royal Flying Corps. He was awarded the MC early in his flying career for destroying two enemy machines and driving down a further five out of control. The award was gazetted on 1 January 1918. He was also mentioned in despatches on 13 May 1917 and throughout that year he raised his score to fourteen victories, earning him the *Croix de Guerre* (France), which was gazetted on 14 July, and making him the most successful pilot in his squadron.

On the evening of 19 August 1917 he and his observer, Lieutenant Ralph Barr CARTER, set off on patrol, but their Bristol F2b was shot down over Langemarck. When Sir Hugh Trenchard, commander of the Royal Flying Corps, heard of CLEMENT's death he sent the squadron a telegram expressing condolences. CARTER's name is also commemorated on the memorial.

Captain Jack Oliver COOPER, 21 Squadron, Royal Flying Corps, is shown as having died between 21 and 23 July 1916. He and Lieutenant Alfred Vernon OLIVER-JONES were reported missing on 21 July after failing to return from a bombing raid on Epéhy station. It was later confirmed by the Red Cross in Geneva that COOPER had been shot down and killed. He was 20 years of age when he died and was educated at Harrow. He was the youngest son of Sir Alfred Cooper, a tea merchant, from Christchurch in Hampshire, and was in Australia when war broke out. In January 1915 he obtained a commission in the Royal Flying Corps and was considered a very promising flyer by those who knew him; in fact, many believed that he would have had a squadron of his own within the year had he survived. Lieutenant OLIVER-JONES is also commemorated on the memorial.

Captain Philip Chalmers COWAN, 56 Squadron, Royal Flying Corps, formerly 8th Manchester Regiment, was killed in action on 8 November 1917, and was the second flying casualty in the family. Philip was a medical student at Trinity College, Dublin, and had enlisted in August 1914. His younger brother, Captain Sidney Edward Cowan MC and two Bars, 29 Squadron, was killed in action on 17 November 1916 after colliding with another British aircraft during an aerial combat with three enemy machines. Both pilots were diving on the same target when they collided and fell behind enemy lines. Sidney is buried at Cagnicourt British Cemetery, but Philip's final resting place remains unknown.

Captain Kelvin CRAWFORD had served in the Machine Gun Corps before flying. From October 1916 to July 1917 he flew with 24 Squadron, Royal Flying Corps, but then returned to the Home Establishment for a time. In March 1918 he returned to the front where he was was posted to 60 Squadron, Royal Air Force. He was killed in action above Bucquoy on the evening of 11 April. He had five victories to his credit, which was the minimum score required to qualify as an 'ace'.

Captain Theodore CREAN, 4 Squadron, Royal Flying Corps, and his pilot, Lieutenant Cyril Gordon HOSKING, were killed in action on 26 October 1914 in tragic circumstances. They were observing enemy batteries and had descended to around 1,000 feet. In those early days, many infantrymen were unfamiliar with aircraft and had great difficulty distinguishing friend from foe. At the beginning of the war British aircraft bore Union Jack markings, which from the ground were often mistaken for the German Maltese Cross. Sadly, but hardly surprisingly, British troops fired on their machine in the mistaken belief that it was an enemy aircraft carrying out a reconnaissance. Their aircraft caught fire and descended in flames, killing both men. French troops also often fired mistakenly at British aircraft for the same reason, and it was the French who then suggested that the Royal Flying Corps adopt the same roundel marking as its aircraft. The Union Jack marking was therefore replaced in favour of the now familiar circular marking, although the red and blue circles were reversed in order to preserve the distinctly separate identity of the Royal Flying Corps. Both men are now commemorated on the memorial.

HOSKING was one of the pilots who had provided vital information regarding the wheeling movement of the German army as it advanced through northern France in late August 1914. He had entered the Royal Military Academy, Woolwich, in 1910, obtaining his commission there in 1913. His artillery background made him ideally suited for the type of duty he and his observer were carrying out on the day they died. His brother, Captain Herbert Edward Hosking, who is buried in Amara War Cemetery, was killed on 3 February 1917 in Mesopotamia supporting an attack on Turkish positions while serving with the 62nd Punjabis.

Captain Francis Richard CUBBON MC, 20 Squadron, Royal Flying Corps, formerly 72nd Punjabis, was one half of a very successful team, the other being Captain Frederick James Harry THAYRE MC. Their first two victories came on 29 April 1916, but the following month they notched up a further fifteen, bringing with it the award of the MC to both men. On one occasion, on 3 May, they had an outstanding encounter with twenty-six enemy Albatros Scouts. They shot down two of them and eventually managed to drive away the others. Towards the end of this engagement they had exhausted their machine gun ammunition and resorted to firing their pistols at the enemy.

They claimed two more victories the following month, which brought THAYRE's total to twenty and CUBBON's to twenty-one, which made him the most successful observer/gunner until well into the final year of the war. CUBBON's citation, gazetted on 18 July 1917, specifically refers to his fine marksmanship, coolness and courage as an observer which he had displayed on numerous occasions. Both men were in the thick of it during the latter part of April and into May 1917. However, both were killed on 9 June that year when their FE2d received a direct hit from an anti-aircraft battery near Warneton.

Captain Arthur Tulloch CULL, 48 Squadron, Royal Flying Corps, was killed in action while on an offensive patrol east of Arras on 11 May 1917. His observer, Air Mechanic 1st Class Arthur TRUSSON, also died when their machine was attacked early into their flight and fell to the ground in flames. TRUSSON is also commemorated on the memorial. CULL was born in Ceylon, and was educated at Uppingham School in England, where he became school captain. In 1914 he joined the Inns of Court OTC and was subsequently commissioned into the 1st Seaforth Highlanders before joining the Royal Flying Corps.

His brother, John Tulloch Cull DSO, served in the Royal Naval Air Service, having joined the Royal Navy in 1909. On 11 July 1915 Flight Commander John Cull and his colleague, Flight Sub Lieutenant Arnold, were engaged in spotting when their machine came under fire causing damage and loss of height. The distance back to base on Mafia Island, just off the coast of East Africa, was such that they needed to return immediately, yet they made no attempt to do so. Arnold continued to send back signals the whole time and, when their machine was hit again, forcing it to descend further, Cull continued to control the machine while Arnold carried on sending spotting corrections regardless of their predicament. Their instruments showed that their machine was failing badly and it became clear to Cull that he would have to land it as best he could. Their biplane finally came down in a river, turning over. Cull almost drowned, but Arnold managed to come to his assistance, and both men were subsequently rescued by a boat launched from HMS *Mersey*.

Captain Donald Alastair Leslie DAVIDSON MC 19 Squadron, Royal Flying Corps, was killed in action on 30 April 1917 aged 25. His family was well connected; his mother was the sister of the Earl of Albemarle and before the war DAVIDSON had been a page of honour to King Edward VII. He was educated at Wellington College and McGill University, Canada, before joining the Royal Flying Corps as an officer in May 1915. He then went to Egypt and Mesopotamia on active service. It was in this latter theatre that he was wounded while carrying out a food drop on the besieged town of Kut, for which he was awarded the MC. Awarded for conspicuous gallantry and determination when attacked by an enemy scout, the citation notes that his machine was heavily damaged, its controls had been shot away and he had been wounded in three places. However, with great skill he managed to reach his aerodrome and landed safely, though he had to be lifted out of his machine before being carried off to hospital. His wounds were so severe that he was invalided home. He returned to the Royal Flying Corps in spring 1917, but was shot down soon after arrival.

DAVIDSON's father also had a distinguished military career and had been mentioned in despatches in the Zulu War of 1879 before going on to serve in the Afghan War the following year. He also served in the South African War in 1899. He was a Gentleman Usher to HM the King and, greatly to his credit, at the age of 63, he had volunteered for war service. He was posted in charge of No. 4 Base Depot at Rouen where he died of heart failure, aged 65. He is buried at St Sever Cemetery, Rouen. Both father and son were members of the MCC.

Captain Edward Barfoot DRAKE, 209 Squadron, Royal Air Force, was previously employed on Home Defence duties, where he was credited with shooting down a Gotha bomber off Dover during a raid over the south of England on 22 August 1917. Soon afterwards, he was posted to 9 Squadron, Royal Naval Air

Service, claiming a further four victories with that unit. His fourth victory was against Leutnant Steinbrecher, who had made the first operational descent by parachute from an aircraft on 27 June 1918. On 29 September DRAKE was brought down when his Camel aircraft was hit by ground fire and he died soon afterwards from his wounds.

Captain Herbert Ruska GOULD MC, 18 Squadron, Royal Air Force, was killed in action on 14 August 1918. His MC was gazetted on 16 September 1918 and was awarded for his service to date, which included carrying out twenty-four successful bombing raids, several of which he personally led. He had also carried out twenty-six low-altitude reconnaissance flights and many low-level harassing and bombing patrols during which many direct hits were scored and severe casualties were inflicted on enemy forces. He had personally destroyed three enemy aircraft and throughout the operations he had always shown great zeal and spirit. His observer, Lieutenant Ewart William Frederick JINMAN, aged 19, was killed with him when their DH4 aircraft came down. JINMAN is also commemorated on the memorial.

Captain Henry Oswald William HILL MC, 52 Squadron, Royal Flying Corps, was killed in action on 21 October 1917, aged 29. He was commissioned in March 1916 from Manchester University OTC. His MC was gazetted on 17 December 1917 and its citation appeared on 23 April 1918. It was awarded for conspicuous gallantry and devotion to duty. It states that he had carried out artillery observation on a hostile battery for three and a half hours, subjected most of that time to heavy anti-aircraft and machine-gun fire. He had also attacked enemy aircraft on twenty-three occasions, once driving away five opponents, even though his observer had been wounded. It concludes that throughout all of these operations he had shown great skill.

Captain Robert Gerald HOPWOOD, 70 Squadron, Royal Flying Corps, was killed on 24 August 1916, aged 31. His gunner and observer that day, Charles Rapley PEARCE, who had previously served with the 1st Division Ammunition Column, Canadian Field Artillery, also perished with him. Both men are now commemorated on the memorial. HOPWOOD's brother, Lieutenant Colonel Edward Byng George Gregge-Hopwood DSO, was killed in action on 20 July 1917 while commanding the 1st Coldstream Guards. He is buried at Canada Farm Cemetery in Belgium.

Captain Richard Watson HOWARD MC, 2 Squadron, Australian Flying Corps, died of wounds on 22 March 1918. He was born in Sydney, Australia, and had studied engineering, a factor which no doubt influenced his decision to join the Australian Army Engineers in September 1915. From March to December 1916 he served in France, but then transferred to the Australian Flying Corps, joining 68 Squadron on 7 April 1917. He also spent a very short period with 57 Squadron and later took part in many ground attack operations, his aeroplane sustaining severe damage from an enemy machine on one of those occasions.

On 22 February 1918 he was promoted to flight commander in what had now become the 2nd Australian Squadron. It was during March, as activity intensified, that he gained six of his eight victories, but he was shot down near Vermand and died as a result of his injuries.

His MC was gazetted on 5 July 1918 and awarded for conspicuous gallantry and devotion to duty after he became separated from his patrol owing to thick mist. Undaunted, he drove one enemy aeroplane out of control and then engaged an enemy two-seater, forcing it to land behind our lines. On another occasion, he was attacked at a height of 400 feet, but managed to manoeuvre, causing his opponent to make a difficult landing after his observer had been shot, although the machine still remained intact. The citation concludes that he had consistently done good work.

Captain Gordon Budd IRVING DFC, 19 Squadron, Royal Air Force, was a Canadian flyer who joined the Royal Flying Corps in 1917. In November that year he was posted to 19 Squadron and in May 1918 he was promoted to captain and flight commander. He scored twelve victories between the end of March and 11 August 1918 when he was shot down in flames near Albert in a dog-fight, the same day on which he had scored his twelfth victory. His DFC was gazetted on 3 August 1918 and was awarded after carrying out numerous offensive patrols and for his leadership against many enemy formations. It concludes that he had personally accounted for six enemy aircraft and had set a fine example by his consistent keenness and fearlessness.

Captain Baron Trevenan JAMES MC, 6 Squadron, Royal Flying Corps, had formerly served with the Royal Engineers. He was 26 years old when he was killed in action on 13 July 1915 near Hooge. He was twice mentioned in despatches and was awarded the MC, which was gazetted on 23 June, just before his death, in connection with his service in the Royal Engineers. After attending Harrow, he entered the Royal Military Academy at Woolwich before going on to obtain his commission in the Royal Flying Corps in 1912.

He quickly made a name for himself in the field of aviation wireless telegraphy, and especially as a pioneer in wireless ranging with the artillery. He and another flyer, Lieutenant Donald Swain Lewis, were pivotal in persuading the many doubters that aircraft with wireless capability were crucial to accurate artillery ranging. The wireless kit itself was bulky and weighed about 75lbs, which meant that both men had to fly solo when carrying this equipment. They also had to fly their machines with one hand while transmitting via a buzzer with the other, often under anti-aircraft fire, which made every flight potentially hazardous.

'Bron' JAMES, whose father was a Member of the Royal College of Surgeons, was a consummate professional who went to the front in August 1914 and whose ideas and initiative were well ahead of his time. On hearing news of his death, his commanding officer, Gordon Shephard, claimed that he was one of the three best flight commanders in France at the time, and by far the best as regards artillery matters. He also acknowledged that the Corps had been slow to recognize this and to accord JAMES the credit he undoubtedly deserved for his work.

The nature of the work in which he and Lewis were engaged meant that their aircraft were soon identified by the Germans. They needed to remain fairly static over targets while accurately transmitting their positions, which made them especially vulnerable, and it was while carrying out ranging for a battery that Captain JAMES was hit by a shell that brought his aircraft crashing to the ground. After his death a message was received from the Germans stating that he had died instantly.

Lewis had also developed a celluloid dial consisting of eight concentric rings around which were the twelve positions of the clock. When overlaid on a map divided into grid squares, it enabled him to transmit the position of targets accurately to the gun batteries for which he was working. Each of the eight concentric circles represented varying distances from the target and each circle was identified by a letter. Therefore, by signalling a single letter followed by a number from one to twelve, he was able, not only to locate targets accurately, but also inform batteries if they needed to adjust their fire.

On 10 April 1916, while taking an artillery officer on a flight to show him the results of his trench mortar fire, Lewis's aircraft received a direct hit from an enemy shell, killing him and his passenger. He is now buried at Lijssenthoek Military Cemetery. He was awarded a DSO in the New Year's Honours List on 1 January 1915 and, like JAMES, had also been mentioned in despatches.

Captain Louis Fleeming JENKIN MC and Bar, 1 Squadron, Royal Flying Corps, was killed in action on 11 September 1917, aged 22. Although he was born in London, he had initially served with the 9th Loyal North Lancashire Regiment. He began his flying career in May 1917 when he joined 1 Squadron and within his first week had scored the first of his eventual twenty-two victories. Two months later, he had notched up a further nineteen victories. His MC was gazetted on 16 August 1917 and was awarded for conspicuous gallantry and devotion to duty. Clearly referring to his quick succession of victories, it notes that whilst engaged on offensive patrols he had continually shown the greatest dash and determination in attacking enemy aircraft in superior numbers, destroying some and bringing others down out of control. The bar to his MC was gazetted on 17 September 1917 and was awarded for conspicuous gallantry and devotion to duty, yet again, continually attacking hostile aircraft at close range, destroying some and driving others down and out of control. The citation concludes that at all times his dash and offensive spirit had been admirable. He was initially posted as missing in action on 11 September, the day on which he scored his twenty-second victory, almost certainly the result of aerial combat with Oberleutnant Schmidt of Jasta 29.

Captain Kenneth William JUNOR MC, 56 Squadron, Royal Air Force, was killed in action on 23 April 1918, aged 24. His MC was gazetted on 13 May 1918 and was awarded for gallantry, destroying two enemy machines in aerial combat and driving down a further two out of control, both of which crashed on landing. The citation concludes that he had always shown the greatest courage, skill and resource.

Captain James Kidston LAW, a pilot with 60 Squadron, Royal Flying Corps, had formerly served with the Royal Fusiliers. He was the eldest son of the Right Honourable Andrew Bonar Law, leader of the Conservative Party between 1911 and 1921, and again between 1922 and 1923 when he was Prime Minister. James was killed on 21 September 1917 whilst his younger brother, Lieutenant Charles John Law, was killed in action on 19 April 1917, aged 20, while serving with the 1/5th King's Own Scottish Borderers in Palestine. He is buried at Gaza War Cemetery.

Captain Henry George Ernest LUCHFORD MC and Bar, 20 Squadron, Royal Flying Corps, had originally joined the Norfolk Regiment in 1914 and was later commissioned in the Army Service Corps. Once in France, he also served with the Indian Cavalry Division, but in January 1916 he transferred to the Royal Flying Corps. He qualified as a pilot in May 1917 and then joined 20 Squadron. All of LUCHFORD's twenty-four victories occurred in the skies above Belgium. His MC was gazetted on 26 October 1917 and the bar gazetted a month later on 26 November. LUCHFORD was eventually shot down on 2 December 1917 near Becelaere, although his observer/gunner, Captain J.E. Johnston, survived and spent the rest of the war as a prisoner.

The citation for LUCHFORD's MC, which was gazetted on 18 March 1918, states that it was awarded for conspicuous gallantry and devotion to duty in carrying out a great deal of extremely useful work during which he proved himself a very capable and determined leader. On one occasion, when on a photographic reconnaissance, he and his observer shot down and destroyed two enemy scouts. He was also responsible for the destruction of a further five machines. The bar to his MC was awarded after an encounter with around fifteen hostile aircraft, one of which he shot down in flames. Later, while on a reconnaissance with three other machines, he shot down one enemy aircraft, and on another occasion he destroyed one of three hostile scouts that were attacking one of our own, after which he also shot down an enemy two-seater. The bar was gazetted on 6 April 1918.

Captain Julian Mackay MacILWAINE, 12 Squadron, Royal Flying Corps, formerly 5th Royal Irish Rifles, was 29 when he was killed in action on 22 March 1918. An Australian by birth, he had worked in stockbroking before the war. After receiving his commission in the Royal Irish Rifles, he became a musketry instructor and for a time was posted to Dublin in that capacity. He was wounded in the stomach in April 1915 while serving with the 1st Royal Irish Rifles in trenches near Festubert. The bullet wound was one that he was lucky to survive and it was two years before he was again passed fit for active service. It was then that he transferred to the Royal Flying Corps. His observer, Second Lieutenant

William Magnus IRVINE, was also killed when their RE8 aircraft came down and he is now commemorated here on the memorial.

Captain Alexander Murchison MacLEAN, 10 Squadron, Royal Air Force, was posted missing, and later presumed dead, following a low level reconnaissance mission during the critical days of the German Offensive in April 1918. His date of death is shown as 12 April. He was a graduate of Glasgow University and a member of its OTC.

When war broke out he was working in Chile. However, it proved impossible for him to book his passage to England from there owing to the presence of enemy warships off the Chilean coast. Undeterred, he and two other friends tried to get to Santiago, but heavy snowfall had blocked the railway line, so they then hired local guides and trekked across the Andes by mule. They eventually boarded a train for Buenos Aires and from there they managed to sail to England. MacLEAN initially served in Egypt and Gallipoli with the Scottish Horse where he was recommended for the MC, although no award ever materialized. After briefly serving with the Black Watch in Salonika, he transferred to the Royal Flying Corps, serving with it in Egypt and France prior to his death.

He was the second son of Professor Magnus MacLean, a distinguished academic in electrical engineering and one time assistant to Lord Kelvin. Professor MacLean was also a keen champion of Celtic Studies. He was the first Celtic lecturer at Glasgow University and also served as President of the Gaelic Society. MacLEAN's observer, Lieutenant Francis Beattie WRIGHT, was killed with him when their AWFK 8 aircraft came down. He is also commemorated on the memorial.

Captain Norman George McNAUGHTON MC and Captain Angus Hughes MEARNS, 57 Squadron, Royal Flying Corps, were killed in action on 24 June 1917 when their aircraft, a DH4, crashed into a German hangar behind enemy lines near Becelaere in Belgium. They had been carrying out a photographic reconnaissance under escort when they were engaged and shot down by Manfred von Richthofen, becoming his fifty-fifth victory.

McNAUGHTON had been in Argentina before the war, but like many who had gone abroad to work, he returned home when war broke out. In the summer of 1915 he obtained a commission in the Royal Flying Corps and by early 1916 he was flying operationally on the Western Front and was wounded that year in Belgium. His MC was awarded for conspicuous gallantry and devotion to duty as a patrol leader in numerous combats, but particularly for one occasion when he led his formation against an enemy patrol, personally driving down two enemy machines and setting a fine example of courage and leadership. The award was gazetted on 1 June 1917. His brother, Hamish, was killed in April 1917 serving with the Royal Field Artillery in Macedonia.

MEARNS, who is also commemorated on the memorial, had studied Medicine at St Andrews University before the war where he had been a member of its

OTC. He gained his commission in the Black Watch and was posted to its 9th Battalion, transferring to the Royal Flying Corps in March 1917.

Captain Kenneth Charles MILLS, 1 Squadron, Royal Air Force, was killed by ground fire on 8 August 1918, the opening day of the Allied advance towards final victory that began east of Amiens, although he was not directly involved in that operation. He had joined the Royal Flying Corps in June the previous year and served with 1 Squadron throughout the spring and early summer of 1918. He scored five victories, all of which were achieved over the front above Ypres and northern Flanders.

Captain John Theobald MILNE MC, 48 Squadron, Royal Flying Corps, was killed in action on 24 October 1917, aged 22. He was an ace with nine victories to his credit and had also been mentioned in despatches. He became a flight commander within a month of scoring his first victory, which was on 6 July 1917. He was wounded in September, but soon returned to action, only to be killed a month later. His MC was gazetted on 17 September 1917 and awarded for his conspicuous gallantry and devotion to duty leading offensive patrols. During these operations he showed great determination and courage when attacking hostile formations, often at close range and against superior numbers. The citation adds that he had also carried out long and arduous reconnaissance flights during which he obtained good photographs under very trying conditions and under heavy fire, displaying at all times fearlessness and energy.

Fellow ace, Captain Keith Rodney Park, who also served with 48 Squadron, paid tribute to his courage and ability as a flyer. Park also served with distinction in the Second World War during the Battle of Britain and the Battle of Malta, ending his career as an Air Chief Marshal.

MILNE's observer, Lieutenant Stanley WRIGHT MC, also perished with him, aged 25, when their Bristol F2b came down. WRIGHT is shown in the CWGC records as serving with the 21st Kite Balloon Section at the time of his death, but is commemorated with MILNE on the memorial. WRIGHT's MC is recorded in *Airmen Died in the Great War*, but I can find no trace of it in any of the gazettes.

Captain Guy Borthwick MOORE MC, 1 Squadron, Royal Air Force, was killed in action on 7 April 1918 when his aircraft was struck by an anti-aircraft shell. He had studied at the University of British Columbia between 1913 and 1916, gaining a Bachelor of Arts degree before joining the Irish Fusiliers of Canada, a militia unit from Vancouver. He joined the Royal Flying Corps in December 1916, gaining his wings in August the following year. At university he was a keen rower and a good rugby player. His MC was gazetted on 13 May 1918 and was awarded for his leadership during an attack on enemy balloons. His patrol brought down three and he personally accounted for one of them. He had also destroyed three enemy aircraft and had driven a further three out of control. He had shown great courage and resource throughout these operations.

Captain Charles George Douglas NAPIER MC, 48 Squadron, Royal Air Force, had previously served with 20 Squadron, Royal Flying Corps, until late 1917. After reaching his ninth victory, he and his observer, Serjeant Pat MURPHY, who is also commemorated on the memorial, were shot down in flames on 15 May 1918 in aerial combat. Originally posted as missing, the Germans confirmed the death of both men a few weeks later. He had also been shot down six days before his death, but on that day he and his observer were unharmed.

His MC was gazetted on 22 June 1918. The citation for it refers to a specific occasion when he dropped four bombs on a body of enemy troops from a height of only a hundred feet causing heavy casualties. It goes on to state that during offensive patrols he attacked an enemy two-seater causing it to crash; then attacked an enemy scout causing it to overturn and fall to the ground; finally, he drove a further four out of control, bringing his tally to six. His final three victories were achieved all on the same day, 9 May 1918.

The CWGC records show that he had also been awarded the DCM, but there appears to be no evidence for this in the gazettes. *Airmen Died in the Great War* credits him with the MM, though this is almost certainly the *Médaille Militaire* (France) referred to in the CWGC notes attached to his register entry.

Captain George Alec PARKER DSO MC, 60 Squadron, Royal Flying Corps, was killed in action on 27 November 1916. His DSO was awarded for attack-ing enemy machines on three separate occasions during the same flight, killing an enemy observer in the process. Then, on another occasion, he drove off three enemy machines three miles behind their own lines. The award was gazetted on 10 January 1917, as was his MC, which was awarded for forcing an enemy scout to land after engaging it in a long aerial combat during which he handled his own machine with great skill.

Captain William Gordon PENDER MC, 40 Squadron, Royal Flying Corps, was killed in action on 15 August 1917, aged 30. *Officers Died in the Great War* also shows the award of the MC against his name, but I can find no reference to it in any of the gazettes. There is a reference to his appointment as second lieutenant in the Royal Flying Corps in the *London Gazette* dated 14 September 1915, but there appears to be nothing further under his full name.

Captain Wilfred PICTON-WARLOW is presumed to have been lost in the Channel on 20 December 1914, aged 30, although *Royal Flying Corps Casualties and Honours during the War of 1914–1917* shows his date of death as 30 December 1914. In any case, he was killed flying a two-seater Blériot monoplane, which even at this early stage of the war had become virtually obsolete, although it was still being used for training purposes in England. It was also customary for officers of the Royal Flying Corps to be allowed to fly these aircraft when going home on leave. On the day of his death he had carried out a short test flight before setting off on what was a clear day, with some high cloud. One theory was that he had flown into the cloud, lost his way and had then run out of fuel, eventually falling into the sea. However, he began his flight with twice the amount of fuel sufficient for his intended journey. Of course, it is equally possible that his machine suffered a mechanical failure.

He had served previously with the Welsh Regiment and had seen action during the South African campaign. His late father, Colonel John Picton-Turbevill, had served on the Staff Corps at Madras in India. The family owned an estate in Glamorganshire, including Ewenny Priory, an unusual and impressively fortified monastic building founded in the twelfth century by Benedictine monks.

Captain Robert Maxwell PIKE, 5 Squadron, Royal Flying Corps, was killed in action east of Ypres on 9 August 1915, aged 28. Educated at Harrow, he entered the Navy in 1902, but a rare medical condition caused him to undergo an operation to remove a knee joint. It left him with a stiff leg and he was invalided out of the service. However, this did not prevent him joining the Royal Flying Corps in September 1914, where he soon showed great promise as a flyer.

His first taste of action came on the night of 19 January 1915 while employed on home defence. He engaged a Zeppelin, but was forced to break off and land after engine problems. Despite hitting a dyke when he landed, he and his observer were miraculously unhurt and he went to the front later that month. In early April that year he was promoted to flight commander with the rank of temporary captain. He was mortally wounded while flying the new DH4 aircraft, one of which he had flown earlier on a test flight in England. He was shot in the head and, although he brought his machine down, it landed heavily causing severe damage as it turned over. He was buried by the Germans, but his grave was lost during later fighting.

Captain Leslie PORTER, 45 Squadron, Royal Flying Corps, was one of six personnel from that squadron reported missing on 22 October 1916. Three of them are commemorated here on the memorial with him: Second Lieutenant George Bernard SAMUELS, who was PORTER's observer, and Lieutenant Oliver John WADE and his observer, Second Lieutenant William Johnson THUELL. The other two were Serjeant Percy Snowdon and his observer, Second Lieutenant William Francis Hannan Fullerton, who are buried next to each other in the Porte de Paris Cemetery, Cambrai.

PORTER is known to have died of wounds in Germany. He was the son of Captain David Porter, who served with the Royal Army Medical Corps, and in civilian life he was a keen motor racing enthusiast who had founded his own company, 'Leslie Porter Limited', based in Northern Ireland. In 1903 he took part in the infamous Paris to Madrid car rally during which his car was involved in an accident resulting in the death of his racing companion and mechanic, William Nixon. In August 1915 he flew from England to Belfast and gave some exhibition flights over the city. PORTER died on 24 October, two days after initially being reported missing. He left three children, one of whom, David, was shot down during the Second World War, but survived as a prisoner of war.

Captain Percy Dickson ROBINSON MC, 57 Squadron, Royal Flying Corps, was killed in action on 31 March 1918. His MC was not gazetted until 16 August that year, well after his death. However, the citation pays a fine tribute to his courage, skill and determination as a pilot, referring to an occasion when, during a photographic reconnaissance, he was attacked by ten enemy aircraft. He handled his machine so skilfully in this encounter that his observer was able to shoot down two of their opponents and disperse the remainder. Even though his own machine was badly damaged and almost unmanageable, he continued taking photographs and finally brought his machine back safely. The citation concludes that he had already taken part in many such photographic missions and had always displayed the same courage and determination. ROBINSON's observer, Lieutenant John Quintin Frederick WALKER, was also killed, aged 18, when their DH4 aircraft came down. He too is commemorated on the memorial.

Captain Frederick Hatherley Bruce SELOUS MC, 60 Squadron, Royal Flying Corps, had formerly served with the Queen's (Royal West Surrey Regiment) and was also the recipient of the Silver Medal for Military Valour (Italy). His MC was gazetted in June 1917 in the King's Birthday Honours List. He was killed in action during an offensive patrol near Menin on 4 January 1918. The wings of his SE5a aircraft were seen to collapse before it plummeted to the ground offering him no chance of survival. Exactly what caused the damage to his machine is not known.

Coincidentally, his father, Captain Frederick Courteney SELOUS DSO, had been killed exactly a year previously, on 4 January 1917, leading an attack on Behobeho at the remarkable age of 65. The father was another colourful character. Like his son he had attended Rugby School and was one of the Rugby School 'Volunteers'. He was present at a review by Queen Victoria at Windsor Great Park. Before his twentieth birthday, he went to South Africa where he became a big game hunter, accounting for over a thousand head of big game, thirty-three of which are preserved in the Natural History Museum in London.

He spent several years mapping Mashonaland and wrote books on hunting and exploration. In 1893 he took part in the first Matabele War and also acted as guide to an expedition organised by Cecil Rhodes. He continued to shoot and hunt and also did some travelling in Asia. As he approached his sixtieth birthday, he joined 'Teddy' Roosevelt in a hunting expedition and went on to write more books.

When the war broke out, Frederick senior enlisted as a private in the 24th Royal Fusiliers and was commissioned as a lieutenant in February 1915. In August that year he was promoted to captain and joined a special draft of 1,166 men who became the 25th (Service) Battalion, Royal Fusiliers (Frontiersmen), an eclectic mix of men of all ages, experience and background, who were sent to join General Smuts in the campaign in South-West Africa. It was here that his pre-war experiences brought him to notice and where he won his DSO and mentions in despatches. He was invalided back to England with sickness, but remarkably he returned to active service on 16 December 1916, arriving in Africa with a draft of 150 men. By this time only around sixty of the original battalion remained.

On 4 January 1917 he was wounded when leading his men in an attack on entrenched positions before being shot dead. These positions were taken, as was Behobeho. An account of this action appeared in the *Fourth Supplement to the London Gazette* dated 17 April 1917. His DSO was gazetted on 26 September 1916 and was awarded for conspicuous gallantry, resource, endurance and the magnificent example that he set to all ranks.

Captain Allan Higson SMITH MC, 21 Squadron, Royal Flying Corps, was killed in action on 21 August 1917, aged 23. His MC is shown next to his name in *Officers Died in the Great War*, but I can find no trace of it in any of the gazettes. There is, however, a reference in Royal Flying Corps Communiqué 122, dated 11 January 1918, noting the award of the MC to a temporary Captain H.A. Smith, but there are no further details to help determine whether this is the man listed here on the memorial.

Captain Sydney Philip SMITH DSO, but shown in the CWGC register as Philip Sydney SMITH, 46 Squadron, Royal Air Force, had served in the Army Service Corps before transferring to the Royal Flying Corps in 1916. In June that same year he qualified as a pilot and was promoted to captain at the end of the year. He joined 46 Squadron as a flight commander on 6 February 1918 and was shot down by Manfred von Richthofen two months later on 6 April. SMITH had five victories to his credit and was awarded a DSO and the *Croix de Guerre* (France). He was severely wounded in the right arm while flying in January 1916. The arm failed to heal and was later amputated.

SMITH was a tireless, courageous and aggressive fighter in the same way that Albert Ball had been. He was killed while carrying out a low-level operation. During the German Offensive in spring 1918 squadrons were ordered to make many such attacks on German troop columns and transport. One of the problems with these kind of attacks was that pilots were vulnerable to attack from above at the very moment that their attention was focused on targets at ground level. This placed them at a significant disadvantage, and even an experienced flyer like SMITH was unable to react quickly enough to give himself a realistic chance of taking evasive action or engaging an aerial opponent.

After the war SMITH's father searched the area where his son's machine had come down, but he was unable to find any trace of his son, even though he did locate parts of his Sopwith Camel. It was known that the Camel had caught fire as it went down and that it continued burning after the crash, so the body would have been badly burnt. SMITH was Richthofen's seventy-sixth victory.

Captain James Maitland STUART and Lieutenant Maurice Herbert WOOD, 59 Squadron, Royal Flying Corps, were killed in action on 13 April 1917 while on a photographic mission. It was a disastrous day and all six aircraft of 59 Squadron that took off that morning fell victim to German fighters, killing all twelve men.

Eight of the twelve are commemorated on the memorial along with STUART and WOOD. They are: Captain George Bailey HODGSON and his observer, Lieutenant Charles Herbert MORRIS; Second Lieutenant Philip Bentinck BOYD and his observer, Second Lieutenant Philip Oliphant RAY; Second Lieutenant Arthur Horace TANFIELD and his observer, Second Lieutenant Andrew ORMEROD, and Second Lieutenant Herbert George McMillan HORNE and his observer, Lieutenant William Joseph CHALK, a Canadian from Winnipeg.

STUART was brought up in Australia where the family had commercial interests, but he finished his education at Sandhurst. He was gazetted in the 1st Royal Inniskilling Fusiliers, but soon moved over to flying and went to France towards the end of 1915. He became a flight commander in November 1916 and joined 59 Squadron, newly arrived on the Western Front, in February 1917. He was considered an experienced pilot and had spent the autumn of 1916 as part of the Home Establishment before returning to the front.

WOOD had completed his education at University College, London, graduating with Honours in French and History. He joined the OTC there and went on to obtain a commission in the 4th Lincolnshire Regiment in 1913. He then went to France with the battalion in March 1915 and later served at the Grenade School at Second Army HQ. It was only in January 1917 that he joined the Royal Flying Corps as an observer. STUART and WOOD became Richthofen's forty-first victory and the first of three that he scored that day.

Captain William Assheton SUMMERS MC, 22 Squadron, Royal Flying Corps, formerly 18th (Queen Mary's Own) Hussars, was aged 20 when he was killed in action on 1 August 1916. His aircraft was subject to a direct hit from anti-aircraft fire. He and Flight Serjeant Norman Thomas CLARKSON, aged 22, are now commemorated on the memorial.

SUMMERS was educated at Eton, then at Sandhurst, before obtaining his commission in the Hussars in March 1914. He went to France with his regiment in the early days of the war. However, in May 1915 he transferred to the Royal Flying Corps and was promoted to flight commander in March 1916. SUMMERS was awarded the MC along with Lieutenant William Owen Tudor Tudor-Hart, his observer on the day, and both awards were gazetted on 27 July 1916. They had single-handedly attacked a flight of ten enemy aircraft, completely breaking up its formation, and had only disengaged many miles into enemy lines when all their ammunition had been expended. During the engagement they came under fire from as many as four enemy aircraft simultaneously, which had resulted in heavy damage to their own machine.

Captain St Cyprian Churchill TAYLER MC, 80 Squadron, had joined the Royal Flying Corps from the Royal Sussex Regiment and was initially posted to 32 Squadron. During the first half of 1917 he flew with Captain Arthur 'Maori' Coningham's DH5 flight, claiming six victories before being wounded on 31 July. Coningham went on to serve during the Second World War and ended his career as an Air Marshal. After recovering, TAYLER was promoted to captain and joined 80 Squadron as flight commander, taking it to France in January 1918. He claimed a further three victories before he was shot down south of Cambrai by Heinrich Kroll on 17 March 1918. His MC was gazetted on 9 January 1918 and was awarded for conspicuous gallantry and devotion to duty in leading his squadron on offensive patrols against enemy aircraft. The citation states that on at least five occasions he and his patrols had been responsible for attacking and bringing down hostile aircraft. TAYLER's observer, Lieutenant Albert Warren, died the same day, aged 25, and is buried at Tincourt New British Cemetery

Captain Samuel Frederick Henry THOMPSON MC DFC, 22 Squadron, Royal Air Force, began his military service with the Army Service Corps. He started flying with 20 Squadron in late 1917 and was known as an aggressive pilot. He suffered a crash on 27 October 1917, but returned to flying, this time with 22 Squadron, scoring his first victory on 22 April 1918. His MC was gazetted on 16 September that year and the citation states that he had destroyed five enemy aircraft in recent operations, during which he displayed fine skill and courage, and that his keenness and dash had set a fine example to all. His DFC, gazetted on 2 November 1918, records that he had carried out numerous offensive patrols displaying the most marked bravery and determination. It goes on to say that his boldness in attack and utter disregard of personal danger had set an inspiring example to his fellow pilots, concluding that since June he had destroyed eleven enemy aircraft.

Twenty-five of his thirty victories came with his observer/gunner, Serjeant Ronald Malcolm Fletcher DFM, who was credited with eleven victories in his own right, although not all of them flying with THOMPSON. Fletcher's DFM was gazetted on the same date as THOMPSON's DFC. The citation for it states that he was a most efficient and keen observer who was implicitly trusted by all the pilots with whom he flew. It goes on to add that he had taken part in numerous combats with enemy aircraft and invariably displayed marked fearlessness and skill, noting that he had accounted for seven enemy machines since 21 May. THOMPSON was killed in action on 27 September 1918 over Cambrai with his observer, Second Lieutenant Clifford John TOLMAN, who is also commemorated on this memorial. THOMPSON was the second most successful Bristol Fighter pilot after Lieutenant Colonel Andrew McKeever, a Canadian, whose tally came to thirty-one.

Captain Hugh Christopher TOWER, 60 Squadron, Royal Flying Corps, was killed on 19 September 1916, aged 30, while his squadron was acting as escort to aircraft from 11 Squadron, which were carrying out reconnaissance work. The formation was attacked by between twenty and twenty-five enemy machines and continuous heavy fighting took place over Quéant and throughout the return flight. The escorts successfully protected 11 Squadron, but Captain TOWER was heavily involved in the fighting and he was eventually brought down.

Before the war he had passed his Surveyors' Institute examination and had been working as a land agent on the estates of Lady Heytesbury and Sir Edward

Antrobus in Wiltshire. On the outbreak of war he volunteered for the Royal Flying Corps, Special Reserve, joining at Farnborough on 15 August 1914, and by April the following year he was flying operationally in France. He then returned to England, where he gained promotion to flight commander, and returned to the front in May 1916. Throughout his time with the Royal Flying Corps he gained a reputation as a fearless flyer.

His brother, Lieutenant Christopher Cecil Tower, died on 2 October 1915, aged 30, when he was killed alongside Major General Frederick Drummond Vincent Wing CB, GOC of the 12th (Eastern) Division. Tower was Wing's ADC at the time and the men are buried next to each other in Noeux-les-Mines Communal Cemetery.

Captain Ronald Travis TOWNSEND, Royal Flying Corps, formerly 5th Highland Light Infantry, Canadian Local Forces, and Canadian Army Pay Corps, was killed in action on 30 November 1917, aged 28. His brother, Captain Eric Travis Townsend, was also killed in action a few weeks earlier on 8 November while serving with the 5th Highland Light Infantry in Palestine. He is buried in Gaza War Cemetery.

Captain Dawyck Moberly Veitch VEITCH, 70 Squadron, Royal Flying Corps, was killed in action on 8 July 1916 with his observer, Lieutenant John Leo WHITTY MC, when the wings of their aircraft were blown off, giving neither any chance of survival. VEITCH went to war in September 1914 with the 9th Lancers before transferring that November to the 4th (Royal Irish) Dragoon Guards. He was invalided home in December that year, but a month later joined the Royal Flying Corps as an observer. In February 1916 he was invited to qualify as a pilot and was successful. He went to France in June the same year, only to die a month later.

WHITTY was born in Cape Town, but was educated at a Jesuit College in Liverpool. He was gazetted from Sandhurst into the Leinster Regiment in February 1913, joining the 1st Battalion at Fyzabad in September. He gained a reputation for being cool and calm under pressure and was mentioned in despatches. His MC was gazetted on 29 June 1915 while he was serving with the 1st Leinster Regiment, though there does not appear to be any citation for it. He was the son of Colonel M.J. Whitty, Royal Army Medical Corps, who died in England on 28 March 1917 and is buried in Liverpool (Yew Tree) Roman Catholic Cemetery.

Captain William WALKER DFC, General List and 6 Squadron, Royal Air Force, formerly 4th Battalion, Royal Scots (Queen's Edinburgh Rifles), was killed in action on 8 October 1918 and had been awarded the *Croix de Guerre* (Belgium). He was aged 24. His DFC was gazetted on 2 November 1918 and was awarded after he had carried out a contact patrol to identify the location of our cavalry on 9 August. The mission called for low-level flying and at times he came under heavy machine-gun fire. Despite all this he brought back the information that was required. He had already carried out two reconnaissance flights that day and this third task meant that he had spent over six hours flying, during which time he had been engaged with enemy aircraft and by ground troops. His observer, Second Lieutenant Michael Anthony Waterer, was killed with him and is buried at Tincourt New British Cemetery.

Captain Noel William Ward WEBB MC and Bar, 70 Squadron, Royal Flying Corps, was killed in action on 16 August 1917, aged 20. His MC was gazetted on 1 January 1917 and the bar followed a year later, appearing in the *London Gazette* on 9 January 1918. It was awarded for gallantry in aerial combats, in particular for the destruction of three enemy machines and for driving down a further four out of control, inspiring those around him to engage enemy formations more numerous than their own. The first five of his fourteen victories occurred between mid-July and mid-September 1916 while posted to 25 Squadron, earning him the award of the MC. After that he was sent home as an instructor, but he returned to the front with 70 Squadron in June 1917. His last three victories were scored on the same day, 13 August 1917, but he was shot down over Polygon Wood three days later by Werner Voss, the German ace.

Captain Lewis Ewart WHITEHEAD was wounded in combat on 26 July 1916 when flying with 60 Squadron, Royal Flying Corps. He transferred to 65 Squadron in 1917, initially serving with it as part of the Home Establishment, but remaining in England when the squadron went to France in November the same year. He rejoined his squadron in France in April 1918 as a flight commander. On 15 May, a few days before his death, he had a narrow escape when his aircraft was forced down by six enemy machines. During the encounter he skilfully handled his own aircraft and, despite losing five of them, he was still left with one on his tail. He again skilfully manoeuvred his machine into a position, firing his machine gun into his opponent from a distance of only twenty yards. His own machine was badly damaged in the fight and his luck finally ran out a few days later on 20 May 1918. His father, Lewis Whitehead, had also been a soldier and ended his career with the rank of lieutenant colonel.

Captain William George Bransby WILLIAMS MC, 19 Squadron, Royal Flying Corps, was killed in action on 12 May 1917, aged just 19. He was the eldest son of the actor Bransby Williams, who was a leading music hall artist of his day, and who later went on to do impersonations of famous actors, as well as characters from the novels of Charles Dickens. In 1903 he gave a Royal Command Performance for King Edward VII at Sandringham and later toured America, taking on a number of serious acting parts, including roles from Shakespeare. He appeared as a guest on *Desert Island Discs* on 4 November 1957 and on *This is Your Life* the following year. Today he is largely forgotten. His son's MC was gazetted in the King's Birthday Honours List on 5 June 1916.

Captain Alfred Clarence YOUDALE MC and two Bars, 21 Squadron, Royal Flying Corps, was killed in action on 23 December 1917, aged 28. His MC was awarded after rendering valuable assistance to our infantry in an attack. He flew several times through our heavy barrage, using his machine gun at very low altitude on enemy targets. Throughout the operation he showed skill and fearlessness. His bar was gazetted on 18 March 1918 and was awarded for conspicuous gallantry attacking enemy troops, again at extremely low altitudes. On one occasion, when our infantry was held up, he carried out an attack on the enemy's position, approaching it from behind and from a height of just 150 feet and engaging it at close quarters. His second bar was won for conspicuous gallantry and devotion to duty whilst engaged on contact patrol and was gazetted on 5 July 1918. Tasked with locating the position gained by our troops, his first attempt was frustrated by a snowstorm. He then made a second attempt and, flying at a height of 200 feet in spite of severe hostile fire, he succeeded in locating all our positions. His observer, Second Lieutenant Jacob Ernest MOTT, is also commemorated on the memorial.

Lieutenant Herbert Cecil AINGER, 19 Squadron, Royal Flying Corps, was killed in action on 4 October 1917, aged 22, a day of extremely bad weather for flying. His first notable piece of work came on 26 August 1917 when he and his squadron set out at dawn to attack Bisseghem and Marcke aerodromes. The sortie was not without incident and involved an engagement with enemy fighters during which AINGER and his men destroyed three of their opponents and drove down several others out of control. The attack on the airfields went well. AINGER also took the opportunity to attack a train leaving Courtrai, and at Marcke he twice attacked eight enemy aircraft on the ground outside their hangars before returning home because of a problem with his gun.

Lieutenant Richard APPLIN, 19 Squadron, Royal Flying Corps, was one of three pilots from that squadron who took off from the airfield at Vert Galant on 29 April 1917. He became the forty-ninth victory of Manfred von Richthofen. One of the other pilots with him that day was Major Hubert Dunsterville Harvey-Kelly, a renowned pilot and larger-than-life character. APPLIN was brought down behind German lines near Lecluse, an area of marshy ground along the River Scarpe, several miles south of Douai. Both APPLIN and Harvey-Kelly were killed that day, but the third pilot, Lieutenant W.N. Hamilton, was taken prisoner after his aircraft was also brought down. APPLIN had joined the Inns of Court OTC in October 1915. He joined 19 Squadron in March 1917 and was relatively inexperienced as a flyer. I can find no record of his body ever having been recovered and it is possible that the crash site was inaccessible owing to the nature of the ground.

Lieutenant Thomas BECK MC, 48 Squadron, Royal Air Force, was killed in action on 1 October 1918. He had previously served with the Argyll & Sutherland Highlanders and the 2nd Highland Light Infantry. His MC was gazetted in the New Year's Honours List 1918. BECK's pilot, Captain W. Buckingham, was taken prisoner.

Lieutenant Enyon George Arthur BOWEN, 22 Squadron, Royal Flying Corps, was reported missing in action on 8 September 1916, but it was later confirmed that he had been killed. He was a pupil at Sherborne School and then entered the Royal Military Academy, Woolwich, in January 1912. In December the following year he was gazetted into the Royal Garrison Artillery and went to the front with a heavy battery in June 1915. In August he became an observer and in May 1916 he qualified as a pilot and returned to the front.

On 21 July he was attacked by an enemy Roland aircraft while on photographic duties with his observer, Second Lieutenant William Stanley Mansell. He skilfully outmanoeuvred it and brought it down after firing three drums of ammunition into it from forty yards. A month later he came to notice for strafing enemy trench positions on the Somme. Mansell was later killed in action on 11 September 1917 when flying with 1 Squadron and is now buried in Pont-du-Hem Military Cemetery, La Gorgue. BOWEN was killed a few weeks later, flying with another observer, Lieutenant Robert Macallan STALKER, who is also commemorated here on the memorial.

Lieutenant Leslie Spencer BOWMAN, 53 Squadron, Royal Flying Corps, and Second Lieutenant James Edward Power-Clutterbuck, became the fifty-sixth victory of Manfred von Richthofen when their aircraft was shot down on 25 June 1917 near Le Bizet, not far from Ploegsteert Wood. They had been working with artillery on a shoot when they were attacked. Their burning wreckage came down in no man's land and BOWMAN's body was never recovered, although Power-Clutterbuck's body was retrieved by some of our own troops who were holding that part of the line. It may have been that BOWMAN's charred remains proved impossible to extricate from the wreckage, whereas his observer had perhaps been thrown clear of the burning craft on impact. Power-Clutterbuck's remains now lie in Strand Military Cemetery on the edge of Ploegsteert Wood.

BOWMAN had previously served with the 4th King's Own (Royal Lancaster Regiment) and went to France with the battalion at the end of December 1915. He was wounded in 1916, though not seriously, and by mid-July that year he had recovered sufficiently to transfer to the Royal Flying Corps. By the end of that year he had qualified as a pilot. He was again slightly wounded while flying on 6 June, the day before the Battle of Messines Ridge. Lieutenant Power-Clutterbuck had been gazetted in the Royal Field Artillery in early January 1915 and, like BOWMAN, he was wounded twice in action, once in Gallipoli and once on the Western Front.

Lieutenant Frederick Henry CANTLON MC, 11 Squadron, Royal Flying Corps, was killed in action on 18 March 1918. He had previously served with the Canadian Infantry and was awarded the MC for gallantry after leading his men with great determination in an assault. His platoon was then ordered to another sector of the line which he put into a state of defence, showing great energy and skill. When all the officers of his company and those of another had become casualties, he collected up the remainder of both companies and held the newly captured position for two days, repelling several determined and well organized counter-attacks. The award was gazetted on 7 March 1918, barely a couple of weeks before his death.

Lieutenant Stanley Winther CAWS, 10 Squadron, Royal Flying Corps, was killed in action on 21 September 1915, aged 36. His observer that day, Lieutenant W.H. Sugden-Wilson, was more fortunate and was taken prisoner. An only son, CAWS was killed in aerial combat and was buried with full military honours by the Germans.

He had previously served in the South African War with Paget's Horse. After serving in South Africa he moved to Canada where he helped to form the Legion of Frontiersmen, an association of adventurous, pioneering individuals, often South African War veterans, who had settled in some of the more remote areas of Western Canada during the early part of the century. The association was organized along military lines and provided a ready source of men with a military background in 1914. He was still in north-west Canada when war broke out and he came over to England with the first Canadian Contingent. He transferred to the Royal Flying Corps in February 1915.

The CWGC records show a Private Henry Churchill Caws, 1st Royal Berkshire Regiment, killed in action on 19 February 1917, and a Private Gordon Frank Caws, 1st Queen's (Royal West Surrey Regiment), killed in action on 23 April 1917. Both men were brothers and came from Sea View Bay on the Isle of Wight, where Stanley's parents lived, making it highly likely that they were cousins of Lieutenant CAWS. The CWGC records also include at least two other men who fell during the war and who may be related to him. Henry is commemorated on the Thiepval Memorial and Gordon on the Arras Memorial.

Lieutenant Bernard Tarrant COLLER, 9 Squadron, Royal Flying Corps, was reported missing in action on 26 September 1916 while over enemy lines. He had been a member of his school OTC and had then studied at University College, Oxford. He obtained a commission in the Norfolk Regiment in October 1914 and joined the Royal Flying Corps in November 1915. The following May he went to the front. He was killed with his observer, Second Lieutenant Thomas Earle Gordon SCAIFE MC, who is also commemorated on the memorial. Their BE2e machine was hit by anti-aircraft fire while they were carrying out a contact patrol over Lesboeufs.

SCAIFE was a very experienced and resourceful observer. His MC was awarded for his conspicuous gallantry and skill while engaged on contact patrols, often at low level and under heavy fire. During one of these a shell fragment pierced the fuel tanks, but SCAIFE managed to carry out a running repair by stopping up the holes, enabling his pilot to get the machine back to their airfield. He had also come to notice on other occasions, most notably on 1 July 1916, when he and his pilot were able to report successfully on the progress of the 30th Division troops near Montauban. They also attacked a German gun battery and some infantry that day, even though their machine was damaged by anti-aircraft fire. Another time, he and his pilot had assisted a party of men from the Royal Warwickshire Regiment who were pinned down by enemy fire near Falfemont Farm. They attacked the enemy's position, which enabled the infantry to advance.

One of COLLER's brothers, Captain Charles Mervyn COLLER, was killed in action, aged 22, during the fighting around Lagnicourt on 21 March 1918 while serving with the 9th Norfolk Regiment. He is commemorated on the Arras Memorial. Another brother, Major Raymond Geoffrey Coller, who served with the Royal Artillery, died from injuries on 10 December 1940 when the train in which he was travelling was hit during an air raid. He is buried in Hethersett (St Remigius) Churchyard in Norfolk.

Lieutenant James CRAFTER MC, 20 Squadron, Royal Flying Corps, and his observer, Serjeant Walter Douglas Ackroyd BACKHOUSE, were killed in action on 7 July 1917 while flying their FE2d aircraft. BACKHOUSE is also commemorated on the memorial. CRAFTER went to France with the 1/14th Battalion, London Regiment (London Scottish) in September 1914 and was later commissioned in the 20th Battalion, London Regiment (Blackheath & Woolwich). His MC was awarded while serving with this unit, but there does not appear to be a citation for it.

CRAFTER's brother, Tom, was also killed in action, at Klein Zillebeke, fighting with the 1/14th London Regiment (London Scottish) on 11 November 1914, the last major attempt by the Germans to break the British line at First Ypres. Tom died of wounds the following day and is now commemorated on the Menin Gate at Ypres. It is highly likely that the brothers were in the line together at Ypres when Tom was killed, although I can find no source to corroborate this.

Lieutenant David Evan DAVIES, 12 Squadron, Royal Flying Corps, was killed in action on 29 April 1917 with his observer, Lieutenant George Henry RATHBONE. Their aircraft crashed near Roeux when they were shot down by Manfred von Richthofen and became his fifty-first victory. DAVIES was working abroad when the war broke out and, like many others, he returned to enlist. He served with the Royal Welsh Fusiliers in France before gaining his commission and transferring to the Royal Flying Corps. RATHBONE was a volunteer in the militia in Canada and came to England with an infantry battalion. However, in February 1917 he too transferred to the Royal Flying Corps and was posted to 12 Squadron at Avesnes-le-Comte during the first week of April.

Lieutenant Robert Hartley DEAKIN, 45 Squadron, Royal Flying Corps, had previously served with the South Lancashire Regiment before receiving his commission in the 10th Jats, an Indian Army regiment. Prior to attending Sandhurst as a cadet in 1915, he had won an Exhibition to Oxford, studying at Jesus College, although he did not complete his time there owing to the outbreak of war. After serving in India, he transferred to the Royal Flying Corps in January 1917. He was killed in action on 22 July that year, aged 22. His brother, Lieutenant George

Deakin, also served during the war and won a bar to his MC. He served with the Royal Engineers and, although severely wounded in the thigh, he survived. DEAKIN's observer, Lieutenant Reginald HAYES, was killed with him and is commemorated on the memorial.

Lieutenant Pruett Mullens DENNETT, 208 Squadron, Royal Air Force, joined the Royal Naval Air Service on 25 March 1917. He received his commission as a flight sub-lieutenant in August that year and was posted to 8 Squadron, Royal Naval Air Service some months later. By June 1918 he had scored eight victories, but was shot down flying his Sopwith Camel near Estaires on 2 June 1918.

Lieutenant Julius DIAMOND MC, 7 Squadron, Royal Flying Corps, formerly King's Own Scottish Borderers, was killed in action on 8 October 1917. His MC was gazetted posthumously on 7 March 1918 and was awarded for conspicuous gallantry and devotion to duty while co-ordinating with our artillery, often under the most adverse conditions, and during which on two occasions he ranged our siege batteries on hostile battery positions causing numerous fires and explosions. Before the war, DIAMOND had studied Mathematics and French at Glasgow University, where he also became a member of its OTC. He was well known in the Jewish community in Great Britain, having served as secretary of the Jewish Representative Council, vice president of the Junior Zionist Society, and was also a member of the Grand Order of Israel. DIAMOND's pilot, Second Lieutenant Cyril Beaven WATTSON, died with him, aged 19, and is also commemorated on the memorial.

Lieutenant Cedric George EDWARDS DFC, 209 Squadron, Royal Air Force, joined the Royal Naval Air Service in June 1917 and went on to complete his training in France with 12 Squadron by the end of the year. In the early days of 1918 he was posted to 9 Squadron, Royal Naval Air Service, which became 209 Squadron, Royal Air Force on 1 April. He scored seven victories and won the DFC with 209 Squadron. He was shot down by anti-aircraft fire above Jigsaw Wood on 27 August 1918. His DFC was gazetted on 23 September 1918 and was awarded for his coolness and fearlessness in carrying out attacks at low altitude. The citation continues by referring to an attack on an enemy aerodrome in which he flew so low that his wheels actually came into contact with the ground as he fired on some hangars. It concludes by stating that he had also destroyed three enemy machines in aerial combat.

Lieutenant Ralph Walter ELLIS, 9 Squadron, Royal Flying Corps, was another of those aviators who had learned to fly at his own expense, although he had already been commissioned in the Royal Garrison Artillery. He was shot down with his observer, Lieutenant Harold Carver BARLOW, on 18 June 1917, the fifty-third victory of Manfred von Richthofen. The wreckage was badly damaged by fire when it came down near Pilckem in the Ypres Salient. Pilckem was in German hands at the time and both men were buried together by the Germans, though BARLOW's body was said to have been burnt beyond recognition. Subsequent fighting during the Third Battle of Ypres, which began barely six weeks later, was the reason why neither grave survived. They were probably obliterated by shell fire and disappeared in a sea of mud. BARLOW is also commemorated on the memorial.

Lieutenant Reginald William FOLLITT, 13 Squadron, Royal Flying Corps, rejoined the Honourable Artillery Company when war broke out, but then gained a commission in the Royal Field Artillery in the summer of 1915. He served with his battery in France until his transfer to the Royal Flying Corps. He and his observer, Second Lieutenant Frederick James Kirkham, took off from their base at Savy on the morning of 28 April 1917 to carry out sound ranging for the artillery. Like FOLLITT, Kirkham had also been commissioned in the Royal Field Artillery, so both men had a very good understanding of their work. They were attacked while flying over Biache-Saint-Vaast and came down somewhere east of Pelves. FOLLITT had been hit whilst in flight and was barely alive when he was pulled from the wreckage of his machine, though he was briefly conscious. Kirkham was injured, but not seriously, and survived the war in captivity. Both men were brought down by Manfred von Richthofen and were his forty-eighth victory. Their fate was conveyed by the dropping of a message over our lines. Kirkham was able to safeguard FOLLITT's wedding ring, returning it to his widow after the war.

Lieutenant Bertie Constantine Ruffell GRIMWOOD MC, 4 Squadron, Royal Flying Corps, was killed in action on 7 November 1917, aged 33. The day was one of low cloud and little flying. His pilot, Second Lieutenant Albert George GROSE, who is also commemorated here, died of wounds two days later on 9 November. GRIMWOOD's MC was gazetted posthumously on 9 January 1918 and was awarded for conspicuous gallantry and devotion to duty. The citation states that having located a strong force of enemy infantry preparing to make a counter-attack, his machine was struck by a shell, wounding him severely and destroying his wireless apparatus. His machine was said to have been so badly damaged that it could barely fly. However, in spite of his wounds, he wrote a message reporting the position of the enemy and dropped it on divisional headquarters, which was then able to direct nine batteries on to the target area. The citation rightly concludes that his pluck and devotion to duty were worthy of the highest praise.

Lieutenant Hallgrimur JONSSON MC, 12 Squadron, Royal Air Force, was killed in action on 3 September 1918. His MC was won for conspicuous gallantry in action while serving with the Canadian Infantry, showing great courage and skill in handling two working parties and setting a fine example to his men. The award was gazetted on 25 November 1916. JONSSON's pilot, Lieutenant Arthur William Macnamara DFC, was also killed, aged 19, and is buried in Morchies Military Cemetery.

Lieutenant Leonard Cameron KIDD MC, 3 Squadron, Royal Flying Corps, was killed in action on 12 October 1916, aged 23, while flying with Second Lieutenant Fenton Ellis Stanley PHILLIPS MC, who was aged 21. In his memoir, *Sagittarius Rising*, the author and fellow airman Cecil Lewis claims that KIDD and PHILLIPS were hit by one of our own shells. KIDD had gained his flying certificate at Hendon prior to the war, but was working in Ceylon when war was declared. He returned from tea-planting and immediately made use of his flying skills by joining the Royal Flying Corps. After a short stint of retraining in England he went to the front in February 1916.

He received news that he had been awarded the MC just a week before he was killed, though it was not gazetted until November that year. It was awarded for conspicuous skill and gallantry in connection with his contact patrol work. The citation refers to one occasion when he carried out three such patrols, each at an altitude of 1,000 feet, in order to gather valuable information under heavy fire. It also mentions that he had attacked enemy reinforcements with a machine gun from 500 feet.

Second Lieutenant PHILLIPS had previously served with the 3rd Devonshire Regiment and had spent some time in the trenches with the Artists' Rifles before joining the Royal Flying Corps. His MC was gazetted just after his death on 20 October and was also awarded for conspicuous gallantry and skill in carrying out contact patrols. The citation refers to an occasion when he flew at very low altitude, in spite of rifle and machine-gun fire, in order to obtain information for his report. His information enabled our artillery to be directed on to enemy troops preparing to carry out a counter-attack. Both men are now commemorated on this memorial.

Lieutenant Edward Llewelyn LEWIS, 24 Squadron, Royal Flying Corps, was killed when his machine, a DH2, came down over enemy lines on 26 December 1916 after an engagement with several enemy aircraft. He managed to bring down one of the enemy machines before he suffered the same fate. He was just 21 when he died and had previously served in the Essex Regiment. In July 1915 he went to Gallipoli, but was invalided home in the November. It was while convalescing that he learned to fly and in March 1916 he was seconded to the Royal Flying Corps. Three months later he was in France where he was wounded in a single-handed fight with several enemy aircraft. On that occasion he had shown great skill, landing his machine on the British side of the lines even though the controls were badly damaged. After two months recovering, he returned to the front, but was killed soon afterwards. By cruel irony, he was gazetted as a lieutenant the day after his death.

Lieutenant John Percy McCONE, 41 Squadron, Royal Flying Corps, was a Canadian who had initially served as a cyclist with the Canadian Engineers. He transferred to the Royal Flying Corps in 1917, becoming a pilot by the end of the year. His SE5a aircraft was brought down behind German lines on 24 March 1918, crashing somewhere near Combles on the Somme. It had been irretrievably damaged and had lost both wings. It fell to earth giving McCONE no chance of survival and his body was never recovered. He was shot down by Manfred von Richthofen and was his sixty-seventh victory.

Lieutenant Ian Cameron MACDONNELL, 9 Squadron, Royal Flying Corps, was a Canadian who had previously served in his father's old regiment, Lord Strathcona's Horse, although he later elected to join the Royal Flying Corps. He was killed on 2 July 1916 with his observer, Second Lieutenant Hugh Albert WLLIAMSON, who had been mentioned in despatches and who is also commemorated on the memorial.

MACDONNELL's father, Lieutenant General Sir Archibald Cameron Macdonnell KCB CMG DSO, began his long and distinguished career in 1886 with the Canadian Militia. He then served briefly as a regular before transferring to the North-West Mounted Police in 1889. In 1900 he again volunteered for service, this time in the South African War with the 2nd Battalion Canadian Mounted Rifles, where he gained successive promotions to captain and then major. On the night of 5/6 May 1900, following the Battle of Vet River, he commanded a composite squadron that blew up a culvert behind the Boer lines and cut telegraph wires. He was then seriously wounded at Diamond Hill on 12 June that year and was invalided home to Canada. His DSO was awarded for distinguished service during the campaign.

He recovered sufficiently to resume his career with the North-West Mounted Police and in March 1907 he again joined his old unit, the Canadian Mounted Rifles, which in 1909 became Lord Strathcona's Horse, and which he commanded until 22 December 1915. He came to England with the First Canadian Contingent in October 1914 and was present at the Battle of Festubert. Between 23 December 1915 and 8 June 1917 he commanded 7 Brigade, Canadian Infantry. On 17 February 1917 he was wounded by a bullet, breaking his upper left arm, followed by a second bullet to the top of the shoulder, which suggests he may have been shot by a sniper.

On 9 June 1917 he was promoted to major general and was awarded the CMG. His KCB came after the war in 1919, as did a *Croix de Guerre* in July that year. He had already been awarded the *Légion d'Honneur* (France) in November 1918. In total he was mentioned in despatches seven times.

The family pedigree was indeed exceptional. Lieutenant MACDONNELL's great grandfather, the Honourable Alexander Macdonnell, had fought in the Revolutionary War of 1776–1783 and had also served as Assistant Paymaster-General in the war of 1812–1814. He was also related via his grandmother, Ellen Brodhead, to one of George Washington's generals, Daniel Brodhead, and also to Colonel Thornton Brodhead, who was mortally wounded at the Second Battle of Bull Run in the American Civil War.

Lieutenant Donald Argyle Douglas Ian MACGREGOR, 41 Squadron, Royal Flying Corps, became Manfred von Richthofen's sixty-third victory when he was shot down between Bapaume and Cambrai on 30 November 1917. This was his last victory of the year. The SE5 aircraft fell in flames and MACGREGOR's body was never recovered. He had immediately volunteered to serve when war broke out and was commissioned in the Army Service Corps in October 1914. He served with motor ambulances in France, but then secured a transfer to the Royal Flying Corps, firstly as an observer, then as a pilot. He also spent some time as a test pilot and turned down the opportunity to serve as an instructor, preferring instead to serve at the front where he was subsequently killed.

Lieutenant James Matthew MACKIE DCM, 25 Squadron, Royal Air Force, was killed in action on 16 July 1918, aged 25. His DCM was won as a sergeant in the infantry and was awarded for conspicuous gallantry after he crawled 200 yards across no man's land in broad daylight to within twenty yards of the enemy parapet in order to carry out a reconnaissance. Later, he entered the German trench with a raiding party, killing three of the enemy with his revolver and wounding others with bombs. Although badly wounded, he helped other wounded men out of the trench. The award was gazetted on 22 September 1916. Canadian army records show his date of death as 16 June, rather than July.

MACKIE's pilot, Captain Eric Waterlow MC DFC, was also killed with him. He had been mentioned in despatches. Captain Waterlow is buried in Ypres Reservoir Cemetery. Their aircraft was a DH4.

Lieutenant Bernard Sanderson MARSHALL MC, 20 Squadron, Royal Flying Corps, was killed in action on 7 June 1917, aged 22. His MC was gazetted on 24 June, a few weeks after his death, the citation appearing on 27 July. It was awarded for gallant conduct and devotion to duty with the 6th South Wales Borderers when consolidating a crater. Though badly hit in the arm, he carried on until exhausted. After having his wound dressed, he returned to carry on overseeing the work of his men. He was initially commissioned from the OTC in January 1915.

Lieutenant Walter Douglas MILLER, 15 Squadron, Royal Flying Corps, was the son of a clergyman and between 1910 and 1914 went to Glasgow University to study Engineering. However, for some reason, he left before graduating. Like many of his generation, he was a keen sportsman and had played rugby for his university in the 1st XV. He was 22 years old when the war broke out and he was quick to enlist with the unit he had been with while serving in the OTC, the 120th Clyde Battery, Royal Garrison Artillery. Soon after gaining his commission, he transferred to the Royal Flying Corps, going to France in August 1916. He was shot down and killed about four miles behind German lines on 2 October that year and, although his observer, Second Lieutenant Carmichael, survived the crash, he was badly wounded. According to Carmichael, they were just turning when they were hit by a burst of fire from an enemy aircraft. On impact with the ground their BE2c caught fire. MILLER's younger brother, Lieutenant Iain Maclellan Miller, was killed in action on 25 September 1915 with the 2nd Argyll

& Sutherland Highlanders. He is buried at Cambrin Churchyard Extension, near La Bassée.

Lieutenant Alan Wilson MOREY MC, 60 Squadron, Royal Flying Corps, was killed in a mid-air collision with an enemy aircraft on 24 January 1918. He had previously served with the 11th Royal Scots, and it was with that unit on 25 September 1915, the opening day of the Battle of Loos, that he won his MC. He did so by volunteering to go across the open ground between the opposing lines to obtain information. Although wounded in the shoulder, he sent back a written report, but then made the long journey on foot in order to make a report in person to his brigade commander before having his wounds dressed. The award was gazetted on 4 November 1915.

Lieutenant James David MOSES, 57 Squadron, Royal Air Force, was a Canadian Native American from the Six Nations Reserve who had served in the infantry before joining the Royal Flying Corps. His death on 1 April 1918, aged 28, gives him the distinction of being one of the first, if not the first Royal Air Force casualty, as the Royal Flying Corps and the Royal Naval Air Service were amalgamated that very day to create the Royal Air Force. He was the observer and he was killed along with his pilot, Lieutenant Douglas Price TROLLIP, when they were shot down near Grévillers.

Lieutenant Osborne John ORR DFC, 204 Squadron, Royal Air Force, was killed in action on 23 October 1918, aged 23, when his machine was shot down. This American-born flyer had scored five victories before his death, which occurred over Termonde, in Belgium. His award was gazetted on 1 January 1919 in the New Year's Honours List. *The Distinguished Flying Cross and How It Was Won 1918–1995* includes no citation for the award.

Lieutenant Leslie PLAYNE, 16 Squadron, Royal Flying Corps, was killed on 27 March 1915, aged 23 and, according to the note in the CWGC register, he went to France with the 1st Canadian Division. If we are to accept that fact at face value, his time with the Royal Flying Corps was extremely brief, as the 1st Canadian Division only began sailing from England to France in February 1915. It is perhaps more likely that the note refers to his leaving Canada for England in the autumn of 1914. However, *Airmen Died in the Great War* offers greater clarity as to his true date of death, which was 27 March 1918, not 1915. It confirms that he had previously served with the 1st Battalion, Canadian Infantry, then with the 27th Battalion. His observer, Second Lieutenant Henry CARBINES, was killed with him in their RE8 aircraft.

Lieutenant Patrick John Gordon POWELL, 13 Squadron, Royal Flying Corps, and Air Mechanic 1st Class, Percy BONNER, were both killed in action on 2 April 1917 while on a photographic operation near Vimy Ridge. Their death marked the thirty-second victory for Manfred von Richthofen. They had tried to evade him by flying low as they attempted to get back behind their own lines, but were forced to land on the edge of the village of Farbus, just east of the main ridge, where their machine hit a house and broke up. POWELL had originally joined one of the University and Public Schools Battalions, Royal Fusiliers, and then went on to Sandhurst, receiving his commission in the Army Service Corps in March 1915. He then trained back in England and transferred to the Royal Flying Corps, where he became proficient at aerial photography. BONNER was a keen mechanic in civilian life and had joined the Royal Flying Corps almost immediately when war broke out. Both men were buried by the Germans, but their graves were later lost.

Lieutenant Arthur Percival Foley RHYS-DAVIDS DSO MC and Bar, 56 Squadron, Royal Flying Corps, was killed in action on 27 October 1917, although initially he was only reported as missing in action. A former head boy at Eton, he was involved in the same encounter as Albert Ball on the day of his fatal crash. Despite his youth, RHYS-DAVIDS was a very capable flyer and was responsible for shooting down the German ace, Werner Voss, later stating that he only wished he could have brought him down alive. He was also a good athlete, a classical scholar, and had joined the Royal Flying Corps virtually from Eton. A protégé of James McCudden VC DSO and Bar, MC and Bar MM, many saw him as a natural successor to Albert Ball VC DSO and two Bars MC, and he quickly gained a reputation as a fearless flyer who would take on any odds. McCudden, in fact, once said that RHYS-DAVIDS would have chased the Huns over to the Russian front if left to his own devices. It was while James McCudden was on leave that RHYS-DAVIDS temporarily took over the flight, shortly before he too was due for a period of home leave. Four days after taking over, RHYS-DAVIDS was reported missing while out on patrol, but two months later the Germans dropped a message stating that he had been killed. In a little over six months he had scored a magnificent twenty-five victories.

Lieutenant Geoffrey Charles Taylor SALTER MC, 20 Squadron, Royal Air Force, was killed in action on 28 May 1918. He was originally commissioned in the 3rd East Yorkshire Regiment (Special Reserve) in May 1915. His MC, which appeared in the *Edinburgh Gazette* on 27 June 1917, was awarded to him whilst nominally still serving with the East Yorkshire Regiment, though attached to the Machine Gun Corps. It is also clear from the citation that he was working with tanks. It states that he had handled his tank with great skill and gallantry and, although under heavy fire, he had cleared an enemy trench before handing it over to the infantry.

Lieutenant Herbert Whiteley SELLARS MC, 11 Squadron, Royal Air Force, received his commission with the Royal Flying Corps in June 1916 and joined 25 Squadron in August that year. On 16 September he was severely injured after his machine crashed, but he returned to the same squadron in July 1917 once he had recovered. After three months he was posted to 11 Squadron and went on to score six victories in March the following year, adding a further victory the following month for which he was awarded the MC.

His usual companion was Lieutenant Charles Crichton Robson, a skilful gunner credited with bringing down the sixteen-victory German ace, Leutnant Ludwig Hanstein; SELLARS was flying with Robson on 15 May 1918 when their aircraft was brought down. SELLARS was killed, but Robson was taken prisoner. The citation for the MC, gazetted on 22 June 1918, records that while on offensive patrol SELLARS attacked a hostile two-seater, which dived vertically and then crashed. Having attacked another two-seater, which was driven back behind enemy lines, he then engaged three hostile scouts, skilfully manoeuvring and enabling his observer to fire two bursts at one of them from a range of seventy-five yards causing it to crash in flames.

Lieutenant Frank Aubrey SHAW MC, 98 Squadron, Royal Air Force, was killed in action on 16 July 1918, aged 18. His MC was won as an infantry officer and awarded for his conspicuous gallantry in action leading a raiding party with great courage and initiative, killing several of the enemy. The award was gazetted on 14 November 1916. His pilot, Captain Edward Basil Gowan MORTON, who was also killed when their DH9 aircraft came down, is commemorated with him on the memorial.

Lieutenant Edward Treloar SMART, 2 Squadron, Royal Flying Corps, was commissioned in the Royal Garrison Artillery (Special Reserve) and served at home with an anti-aircraft battery until he moved to the Royal Flying Corps in spring 1917, just before the Battle of Arras. After training, he transferred to his squadron in France, arriving in August 1917. He and his observer, Lieutenant Kenneth Purnell BARFORD, were brought down in flames on 27 March 1918, a few miles south of the River Somme, east of Amiens, in the midst of the German Offensive. They were Manfred von Richthofen's seventy-second victory.

Lieutenant Donald Graham SMITH, 42 Squadron, Royal Air Force, formerly 4th Middlesex Regiment and Royal Army Medical Corps, was killed in action on 10 April 1918, aged 23. He enlisted in August 1914 and had served in Egypt, Salonika and Italy. His pilot, Second Lieutenant Arthur Reginald HOLT-HOUSE, was killed with him and is also commemorated on the memorial.

Lieutenant Wilfred Henry 'Harry' SNEATH, 208 Squadron, Royal Air Force, was born in Hendon, London, and had joined the Royal Naval Air Service as a sub lieutenant in late 1917, whereupon he was posted to 8 Squadron, Royal Naval Air Service, re-designated as 208 Squadron after 1 April 1918. He was shot down in flames on 6 April over Lens after scoring five victories.

Lieutenant Victor Arthur STRAUSS was the elder son of Arthur Strauss, MP for North Paddington between 1910 and 1918. He was educated at Rugby School and spent time in France and Germany learning both languages before joining his father's business. In January 1915 he joined the Inns of Court OTC and received a commission in the Army Service Corps in May of that year before proceeding to France in the October. In June 1916 he was attached to the Royal Flying Corps as an observer and served with 9 Squadron until he and his pilot, Lieutenant James Talmage HANNING, were reported missing on 27 November the same year while flying a reconnaissance mission over the Somme.

HANNING had paid his own passage to England in order to join the Royal Flying Corps, having declined a commission in the Canadian Engineers back home in Canada. HANNING is also commemorated on the memorial. There was, and still is, no explanation of their fate, but flying conditions on the day they went missing had been generally poor owing to fog, which prevailed for the next four days. It is believed that their aircraft may have been shot down by ground fire, since conditions would have forced them to fly at low altitude.

Lieutenant Edgar TAYLOR, 79 Squadron, Royal Air Force, was an American from Long Island who joined the squadron on 24 April 1918. All of his five victories came between 4 and 24 August that year, four of which were credited for bringing down enemy balloons. His aircraft failed to return after claiming his fourth balloon on 24 August. It is believed that anti-aircraft fire was the most likely cause of death. A book of letters written by TAYLOR was published in 1976, together with his flying log and diary.

Lieutenant Merrill Samuel TAYLOR, 209 Squadron, Royal Air Force, was yet another Canadian pilot. He was educated at Toronto University where he was a keen rugby player. He joined the Royal Naval Air Service in February 1917, receiving his commission in July that year as a flight sub lieutenant, before being posted to 9 Squadron towards the end of the year. He flew with that unit until July 1918, during which time he accounted for the sixteen-victory German ace, Hans Weiss, eventually bringing his own total to seven victories by the time of his last flight on 7 July. He was killed in aerial combat by another German ace, Franz Büchner, who went on to score a total of forty victories, TAYLOR being his eighth. TAYLOR was awarded the *Croix de Guerre* (France).

Lieutenant Harold TOULMIN MC, 46 Squadron, Royal Air Force, formerly 6th Loyal North Lancashire Regiment, was killed in action on 17 September 1918, aged 21. He had also served in Gallipoli and Mesopotamia. In Mesopotamia he lost a leg, although this did not prevent him from transferring on recovery to the Royal Flying Corps. His MC was awarded in the King's Birthday Honours List on 3 June 1916.

Lieutenant Douglas Price TROLLIP, 57 Squadron, Royal Air Force, was killed in action, aged 23, on 1 April 1918, the day on which the Royal Air Force came into being. He was flying a DH4 aircraft that day with his observer, Lieutenant James David MOSES, who is also commemorated on the memorial. It is believed that they were shot down by Leutnant Hans Joachim Wolff of *Jasta* 11, whose first victim had been Second Lieutenant John Anthony McCudden, the younger brother of ace James McCudden. TROLLIP's brother, Trooper Noel Roland

Price Trollip, also died in the war on 18 January 1915, aged 21, serving with the 8th Mounted Rifles (Midlandse Ruiters). He is buried in Bedford Cemetery in the Eastern Cape, South Africa.

Lieutenant John Seymour TURNBULL, 41 Squadron, Royal Air Force, had previously served with the Worcestershire Regiment before joining 56 Squadron, Royal Flying Corps, in May 1917. He was shot down and wounded after his first two victories, recorded in May and July that year, and it was in April 1918, after recovering, that he went to 41 Squadron, Royal Air Force. On 17 June he was shot down and killed, but not before he had added a further three scores to his tally.

Lieutenant Kenneth Mackenzie WALKER, 209 Squadron, Royal Air Force, was another flyer with five victories, all of which occurred during the summer of 1918. He was brought down near Péronne on 12 August, the same day that his captain, John Kenneth Summers, was also shot down, although he survived as a prisoner of war. Captain Summers, who was Lothar von Richthofen's fortieth and final victory, was entertained by the German ace before being handed over formally as a prisoner of war, a custom which was not uncommon.

Lieutenant Eric Seth WARD, 32 Squadron, Royal Flying Corps, who had formerly served with the Oxfordshire & Buckinghamshire Light Infantry, was killed in action on 10 August 1917, aged 19, flying a DH5 aircraft. His father, Captain Melville Seth Ward, also served in the Royal Flying Corps.

Second Lieutenant Morton ALLPORT, 70 Squadron, Royal Flying Corps, was the elder son of a Tasmanian barrister-at-law and had originally joined his father in the legal profession. Before the war he was also a keen athlete and a good golfer. He came to England in November 1915 and in the spring of 1916 he became a pilot, going to France on 16 September. He was shot down in a Sopwith Pup with his observer, Lieutenant Trevor Moutray Bennet MC, on 10 November 1916 when his patrol engaged five enemy scouts above the village of Ytres. Bennet, who was just 19, is buried at Hermies Hill British Cemetery. He had joined the Ulster Volunteer Force in 1913 and had fought with the 10th Royal Irish Rifles on the opening day of the Battle of the Somme. It was there that he won his MC after his platoon suffered heavy casualties. He rallied the remainder and led them forward into the enemy trenches. Later, he led another attack and took his objective, consolidated it, and then held it against repeated bombing attacks. The award was gazetted on 20 October 1916.

Second Lieutenant George Andrew BENTHAM, 18 Squadron, Royal Flying Corps, was killed in action on 3 November 1916. On the outbreak of war he joined the 10th Royal Fusiliers and was later commissioned in the Queen's Own (Royal West Kent Regiment). He also served with the 7th East Surrey Regiment, then the Royal Flying Corps, which he joined as an observer. Manfred von Richthofen claimed him as his seventh victory. He was attacked while on patrol above the Somme, while also under enemy shell fire. His machine, therefore, may also have been hit and damaged by shell fire, which is the account given in *Royal Flying Corps, Casualties and Honours during the War, 1914–1917*. In any case, it was seen to come down out of control. His pilot that day, Sergeant Cuthbert Godfrey BALDWIN, died with him when the aircraft crashed behind enemy lines. Both men were initially reported as missing in action. The grave of neither man has been found and both are now commemorated on the memorial.

Second Lieutenant Patrick Anthony Langan BYRNE DSO, 24 Squadron, Royal Flying Corps, was killed in action on 17 October 1916, aged 21. His DSO was gazetted posthumously on 14 November 1916 and was awarded for conspicuous skill and gallantry, attacking hostile machines with great pluck, often against great odds. It goes on to add that he had accounted for several of these and that on one occasion with two other machines, he had attacked seventeen enemy aircraft, shooting one down in flames and forcing another to land. The CWGC register states that he had been mentioned in despatches.

Second Lieutenant Eugene CRUESS-CALLAGHAN, 19 Squadron, Royal Flying Corps, was recorded as missing in action on 26 August 1916, along with four others from his squadron, and was later presumed to have been killed. CRUESS-CALLAGHAN was just 18 years old when he died. On the date of his presumed death, 19 Squadron had been on a bombing raid over Havrincourt Wood. The weather had not been favourable for flying until later in the day. By evening it had cleared sufficiently for the squadron to depart, but after delivering some bombs onto the target, it ran into a storm and five of the flight failed to return. One of those, Second Lieutenant Reginald Fitzroy TALBOT, is also commemorated on the memorial. Another, Lieutenant Henry Maurice Corbold, is buried in Roisel Communal Cemetery Extension, while Lieutenant S.P. Briggs and Second Lieutenant A.W. Reynell were taken prisoner.

Two other members of the family lost their lives while flying during the war. Eugene's brother, Captain Stanislaus Cruess-Callaghan, was killed on 28 June 1917, aged 20, while flying a Curtiss JN4 training aircraft in Canada. He is buried at Barrie (St Mary's) Roman Catholic Cemetery in Canada. He was flying with a cadet who was uninjured in the tragic accident. A third brother, Major Joseph Cruess-Callaghan MC, 87 Squadron, Royal Air Force, formerly 7th Royal Munster Fusiliers, was killed in action on 2 July 1918, aged 25, and is buried at Contay British Cemetery. He had won his MC for his marked skill in carrying out bombing raids at night, and on one occasion destroying an enemy searchlight.

Second Lieutenant Donald CAMERON, 3 Squadron, Royal Flying Corps, became Manfred von Richthofen's sixty-eighth victory when his Camel aircraft was shot down above the village of Contalmaison on 25 March 1918. He was gazetted in the Royal Flying Corps in August 1917 and was flying by early 1918. He went to France in February that year and was killed soon afterwards, aged 18. He took off from the airfield at Vert Galant, a farm that still exists next to a flat field that was the aerodrome. CAMERON and his colleagues were on a mission to bomb German transport lines and troop columns as they advanced during the German March Offensive. It is not surprising that his body was never recovered; his aircraft came down carrying a full load of bombs and exploded on impact with the ground.

Second Lieutenant Leonard Heath CANTLE, 43 Squadron, Royal Flying Corps, was killed in action while on patrol near Farbus, just east of Vimy. His pilot, Second Lieutenant John Seymour Heagerty, survived the crash on 8 April 1917 when their machine came down, marking the thirty-eighth victory for Manfred von Richthofen. It appears that a burst of fire had damaged their engine and controls. Heagerty did extraordinarily well even to have landed it, sustaining only cuts and bruises, but CANTLE was killed. Heagerty was made a prisoner-of-war and was eventually repatriated after the Armistice.

CANTLE was educated at Charterhouse and Trinity Hall, Cambridge, before joining the 2/1st Surrey Yeomanry at the end of 1914. He was then posted to the 11th Queen's (Royal West Surrey Regiment) and served in the trenches south of Ypres. He subsequently joined the Royal Flying Corps in February 1917. Heagerty briefly served at Gallipoli, although by the time he arrived there in November 1915 from the 3rd East Kent Regiment (The Buffs), the campaign was closing down and his battalion was then posted to Egypt. He and CANTLE were posted to 43 Squadron at the same time, in March 1917, and had only been with their unit for a couple of weeks before their flying careers ended.

Second Lieutenant William Martin Vernon COTTON, 7 Squadron, Royal Flying Corps, was reported missing on 21 December 1916, along with Second Lieutenant D.W. Davis, after their machine failed to return from assisting 72nd Siege Battery, which succeeded that day in registering four direct hits on an enemy position, damaging one of the gun pits. COTTON had carried out similar work for the 94th Siege Battery on 10 October when all four gun pits of an enemy battery were hit. All in all, 10 October was a successful day for co-operation between the artillery and the Royal Flying Corps, resulting in the destruction of nine gun pits. Seventeen more were damaged, six ammunition dumps were blown up and several enemy batteries were silenced. Davis survived as a prisoner of war.

Second Lieutenant George Robin CUTTLE MC, 49 Squadron, Royal Air Force, was killed in action on 9 May 1918, aged 22, and had previously served with the Royal Field Artillery. He won his MC while serving as a forward observation officer when he went to the relief of a wounded officer under intense fire. The citation continues that, from time to time during that posting, he was able to send back information by means of a signal lamp and remained on duty for around twenty hours. The award was gazetted on 12 January 1917. His pilot, Lieutenant George Arthur LECKIE, was also killed and is commemorated on the memorial.

The 20th December 1916 proved a difficult day for 18 Squadron, Royal Flying Corps, when six of its members were reported missing, including Second Lieutenant Lionel George D'ARCY and his observer, Second Lieutenant Reginald Cuthbert WHITESIDE, both of whom are commemorated on this memorial. The others were Lieutenant Reginald Smith, who is buried at Achiet-le-Petit Communal Cemetery Extension, and Lieutenant Harold Fiske, who is commemorated within the same cemetery on the Beugny German Cemetery, Memorial 11. The other two, Lieutenant C.H. Windrum and Lieutenant J.A. Hollis, were taken prisoner after their machine had crashed.

D'ARCY and WHITESIDE were Manfred von Richthofen's fourteenth victory. D'ARCY was commissioned in the Connaught Rangers; his father was Deputy Lord Lieutenant of County Galway. He went to France in June 1916 with the 6th Connaught Rangers and took part in a successful raid on German positions at Hulluch on the night of 26/27 June, just a few weeks after his arrival in France. He led one of two parties tasked with consolidating the newly-won position after two craters had been blown in the German lines. However, when he went on to train as a pilot, he did so at his own expense and then joined the Royal Flying Corps, which was quite an unusual route to take by that stage of the war. On 20 December, the day of his death, records show that D'ARCY was duty officer for his squadron and therefore he had actually chosen to fly, even though there was no requirement for him to do so.

WHITESIDE, an Ulsterman by birth, had been working for the Hong Kong and Shanghai Bank before the war. After the outbreak of war, he gained a commission in the Royal Naval Volunteer Reserve, joining Nelson Battalion, which was part of the Royal Naval Division. He transferred to the Royal Flying Corps just two months before his death.

Second Lieutenant Allan McNab DENOVAN, 1 Squadron, Royal Flying Corps, was shot down on 26 March 1918, crashing in a copse south of the ruined village of Contalmaison. He had joined the militia in Canada, but then transferred to the Canadian infantry early in 1916. He remained in Canada until he joined the Royal Flying Corps in November that year. After receiving his commission and completing his training, he went to France in May 1917 where he served with 3 Squadron. He was subsequently wounded in the hand while flying, but after recovering, he returned to the front in February 1918, this time posted to 1 Squadron. His machine was seen to fall apart before it hit the ground and was clearly out of control, suggesting that he may have been badly wounded, or even killed outright, before it fell and crashed.

Second Lieutenant Hubert George DOWNING MC, 29 Squadron, Royal Flying Corps, was killed in action on 6 November 1917. His MC was gazetted on 18 June 1917 and awarded for consistent skill and gallantry as an observer. On one occasion when on patrol, by holding his fire until his opponents were within very short range, and by skilful co-operation with his pilot, he successfully shot down two hostile machines. DOWNING's brother, Serjeant Richard Leslie

Downing, died of wounds on 11 May 1917 while serving with 'D' Battery, 63 Brigade, Royal Field Artillery. He is buried at Duisans British Cemetery, Étrun.

Second Lieutenant Wallace Sinclair EARLE, 9 Squadron, Royal Flying Corps, was killed on 16 April 1916 when his machine was brought down in aerial combat behind German lines, near Maricourt on the Somme, whilst engaged on a reconnaissance for the artillery. His partner and observer that day, Second Lieutenant C.W.P. Selby, was wounded and taken prisoner. Before the war, EARLE attended Queen's University in Canada and had embarked on a career as a land surveyor, working from Vancouver until the outbreak of war. After a short spell with a Canadian engineer unit, he transferred to the Royal Flying Corps in October 1915, gaining his 'wings' in December that year.

Second Lieutenant Henry Cope EVANS DSO, 24 Squadron, Royal Flying Corps, was killed in action on 3 September 1916. A former pupil at Haileybury College, he had originally served with the Alberta Dragoons in 1914 before gaining a commission in 1915. Prior to that, he had previous military service having served in the South African War. During his time on the Western Front between February and September 1915 he was gassed. It was after this that he transferred to the Royal Flying Corps, initially as an observer. The following year he became a pilot and during the summer of 1916 he scored a total of five victories. His DSO, gazetted on 22 September 1916, was awarded for conspicuous gallantry and skill on many occasions in attacking hostile aircraft, frequently against large odds. In one fortnight he brought down four enemy machines, returning on one occasion with his own machine badly damaged.

Second Lieutenant William Cecil FENWICK, 21 Squadron, Royal Flying Corps, became Manfred von Richthofen's fourth victory when he was shot in the head and killed on 7 October 1916 during an encounter that began over Rancourt, a small village between Bapaume and Péronne. From there, Richthofen had doggedly pursued him, eventually firing the fatal shot that brought him crashing down near Ytres, a village well behind German lines. His body was recovered and buried there, but unfortunately his grave was lost, probably destroyed during subsequent fighting.

Second Lieutenant Julien Percy FERREIRA, 57 Squadron, Royal Air Force, was shot down in aerial combat over Marcoing on 16 September 1918, aged 18. His parents lived in South Africa. He had volunteered while still at school in April 1917 and soon left to take up training in England. He began operational flying in May 1918. His observer, Second Lieutenant Leslie Bernard SIMMONDS, was killed with him, aged 21, and is commemorated on the memorial.

Second Lieutenant Godfrey Benjamin Joseph FIRBANK, 23 Squadron, Royal Flying Corps, is shown as having died on 11 September 1916 after being shot down in aerial combat. News of his death, and that of Second Lieutenant Leslie

Godfrey Harcourt VERNON, who was flying with him that day, was received via the American Embassy in Berlin. Their aeroplane was reported as wrecked, killing both men outright. FIRBANK had attended Clifton College and had then gone out to South Africa to farm. When the war broke out he joined the Eastern Rifles and served during the Rebellion in South-West Africa. After that campaign he returned home and was gazetted in the Welsh Regiment, eventually transferring to the Royal Flying Corps. VERNON had also served with a Welsh regiment before joining the Royal Flying Corps, but in his case it was the Royal Welsh Fusiliers.

Second Lieutenant George Mortlock GOODE, 43 Squadron, Royal Flying Corps, and his observer, Second Lieutenant John GAGNE, were both killed in action on 24 May 1917 while carrying out a long-range photographic reconnaissance.

Second Lieutenant Thomas Sydney Curzon HOWE MC, 54 Squadron, Royal Air Force, died on 18 April 1918. He was gazetted on 6 September 1915 as a temporary second lieutenant in the Connaught Rangers, but later transferred to the Royal Flying Corps. On 18 April he failed to return from a sortie and was presumed to have been killed. I have been unable to locate any trace of his MC in any of the gazettes.

Second Lieutenant Ernest David JONES, 52 Squadron, Royal Air Force, and his observer, Second Lieutenant Robert Francis NEWTON, were killed in aerial combat above Moreuil Wood on 2 April 1918 when they were attacked by Manfred von Richthofen shortly after taking off from their base at Abbeville. JONES and NEWTON had little time to react and their aircraft caught fire while in the air. Richthofen described how both men had tried to lean out of their machine as the flames took hold and how NEWTON had gallantly kept on firing at him at very close range. When their aircraft hit the ground it exploded and carried on burning fiercely. Neither body was recovered. JONES, who had only arrived in France at the end of February 1918, had little operational or combat experience. He and NEWTON became the seventy-fifth victory for Richthofen.

Second Lieutenant Stanley Walter MANN, 9 Squadron, Royal Flying Corps, went to the front in June 1916 after gaining his commission in March that year. He was killed in action, aged 21, after going out on a mission to photograph German trench positions with Second Lieutenant Arthur Ernest WYNN. The day on which they were posted missing in action was a stormy one. Their machine was attacked by four enemy machines, and it may be that they accounted for one of them, as only three were seen behind their machine when it went down. Second Lieutenant WYNN, who was 20 years old, is known to have died in a German hospital as a prisoner of war. He would have been buried, but evidently, and for whatever reason, his grave was lost. Both are commemorated on the memorial. The date of death for both men is shown as 1 November 1916.

Second Lieutenant Maurice Edward MEALING MC, 56 Squadron, Royal Flying Corps, had previously served with the King's (Shropshire Light Infantry). He was commissioned in May 1916 and posted to 15 Squadron as an observer in August that year, remaining so until May 1917. After that, he trained as a pilot and was then posted to 56 Squadron. It was in March 1918 that he suddenly began to increase his score, gaining ten of his fourteen victories that month, a feat for which he was posthumously awarded his MC. He was last seen on 24 March chasing a pair of two-seater aircraft, though there remains some uncertainty as to whether he was shot down from the air or by ground fire. His MC was gazetted on 13 May 1918 and was awarded for his keenness, courage and determination, as well as for conspicuous gallantry and devotion to duty. The citation adds that he had destroyed three enemy machines and had driven a further three out of control, added to which he had also driven down an enemy balloon in flames.

Second Lieutenant John Ingram Mullaniffe O'BEIRNE, 25 Squadron, Royal Flying Corps, died of wounds when he and his pilot, Second Lieutenant Donald Peter McDonald, were shot down over Vimy Ridge on 3 April 1917 by Manfred von Richthofen. They were on a photographic sortie and McDonald was fortunately taken prisoner and survived the war. He had served earlier in the war against the Germans in South West Africa before returning to Britain and joining the Lovat Scouts, attached to the Cameron Highlanders. He transferred to the Royal Flying Corps in 1917.

O'BEIRNE gained his commission in his father's old regiment, the Royal Warwickshire Regiment, at the outbreak of war in 1914. He arrived in Belgium in November 1914 and joined the 2nd Battalion, which was then at Ypres. However, he was soon invalided home with poisoning, believed from a contaminated water source. In 1916 he transferred to the Royal Flying Corps and began his flying career as an observer. He again fell sick and was posted home where he spent the second part of 1916 recovering, returning only at the end of the year. He was 24 when he died. His brother, Arthur James Lewis O'Beirne, was also killed in action in late July 1917 while serving as a lieutenant with 57 Squadron, Royal Flying Corps. He is buried at Coxyde Military Cemetery in Belgium.

Second Lieutenant Arthur John PEARSON MC, 29 Squadron, Royal Flying Corps, was killed in action on 9 March 1917 and had previously served with the Royal Fusiliers. After receiving his commission he joined the 8th Northamptonshire Regiment. He was subsequently posted to the Machine Gun Corps and was awarded the MC on the Somme in 1916 for conspicuous gallantry in action. When held up by wire during an advance, and in the face of heavy fire, he managed to get himself into a shell hole where he held on for several hours with his gun. He later brought it back, along with his batman who had been wounded. When he was shot down on 9 March 1917, he became Manfred von Richthofen's twenty-fifth victory. The aircraft came down somewhere between Roclincourt and Bailleul-Sir-Berthoult, and both pilot and machine were badly burnt.

Second Lieutenant James Lewis PULLYEN, 11 Squadron, Royal Flying Corps, was one of four from that squadron reported missing on 17 October 1916. He was only 19 years old when he died. The other three were: Second Lieutenant C.L. Roberts, Lieutenant William Powell Bowman, and Second Lieutenant George Clayton. These last two are buried in HAC Cemetery, Écoust Saint-Mein. Roberts was taken prisoner.

Second Lieutenant Vernon Jack READING and Second Lieutenant Matthew LEGGAT, 15 Squadron, Royal Flying Corps, were intercepted and shot down soon after taking off from their new base at Fienvillers. They were the seventieth victory for Manfred von Richthofen; their aircraft came down in flames just outside Albert on the afternoon of 26 March 1918. READING had only begun flying operationally with his squadron in early February 1918 and was not an experienced pilot, though he had shown plenty of promise during training. His observer, LEGGAT, had joined the Royal Engineers in October 1915 and had then gone to France the following February. It was only in spring 1917 that he returned home to train as an officer, after which he was gazetted a second lieutenant in the 5th Lancashire Fusiliers. In reality, he spent very little time with his battalion before transferring to the Royal Flying Corps. He eventually returned to France at the end of January 1918 and remained operational with his squadron until his death.

Second Lieutenant William Spencer Fitzrobert SAUNDBY, 29 Squadron, Royal Flying Corps, had formerly served with the Yorkshire Regiment. He and Captain Sidney Edward Cowan MC and two Bars, were both reported missing on 17 November 1916. Cowan is buried at Cagnicourt British Cemetery and an account of their final action is covered in the chapter covering that cemetery. However, Cowan's brother and fellow flyer, Captain Philip Chalmers COWAN, is commemorated on this memorial.

Second Lieutenant Maurice SHARPE, 21 Squadron, Royal Flying Corps, was the youngest son of Sir Alfred Sharpe KCMG CB, a British colonial administrator. Maurice was a pupil at Haileybury College near Hertford before taking up a career in engineering, working in Preston before the war, near to the family home. During that time he also served as a lieutenant in the Territorial Army (Royal Horse Artillery) and spent a year in America and Canada before going to Nigeria as an engineer for the British Cotton Growing Association. On the outbreak of war he was attached to the Nigerian Regiment, serving with it throughout the campaign in the Cameroons. At its conclusion, he joined the Royal Flying Corps and went to France on 6 September 1916. He was killed in action on 28 October 1916 while out on a patrol with four other machines. His aircraft was shot down over enemy lines and destroyed by fire. His partner and wireless operator that day was Air Mechanic Charles Frederick Heatley. He died from his injuries the following day, aged 19, and is buried in Euston Road Cemetery, but is shown as serving with 5 Squadron rather than 21 Squadron.

Second Lieutenant Alfred Seymour SHEPHERD DSO MC, 29 Squadron, Royal Flying Corps, was born in New South Wales, Australia. He enlisted in September 1915, initially serving with the 30th, then the 46th Battalion, Australian Infantry. In October the following year he transferred to the Royal Flying Corps. He went on to score ten victories, many of them in the skies above Arras, Lens and Douai. He was killed in action on 20 July 1917. His MC was gazetted on 16 August 1917 and was awarded for conspicuous gallantry and devotion to duty whilst attacking an enemy balloon. As he did so, he came under heavy fire from a rocket battery, which he then attacked at low altitude, silencing it and causing those operating the battery to abandon it. After that he returned and attacked the balloon, firing all his ammunition. The citation concludes by stating that although his machine was badly hit, he had crossed the lines at a height of only 100 feet during the attack.

His DSO was gazetted on 17 September that year and was awarded for conspicuous gallantry and devotion to duty on numerous occasions when engaged in combat with hostile aircraft. In one instance, though surrounded by enemy machines, he continued to fight for almost an hour with the utmost gallantry and determination against two hostile formations, finally bringing down one of their machines. The citation notes that he had brought down a total of seven enemy aircraft, again completely out of control, within the space of a month.

Second Lieutenant Robert Hugh SLOLEY, Royal Garrison Artillery, attached 56 Squadron, Royal Flying Corps, was killed in action on 1 October 1917, aged 20. He was the son of Sir Herbert Sloley KCMG, from Cape Town, who had served in South Africa during the campaigns of 1877–1879, 1880–1881 and 1899–1900 before going on to pursue a career in policing in Basutoland where he eventually became Commissioner in Residence. His son had emerged as a promising pilot after transferring to the Royal Flying Corps in 1917, notching up nine victories during August and September that year. His death came when he was attacked by four enemy Albatros DVs, one of which shot his tail fin away causing his machine to lose control. The incident was witnessed by James McCudden VC.

Second Lieutenant George Orme SMART, 60 Squadron, Royal Flying Corps, was shot down near Mercatel, south of Arras, on 7 April 1917. So close to the opening of the Arras offensive, his was yet another mission to obtain photographs of German positions in order to gain accurate information and intelligence, usually for the artillery. SMART was brought down by Manfred von Richthofen and was his thirty-seventh victory. He was buried in a marked grave near to where his aircraft had crashed and burst into flames, but subsequent fighting obliterated any trace of it and his body has never been identified. SMART had made several attempts to throw off his pursuer, but to no avail. Before the war he worked in the family business, which was a cotton mill in Lancashire. He initially joined the Royal Flying Corps as a mechanic, later learning to fly at his own expense. He first flew as a serjeant before eventually receiving his commission. His brother, Charles, also flew and won the MC.

Second Lieutenant Robert Archibald STEEL, 16 Squadron, Royal Flying Corps, who had formerly served with the Rifle Brigade, was killed in action on 27 March 1918, aged 18. His father was a journalist working for *The Scotsman* newspaper. His pilot, Second Lieutenant George GORNALL, was killed with him and is also commemorated on the memorial.

Second Lieutenant Guy Somerville STEWART, 49 Squadron, Royal Flying Corps, had been a member of the OTC at the University of London where he was a student. He was killed in action on 28 March 1918, aged 19, when he was shot down near Guillaucourt, east of Amiens, while flying low over the enemy, harassing them with machine-gun fire. His observer, Lieutenant D.D. Richardson, was taken prisoner.

Second Lieutenant Edward Dickinson STEYTLER, 7 Squadron, Royal Flying Corps, formerly 7th Battalion, South Lancashire Regiment, was reported missing in action on 25 July 1916, along with Second Lieutenant J.G. Robertson, while they were flying above Courcelette on the Somme. It was subsequently discovered that Robertson had been taken prisoner. STEYTLER was 19 years old when he died. His parents lived in South Africa.

Second Lieutenant Reginald Fitzroy TALBOT, 19 Squadron, Royal Flying Corps, was killed in action on 27 August 1916. TALBOT's grandfather was Rear Admiral Sir Charles Talbot KCB, and his great grandfather, Major General the Honourable Sir William Ponsonby, had served in the Peninsular War with Wellington and was killed in action at Waterloo in 1815. Another four members of the same squadron were lost that day, including Lieutenant Eugene Creuss CALLAGHAN, who is also commemorated on the memorial.

Second Lieutenant Joseph Bertram TAYLOR and Second Lieutenant Eric BETLEY, 82 Squadron, Royal Flying Corps, became Manfred von Richthofen's seventy-fourth victory when they were brought down on 28 March 1918 near Méricourt, close to the River Somme. TAYLOR, the pilot, had very little experience of operational flying, while BETLEY, his observer, was one of those bright boys who, thanks to the scholarship system, had won a place at Manchester Grammar School and who then went on to gain a place at Hertford College, Oxford, to read Classics. The war interrupted all that and in January 1916 he accepted a commission instead in the Royal Garrison Artillery. He then transferred to the Royal Flying Corps and was posted to 82 Squadron in France. His usual pilot had been wounded a few days earlier and it is interesting to wonder whether the outcome might have been different on that fateful day had he been flying with his usual partner.

Second Lieutenant Allan Switzer TODD, 8 Squadron, Royal Naval Air Service, became Manfred von Richthofen's sixteenth victory when he was shot down and crashed near Havrincourt Wood on 4 January 1917. He was a Canadian and was, in fact, the first Canadian pilot to be killed in action. He began flying at home in

Canada in 1915, and once he arrived in England he served at Dover, then on the French coast with No. 1 Wing, Royal Naval Air Service, before transferring later to 8 Squadron.

Second Lieutenant George Milne UNDERWOOD, General List and 16 Squadron, Royal Flying Corps, was killed in action on 6 March 1917, aged 19. His father worked as a missionary in Kiukiang, China. His observer, Second Lieutenant Albert Edward WATTS, was killed with him and is commemorated on the memorial.

Second Lieutenant John Syers WALTHEW, General List and 4 Squadron, Royal Flying Corps, was killed in action on 19 September 1917, aged 19. He was educated at Cranleigh School and had initially enlisted in the Public Schools Battalion (16th Battalion, Middlesex Regiment). His observer, Lieutenant Michael Charles Hartnett, was killed with him and is buried at Harlebeke New British Cemetery.

Second Lieutenant John Francis WIGHTMAN, 11 Squadron, Royal Flying Corps, enjoyed only the briefest of flying careers, despite being highly rated on leaving flying school, even though he was only 18 years old. However, the requirement to send pilots to the front as quickly as possible often meant that they were sent out before they were truly ready, let alone experienced enough. So it was that WIGHTMAN joined his squadron in France on 27 August 1917. Tragically on 4 September, just nine days into active service, he was shot down in flames in aerial combat; it was only his second operational flight. He and his observer, Air Mechanic 2nd Class, John HEEDY, both perished. Both are commemorated on the memorial.

Second Lieutenant Coningsby Philip WILLIAMS, 19 Squadron, Royal Flying Corps, was shot down on 26 August 1917 flying in his single-seat SPAD, the victor in this instance being Manfred von Richthofen. The squadron had been tasked with attacking enemy airfields and WILLIAMS was intercepted while returning from that mission. His machine came down near Poelcapelle in the northern part of the Ypres Salient. His body was never recovered, almost certainly because his aircraft broke up in an explosion before it hit the ground. The victory was Richthofen's fifty-ninth.

Second Lieutenant Francis Chisholm YOUNG, 3 Squadron, Royal Flying Corps, was killed in action on 14 February 1917, aged 19. He was shot down in flames near Gueudecourt while carrying out observation work for the artillery. His aircraft was attacked by an enemy formation and he and his observer, Second Lieutenant Adam Gower Sutherland De ROSS, both perished in the wreckage. De ROSS is also commemorated here on the Flying Services Memorial. YOUNG's father was a distinguished mathematician who became an Honorary Fellow of Peterhouse College, Cambridge, while his mother, also a respected academic, was proposed for an Honorary Fellowship at Girton College, Cambridge, but she died in 1944 before she could receive it. A distant relative, Thomas Bolton, had married Susannah Nelson, sister of Admiral Horatio Nelson.

Serjeant Herbert BELLERBY, 27 Squadron, Royal Flying Corps, was shot down and killed in action behind German lines while returning from an offensive patrol between Bapaume and Cambrai on 23 September 1916. He was 28 when he died and had been with the Royal Flying Corps since 1915. Although he was an experienced pilot, he was shot down by Manfred von Richthofen and was the second of his eighty victories. BELLERBY was buried by the Germans, but his grave was eventually lost during later fighting. The previous day he had flown on a bombing raid to Havrincourt where he was attacked and, although he managed to return uninjured, his machine was damaged. However, the following day his luck finally ran out.

Serjeant William Joseph BENGER MM, 20 Squadron, Royal Flying Corps, is mentioned on a number of occasions between 25 September and 11 October 1917, a period during which he and his squadron were heavily involved in the skies above Ypres. The Royal Flying Corps Communiqués, however, refer to him incorrectly as Serjeant A.N. Benger. His MM was gazetted on 20 October 1917, a few days after his death. He had been injured on 25 June that year when he was brought down by anti-aircraft fire.

On 25 September 1917 he and his squadron were involved in a fight with six Albatros fighters over Becelaere. Four of these were shot down, including one by BENGER and Lieutenant Dally. Two days later, above Moorslede, BENGER and a Canadian flyer, Lieutenant William Durrand, shot down one of eight enemy aircraft in flames, while two more were accounted for by other members of the squadron. On 3 October his squadron again encountered six Albatros scouts and, in the engagement that ensued, BENGER and Lieutenant Arthur Gilbert Vivian TAYLOR brought down one of them out of control. On the 11th of that month, he and Lieutenant LUCHFORD were responsible for shooting down one enemy machine and bringing down another out of control. Unfortunately, a few days later on 17 October, this brief, but very eventful, life came to an end when he was shot down over Poelcapelle, Belgium, and died from his wounds. Lieutenant Arthur Gilbert Vivian TAYLOR was flying with him that day and was also killed. TAYLOR is commemorated on the memorial with BENGER, but the CWGC records show his primary regiment as the 41st Dogras rather than the Royal Flying Corps.

By September 1917, 20 Squadron had claimed 220 victories and was a fighter-reconnaissance unit with a very good reputation. It was a reputation that continued right the way through to the end of the war, by which time its total claims had risen to 630; the highest total for any British scout unit.

Serjeant Henry Philip BURGESS, 18 Squadron, Royal Flying Corps, was killed on 11 March 1917, aged 30. His parents lived in the 'well-heeled' location of Gloucester Terrace, close to Hyde Park, in London. The CWGC register contains an extract from a letter sent to them by the officer then commanding their son's squadron, remarking that '*he was a sound pilot, and though the other four machines on his job all suffered, except one, the whole lot put up a splendid exhibition and the job was completed*'. The Royal Flying Corps Communiqué for the day that he died fails to shed further light on the nature of the task on which BURGESS and the others were engaged. His observer, Second Lieutenant Herbert Marshall Headley, was killed with him and is buried at Mory Abbey Military Cemetery.

Serjeant Thomas Frederick STEPHENSON DCM, 11 Squadron, Royal Flying Corps, was awarded his DCM for a single incident on 31 October 1917 in which he demonstrated conspicuous gallantry and devotion to duty after coming under attack from an enemy formation consisting of twelve aircraft. He engaged four and destroyed one of them. He was then attacked by another enemy machine. Even though his observer, Air Mechanic 1st Class, S.H. Platel, had been wounded, STEPHENSON engaged and destroyed his new opponent. Just then, a shell struck his machine causing severe damage to the right wing, which had almost been shot off. Though he found it extremely difficult to maintain control of his machine, STEPHENSON skilfully managed to bring it down without further mishap, landing it in the wire of our front line. Oddly, there is no mention of this series of incidents in the communiqué for that day, though other incidents involving 11 Squadron are recorded.

By the time he and Lieutenant T. William Morse were reported missing on 20 November 1917, somewhere west of Beaurevoir, STEPHENSON had five victories credited to him. Despite very low cloud and mist that day, a great deal of aerial activity took place in support of the opening of the Battle of Cambrai, almost all of it consisting of low level attacks on enemy troops. It was in such difficult and hazardous flying conditions that STEPHENSON and Morse are believed to have been brought down by anti-aircraft fire. Lieutenant Morse, who was wounded when their machine came down, was taken prisoner.

Serjeant Robert Charles TAYLOR DCM, 13 Squadron, Royal Flying Corps, was killed in action on 20 November 1917, aged 19. On 2 September 1917 he and Lieutenant STEEL were sent out on a photographic mission, but were spotted over their target by seven enemy aircraft. Six of them then swooped down to attack. Knowing the importance of the work with which he had been tasked and, with the weather becoming increasingly cloudy, making it unlikely that the task could be carried out later that day, TAYLOR chose to continue taking photographs until one of the enemy aircraft came within about fifty yards of them, at which point he showed great skill and coolness by manoeuvring, turning so as to give his observer, STEEL, the opportunity to fire at it at point blank range, causing it to overturn and crash. TAYLOR then attacked another one of the enemy formation, driving it down in a spin. At this point, the remaining four withdrew from the fight and TAYLOR completed the task of photographing his objective. TAYLOR's DCM was gazetted on 22 October 1917.

Serjeant Hubert Arthur WHATLEY, 53 Squadron, Royal Flying Corps, was killed in action with his observer, Second Lieutenant Frank Guy Buckingham PASCOE, on 2 July 1917. They were shot down in flames by Manfred von Richthofen, which brought his tally to fifty-seven. Their RE8 aircraft came down behind British lines and had been on an escorted flight, tasked with carrying out photographic reconnaissance. Although both men were recovered from the wreckage and then buried, their graves were subsequently lost, probably owing to shell fire. WHATLEY was another of those who had learnt to fly at his own expense and, after qualifying as a pilot, he was soon flying operationally in France with his squadron. PASCOE had previously served as a second lieutenant with the 7th Battalion, Royal Irish Fusiliers, before transferring to the Royal Flying Corps.

Corporal Alfred BEEBEE was just 18 years old when he was killed in action on 29 April 1917 when serving with 18 Squadron, Royal Flying Corps. Despite his youth, he had been awarded the *Croix de Guerre* (France) for his energy and fearless spirit in shooting down an enemy aircraft. The award, however, was gazetted posthumously on 14 July 1917, a few months after his death, so he may well have been unaware of it. His partner on 29 April was Serjeant George STEAD, who, aged 19, was only a fraction older than BEEBEE, and who had only been posted to the squadron a week earlier. Both men were engaged in a photographic reconnaissance when they were attacked by Manfred von Richthofen above Marcoing, near Cambrai. Their machine began to burn as it fell and neither body was ever recovered. Their deaths marked the Red Baron's fiftieth victory.

Corporal Ernest Frank LANGRIDGE DCM, 8 Squadron Royal Flying Corps, was killed in action on 6 April 1917 during a period of intense activity in the days leading up to the Arras offensive. His DCM was awarded not for any specific incident of note, but for his continuous gallantry and devotion to duty. The citation, gazetted on 9 July 1917, concludes that his work throughout had been splendid and of great value. The award was gazetted in the King's Birthday Honours List on 4 June 1917. His pilot, Lieutenant George John Hatch, died on the same date and is buried at Cabaret Rouge British Cemetery.

Corporal Charles George Sedgwick WARD, 11 Squadron, Royal Flying Corps, was killed on 9 November 1916, aged 22. He was an observer and died in aerial combat while escorting British aircraft on a bombing mission. His aircraft was flown by Lieutenant J.D. Cowie who was wounded and only just evaded capture when their aircraft came down close to the British lines.

There are two casualties on the memorial dating from 1919. Aircraftman 1st Class, Christopher Thomas FORREST, 5 Squadron, Royal Air Force, died on 13 February, while Serjeant George FISHER, of 29 Squadron, died on 16 June that year.

Of the five recipients of the Distinguished Service Cross listed on the memorial, four of them died serving with the Royal Naval Air Service. They are as follows:

Flight Commander Frederick Carr ARMSTRONG DSC, 3 Squadron, Royal Naval Air Service, was killed in action on 25 March 1918. His DSC was awarded in recognition of services while stationed at Dunkirk between January and September 1917, during which time he destroyed several enemy machines and drove down numerous others. He had joined the Royal Naval Air Service in 1915 and was an experienced flyer. He was eventually shot down over the village of Ervillers, his machine ablaze as it fell to the ground, but not before he had achieved thirteen victories. His award was gazetted on 30 November 1917.

Flight Commander Guy William PRICE DSC and Bar, 8 Squadron, Royal Naval Air Service, was killed in action when he was shot down on 18 February 1918 near La Bassée, aged 22. His Sopwith Camel was brought down whilst strafing enemy positions. He went on to score a total of twelve victories between 5 December 1917 and his death, the majority of them in the skies above Lens and La Bassée. Although he gained his flying certificate in 1914, three years elapsed before he achieved his first victory. By coincidence, his DSC was gazetted on the day he died and was awarded in recognition of his gallantry and determination whilst leading offensive patrols which had constantly engaged and driven away enemy aircraft. It cites 2 January 1918 when he had crossed the lines using cloud cover before attacking one of seven enemy machines, which then burst into flames as it fell to the ground. It adds that on other occasions he had driven enemy machines down and out of control.

The bar was gazetted on 16 March, shortly after his death. This time, the award was conferred for consistency and determination in attacking enemy formations, often superior in numbers. On 22 January 1918, whilst on offensive patrol, he again engaged seven Albatros scouts. He attacked one of them, firing at it and causing it to stall, side-slip, then flip over out of control before falling to the ground. Again, the citation notes that he had previously attacked several enemy machines, either destroying them or bringing them down out of control. He came from Rostrevor in County Down.

Flight Lieutenant Thomas Grey CULLING DSC, 1 Squadron, Royal Naval Air Service, a New Zealander from Auckland, was killed in action on 8 June 1917, aged 21. His DSC was awarded in recognition of his services on 23 April 1917 when, in conjunction with two other aircraft, he engaged an enemy formation consisting of nine scouts and some two-seater machines. Two of the two-seater machines were shot down, one of them by CULLING. He had studied at King's College in London between 1909 and 1913, but also had the distinction of becoming the first New Zealand ace, scoring three victories in April 1917, followed by a further three in May. During that time he flew with Major Roderic Stanley Dallas DSO DSC and Bar, who succeeded in scoring thirty-two victories before he was eventually shot down and killed near Liévin on 1 June 1917. Dallas, whose tally made him Australia's second highest ace, was also awarded the *Croix de Guerre* (France). He is buried in Pernes British Cemetery.

Flight Sub Lieutenant Ellis Vair REID DSC, 10 Squadron, Royal Naval Air Service, was killed in action on 28 July 1917. A graduate of Toronto University where he gained a degree in Architecture, he came over to England in 1916 where he learned to fly, subsequently joining the Royal Naval Air Service. After completing his training, he went to the front and quickly established himself as a very competent and aggressive flyer with 10 Squadron. It was there, along with fellow flyers Raymond Collishaw, John Edward Sharman, W. Melville Alexander and Gerard Ewart Nash, that he became part of a team known as Black Flight. Nash was shot down by Karl Allmemröder on 26 June 1917 and taken prisoner. Sharman was shot down almost a month later on 22 July, whilst REID was reported missing in action six days later on 28 July. REID's impressive tally of nineteen victories was achieved in the skies above Ypres and northern Flanders between 1 June 1917 and 28 July 1917. There were successive victories on 1, 2, 3 June; 5, 6, 7 June; then two on 15 June; two on 12 July and three on 27 July. His last score was achieved on the day he was reported missing in action, presumed killed. All of his nineteen victories were made in the same aircraft, a Sopwith Triplane affectionately known as Black Roger.

His DSC, gazetted on 11 August 1917, the same day as the bar to Sharman's DSC and Collishaw's DSO, was awarded for having shown the greatest bravery and determination at all times. The citation picks out two occasions: firstly on 6 June 1917 when he attacked four hostile scouts, driving down one of them which then nose-dived to the ground and was destroyed on impact; then, on the afternoon of 15 June, whilst leading a patrol of three scouts, they encountered a formation of ten enemy aircraft. During the ensuing combat he forced one machine down, out of control, before attacking another of the enemy scouts at a range of just thirty yards, killing the pilot.

Chapter Three

'Make dust our paper, and with rainy eyes write sorrow on the bosom of the earth'

The Vimy Memorial, Vimy Ridge

This, for many people, is the highlight of any visit to the Arras battlefields. For me, it is the finest of all the British and Commonwealth memorials on the Western Front. It sits on the highest point of the ridge, known to the troops as Hill 145. The Canadian Battlefields Memorials Commission chose the site, not least because of its prominent position overlooking the Douai Plain. The view today is almost the same one that men of the Canadian 4th Division would have witnessed after they had captured all but the very northern edge of the ridge on 9 April 1917. The other important factor behind the choice of site was more symbolic. It was here on that date, for the very first time (and the only time), that all four divisions of the Canadian Corps lined up for battle side by side. For a national memorial there could hardly be a better choice.

The memorial commemorates the 60,000 or so members of the Canadian Expeditionary Force who were killed on the Western Front. Much against the wishes of the architect, the names of the missing in France were inscribed on the walls at the base of the monument (in Belgium these are on the Menin Gate). The method adopted precluded the removal of the names of men subsequently found and identified.

The memorial was designed by the Canadian architect Walter Seymour Allward, who came from Toronto. He had already made his name as an architect and sculptor, including a handful of works commemorating military campaigns, such as the memorial in Portland Park, Toronto, dedicated to the War of 1812 and referred to as 'The Old Soldier'. He had also designed the Boer War Memorial Fountain at Windsor, Ontario. By 1918 he was already a full member of the Royal Canadian Academy, and in many ways the obvious, if not the perfect choice for the commission of the proposed national memorial in France. Work began in 1921 and the memorial was only completed in 1936 when it was officially inaugurated on 26 July in a ceremony attended by King Edward VIII. Walter Allward died in 1955.

It is not difficult to understand why the memorial park in which the monument sits is one of the iconic sites on the Western Front. The park includes a section of preserved trench lines, or more accurately a crater outpost line, and as such more or less authentic. Close by are the remains of several mine craters, including Broadmarsh Crater, and among the grassed and wooded areas of the park are the countless indentations of shell holes, some of which show evidence of having been joined together to form new trenches. Finally, there is the section of tunnel, visits to which can be arranged at the adjacent visitor centre. The tunnel is part of the Grange Tunnel complex and is always worth a visit, though it is advisable to book in advance.

The memorial park is around five miles north-east of Arras. Many visitors choose to arrive from the D937, coming off at one of the turnings for Neuville-Saint-Vaast, either the D49 or the D55. However, it is also worth approaching the memorial and memorial park from the north-east along the D55. The view up to the memorial is extremely impressive.

First of all, a little guidance on how to locate the names on the memorial. The names are arranged differently to those on British memorials. The first difference is that there is no regimental order of precedence. Secondly, the face of the memorial, as approached by the visitor from the car park, is actually the back of the memorial, not the front. The front of the memorial is the face that looks out over the Douai Plain to the east.

The names begin on the north-east corner of the memorial by the sculpture known as 'Breaking the Sword', which is the one to the left of the front face. From there the names run anti-clockwise. The names are listed in alphabetical order according to rank. Names beginning 'A' to 'E' are to the left of the central steps, 'F' to 'L' to the right of them.

This should save time for the visitor looking for several individuals on the memorial. The names referred to below are arranged sequentially in the same order as they appear on the memorial.

The highest rank commemorated on the memorial is that of major; there are thirty-one of them, six of whom hold decorations for distinguished service or acts of gallantry. Twenty-two of them were killed in action on the Somme between September and November 1916. Only one of the thirty-one fell on 9 April 1917 here at Vimy Ridge: Major Horace HUTCHINS, 21st Battalion, Canadian Infantry. There is also one who fell in action at Festubert in May 1915: Major Allan Crawford SHAW. Two more died in 1918, but the remainder are all 1917 casualties. Thirty of the thirty-one fell whilst serving with infantry units.

With regard to gallantry awards, there are two holders of the DSO, twenty-three holders of the MC and thirty-four holders of the DCM, together with 187 men who were awarded the MM, three of whom also held the DCM. Seven men on the memorial were awarded a bar to their MM and a further two are credited with two bars. There are also four holders of the VC.

There are forty-two captains and 248 lieutenants. The Canadian Expeditionary Force did not include the rank of second lieutenant. Another point worth noting is that Canadian infantry companies were often commanded by officers holding the rank of major or temporary major.

Major Alfred James ANSLEY, 15th Battalion, Canadian Infantry, was killed in action on 14 October 1916. He was a jeweller before the war and had enlisted in

June 1915. The battalion's war diary makes no reference to his death, which is unusual to say the least. It records only that the battalion was in trenches near Courcelette that day and that there was some shelling by both sides. His brother, Captain Fredrick Campbell Russell Ansley, was initially reported as having been killed in action, but this was then changed to 'missing in action, believed killed'. However, it would appear from Canadian records, supported by those held by the CWGC, that he survived the war.

Major William Norman ASHPLANT, 1st Battalion, Canadian Infantry, was killed in action on 22 September 1916, aged 39. He had previously served in the South African War. A civil engineer by profession, he had worked abroad quite extensively, including in South Africa, Nigeria and the British West Indies, but prior to his enlistment in 1915 he was working closer to home in Ontario. The battalion war diary for 22 September 1916 is extremely detailed, but with regard to Major ASHPLNT it only notes that he was last seen leading his men as they advanced and that he was later reported missing in action, although he was believed to have been killed.

Of the eight officers commemorated on the memorial who were awarded the MM prior to receiving their commission, Lieutenant Norman APPLEBY, MM and Bar, 31st Battalion, Canadian Infantry, is one of just two to have been awarded a bar. He was born in Leeds and his parents lived in Harrogate. He enlisted in November 1914. His MM, which he had won at Mount Sorrel in June 1916, was awarded for conspicuous gallantry as a sergeant with the same battalion. The initial award was gazetted in July that year and the bar followed on 9 December. He was killed in action on 29 March 1917. Surprisingly, the war diary makes no reference to his death other than to state that the battalion came under bombardment that day and that six men were killed and six were wounded.

Private Beresford ADDY, 27th Battalion, Canadian Infantry, was the youngest of three brothers to serve with the Canadian Expeditionary Force. According to the CWGC and Canadian army records, he appears to be the only one to have died during the war. He was killed in action on the Somme on 15 September 1916 near Courcelette, aged 22. He was born in Ireland and was the son of a clergyman from Tyrone.

Private Hugh Arbuckle ANDREW, 78th Battalion, Canadian Infantry, was recommended for a gallantry award following his death on 19 February 1917 after he and men from his battalion had carried out a raid that morning in broad daylight lasting just ten minutes. Three prisoners were captured and some damage was done to the enemy's dug-outs and other infrastructure, including a mine shaft that was destroyed when it blew up creating a crater eighty feet in diameter and twenty-five feet deep. After the raid Private ANDREW, together with Lieutenant Derbyshire and another man, Private Fulton, went back out to rescue a wounded comrade from no-man's land, but ANDREW was killed in the process. Unfortunately, he received no decoration for his gallantry, although he was mentioned in despatches in connection with the operation.

Fulton, who was severely wounded, appears to have survived the war. The raid itself proved fairly costly and resulted in nine men killed and fifteen wounded. Most of these casualties occurred when Lieutenant Derbyshire's men ran into stiff resistance in a sap near Kennedy Crater. Lieutenant Wilfred Derbyshire, who received the MC for his part in the raid, survived the war, but died six months after the Armistice on 20 May 1919. He is buried in St Helens Cemetery on Merseyside.

Private James ANGUS, 29th Battalion, Canadian Infantry, was killed in action on 11 September 1916, aged 29. His brother, Private Robert George Angus, was killed in action near Passchendaele on 30 October 1917. Like that of his brother, his body was never recovered and he is now commemorated on the Menin Gate at Ypres.

Major William Falconer BATTERSBY MC, 1st Canadian Motor Machine Gun Brigade, was killed in action on 25 March 1918. His MC was gazetted on 14 November 1916 and was awarded for conspicuous gallantry during an engagement in which he handled his team of eight machine guns with great skill and courage, inflicting heavy casualties on two enemy field gun batteries. He was killed by enemy shrapnel whilst travelling in an armoured car just west of the River Somme between Licourt and Marchelpot, not far from Villers-Carbonnel, south of the main Amiens–Saint-Quentin road. He is one of the six majors commemorated on the memorial to have been decorated for military service or gallantry.

Captain Reginald John Godfrey BATEMAN, 46th Battalion, Canadian Infantry, had spent the years before the war as an academic at Saskatchewan University where he was Professor of English. Having graduated from Trinity College, Dublin, with a Bachelor of Arts degree in 1906, he moved to Canada three years later to take up the post at Saskatchewan University. He initially enlisted as a private in the 28th Battalion, Canadian Infantry, but returned from active duty in 1916 in order to take command of one of the companies of the 196th (Western Universities) Battalion. Whilst in Canada he made the decision to return to the front and was wounded during the fighting at Hill 70, near Loos, in August 1917. He was killed in action on 3 September 1918, the day after his battalion had captured the village of Dury, which formed such a key part of the Drocourt–Quéant defences on the north side of the Arras–Cambrai road. He was standing outside the Battalion HQ when a shell landed close to the entrance, killing him more or less instantly.

Captain William Evans BEATON MC, 14th Battalion, Canadian Infantry, was killed in action near Courcelette on 26 September 1916, aged 22. His MC was gazetted on 19 August 1916 and was awarded for conspicuous gallantry during a counter-attack against the enemy in which he led his company with great coolness under heavy fire. Despite being wounded, he remained on duty with his company and held the newly won position throughout the entire day. Later, he took a party of men out to rescue the wounded.

Lieutenant Lancelot Joseph BERTRAND MC, 7th Battalion, Canadian Infantry, was killed in action at Hill 70, near Loos, on 15 August 1917 whilst advancing from one objective to another under heavy sniper and machine-gun fire. His MC, gazetted on 18 July that year, was awarded for conspicuous gallantry and devotion to duty during an advance in which all the remaining officers in his company had become casualties. He then took command of the company and led it to its objective showing great determination and courage, followed by a marked ability when it came to reorganizing and consolidating the new position. The citation ends by stating that the example he set throughout these operations was splendid. He was born in Grenada, British West Indies, and was unusual in so far as he was a black officer of African-Caribbean origin.

Lieutenant Mossom Richard BOYD, 50th Battalion, Canadian Infantry, was killed in action on 18 November 1916, aged 30. The CWGC register notes that his father served as a major with the Canadian Army Medical Corps. Mossom's brother, Private Henry Ormsby Boyd, died on 9 May 1916 in Mesopotamia when serving with the 6th Battalion, South Lancashire Regiment, and is commemorated on the Basra Memorial. Another member of the extended family also served; Lieutenant Herbert Thornton Cust Boyd died in Canada on 17 February 1918, aged 20. He had enlisted in the Army Service Corps, but was attached to the King's Own (Yorkshire Light Infantry) at the time of his death. The family was descended from Mossom Boyd who, from very humble beginnings in Ireland, went on to become a wealthy tycoon in the Canadian timber industry.

Lieutenant George Herbert BURNS MM and Bar, 43rd Battalion, Canadian Infantry, won his MM near Courcelette in October 1916. It was awarded for conspicuous gallantry and devotion to duty whilst treating the wounded under heavy fire and was gazetted on 24 January 1917. He had also been awarded the Italian Bronze Medal for Military Valour. He was killed in action on 28 August 1918 east of Arras. I can find no mention of the bar in any of the gazettes and no accompanying citation for it, though there is reference to it in *Officers of the Canadian Expeditionary Force who Died Overseas 1914–1919*.

Sergeant Louis BOVINEAU MM and Bar, 19th Battalion, Canadian Infantry, was awarded his MM for conspicuous gallantry and devotion to duty at Loos between 15 and 17 August 1917 during operations to capture Hill 70. On two occasions he crossed open ground under heavy shell, rifle and machine-gun fire in order to establish communication with the one of the flanking battalions, and on both occasions he was successful. Later, he volunteered to go through the enemy's barrage to find a platoon that had become lost. Having found the platoon, he then guided it to its correct position. The citation notes that throughout this entire period his coolness and cheerfulness greatly contributed towards maintaining the spirits of the men. The award was gazetted on 2 November 1917. The bar to his MM was gazetted the following year on 29 August, just two weeks after he was killed in action on 16 August 1918 near Fransart, just east of Fouquescourt. His brother, Private Eli Bovineau, served with the 50th Battalion, Canadian Infantry, and was killed in action on 28 September 1918. He is buried at Raillencourt Communal Cemetery Extension.

Lance Corporal John English BRAYLEY DCM, 5th Battalion, Canadian Mounted Rifles, was killed in action between 15 and 16 September 1916. His DCM was won as a private and was awarded for conspicuous gallantry. When all his officers had been killed or wounded, he collected part of his company and led it under heavy fire to join the rest of the company in the front line. He also showed great coolness and courage when carrying messages under trying circumstances. The award was gazetted on 19 August 1916.

Private Gordon Keith BEACH and his brother, Private Herbert Freeman BEACH, enlisted together and then fought together as part of the 25th Battalion, Canadian Infantry, until Gordon was killed in action at Hill 70 on 15 August 1917, aged 19. Herbert fell a year later, east of Arras, on 27 August 1918, aged 21. The brothers are both commemorated here on the memorial where, in a sense, they are again reunited. They came from King's County, Nova Scotia.

Private Alexander BIGGAN, 16th Battalion, Canadian Infantry, was killed in action on the Somme between 4 and 7 September 1916, aged 19. His father, Pioneer Andrew Burns BIGGAN, who had served with the Imperial Yeomanry during the South African campaign, was killed a few days later on 16 September 1916, aged 41, whilst serving with 'B' Company, 1st Battalion, Canadian Pioneers. He is listed in Canadian army records under the surname 'Biggar'. He and his son were both killed near the village of Courcelette and are now commemorated here on the memorial.

The memorial carries the names of several Canadian Native Americans, although not all of them are obvious from the surnames under which they served. One man whose name does suggest his origins is Private George BLACKFACE, 8th Battalion, Canadian Infantry, who came from the Bird Tail Sioux Reserve. He was killed in action on 14 October 1918 and had been wounded in September the previous year.

Private Claude BLAKEMAN DCM, 14th Battalion, Canadian Infantry, was killed in action on 1 October 1918. His DCM was awarded for most conspicuous gallantry and devotion to duty during an attack near Sains-les-Marquion on 27 September 1918. The citation records that after his entire section had become casualties from enemy machine-gun fire on a flank, he immediately crawled forward and eventually reached the rear of the emplacement that was responsible.

After throwing a grenade, he rushed it single-handed with fixed bayonet and succeeded in killing some of the gun crew, wounding others and capturing two guns. This fine action undoubtedly saved many casualties. The award was gazetted on 2 December 1919.

Private Robert James BOYD, 72nd Battalion, Canadian Infantry, who was killed in action on 9 April 1917, aged 20, was one of four brothers who served during the war, two of whom lost their lives. Private Thomas William Boyd fell in action near Ypres on 6 June 1916 whilst serving with the 28th Battalion, Canadian Infantry. He also has no known grave and is commemorated on the Menin Gate at Ypres.

Private Patrick BRENNAN, 24th Battalion, Canadian Infantry, was killed in action on 17 September 1916, aged 23. His brother, Private William Brennan, was killed in action on 22 August 1915 at Gallipoli when serving with the 5th Connaught Rangers. He is commemorated on the Helles Memorial.

Private David Barclay BROWN, 3rd Battalion, Canadian Infantry, was killed in action on 8 October 1916, aged 21. The CWGC register notes that he had been recommended for the VC during fighting at Regina Trench. The war diary makes no specific mention of him or any particular action from which he could be identified, but it does narrate in some detail how the battalion was forced to withdraw from its newly won position in the face of an enemy counter-attack, but only after desperate fighting and after it had exhausted its supply of bombs.

The account refers to the gallantry of Lieutenant Willoughby Eyre Chatterton who was badly wounded in the shoulder whilst leading a bayonet charge and who was killed by a sniper soon afterwards. In the end, the only Lewis gun ran out of ammunition and many of those holding on were forced to fight hand to hand, in some cases using only their fists. Corporal WALSH managed to gather up a few bombs from the dead and wounded in an effort to cover the retirement, but was killed whilst doing so as remnants of the battalion made their way back to their jumping off trench. Chatterton, who originally came from Wimbledon, is buried at Adanac Military Cemetery on the Somme and Corporal William Joseph WALSH MM is commemorated here on the Vimy Memorial. From the description of the fighting it is easy to imagine the circumstances in which Private BROWN might have been recommended for the highest bravery award, even if, in the end, it never materialized.

Private George BROWNIE, 72nd Battalion, Canadian Infantry, was killed in action on 9 April 1917, aged 27. His younger brother, Private John BROWNIE, was killed in action on 21 August 1917, aged 19, serving with the 50th Battalion, Canadian Infantry. He also has no known grave and is commemorated here on the Vimy Memorial.

Private Thomas BURKE, 31st Battalion, Canadian Infantry, was killed in action between 24 and 30 September 1916, aged 26. His younger brother, Private

William BURKE, also fell during the war. He was killed on 31 March 1917 whilst serving with the 50th Battalion, Canadian Infantry, and is also commemorated on the memorial.

Lieutenant Charles Frederick CASEY MC, 1st Battalion, Canadian Mounted Rifles, was killed in action near Courcelette on 15 September 1916, aged 36. His MC was gazetted on 22 August 1916 whilst serving as a sergeant major in the regiment. It was awarded for consistent good work. The citation goes on to add that during several bombardments he set a fine example to all under him by his coolness and devotion to duty.

Lieutenant Robert Grierson COMBE VC, 27th Battalion, Canadian Infantry, was killed in action on 3 May 1917, aged 35. He was born in Aberdeen, Scotland, and attended Aberdeen Grammar School. After leaving school he was apprenticed as a chemist and worked in Aberdeen and London before moving to Canada in 1906. He continued working as a chemist, eventually running his own pharmacy until the outbreak of war intervened. Having obtained his commission, he initially became an instructor, but decided that he wanted to serve at the front and so reverted to the rank of lieutenant. He was posted to the 27th Battalion, Canadian Infantry, where he served until his death in May 1917 near Fresnoy.

His VC, won near Acheville on 3 May 917, was awarded for most conspicuous bravery and example when, under intense fire, he steadied his company and led it through the enemy's barrage, eventually reaching his objective with just five men. With great coolness and courage, he then bombed the enemy, inflicting heavy casualties on them, before collecting up small groups of men and capturing his company's objective along with eighty prisoners. Having seized the objective, he repeatedly charged the enemy, on each occasion driving them before him, but as he was leading his bombers in a counter-attack he was killed by a sniper. The citation concludes that his conduct that day inspired all ranks and that it was entirely due to his magnificent courage that the position was carried, secured and then held. The award was gazetted on 27 June 1917. Lake Combe in Saskatchewan is named in his honour.

Sergeant William COOPER DCM MM, 10th Battalion, Canadian Infantry, was killed in action on 3 September 1918. His DCM was won as an acting corporal and was awarded for conspicuous gallantry and devotion to duty in action. When a strongly entrenched party of the enemy with two machine guns was holding up his company, he led eight men forward and captured the post together with fifty prisoners and both machine guns. His prompt act of courage and determination enabled his company to continue its advance. The award was gazetted on 15 November 1918. *The Distinguished Conduct Medal Awarded to Members of the Canadian Expeditionary Force 1914–1920* makes no reference to his MM, but it was certainly awarded and was gazetted on 11 February 1919.

Private Alan Robert Sinclair CAMPBELL was killed in action on 2 September 1918 during the fighting to capture the Drocourt–Quéant Line. He was 20 years old when he died and was serving with the 72nd Battalion, Canadian Infantry, at the time. The CWGC register notes that his father, Colonel Alan James Campbell, was awarded the DSO. Colonel Campbell survived the war, but was seriously wounded near Aden whilst serving with the Indian Army in the Near East. His DSO, gazetted on 17 October 1917, was awarded for distinguished service in the field and he was also mentioned in despatches. He ended the war as a temporary brigadier general commanding 55 Infantry Brigade. His long military career began when he was gazetted as a second lieutenant in the East Lancashire Regiment in May 1885. Private CAMPBELL's maternal grandfather, who had also served as a colonel in the Indian Army, was in turn the son of a major who had served with the 80th Regiment of Foot.

Private David Adam CANTELON MM, 1st Battalion, Canadian Infantry, was killed in action on 3 May 1917 during the attack on the village of Fresnoy, east of Vimy Ridge. He is one of two holders of the MM on the memorial who were killed in action, aged just 18. The other is Private Andrew CUTHBERT MM, 47th, Battalion, Canadian Infantry, who was killed in action a few days later on 8 May 1917.

Private Guy Francis CHAPMAN, 43rd Battalion, Canadian Infantry, was killed in action on 8 August 1918, aged 28. His brother, George Chapman, also fell during the Great War, but Canadian army records appear to offer no exact match, nor do CWGC records.

Private Harold CHAPMAN, 7th Battalion, Canadian Infantry, was killed in action on 15 August 1917 at Hill 70, near Loos. He was 40 years old when he died and had previously served in the South African campaign. He also served in Gallipoli as a major with the British Expeditionary Force until he was wounded and invalided back to Canada. He subsequently re-enlisted with the Canadian Expeditionary Force in Vancouver in October 1916 and returned to action on the Western Front.

Private Cyril Carey COLPITTS was just 18 years old when he fell in action near Courcelette serving with the 5th Battalion, Canadian Mounted Rifles, some time between 14 and the 16 September 1916. His brother, Private Bela Alonzo Colpitts, was killed in action at Ypres on 30 October 1917 whilst serving in the same battalion. He is buried in Poelcapelle British Cemetery in Belgium.

Private Henry COTTRELL DCM, 28th Battalion, Canadian Infantry, was killed in action on 6 July 1917, aged 32. His DCM was awarded for conspicuous gallantry and devotion to duty whilst attached to a trench mortar battery. When a round misfired, he extracted it from his trench mortar and threw it over the parapet where it immediately exploded. He undoubtedly saved the lives of his gun crew. The award was gazetted on 26 May 1917.

Private Albert COTTRILL MM was just 17 years old when he was killed in action on 6 October 1916. He is shown in the CWGC register as serving with the

60th Battalion, Canadian Infantry. According to CWGC records, he is one of only two Canadian recipients of the MM who fell in action aged 17. According to Canadian army records, he is the younger of the two, though the date of birth in the case of both men suggests that they were actually 19 years old when they died. However, both men may have given a false date of birth in order to enlist.

Private George CRAIGIE and his brother, Private John CRAIGIE, served with the 75th Battalion, Canadian Infantry. Both men were killed in action on the same day, 31 March 1917. They have consecutive army numbers, although Canadian army records show the younger brother, John, enlisting on 1 October 1915, seven weeks earlier than his brother. Both brothers are commemorated on the memorial.

Private Robert CRICHTON, 50th Battalion, Canadian Infantry, was killed in action on 11 May 1917, aged 29. His younger brother, Private William CRICH-TON, 44th Battalion, Canadian Infantry, was killed in action a few months earlier on 2 January 1917, aged 20. They also have consecutive army numbers. William is commemorated on the memorial with his brother.

Company Sergeant Major John DOUGALL DCM, 16th Battalion, Canadian Infantry, was killed in action on 8 October 1916, aged 35. His DCM was awarded for conspicuous gallantry at St Julien on the night of 22/23 April 1915. During an attack on a wood, he placed himself at the head of a party of men belonging to another battalion that had no officer or recognized leader. Leading them forward, he cleared a far superior number of the enemy from a farm that lay beyond the wood. The award was gazetted on 30 June 1915. The wood referred to in the citation is Kitcheners' Wood, which no longer exists. It was named as a translation of Bois de Cuisinières and not Field Marshal Earl Kitchener.

Lance Sergeant Frederick DIEHL DCM, 1st Battalion, Canadian Mounted Rifles, was killed in action on 26 August 1918. His DCM was awarded for conspicuous gallantry and devotion to duty during the attack on Hangard on 8 August 1918 when he led his section under heavy shell and machine-gun fire. When the attack was temporarily checked by a number of enemy snipers and two machine-gun posts, he rallied his section and rushed the posts, killing eight of the enemy and capturing six prisoners and two heavy machine guns. The citation adds that he showed skilful leadership and coolness during the attack and goes on to say that his prompt action at a critical period proved to be of great assistance, contributing to the success of the operations and averting many casualties amongst our troops. The award was gazetted on 16 January 1919.

Trooper Frank DALY, Royal Canadian Dragoons, fell in action during the famous cavalry charge at Moreuil Wood on 30 March 1918, aged 18. The CWGC records show that he was one of four brothers who served during the war. The regiment sustained just over ninety casualties in the charge, considerably fewer than Lord Strathcona's Horse, which suffered 157. There are sixty-four Royal

Canadian Dragoons on the memorial, including Daly, twenty-eight of whom fell in the attack on Moreuil Wood.

Private Baptiste DEMERY, 52nd Battalion, Canadian Infantry, was killed in action on 10 August 1918. There are variations on the spelling of his surname and it is sometimes recorded as 'Demerais'. He was of Native American origin and came from Sandy Bay Reserve, which in turn came under the Portage La Prairie Agency. He was born at Fort Ellice and was 52 years old when he died. The CWGC register shows him as 'Betice Demery', which is clearly a phonetic misrepresentation of his name. Despite such variations, his army number indicates that all the records relate to the same man.

There are also discrepancies in the case of Private Hébert DESJARLAIS, 2nd Battalion, Canadian Infantry. His first name, as recorded in the CWGC register, is anglicised and appears as Herbert, but it also shows his unit as the 8th Battalion, Canadian Infantry. Canadian and CWGC records agree that he was killed in action on 15 August 1917 during the Canadian attack on Hill 70, near Loos, and both records show the same army number, 234958. He had a brother, Alexander, who also served, but he was more fortunate and survived the war. The CWGC register shows his father as Gilbert, Chief of the Broken Head Reserve. Another source, *Warriors of the King*, claims that his father was killed in action on 25 October 1918 serving as Corporal 234960 with the 2nd Battalion, Canadian Infantry, and yet there appears to be no trace of the father's death in CWGC records. There is, however, a Lance Corporal Gilbert Des Jarlais shown in the CWGC records who died on 25 October 1918 serving with the 2nd Field Company, Canadian Engineers. He is buried in Chichester Cemetery, but he was 24 years old when he died. His army number is 234960, but he was clearly Hébert's brother, not his father, as claimed in *Warriors of the King*.

Private Frank Nickle DREAVER, 5th Battalion, Canadian Infantry, was also of Native American origin and came from the Mistawasis Reserve. He initially enlisted in Canada with the 188th Battalion before transferring to the 5th Battalion. He was killed in action on 5 April 1917.

Company Sergeant Major Michael George ELLIS DCM, 49th Battalion, Canadian Infantry, was killed in action some time between 15 and 16 September 1916. His DCM was won as an acting company sergeant major and was awarded for conspicuous gallantry and ability after all the officers of his company had been killed or wounded. He then took command and, by his coolness and example under heavy fire, enabled his company to consolidate a newly captured position. The award was gazetted on 19 August 1916.

Lance Sergeant John EVANS DCM, Canadian Machine Gun Corps, was killed in action on 28 April 1917. His DCM was awarded for conspicuous gallantry and devotion to duty after bringing his gun into action at close range under heavy fire. The award was gazetted on 9 July 1917.

Lance Corporal Fred EARL DCM, 28th Battalion, Canadian Infantry, was killed in action on 26 August 1918, aged 22. His DCM was won as a private and awarded for conspicuous gallantry and devotion to duty. When the enemy was attacking one of our posts, he noticed that another party had managed to work its way about a hundred yards to the rear of the position. At this point he crept out and bombed them, compelling them to retire. He then turned on the first party, engaging it from the rear, and when its men also retired, he followed them for over a hundred yards, even though it was broad daylight, inflicting further casualties on the group. The citation rightly concludes that his energy and initiative materially assisted in foiling the enemy's plans. On several other occasions he had shown similar qualities. The award was gazetted on 3 September 1918.

Private George Davis FANNING, 2nd Battalion, Canadian Infantry, was one of four brothers who served during the Great War, but he was the only one to lose his life in the conflict. He was killed in action on the opening day of the Battle of Amiens, 8 August 1918, aged 20.

The oldest of the thirty-one majors commemorated on this memorial is Major Harold Leonard GAETZ. He was killed in action on 26 September 1916, aged 47, whilst serving with the 5th Battalion, Canadian Infantry. He was initially wounded shortly after leading his men in an attack, but as his batman was dressing his wound he was hit again, this time fatally. He was originally buried near to where he fell on the battlefield, not far from Courcelette, but his grave was subsequently lost. The CWGC register tells us that he held the Colonial Auxiliary Forces Long Service Medal.

Lance Corporal David GORDON, 2nd Battalion, Canadian Infantry, was killed in action on 9 September 1916, aged 22. His elder brother, George F. Gordon, was also killed serving with the same battalion, although he fell earlier in the year on 25 April 1916, aged 25. Both men enlisted at Valcartier on the same day, 17 September 1914, and have consecutive army numbers. George was killed near Ypres and is buried in Woods Cemetery in Belgium.

Lance Corporal Bert GUIGNION, 87th Battalion, Canadian Infantry, was killed in action on 9 June 1917, aged 36. His younger brother, Private John GUIGNION, was killed in action on 30 September 1916, aged 23, when serving with the 26th Battalion, Canadian Infantry. Both men are now commemorated here on the memorial.

Private Gerald Joseph GIBBS, 7th Battalion, Canadian Infantry, was one of five brothers who served during the war. Records appear to indicate that Gerald was the only one to lose his life during the conflict. He was killed in action on 15 August 1917 at Hill 70, near Loos. His father served as a serjeant major in the Royal Marine Light Infantry.

Private Robert George GOWANLOCK, 2nd Battalion, Canadian Infantry, was killed in action near Loos on 18 August 1917, aged 30. His brother, Private James

Laidlaw Gowanlock, also fell in action whilst serving with the 116th Battalion, Canadian Infantry. He died of wounds on 24 August 1917 in the days following the capture of Hill 70 and is buried at Aix-Noulette Communal Cemetery Extension. Before the war both men had been farmers in Ontario.

Private Thomas John GRATTON MM, 29th Battalion, Canadian Infantry, was one of four brothers killed during the war. Thomas fell on 21 August 1917, aged 37. His brother, Private Alfred Frank Gratton, served with the 2nd Devonshire Regiment and was killed in action near Loos on 6 October 1916, aged 22. His death occurred during a large raid on German trenches carried out by his battalion and the 1st Sherwood Foresters. He is buried at Philosophe British Cemetery, Mazingarbe. Their brother, Private Sydney James Gratton, 22nd Battalion, Australian Infantry, died in England on 14 December 1916, aged 33, and is buried in Landkey (St Paul's) Cemetery in Devon. Private Lewis William Gratton was the eldest of the four and was killed in action at Neuve Chapelle on 13 March 1915 serving with the 2nd Devonshire Regiment. Like Thomas, he has no known grave, but is commemorated on the Le Touret Memorial.

Major Horace HUTCHINS, 21st Battalion, Canadian Infantry, is the only officer on the memorial of that rank to have lost his life on 9 April 1917, the opening day of the Battle of Arras. He was 49 years old when he was killed by a shell.

Captain Ernest Hudson HOLLAND MC, 'B' Battery, 1st Canadian Motor Machine Gun Brigade, was killed in action on 24 March 1918. His MC was gazetted on 4 June 1917 in the King's Birthday Honours List and was awarded for distinguished service in the field. He had also served in the South African campaign. He initially went to war as part of Borden's Motor Machine Gun Battery under Major Edward James Gibson Holland VC. I have not been able to confirm whether the two men were related, though Ernest's mother's middle name was 'Gibson'.

Lieutenant Francis HART DCM, Canadian Cavalry Machine Gun Squadron, fell in action on 1 April 1918, aged 25. His DCM was won as a sergeant with the Canadian Machine Gun Corps. It was awarded for conspicuous gallantry and devotion to duty in an attack where he was in charge of a machine gun. He brought it into action time after time on the enemy's flank, inflicting heavy casualties; on one occasion, after he had taken his gun forward, he opened fire with great effect at a critical moment and showed great courage and initiative under continuous fire from the enemy. The award was gazetted on 28 March 1918. He had enlisted in September 1914 and initially served with the 20th Border Horse before transferring to the 6th Battalion, Canadian Infantry. He later served with the Fort Garry Horse and transferred to the Canadian Cavalry Machine Gun Squadron after receiving his commission.

Lieutenant Stephen George HOBDAY DCM, 3rd Battalion, Canadian Infantry, was killed in action on 8 October 1916. His DCM was won whilst serving as a corporal with the same battalion. It was awarded for conspicuous gallantry on 15 June 1915 at Givenchy after two men had been killed and one wounded in an attempt to dig out an officer and six men who had been buried in a trench by a high explosive shell. In spite of the continuing risk to himself, Corporal HOBDAY took over the work whilst under heavy fire and succeeded in extricating the entire party who would otherwise have perished. The following day he took part in an attack on the German trenches and was one of the first to go forward during the advance. In the subsequent retirement, he rendered assistance to four men who were badly wounded and who were later brought in. On every occasion during these operations, his coolness and great bravery provided a splendid example and gave encouragement to all ranks. The award was gazetted on 6 September 1915. In civilian life he was employed as a butler. The CWGC register shows that his brother, Private Walter James Hobday, was killed in action near Mount Sorrel on 16 June 1916 when serving with the 24th Battalion, Canadian Infantry. He is commemorated on the Menin Gate.

Sergeant Frederick HOBSON VC, 20th Battalion, Canadian Infantry, was killed in action on 18 August 1917, aged 43. HOBSON, who was born in London, but lived in Brigg, Lincolnshire, had served in the South African War with the 2nd Wiltshire Regiment before moving to Canada in 1904 where he became a storekeeper. He initially enlisted there in November 1914 with the Norfolk Rifles, but later transferred to the 20th Battalion, Canadian Infantry, and served with the battalion until his death.

His VC was won on 18 August 1917 during a strong enemy counter-attack near Lens. A Lewis gun in a forward post, located in a communication trench leading to the enemy lines, was buried by a shell and its crew killed, with the exception of one man. Although Sergeant HOBSON was not a gunner, he recognized the importance of the post and rushed from his trench, digging out the gun. He then brought it into action against the enemy who were now advancing down the trench and over the open ground on either side of it. When the gun jammed, he left another man to deal with the stoppage whilst he charged the enemy with the bayonet and held them off until he was shot. However, by the time he fell, the gun was back in action and reinforcements had arrived. It was his valour and devotion to duty, not to mention self-sacrifice, that allowed the gun to be brought back into action and undoubtedly saved a critical situation. His award was gazetted on 17 October 1917.

Private Robert HAIRE, 44th Battalion, Canadian Infantry, was killed in action on 7 May 1917. His brother, Lieutenant George Haire, was killed in action on 7 January 1917, aged 26, whilst serving with the 6th Connaught Rangers. He is buried in Kemmel Château Military Cemetery in Belgium.

Private Percival Egerton HARVEY, 58th Battalion, Canadian Infantry, was one of four brothers who served during the war. The CWGC records give no indication as to who they were, nor does Percy's army record. However, we do know that Percival had only been in France for around seven weeks before he was killed in action on 20 September 1916, aged 32.

Private John Bruno HEBB, 26th Battalion, Canadian Infantry, was the youngest of four brothers to serve. He was killed in action on 16 September 1916, aged 18. Canadian army records and CWGC records tend to suggest that he was the only one of the four to have been killed during the war.

Private Herbert HENDERSON, 58th Battalion, Canadian Infantry, was killed in action on 17 September 1916, aged 38. The CWGC register notes that he was one of three brothers to serve. Again, records suggest that he was the only one killed.

Private Bertie HODGIN, 24th Battalion, Canadian Infantry, was killed in action on 27 August 1918, aged 20. His father, Private William Henry HODGIN, 1st Battalion, Canadian Infantry, also served during the war and was killed in action on the Somme on 22 September 1916, aged 42. Both father and son are commemorated here on the memorial. Prior to the war, Bertie had spent four years with the 55th Irish Canadian Rangers as part of the militia. Both Bertie and his father were born in Manchester.

Driver James HUGHES, 3rd Division Ammunition Column, Canadian Field Artillery, was killed in action on 21 March 1917, aged 19. His two brothers were also killed whilst serving. One of them, Private Robert Eben Hughes, 2nd Battalion, Canadian Infantry, was killed in action near St Julian on 22 April 1915, the opening day of the Second Battle of Ypres, when the Germans released chlorine gas prior to their attack. He was 24 years old when he died and is commemorated on the Menin Gate in Ypres. CWGC records for James and Robert provide no clues as to the identity of the other brother, nor do Canadian army records.

Company Sergeant Major John Bercy IRONSIDE MM and two Bars, 1st Battalion, Canadian Infantry, was killed in action in the attack on Fresnoy-en-Gohelle on 3 May 1917, aged 26. His MM was gazetted on 23 August 1916, the bar to it on 12 December 1916 and the second bar posthumously on 9 July 1917. The bar is incorrectly ascribed in the gazette to a 'J.P. IRONSIDE', but the army number indicates that this is simply a typographical error. The *Croix de Guerre* (France) is listed under his correct full name in the *London Gazette* of 14 July 1917.

Corporal Charles Burton INCH, 20th Battalion, Canadian Infantry, was killed in action on 15 September 1916, aged 25. His brother, Private Frank William Inch, died of wounds whilst serving with Princess Patricia's Canadian Light Infantry. He was evacuated as far as Étaples, but died there on 12 November 1917, aged 19, and is now buried at Étaples Military Cemetery. He was wounded during the fighting at Passchendaele.

Private Adam Francis Rankine INKSTER, 31st Battalion, Canadian Infantry, and Lance Corporal Alexander INKSTER, 72nd Battalion, Canadian Infantry, were very likely related, as the families of both men came from the Shetland Isles. The same is likely to be the case with regard to Private George James JESSIMAN and Private Thomas JESSIMAN, whose families lived in the small Aberdeenshire town of Huntly.

Private Robert Wray JOSLYN DCM, 5th Battalion, Canadian Infantry, was killed in action on 24 May 1915. His DCM was awarded for gallant conduct and devotion to duty whilst employed as a battalion runner carrying despatches under fire. The award was gazetted on 30 June 1915 and the citation provides no further details.

Corporal Walter KELLY MC, 27th Battalion, Canadian Infantry, was killed in action on 19 August 1917, aged 27. At face value, the award of the MC appears very unlikely, although men did sometimes revert to the ranks, having previously served as commissioned officers. However, I can find no trace in any of the gazettes of any award of the MC under that name, including a number of variations.

Private Frederick Arthur KEENE, 5th Battalion, Canadian Infantry, and his brother, Private Wilford KEENE, 47th Battalion, Canadian Infantry, were both killed in action. Frederick was killed on 17 September 1916, aged 20, whilst Wilford fell almost a year later on 3 September 1918, aged 23. Both are commemorated together here on the memorial.

Major Henry Rupert LINNELL DSO, 78th Battalion, Canadian Infantry, was killed in action on 11 August 1918, aged 34, during operations east of Amiens. He was also mentioned in despatches and had been an architect in civilian life. The war diary records that he died holding the railway embankment at Hallu against German counter-attacks. The German bombardment on Hallu was very effective, but shells from our own artillery also fell short, which only added to LIN-NELL's problems after he was ordered to hold the position until reinforcements arrived. His DSO was gazetted on 16 August 1917 and was won when he took charge of a very critical situation shortly after he and his men had gained their objective. With great bravery and skill he organized the defence of the position with scattered forces under intense shell fire. He then held the position successfully for five days and was, in fact, the only officer of his battalion who was not killed or wounded during these operations.

Captain Charlewood Derwent LLWYD MC, 13th Battalion, Canadian Infantry, was killed in action on 1 October 1918, aged 24. His MC was gazetted on 14 November 1916 under the surname 'Lloyd', but was then corrected two weeks later on 26 November. It was awarded for conspicuous gallantry in action after holding a barricade on the left flank of his company under heavy fire with great courage and determination. The citation notes that he later performed fine work rescuing wounded men.

Lieutenant Harold Oakley LEACH MC, 4th Battalion, Canadian Machine Gun Corps, was killed in action near the Drocourt–Quéant Line, east of Arras, on 2 September 1918, aged 28. His MC was gazetted on 6 February 1918 and the citation for it appeared later that year on 8 July. It was awarded for conspicuous gallantry and devotion to duty when going forward with the attacking troops and getting his guns into action in a commanding position, materially assisting the infantry by destroying enemy units as they retreated and dispersing others that were gathering for a counter-attack. The aggressive manner in which he handled his guns attracted hostile fire, but he carried on regardless, firing and inflicting severe casualties on the enemy. Throughout the day he showed great determination and initiative. He was a graduate of Toronto University and had been a civil engineer before the war.

Lieutenant John LEONARD MC, 75th Battalion, Canadian Infantry, was killed in action on 13 July 1918, aged 21, when a machine-gun bullet passed through his neck whilst he was on a scouting patrol near Trent Trench, south-west of the village of Gavrelle. His MC was gazetted on 9 August 1918 and was awarded for conspicuous gallantry and devotion to duty when his position came under heavy bombardment during a raid by the enemy against the unit to the right of his battalion. Seeing some of the enemy near the wire, he went forward with a few men and captured two prisoners, thereby obtaining valuable identification. Later, in preparation for a raid on the enemy's lines, he twice led patrols forward, reconnoitring the enemy's wire, cutting a passage through it and again obtaining valuable information. His careful preparations enabled the raiding party to carry out a successful operation during which he showed a splendid example of courage and initiative.

Sergeant St George Otway LLOYD, 78th Battalion, Canadian Infantry, was killed instantly on 19 February 1917, aged 23, when he and a party of men carried out a raid on enemy positions near Vimy Ridge. Reference has already been made to another member of the same raiding party, Private Hugh Arbuckle ANDREW, who is also commemorated here on the memorial. LLOYD's body was never recovered, as he was buried under tons of debris after hurling a mobile explosive charge into a mineshaft, completely unaware that the Germans had stacked their own explosives at the bottom of the shaft in preparation for charging one of their mines. The explosion created a new crater on Vimy Ridge measuring eighty feet in diameter, known thereafter as Winnipeg Crater. As with Private ANDREW, Sergeant LLOYD received a mention in despatches for his part in the raid. Although LLOYD's parents came from the Morningside district of Edinburgh, their son was educated in England at Ellesmere College in Shropshire, where he excelled at sports and was considered to be a good academic student. He moved to Canada in 1912 where he worked for the Canadian Bank of Commerce. A fitting tribute would have been to have named the new crater after him.

Lance Corporal Edouard LEGER DCM, 22nd Battalion, Canadian Infantry, was killed in action on 15 September 1916, aged 27. His DCM was won as a private in the battalion and was awarded for conspicuous gallantry when repairing telephone wires under continuous sniper fire and occasional machine-gun fire. It was gazetted on 21 June 1916. His battalion suffered heavy casualties during the fighting that took place between 14 and 18 September; in fact, on the day he was killed, it faced no fewer than seven counter-attacks.

Private Noe LAFRANCE, 22nd Battalion, Canadian Infantry, was killed in action on 4 October 1916 near Courcelette. He was one of four brothers who served during the war, though it would appear that he was the only one to have been killed.

Private Eben Nelson LANGILLE, 24th Battalion, Canadian Infantry, was killed in action on 17 September 1916, aged 23. He was one of three brothers who served during the war, but he too appears to be the only one to have died during the conflict.

Gunner Arthur LAST, 4 Brigade, Canadian Field Artillery, was killed in action on 27 September 1918, aged 17. He was the youngest of three brothers who served during the war. Records suggest that one brother survived, but Private William Charles Last, who served with the 15th Battalion, Canadian Infantry, was killed in action on 3 June 1916, aged 19. He fell during the unsuccessful counter-attack by the Canadian 1st Division to recapture Mount Sorrel after the Germans had taken it the previous day. William also has no known grave and is commemorated on the Menin Gate.

Private Ernest Ivon LEADEN, 18th Battalion, Canadian Infantry, was killed in action near Courcelette on 3 October 1916, aged 20. His brother, Private Albert Edward Leaden, was killed near Passchendaele on 10 November 1917, aged 23, whilst serving with the 8th Battalion, Canadian Infantry. Like his brother, he has no known grave, but is now commemorated in Belgium on the Menin Gate. Canadian army records show Albert's middle name as 'Edwin' rather than Edward.

Private Robert James LEGGOTT, 5th Battalion, Canadian Infantry, was killed in action on 22 May 1915, aged 30. His brother, Private Arthur Leggott, died on 4 June 1916 as a result of wounds received the previous day at Mount Sorrel. He was taken all the way to Lijssenthoek, where he subsequently died, and is now buried at Lijssenthoek Military Cemetery. He was the same age as Robert when he fell.

Private Charles Alfred LYDIARD and his brother, Corporal George Gilmore LYDIARD, were both killed in action serving with the 43rd Battalion, Canadian Infantry. Charles died, aged 25, near Courcelette on 21 September 1916 following his battalion's attack on Zollern Trench the previous day. George fell two weeks later on 8 October, aged 24, during the attack on Regina Trench, which lay just to the rear of Zollern Trench.

Major Norman George Morrison McLEOD MC, 8th Battalion, Canadian Infantry, was killed in action on 26 September 1916. He had previously served with the 1st Gordon Highlanders before joining the Canadian Expeditionary Force. He was born at Stornoway, on the Isle of Lewis, but at some stage he moved to Canada where he enlisted in January 1915. Scottish records show his surname as 'MacLeod' although the spelling of his surname in the *London Gazette* is the same as that in the CWGC records. His MC was gazetted on 23 June 1915, but appears to be without a citation.

Captain Arthur Beamer McCORMICK MC, 3rd Battalion, Canadian Infantry, was killed in action on 10 April 1917, aged 22. His MC was gazetted on 14 February 1917 and was awarded for conspicuous gallantry in action whilst leading a raid on the enemy's trenches. Prior to this, he carried out several daring reconnaissance patrols, each time obtaining valuable information. His father, Lieutenant Colonel Byron James McCormick, was the commanding officer of the 213th Battalion, Canadian Infantry, otherwise known as 'The American Legion'. Colonel McCormick, who came from Michigan, had previously spent sixteen years in the National Guard. When war broke out he volunteered for overseas service and was at Ypres in 1915 during the German gas attack on 22 April. After that he was employed up and down the line instructing troops on the use of the gas mask.

Captain Charles Edward McGEE, 5th Battalion, Canadian Infantry, was killed in action on 26 May 1915, aged 39. He had also served during the South African campaign. His brother, Lieutenant Francis Clarence McGEE, is also commemorated here on the Vimy Memorial. He fell in action at Courcelette on 16 September 1916 when serving with the 21st Battalion, Canadian Infantry. Before the war Francis had been a talented hockey player and was well-known throughout Canada. He lost an eye during a game in 1900, but was still able to enlist in spite of the apparent handicap. He was later wounded in the knee and subsequently served as a dispatch rider. The boys' uncle, Thomas D'Arcy McGee, a Canadian politician, was assassinated in 1868.

Lieutenant Harold Philip MacGREGOR MC, 73rd Battalion, Canadian Infantry, was killed in action during the unsuccessful raid carried out by the Canadian 4th Division at Vimy Ridge on 1 March 1917 in an area between The Pimple and Hill 145. Though initially reported as missing, he was later recorded as having been killed in action. His MC was gazetted on 28 March that year and was awarded for conspicuous gallantry and devotion to duty during another raid on German trenches in which he handled his men with marked ability, inflicting many casualties on the enemy. He was the last of the raiding party to leave the enemy's lines and brought back most valuable information.

Lieutenant Gordon King MacKENDRICK, 58th Battalion, Canadian Infantry, was killed in action near Regina Trench on 8 October 1916, aged 22. His father, Lieutenant Colonel William Gordon MacKendrick, was awarded the DSO in the New Year's Honours List on 1 January 1918 whilst serving with the Canadian Engineers.

Lieutenant John MOTT MC, 1st Canadian Mounted Rifles, was killed in action on 26 August 1918. His MC was gazetted on 13 January 1919 and was awarded for conspicuous gallantry over four days of operations. Owing to dense fog, which made it very difficult to maintain direction, he took up a position in front of his platoon during an attack and then, by his skilful leadership and courage, led it under heavy fire to its final objective where he captured three machine guns, inflicting many casualties on the enemy. On another occasion he showed splendid gallantry leading his men under heavy fire against a strongpoint, setting a fine example to all those under him. He had also been mentioned previously in despatches.

Company Sergeant Major Alexander McVEAN, 75th Battalion, Canadian Infantry, was killed in action on 18 November 1916, aged 27. His brother, Bombardier Malcolm McVean, died of wounds at Étaples on 16 April 1918, aged 24, whilst serving with 'D' Battery, 38 Brigade, Royal Field Artillery. He is buried at Étaples Military Cemetery.

Sergeant Donald MACRAE DCM, 31st Battalion, Canadian Infantry, was killed in action on 27 September 1916, aged 28. His DCM was awarded for conspicuous gallantry whilst rescuing men buried by a shell. During the rescue he was exposed to enemy observation and was under continuous fire. The award was gazetted on 21 June 1916. He had previously spent three years in the Army Service Corps, as well as three years in the Royal Garrison Artillery, and was wounded on 13 June 1916 during the recapture of Mount Sorrel, near Ypres.

Sergeant Hector George MacECHERN, 75th Battalion, Canadian Infantry, was killed in action on 18 November 1916, aged 28. He was one of five brothers who served during the war. Again, records held by the CWGC and the Canadian army suggest that he was the only one of the five to have been killed.

Sergeant Lanchie McDONALD DCM, 15th Battalion, Canadian Infantry, was killed in action on 15 August 1917. His DCM was won as a corporal and was awarded for conspicuous gallantry and devotion to duty when leading an assault party against an enemy machine gun located inside an emplacement. He alone reached the dug-out, entering it from the rear, where he killed the entire crew, despite being seriously wounded. The award was gazetted on 26 July 1917. He had previously served as a private in the 2nd Battalion, Canadian Infantry.

Corporal Hamish Kinnear MAITLAND-DOUGALL, 102nd Battalion, Canadian Infantry, was killed in action on 9 April 1917, aged 19. His brother, Acting Lieutenant William McKinstry Maitland-Dougall, died on 15 March 1918, aged

23, whilst serving with the Royal Canadian Navy aboard HM Submarine *D.3*. On 12 March the submarine was bombed off the coast of France by a French airship when it was mistaken for an enemy vessel. The submarine fired rockets for the airship to see but perhaps not surprisingly, these were mistaken for hostile fire.

After the attack the airship descended to just above sea level and, although survivors could be seen in the water, it was obviously unable to rescue them, although it did drop life rafts. The subsequent court of enquiry concluded that the airship's commander, Lieutenant Saint-Remy, was not to blame and accepted that the signal fired by the submarine had not been recognized by the French vessel, which had then acted in reasonable self-defence. Sadly, all of the submarine's crew perished before help could arrive. Although the CWGC records show his death occurring on 15 March, it is far more likely that he died on 12 March when the vessel sank.

William has the distinction of being not just the first, but also the only Canadian submarine commander to lose his life in action. He is still recognized as the youngest commander of a submarine ever to have served in either the Royal Navy or any of the Commonwealth navies and is now commemorated on the Halifax Memorial. The wreck of Submarine *D.3* was eventually located in the English Channel in 2007.

Corporal George Reginald McCLELLAND and Private Norman Leslie McCLELLAND both served with the 16th Battalion, Canadian Infantry. Norman was killed in action during the fierce contest for Regina Trench on 8 October 1916. Norman's exact date of death cannot be determined, only that he fell sometime between 8 and 9 October. George was killed in action a few weeks before his brother, and again no precise date can be determined. All that is known in his case is that he fell between 4 and 7 September during the very early part of the struggle for the same system of German trenches, close to the village of Courcelette. Both men are now commemorated on the memorial.

Lance Corporal Neil Archibald MacLEAN, 25th Battalion, Canadian Infantry, was killed in action on 16 September 1916, aged 27. His brother, Private Hector Norman MacLean, also fell in action during the war. He was killed on 12 January 1918 when serving with the 85th Battalion, Canadian Infantry. He is buried at Thélus Military Cemetery, east of Vimy Ridge. Private James MacGlashen MacLean was the second of the three brothers to die. He died of wounds on 21 June 1917 serving with Hector in the 85th Battalion and both men had enlisted on the same day, 19 October 1915. James is buried at Barlin Communal Cemetery Extension. The 25th Battalion and the 85th Battalion were both from Nova Scotia.

Private John McKenzie MacFIE, 1st Battalion, Canadian Infantry, was killed in action on 3 May 1917, aged 19. He was one of three brothers who served during the war and a book containing his letters was published after his death. His two brothers, Arthur Gill MacFie and Donald Roy MacFie, both survived the war.

Donald, like John, served with the 1st Battalion, Canadian Infantry, whilst Arthur served with the 162nd Battalion.

Private William Heywood MacKINTOSH, 13th Battalion, Canadian Infantry, was one of five brothers who served during the war. He was killed in action on 15 August 1917 during the attack on Hill 70 and was 18 years old when he died. Canadian and CWGC records provide insufficient details to determine whether any of the remaining four brothers died or survived.

Private Samuel MACDONALD DCM, 28th Battalion, Canadian Infantry, was killed in action on 15 September 1916. His DCM was awarded for conspicuous gallantry in action. After all the NCOs in his section became casualties, he took command and carried on working under heavy fire. Later, he again took command of his section, protecting the flank of another battalion with great skill and determination until he was severely wounded. The award was gazetted on 14 November 1916.

Private George MANN, 3rd Battalion, Canadian Infantry, was killed in action at Regina Trench on 8 October 1916. His brother, Private Jack MANN, also served in the same battalion and was killed in action five weeks earlier on 3 September. Both men enlisted together and are now commemorated here on the memorial.

Private Bert MANSFIELD, 1st Battalion, Canadian Infantry, and his brother, Private Cyril MANSFIELD, were both killed in action on the Somme during the fighting around Courcelette. Bert fell on 23 September 1916 and Cyril was killed two weeks later on 6 October just north of the village. Cyril also served with the 1st Battalion.

Sergeant William McCANDLISH DCM, 8th Battalion, Canadian Infantry, was killed in action on 14 August 1917. His DCM was awarded for conspicuous gallantry and devotion to duty during a raid. When his platoon was held up by a hostile machine gun, he skilfully surrounded it and put the gun and its crew out of action, having personally led a bombing party around its flank under heavy fire with the utmost determination. The award was gazetted on 17 September 1917.

Sergeant Roland Alec MERRETT DCM, 43rd Battalion, Canadian Infantry, was killed in action on 16 August 1918, aged 22. During the attack on the village of Domart on 8 August 1918 he was in charge of a platoon and, although things generally went well that day, not every aspect of the advance ran smoothly. A thick fog had set in overnight, reducing visibility, and some of the tanks accompanying the advance fired on our own men mistaking them for those of the enemy. It was under such trying conditions that he displayed the greatest coolness and courage in leading his platoon forward in an attack on Dodo Wood. During the advance he had to change direction twice and but for his clever leadership and gallantry the situation might well have become serious. Whilst doing so he was constantly under machine gun fire from the enemy, as well as fire from our tanks. He was also personally responsible for putting a machine gun out of action when it threatened to hold up the advance. The award was gazetted on 16 January 1919. Canadian army records show his surname as 'Merritt'.

Gunner Thomas McDONALD, 1 Brigade, Canadian Field Artillery, was killed in action at Festubert on 15 June 1915, aged 48. The CWGC register notes that he had already served for twenty-one years in the British Army.

Private John Albert McHERNESS and his brother, Private William David McHERNESS, were both killed serving in the Canadian Expeditionary Force. John served with the 27th Battalion and William with the 38th Battalion. John was killed in action near Courcelette on 15 September 1916, aged 27; William, on 26 April 1918, aged 36. A third brother, Sergeant Benjamin Wells McHER-NESS, also died during the war. He was killed in action on 13 August 1918, aged 30, serving with the 49th Battalion, Canadian Infantry. All three brothers are commemorated together on the memorial here. The family came from Ontario.

Private Frank McLEISH, 8th Battalion, Canadian Infantry, was killed in action on 27 November 1916, aged 25. His brother, Private George Leslie McLEISH, 27th Battalion, Canadian Infantry, was killed in action on 3 May 1917, aged 27. Both brothers are commemorated on the memorial.

Private William Johnstone MILNE VC, 16th Battalion, Canadian Infantry, was killed in action on 9 April 1917, aged 24. He was born in Cambusnethan, Lanark-shire, in Scotland, but moved to Canada in 1910, where he became a farmer in Moose Jaw, Saskatchewan. It was there that he enlisted in September 1915.

His VC was won on 9 April 1917, the opening day of the Battle of Arras. As he and his men were approaching their first objective, he noticed an enemy machine gun firing on our advancing troops. He crept up to the gun and put it out of action using bombs, killing the crew and capturing the gun. He then saw another machine gun in the enemy's support line and stalked it in similar fashion, again killing its crew and capturing the gun. He was killed soon afterwards, but his actions earlier had undoubtedly saved many lives. His award was gazetted on 8 June 1917.

Private Alexander MITCHELL, 78th Battalion, Canadian Infantry, was killed in action on 9 April 1917. He was another Canadian soldier of Native American origin. Back in Canada he was a farmer and came from the Poplar River Reserve, part of the Portage La Prairie Agency. He enlisted in early January 1916.

Lance Corporal Claude William MOORE MM and two Bars, 52nd Battalion, Canadian Infantry, was killed in action on 27 August 1918, aged 20. His gallantry awards were gazetted on 18 June 1917, 12 December 1917, and 11 February 1919. The bar to his MM was won after he had taken part in a raid on the enemy's positions near Lens on the night of the 3/4 September 1917. He and another bomber captured a machine-gun post, killing several of the enemy and forcing the remainder to withdraw, leaving behind their machine gun. The battalion war diary for September 1918 shows the citation to the second bar. On 15 August

1918 he was in charge of a detached Lewis gun post on the right flank in front of Damery when the Germans made a counter-attack against his battalion's position. Seeing an officer in the forward line calling for assistance, he led his section forward with great skill to a position from which he and his men could bring to bear Lewis gun and rifle fire against the advancing enemy line. Despite heavy machine-gun fire, he handled his own men with such skill that no casualties were incurred by his section, although he and his men succeeded in inflicting very heavy casualties on the enemy.

Private William James MORRISEAU, 16th Battalion, Canadian Infantry, came from the Fort Alexander Reserve and had enlisted under the alias of 'James Marshall'. Records show that on 1 May 1918 he reverted to his original and true name, 'Morriseau'. The CWGC records show his date of death as 1 October 1918. However, another source records him missing in action, but presumed dead, on 28 October 1918, although he was only declared dead officially on 21 November the following year. He was another Canadian soldier of Native American origin.

Bombardier James Stuart MUIR, 4th Trench Mortar Battery, Canadian Light Trench Mortar Battery, was killed in action during the fighting near Cambrai on 27 September 1918, aged 19. His brother, Private John Elliott MUIR, Lord Strathcona's Horse, fell in action earlier that year on 30 March in the Canadian Cavalry Brigade's action at Moreuil Wood. He was 26 years old when he died and is also commemorated here with his brother James.

Captain Phillip NEALE MC, 44th Battalion, Canadian Infantry, was killed in action near Amiens on 10 August 1918. His MC was gazetted on 16 August 1917 and was awarded for conspicuous gallantry and devotion to duty whilst commanding his company after casualties had occurred amongst the other officers. He consolidated his company's position under heavy fire and later established forward posts. The citation concludes that by his own personal example he kept his men together under very trying circumstances.

Captain Arthur Thomas NEWBY MC, Fort Garry Horse, was killed in action on 10 August 1918, aged 33. His MC, gazetted on 2 December 1918, was awarded for conspicuous gallantry and devotion to duty after leading his troop with great dash and courage under heavy artillery fire against a position that was strongly held by machine guns. During that action he was wounded, but set a splendid example to those under his command. He is one of thirteen men from the regiment who died in action on 10 August, eleven of whom are commemorated here on the memorial.

The line of the regiment's advance ran close to and parallel with the Amiens–Roye road, currently the D.934. When it encountered strong enemy resistance, it found that the fields on either side of the road had been wired and were entrenched. This was probably deliberate on the part of the Germans and served to funnel the cavalry into the only gap, which was the road itself. When three troops from 'C' Squadron came charging down the road and through the gap they were cut down by machine-gun fire and shells before they could get to grips with the enemy.

Lieutenant Hugh Wilson NORTON-TAYLOR, 21st Battalion, Canadian Infantry, was killed in action on 16 September 1916, aged 33. His father, the late Lieutenant Colonel Duncan Norton-Taylor, had served with the Royal Artillery.

Private Henry Bertram NASON and his brother, Private Joseph Percival NASON, were both killed serving with the same regiment, Lord Strathcona's Horse. Henry served with 'A' Squadron, Joseph with 'B' Squadron. Henry was killed in action at Cambrai on 1 December 1917, whilst Joseph died the following year on 2 April 1918, almost certainly from wounds received during the action at Moreuil Wood. Both brothers are commemorated on the memorial.

Private Stanley McKay NESBITT was killed in action with the 75th Battalion, Canadian Infantry, on 9 April 1917, aged 18. His brother, Sapper Kenneth Nesbitt, died whilst serving with the Canadian Engineers Training Depot on 4 November 1918 and is buried in Seaford Cemetery, Sussex.

Sergeant Oluf Christian OLSEN DCM, 2 Brigade, Canadian Field Artillery, was killed in action on 4 June 1915, aged 30. His DCM was awarded for conspicuous gallantry and resource as a corporal between 22 April and 4 May 1915, when he repaired telephone wires under heavy shell fire, and also for acting as a scout and obtaining valuable information on 2 May 1915 after all the wires had been cut. The award was gazetted on 5 August 1915.

Private Howard Clifford ODLUM DCM, 7th Battalion, Canadian Infantry, was killed in action on 15 August 1917, aged 20. His DCM was awarded for conspicuous gallantry and resource near Messines on the night of 16/17 November 1915. The citation records that Corporal ODLUM and three other NCOs, Corporal Weir, Corporal Babcock and Lance Corporal Berry, worked for four hours under bright moonlight cutting wire close to a heavily manned German trench. They then assisted a raid by placing a bridge over the River Douve about sixteen yards from the German parapet and guiding bombing parties through the gaps they had just cut. The citation concludes that it was largely due to their coolness and resource that the raid on the enemy's trench was a success. The award was gazetted on 22 January 1916.

Corporal Ernest Babcock and Corporal Kenneth Weir also received the DCM for their role in this exploit. Lance Corporal Arthur Charles Berry may be the man referred to in the citation although, if so, his record shows that he did not receive any award. Weir was subsequently killed in action on 20 April 1916 and is buried at Dickebusch New Military Cemetery in Belgium. He was also awarded the MM for gallantry on the night of 30 January 1916 when, despite being wounded, he volunteered to return to the front trenches to rescue one of his officers, Lieutenant Owen. The citation also notes that he had consistently shown courage and devotion to duty over many months. Lance Corporal Berry was killed in action at Mount Sorrel on 3 June 1916 and is commemorated on the Menin Gate. Babcock managed to survive the war.

Private John Henry OUTHWAITE and Sergeant William Frederick OUTH-WAITE were almost certainly related, probably as cousins, although records are not conclusive. John was killed in action on 9 April 1917 at Vimy Ridge with the 38th Battalion, Canadian Infantry, but William, who had been involved in fighting during the Second Battle of Ypres, was killed nearly two years earlier on 16 June 1915 at Givenchy when serving with the 4th Battalion, Canadian Infantry. In a letter written home in April he had expressed the hope that the war might be over by Christmas and commented briefly on his experiences with regard to sniping. Both men are now commemorated here on the memorial.

Private Peter Alexander OWEN, 43rd Battalion, Canadian Infantry, was killed in action during the fighting for Regina Trench on 8 October 1916, aged 22. He was one of three brothers who served, two of whom fell. CWGC and Canadian army records do not identify the brother who was killed. There is a Corporal John Owen, 27th Battalion, Canadian Infantry, from Winnipeg, whose parents' names are identical to Peter's, but the match still cannot be regarded as conclusive.

Lieutenant Raymond B. PENNIMAN MC, Royal Canadian Regiment, was killed in action on 8 October 1916, but he had also been wounded a few weeks earlier on 16 September near Courcelette. He was initially reported missing in action near Regina Trench on 8 October, but was subsequently presumed to have been killed. His MC was gazetted on 18 August 1916, but the citation for it is extremely brief, simply stating that it was awarded for conspicuous gallantry and devotion to duty, repelling three hostile counter-attacks under difficult circumstances. The citation almost certainly fails to do justice to the action for which it was awarded, though it is not possible to determine when or where that action took place.

Company Sergeant Major Thomas PATTERSON DCM and Bar, 27th Battalion, Canadian Infantry, was killed in action on 3 May 1917, aged 43. His DCM was awarded for consistent good work and devotion to duty, adding that he had always set a fine example of coolness and courage. The award was gazetted on 21 June 1916. The citation for the bar to his DCM was gazetted in November 1916 and refers to an occasion when, as the most senior commander in the front line trenches, he showed courage and utter disregard for danger. It goes on to note that he inspired and organized consolidation work under the most trying of circumstances whilst under intense artillery fire. He was born in Dundee, Scotland, and had previously served for eighteen years with the Gordon Highlanders before moving to Canada.

Company Sergeant Major Charles Henry POPE DCM MM, Royal Canadian Regiment, was killed in action on 30 September 1918, aged 35. His DCM was awarded for conspicuous gallantry and devotion to duty whilst carrying an important message through several sectors under intense bombardment. He exhibited the greatest courage and determination and a total disregard for all personal danger. The award was gazetted on 19 August 1916 and his MM on 6 January 1917. He was born in Falmouth, Cornwall, and was a mariner before the war.

Sergeant James Allen PROFIT DCM, 31st Battalion, Canadian Infantry, was killed in action on 26 September 1916. His DCM was awarded for conspicuous gallantry and ability in action. After Lieutenant Holden, the machine gun officer, was wounded, command of the section devolved to Sergeant PROFIT. He displayed great bravery and executive ability in bringing all his guns safely out of action and even capturing an enemy machine gun. He also showed great coolness and courage when carrying wounded men over 150 yards to safety under heavy shell fire. The award was gazetted on 14 November 1916. He was killed in action during his battalion's attack on Courcelette Trench. In civilian life he was a trapper and had enlisted in November 1914.

Lance Corporal Cecil PRATT, 20th Battalion, Canadian Infantry, was killed in action on 12 May 1917, aged 26. His brother, Private Joseph Henry Frederick Pratt, was killed in action during the retreat on 23 March 1918 serving with the 5th Oxfordshire & Buckinghamshire Light Infantry. He also has no known grave and is now commemorated on the Pozières Memorial on the Somme.

Private Eber Ruel PARKER, 50th Battalion, Canadian Infantry, was killed in action on 25 August 1917, aged 26. His younger brother, Private Emery Hubert PARKER, 31st Battalion, Canadian Infantry, was killed in action a few months earlier, on 7 May 1917, aged 20. He is also commemorated here on the memorial.

Private John PATTERSON, 1st Battalion, Canadian Mounted Rifles, was killed in action on 29 September 1918, aged 28. His brother, Private Henry Duncan Patterson, also fell in action, serving in the same battalion. He died of wounds the following day, 30 September, and is buried at Duisans British Cemetery. Both fell near the village of Saint-Olle during the fighting for Cambrai.

Private Charles Herbert PAYNE, 87th Battalion, Canadian Infantry, was killed in action on 12 October 1918, aged 28. His brother, Private Arthur Payne, died at home on 28 February 1919 and is buried at Tilbrook (All Saints) Churchyard, close to the family home in Huntingdonshire. He was 41 years old and had previously served with the Queen's (Royal West Surrey Regiment) and the 16th Labour Company, but died after his transfer to the 436th Agricultural Company, Labour Corps.

Private Arthur Albright PILLING and his brother, Private Harold Hudson PILLING, were both killed in action within three weeks of each other. Arthur served with the 27th Battalion, Canadian Infantry, and Harold with the 44th Battalion. Harold was the first to die when he was killed on 17 September 1918, aged 23. His younger brother, Arthur, died on 8 October 1918, aged 19. Both are commemorated on the memorial.

Private Sidney Henry PROCTOR, 4th Battalion, Canadian Infantry, was killed in action on 3 May 1917, aged 16. His father, Sergeant William Henry Proctor, was also killed in action just over a week later on 14 May serving with the Canadian Labour Corps. Canadian army records show his father's rank as that of private. The unit's war diary notes that he was one of several men killed when a shell struck an iron fence as they were working on a railway construction site near Kemmel. The explosion also wounded another fifteen men, some of whom later died. William is buried in Kemmel Château Cemetery.

Private Harry PUDDLE DCM, 5th Battalion, Canadian Machine Gun Corps, was killed in action on 3 April 1918. His DCM was awarded for conspicuous gallantry and devotion to duty when in charge of a Vickers machine gun crew during an attack. Owing to the nature of the ground, his gun was in a very exposed position, but even when his gun was hit and damaged and all of its crew had become casualties, he remained with it in order to support the infantry, firing it continuously whilst under very heavy shell fire. The citation notes that his work to date had been characterised by great coolness and courage. The award was gazetted on 21 October 1918.

Major John Alexander ROSS DSO, 24th Battalion, Canadian Infantry, was initially reported as wounded and missing on 17 September 1916, aged 23, though later he was presumed to have died that day. His DSO was gazetted on 24 June 1916 and was awarded after he and a fellow officer had volunteered to carry out a very dangerous reconnaissance under heavy fire, returning later with important information as to the enemy's position.

Back home, he and his family were ranchers, but in 1911 he gained a place at the Royal Military College, Kingston, in Canada, where he excelled at his studies. He received his commission soon after enlisting in December 1914 and went to the Western Front as a major in charge of a company in May 1915, aged 21. He was killed in action whilst leading his men in an attack at Courcelette. Shortly before 5.00pm, just prior to the start of the attack, he was wounded by shrapnel when a shell exploded close to him. In spite of his injuries, he refused to attend the dressing station and insisted on remaining with his company. Unfortunately, opposite his company's front the artillery barrage fell behind the enemy's line rather than on it, and consequently he and his men faced heavy machine-gun fire as soon as they left their trenches. The other two companies involved in the attack reached their objectives, but Ross and his men became caught up in the enemy's wire and were cut down. His body was never found. He was also twice mentioned in despatches.

Lance Sergeant Charles Francis ROUTLEDGE DCM, 4th Canadian Mounted Rifles, was killed in action on 15 September 1916, aged 21. His DCM was awarded for conspicuous gallantry during a bombardment. Whilst retiring he rescued a Lewis gun, which he brought across the open under heavy fire, firing at enemy bombers from shell holes as he went. He also carried in many wounded men during the same operation. His award was gazetted on the 19th August 1916. Prior to enlisting in November 1914 he served as a trooper with the 124th Battalion, Canadian Infantry, also known as the Governor General's Body Guard.

Major James Loutit SCLATER, 7th Battalion, Canadian Infantry, was killed in action during the capture of Hill 70 on 15 August 1917, aged 22. His father, Lieutenant Colonel James Sclater DSO VD, was the commanding officer of the 29th Battalion, Canadian Infantry. His father's DSO was gazetted on 1 January 1918 in the New Year's Honours List.

Major Allan Crawford SHAW, 14th Battalion, Canadian Infantry, was the first of the thirty-one majors listed on the memorial to lose his life. He was killed in action on 19 May 1915, aged 37. The battalion's war diary makes no reference to his death, despite containing quite a lot of detail for that day.

Major Frederick Temple SPENCER DCM, 1st Battalion, Canadian Infantry, was killed in action on 4 April 1917, aged 26. He won his DCM as a sapper serving with No. 2 Section, 1st Division Signals, Canadian Engineers. It was awarded for conspicuous gallantry and devotion to duty laying and repairing telephone lines under heavy shell and rifle fire. The citation notes that he had always set a fine example in times of great danger. The award was gazetted on 11 March 1916. He had also been mentioned in despatches.

Lieutenant James Nimmo SCOTT MC, 8th Battalion, Canadian Infantry, was killed in action in trenches near Festubert as a result of enemy shelling on 22 May 1915. His MC was gazetted two weeks after his death in the King's Birthday Honours List. He was also mentioned in despatches.

Lieutenant Allen SHORTT MC, 58th Battalion, Canadian Infantry, was killed in action on 10 December 1916, aged 20, and was commissioned from within the ranks of the battalion. His MC was gazetted on 26 December 1916 and awarded for conspicuous gallantry in action. When his company was held up, he and five other men succeeded in bombing a machine-gun post, putting it out of action. Later, he returned across no man's land in daylight under heavy fire to give a report on the situation ahead. He was an American citizen who was born in New York.

Lieutenant Henry Albert SMITH MC, 1st Canadian Mounted Rifles, was killed in action on 1 October 1916, aged 25. His MC was gazetted on 19 August 1916 and awarded for conspicuous gallantry after rallying approximately sixty men from different units and taking up a strong defensive position. When the enemy later attacked the position, it was largely due to his actions that they failed to break through and, although wounded, he remained in command of his detachment until relieved.

Sergeant Robert SPALL VC, Princess Patricia's Canadian Light Infantry, was killed in action on 13 August 1918, aged 25. He was born in Brentford, Middlesex, but moved to Canada with his parents. He enlisted in July 1915 and eventually joined his battalion in France in September 1916. His VC was won over two days on 12 and 13 August 1918 near Parvillers and was awarded for most conspicuous bravery and self-sacrifice. When his platoon became isolated during an enemy counter-attack, Sergeant SPALL picked up a Lewis gun and stood on the parapet, firing at the advancing enemy and inflicting many casualties. He then returned down the trench to his men and directed them to a sap seventy-five yards from the enemy's position. Picking up another Lewis gun, he again climbed onto the parapet, firing at the enemy and preventing their advance. It was whilst holding them up that he was killed. The citation acknowledges that it was his self-sacrifice and valour that enabled his platoon to extricate itself from a very difficult situation. The award was gazetted on 26 October 1918.

Lance Corporal Percy Charles Kingsford SIMMONDS DCM, 4th Battalion, Canadian Infantry, was killed in action on 24 April 1917, aged 37. His DCM was awarded for conspicuous gallantry and devotion to duty during a daylight patrol when he and his party came under heavy fire. Owing to lack of immediate cover, his party became pinned down and was unable to extricate itself. He then stood up alone in order to draw the enemy's fire on himself whilst the remainder of the party found cover. Only after they had found shelter, did he find cover for himself. The award was gazetted on 26 July 1917.

Private Halmer SIGURDSON, 16th Battalion, Canadian Infantry, was one of three brothers who served and died during the war. Halmer was killed in action on the Somme on 25 September 1916, aged 20. His brother, Private Stonie Halm Sigurdson, 8th Battalion, Canadian Infantry, died of wounds as a prisoner of war on 30 October 1918. He is buried at Niederzwehren Cemetery in Germany. Neither CWGC records, nor Canadian army records, provide any definite clues as to the identity of the third brother, though I believe the most likely candidate is Private Sytryggur Sigurdson, 44th Battalion, Canadian Infantry, who was killed in action near Arleux on 3 June 1917 and who is now buried at La Chaudière Military Cemetery.

Private Francis SMITH, 4th Battalion, Canadian Infantry, was killed in action near Courcelette on 19 September 1916, aged 50. His son, Private John Leggit SMITH, was also killed in action and fell on 29 June 1917, aged 25, serving with the 52nd Battalion, Canadian Infantry. Both father and son are now commemorated here on the memorial.

Private Philip SOMERVILLE, 58th Battalion, Canadian Infantry, was killed in action near Regina Trench on 8 October 1916. The CWGC register points out that his two brothers also served in the Great War, but with the American Army. It also notes that some of his family had been British sailors, though it does not indicate whether this refers to service in the Royal Navy or some other capacity. His parents are shown living in Toledo, Ohio, where his father was a church minister.

Private Gordon James STOCKALL was one of six brothers to serve in the Great War. He was killed in action on 1 September 1918, aged 19, whilst serving with the 4th Battalion, Canadian Machine Gun Corps. His brother, Private David Robert Stockall, served with Princess Patricia's Canadian Light Infantry and survived the war, despite being wounded and taken prisoner on 2 June 1916 when the Germans attacked and captured Mount Sorrel, near Ypres. He was repatriated soon after the Armistice on 15 December 1918. Another brother, Private Frank Stockall, died of wounds on 10 October 1918, aged 24, serving with the 10th Battalion, Canadian Infantry, and is buried at Bucquoy Road Cemetery.

Private David STRANGER, 1st Canadian Mounted Rifles, was of Native American origin and came from the St Peter Reserve. He was 42 years old when he was killed in action on 29 March 1917, aged 23.

Captain Gordon Harrison TUFTS MC, 27th Battalion, Canadian Infantry, was killed in action on 21 August 1917. His MC, gazetted on 18 July 1917, was awarded for conspicuous gallantry and devotion to duty whilst commanding a strong advanced patrol. By pushing forward under heavy shell fire and establishing himself 400 yards ahead of his battalion, he was able to capture three machine guns that might otherwise have hindered its advance. His position also enabled his battalion to hold the ground it had gained.

Private Cecil Mather TELFER and his brother, Private Eric TELFER, are both commemorated here on the memorial at Vimy. Eric was the younger of the two and was killed in action with the 49th Battalion, Canadian Infantry, during operations south-west of Vis-en-Artois on 28 August 1918, aged 22. Cecil was killed in action two days later on 30 August south-east of Vis-en-Artois with the 8th Battalion, Canadian Infantry, and was 27 years old when he died.

Private George William TOMKINSON MM, was killed in action on 15 September 1916, aged 49. He had previously served for twenty-seven years in the Royal Navy, retiring as a Chief Petty Officer in 1905. He was killed in action with the 49th Battalion, Canadian Infantry, near the village of Courcelette.

Private Charles James TOOGOOD, 47th Battalion, Canadian Infantry, was killed in action on 11 November 1916, aged 29. His brother, Lance Corporal Frederick George TOOGOOD, fell in action the following year on 15 August 1917. He was killed serving with the 7th Battalion, Canadian Infantry, during the capture of Hill 70, near Loos. Both men are now commemorated here on the memorial.

Captain Francis Bassell WINTER MC, 'C' Company, 26th Battalion, Canadian Infantry, was also killed in action on 15 August 1917, at Hill 70. I can find no trace of his MC in any of the gazettes, though Canadian army records confirm the award, as does *Officers of the Canadian Expeditionary Force who Died Overseas 1914–1919*.

Sergeant Frederick Bert WAKELIN DCM, 1st Battalion, Canadian Infantry, was killed in action on 15 June 1915, aged 25. His DCM was awarded for conspicuous gallantry at Pilckem Ridge on 23 April 1915 when, as a lance corporal, he took his platoon into the firing line under heavy shell and rifle fire after all the senior NCOs had been killed or wounded. The award was gazetted on 30 June 1915. His brother, Lance Serjeant Thomas WAKELIN, also 1st Battalion, Canadian Infantry, was killed in action the same day, aged 28. Both of them are now commemorated here on the memorial.

Sergeant William WILLIS DCM MSM, Fort Garry Horse, died on 1 April 1918 from wounds received two days earlier during the cavalry action at Moreuil Wood. Canadian records refer to his surname as 'Wells', despite acknowledging that he had enlisted under the name of 'William Willis'. Prior to joining the cavalry he served with the 6th Battalion, Canadian Infantry. His DCM was awarded for conspicuous gallantry and devotion to duty whilst commanding his squadron in an attack on a wood during which he personally led a charge against two enemy machine guns. Though initially wounded, he continued to lead his men and, after reaching his objective, he organized the defence of the position and was again seriously wounded. His courage, determination and skilful leadership contributed greatly to the success of the operation. The award was gazetted on 26 June 1918. He had enlisted in Canada in September 1914.

Sergeant William Arthur WITHERINGTON DCM, 7th Battalion, Canadian Infantry, was killed in action during the attack at Hill 70 on 15 August 1917, aged 37. His DCM was awarded for conspicuous gallantry and devotion to duty whilst commanding his platoon, leading it to its objective and connecting up with the troops on his flank. He was also wounded later in the day. His award was gazetted on 6 February 1918.

Corporal Murray WELSH DCM, Royal Canadian Dragoons, was killed in action during the cavalry charge at Moreuil Wood on 30 March 1918, aged 30. His DCM had already been awarded for conspicuous gallantry and devotion to duty whilst in charge of a second Bangalore torpedo party during a raid in which he rushed to the far end of the enemy's wire in order to explode the device. The citation then notes that he went on to assume command of the left blocking party in the enemy's front trench where he performed most valuable work. The award was gazetted on 1 May 1918.

Corporal Harry WILSON DCM MM, 10th Battalion, Canadian Infantry, was killed in action on 28 September 1918 during operations near Cambrai. His DCM was awarded for conspicuous gallantry and devotion to duty at Villers-lès-Cagnicourt on 2 September 1918. After a large party of the enemy had been driven out of a position, he followed them down a trench with his Lewis gun and brought accurate fire on them from close range, killing many and throwing the remainder into utter confusion. Following closely on their heels, he brought such severe fire to bear that, when they did attempt to rally for a counter-attack, they were forced instead to make a further retirement. Shortly afterwards he was knocked out by a shell burst but, after regaining consciousness, he insisted on remaining with his company. The following day, he led the platoon successfully when all the other NCOs had become casualties. His DCM was gazetted on 16 January 1919 and his MM on 19 November 1917. His MM was won at Hill 70 where he acted as a runner between 14 and 18 August 1917. The citation records that he made numerous trips under the most dangerous conditions and worked tirelessly and with complete disregard for his own personal safety.

Private William WALKLING DCM, 43rd Battalion, Canadian Infantry, was killed in action on 28 August 1918, aged 23. His DCM was gazetted on 16 January 1919 and awarded for his role during his battalion's attack at Domart on 8 August 1918. After his platoon commander and sergeant had both been killed, he took charge of the men and successfully carried them on to their objective. By his prompt action, leadership and initiative, he and his platoon completed a very difficult flanking movement whilst an attack was in progress against Dodo Wood. During the operation he had to lead the men through stiff enemy resistance in order to reach his objective. His brother, Frederick Walkling, also served, but survived the war.

Brothers Frank and Manson WANNAMAKER both served as privates with the 2nd Battalion, Canadian Infantry, and were both killed in action. Frank was killed on 12 April 1917 during operations to eliminate The Pimple, a small knoll at the north end of Vimy Ridge that had eluded capture on the opening day of the Battle of Arras. Manson was killed in action a few weeks later on 3 May during fighting at Fresnoy, near Arleux, east of Vimy. Both men are now commemorated here on the memorial.

Private Albert WARNER DCM, 2nd Battalion, Canadian Infantry, was killed in action on 3 May 1917, aged 23. His DCM was gazetted on 16 November 1916 and awarded for several acts of conspicuous gallantry in action. On one occasion he rescued wounded men under intense fire, and on another carried a machine gun forward after its team had all become casualties, subsequently bringing up bombs and ammunition through a heavy barrage. Throughout all of these actions he showed great courage and initiative.

Private Thomas WESLEY, 16th Battalion, Canadian Infantry, died on 16 August 1917, the day after the capture of Hill 70 near Loos. He had enlisted on 22 December 1915 and was one of the many Native Americans who served with the Canadian Expeditionary Force during the war. He came from the St Peter Reserve, which was part of the Clandeboye Agency in Manitoba.

Private Jack James WHISKEY, 8th Battalion, Canadian Infantry, came from the Cross Lake Reserve, which was part of the Norway House Agency, and was another soldier of Native American origin. He enlisted on 1 May 1916, originally in the 203rd Battalion, but later transferred to the 8th Battalion which was already in France. He was killed in action during operations carried out by the Canadian 1st and 2nd Divisions at Hill 70 on 15 August 1917. He was 24 years old when he died. The CWGC register shows him under the name of 'St James Whiskey'.

Private Cyril Henry James WINDLE, 'D' Company, 10th Battalion, Canadian Infantry, was killed in action on 26 September 1916, aged 24. Private John Gilbert William WINDLE also served in 'D' Company with his brother and was killed in action the same day, aged 38. Both brothers are commemorated on the memorial.

Private Joseph Stewart WOODS, 8th Battalion, Canadian Infantry, was killed in action near Courcelette on 26 September 1916, aged 23. His brother, Lance Corporal Walter Ralph Woods, was killed in action with the 27th Battalion, Canadian Infantry, at Passchendaele on 6 November 1917, aged 20. He is buried in Tyne Cot Cemetery in Belgium.

The brothers came from a large family of ten children. In 1902 their father, Russell, was found drowned in the docks at Kenora, the town where the family had settled. Two years later, one of their older brothers, Clarence, died during an accident at work. When the war broke out, Joseph, Milfred and Walter enlisted and went overseas. Walter saw action at Saint-Eloi in March 1916, then at Courcelette on the Somme later that year. During the winter of 1916–1917 he was temporarily attached to the 255th Tunneling Company, Royal Engineers, but returned to the 27th Battalion, Canadian Infantry, in March 1917. Although Joseph was killed in action near Courcelette in 1916, Milfred was more fortunate and went on to survive the war.

Lieutenant Guy Randolph YERXA MC, 50th Battalion, Canadian Infantry, was killed in action on 10 April 1917, aged 27. His MC was gazetted on 18 June 1917 and was awarded for conspicuous gallantry and devotion to duty, leading his men to the enemy's second line with great courage and skill under heavy fire. Later he supervised the collection of the wounded, setting a splendid example throughout the operation.

Chapter Four

'We are but warriors for the working day'
The Vis-en-Artois Memorial

Vis-en-Artois and Haucourt were captured by Canadian troops on 27 August 1918. However, there are no soldiers of the Canadian Expeditionary Force commemorated on this memorial. All Canadian soldiers who fell in France and who do not have a known grave are commemorated on the Vimy Memorial. The Vis-en-Artois Memorial records the names of over 9,800 soldiers who fell between 8 August and 11 November 1918 on this part of the Western Front during the Advance to Victory in Picardy and Artois and who have no known grave. This covers a wide area between the Somme and Loos. As with the Canadian Expeditionary Force, there are no members of the New Zealand Expeditionary Force, nor any from the Australian Imperial Force, but men of the South African Brigade are included here with their British counterparts.

It is worth considering the number of engagements and operations that took place between 8 August and 11 November 1918. These are engraved on the memorial: Amiens, Albert, Bapaume, Scarpe, Drocourt–Quéant Line, Havrincourt, Epéhy, Canal du Nord, Saint-Quentin Canal, Beaurevoir Line, Selle, Valenciennes, Sambre, Grande-Hirondelle and Mons. Although the memorial happens to be on the Arras battlefield, it is not unique to Arras, though in this respect it is similar to the Flying Services Memorial. Some people might be surprised to find Mons included, which of course is in Belgium, but it would have made no sense to create a distinction between those who fell in France and those who were killed just a few miles over the border in neighbouring Belgium; for once, geographical divides were deemed to be less important than the idea of commemorating a single victory and the liberation of both countries.

The memorial's design and architectural features are very classical in style. Behind the two rows of ionic columns are the panels containing the names of the missing, but it is worth glancing up from the carved figure of St George and the Dragon to notice the oil lamp, symbol of the CWGC, which as an organisation is a modern day keeper of the flame of remembrance. Above each of the two vertical pillars is a sarcophagus, each adorned with the laurel wreaths of victory. Other neo-classical touches have also been included in what is a very well thought out design. The memorial's creator was John Reginald Truelove, but the sculptures are by Ernest Gillick.

Gillick was born in Bradford, but his family later moved to Nottingham. He went on to study there at the Nottingham School of Art, then at the Royal College of Art in London. As well as exhibiting regularly at the Royal Academy, he also worked at the British School in Rome. He later became an associate member of the Royal Academy, though never a full member. He died in 1951. Other works by Gillick include the Cenotaph in George Square, Glasgow, a sculptural group featuring Henry VII at Bosworth Field for the City Hall in Cardiff, and the chapel that forms part of the war memorial at Winchester College. He also designed the Polar Medal in 1904.

The memorial was unveiled by the Right Honourable Thomas Shaw CBE, on 4 August 1930. It is a very fine memorial and a very fitting tribute to all those commemorated on it who helped to carve out final victory and bring the war to a close.

There are 279 holders of the MM recorded on the panels, far too many to list separately. I have made references to some of them, particularly the nine recipients who also held the DCM and the one man who held the VC, but in many cases it is simply not possible to determine the actions or circumstances in which they were won. There are also forty-eight holders of the DCM and twenty-nine holders of the MC, two of whom were also awarded a bar.

The Royal Naval Volunteer Reserve

Lieutenant Archibald George BAREHAM MC, 1st Battalion, Royal Marine Light Infantry, was killed in action near Niergnies on 8 October 1918, aged 38. His MC was gazetted on 1 August 1919. It was awarded for conspicuous gallantry and devotion to duty at Niergnies on 8 October 1918 when the enemy, accompanied by tanks, attacked our positions. The assault compelled the posts on either side of his battalion to withdraw, which in turn enabled the enemy's tanks to take up a position to the rear of his company. He immediately rallied all the available men, including some from other units, and succeeded in forming a defensive flank to the left. He inflicted heavy casualties on the enemy and later succeeded in re-establishing the entire line, taking back the original positions in a show of great courage and initiative.

Lieutenant Herbert Benjamin BIGGS MC and Bar, Hawke Battalion, Royal Naval Volunteer Reserve, was killed in action near Inchy on 3 September 1918. His MC was gazetted on 4 March 1918 while he was serving as a temporary lieutenant, though it appears to be without citation. The bar to it was gazetted on 11 January 1919 and was awarded for personally supervising the tactical dispositions of the Lewis guns in his battalion over many days during operations between Ligny-Thilloy and Thilloy. His ability and technical knowledge were invaluable, and his coolness under fire, his unflagging energy and devotion to duty were a splendid example, inspiring all ranks with confidence.

Sub Lieutenant Andrew ROSS DCM, Drake Battalion, Royal Naval Volunteer Reserve, was killed in action during the attack on Niergnies on 8 October 1918, aged 24. His DCM was gazetted on 20 July 1917 and was awarded for conspicuous gallantry and devotion to duty whilst serving as an acting Petty Officer when, despite having been wounded twice, he remained in action for forty-eight hours, assisting in the capture of a machine gun and forty prisoners, setting a fine example to all ranks.

Chief Petty Officer George PROWSE VC DCM, Drake Battalion, Royal Naval Volunteer Reserve, was killed in action near Arleux on 27 September 1918, aged 32. His DCM was gazetted on 16 January 1919. It was awarded for actions at Logeast Wood on 21 August 1918 when he led his men with great gallantry against a machine gun that was holding up the advance on his company's flank. In spite of difficulties caused by heavy mist, he captured it and disposed of its crew. On a subsequent occasion he held a position against repeated counter-attacks that were supported by an intense bombardment for twenty-four hours. The citation notes that his courage, leadership and cheerful disposition had an incalculable effect on his men.

His VC was the last one to be issued with a blue ribbon, which until then had been the custom with regard to recipients from the Royal Navy. It was awarded for conspicuous bravery and devotion to duty during operations around Pronville on 2 September 1918. During the advance, part of his company became disorganized by heavy machine-gun fire from an enemy strongpoint. He collected together what men he could and led them with great bravery and coolness against the position, capturing it along with twenty-three prisoners and five machine guns. Following that, he took a patrol forward in the face of much opposition and established it on an important section of high ground.

On another occasion he displayed great heroism by attacking single-handed the crew of an ammunition limber that was trying to recover ammunition, killing three of the team and capturing the limber. Two days later he rendered valuable service whilst covering the advance of his company with a Lewis gun and later located two machine gun positions in a concrete emplacement that had been holding up the advance of the battalion to his right. With complete disregard for his personal safety, he rushed forward with a small party, attacking and capturing the posts, killing six of the enemy and capturing thirteen prisoners and both machine guns; he was the only one out of the assault party to survive. This action enabled the battalion on the right to push forward without incurring further machine-gun fire from the village. The lengthy citation concludes that his magnificent example and leadership throughout the entire operations were an inspiration to all, and that his courage was superb. He had been wounded on two previous occasions during his service.

Leading Seaman Norman Edmund SEAMAN, Hawke Battalion, Royal Naval Volunteer Reserve, was killed in action on 3 September 1918, aged 19. He enlisted in 1915 and had served in Gallipoli.

The Cavalry

Contrary to popular myth, the cavalry had not quite had its day and was able to play a small, but useful part in the final advance, particularly during the opening stages. There are fifty-five cavalrymen listed on the memorial, thirty-five of whom fell between 8 August and 10 August 1918. A further nine died during the rest of August. Whilst many of the cavalry regiments have just a couple of casualties, the 7th (Princess Royal's) Dragoon Guards has nine, the 5th (Princess Charlotte of Wales's) Dragoon Guards has six, and the 19th (Queen Alexandra's Own Royal) Hussars has five.

The only cavalry officer is Lieutenant George William Russell CHIBNALL, 3rd (Prince of Wales's) Dragoon Guards. He was killed in action on 26 August 1918, aged 20. His older brother, Lieutenant Ronald Stanley Chibnall, 8th Suffolk Regiment, was killed in action on the opening day of the Third Battle of Ypres, 31 July 1917. He also has no known grave and is commemorated on the Menin Gate.

Serjeant Frederick Walter HARRIS DCM, 4th (Royal Irish) Dragoon Guards, was killed in action on 21 August 1918, aged 34. His DCM was gazetted on 3 September 1918 and was awarded for conspicuous gallantry and devotion to duty in getting men quickly into position to meet a hostile attack. Later, with the greatest courage and determination, he rallied, re-equipped and led thirty infantrymen in a counter-attack, thereby enabling a line to be re-established at a most critical time.

Private Albert Ernest ENTWISTLE, 5th (Princess Charlotte of Wales's) Dragoon Guards, was killed on 8 August 1918, aged 25. His brother lived at No. 9, Rue Auguste Beernaert, Boitsfort, Brussels, Belgium.

Serjeant Tom SAXON, 'B' Squadron, 3rd (King's Own) Hussars, died of wounds on 10 August 1918, aged 29. He had eleven years' service.

The Royal Horse Artillery
Corporal Daniel Fletcher TURTON, 'A' Battery, Royal Horse Artillery, was killed in action near Péronne on 2 September 1918, aged 32. He was an experienced soldier who had enlisted in 1904 and had previously served in India.

The Royal Field Artillery
Major Ernest Arnold Lovell COOK MC, 'C' Battery, 122 Brigade, Royal Field Artillery, was killed in action on 1 November 1918, aged 26. His MC was gazetted on 26 September 1917, though its citation only appeared on 9 January 1918. It was awarded for conspicuous gallantry and devotion to duty on several occasions as a temporary lieutenant, during which he behaved with fearlessness and energy as a forward observation officer, continually sending back valuable information under fire. On one occasion he remained out in the open all night through a very heavy enemy barrage and signalled back to HQ by means of a lamp. He also went through heavy hostile fire to rescue some of his men who had been gassed and wounded, managing to get three of them back to safety. The citation ends by stating that his gallantry had been noticeable at all times, particularly when assisting his battery in action.

The Grenadier Guards

Serjeant John Henry JARMAN DCM, King's Company, 1st Grenadier Guards, was killed in action near the village of Saint-Léger on 25 August 1918, aged 26. His DCM was gazetted on 5 December 1918 and was awarded in connection with an attack when his company was held up by machine-gun fire. After his captain and another officer had become casualties, he took charge of all the men he was able to collect and led them forward under heavy fire, capturing five machine guns, thirty prisoners and gaining his objective. The attack involved an advance of around 1,000 yards. The citation concludes that his magnificent example of courage and fortitude were worthy of the highest praise.

Private Harry BIRTLES, King's Company, 1st Grenadier Guards, was killed in action on 11 October 1918, aged 25. The battalion was involved in an attack that day near the River Selle in which the King's Company successfully cleared a spur south of Solesmes. His family came from Stoke-on-Trent, but at the time of his enlistment he was working at Alnwick Castle where he held the position of second footman to the Duke of Northumberland.

The Royal Scots (Lothian Regiment)

Several of the regiment's battalions are represented here amongst the 104 men listed. A number of them fell during the fighting around the Albert–Arras railway line in late August 1918 and belong to the 2nd Battalion, which was part of the 3rd Division. Others, belonging to the 52nd (Lowland) Division, fell around Hénin and Hénin Hill a few days later. The regiment also has some casualties from these divisions dating to September and early October. The earliest, however, are men from the 5/6th Battalion, which was part of the 32nd Division. The majority fell on 11 August 1918 in an attack on Parvillers, south-east of Amiens.

Lieutenant Robert Elder MURRAY, 5/6th Royal Scots, was one of twelve officer casualties from the battalion on 11 August 1918, nine of whom were killed. The German defences around Parvillers were strongly wired and proved more than a match for the weak artillery barrage that accompanied the attack. A number of tanks, which were intended to support the attack, were nearly an hour late and were all out of action by the time they reached our own front line. The battalion was relieved by Canadian troops the following day and did not return to action until the end of the month.

Private John Grainger NOBLE MM, 1/4th Royal Scots, is one of two holders of the MM commemorated on the memorial from this regiment. His MM was won in Palestine with the 52nd (Lowland) Division. The roll of honour for the Union Assurance in Edinburgh wrongly refers to his death occurring at Kemmel Hill; he was killed in action near Hénin Hill on 27 August 1918.

The Queen's (Royal West Surrey Regiment)

Company Serjeant Major Benjamin REYNOLDS DCM, 7th Queen's (Royal West Surrey Regiment), formerly Royal Fusiliers, was killed in action on 8 August

1918, aged 28. His DCM was won as a company serjeant major with the 9th Royal Fusiliers. It was gazetted on 9 July 1917 and was awarded for conspicuous gallantry and devotion to duty. The citation does not go into detail and merely states that he had rendered valuable service during raids and had performed consistently good work.

He was killed on the high ground north of the River Somme, north-east of Sailly-le-Sec, and in the same action that claimed the life of Lieutenant Colonel Christopher Bushell VC DSO. REYNOLDS's brigade, 36 Brigade, was lent by the 12th (Eastern) Division to the 18th (Eastern) Division as a replacement for 54 Brigade. The 7th Queen's (Royal West Surrey Regiment) was initially tasked with acting as a defensive flank during the advance, but soon found itself attacked by significant numbers of Germans hurling bombs as they advanced through the mist. Bushell counter-attacked and drove the enemy out of the old front line, but was killed soon afterwards. *Military Operations, France and Belgium 1918, Volume 4* describes the fighting as a *'soldier's battle in which small parties of infantry co-operated with each other as best they could'*.

The Germans who attacked were almost certainly from the same unit that had made a small, but worrying incursion into the British lines just before dawn on 6 August where the front held by the 58th (2/1st London) Division met that of the 18th (Eastern) Division south of Morlancourt. The 27th Würtemberg Division was an efficient unit with a good reputation for fighting and had recently been brought into the line north of the Somme. The attack penetrated half a mile deep on a 4,000 yard frontage. Despite the capture of over 200 prisoners, it would appear that none of them gave away details of the impending Allied offensive that was to take place in two days' time.

Lance Corporal Francis Sydney GOACHER MM, 1st Queen's (Royal West Surrey Regiment) was killed in action on 21 September 1918, aged 25. He had been awarded the *Croix de Guerre* (Belgium), in addition to the MM. He was killed in operations to clear German positions west of the Hindenburg Line following the fighting at Epéhy. The battalion encountered heavy machine-gun fire from two strongpoints, one at Meath Post, the other at Limerick Post. It also faced sniper fire and was eventually forced to dig in. The right hand company, in particular, suffered many casualties after it lost direction and veered off to the right. Lance Corporal GOACHER was the son of a clergyman from Upper Edmonton, north London, and had formerly served with the East Surrey Regiment.

The Buffs (East Kent Regiment)

Serjeant Arthur James AYRES DCM MM, 1st East Kent Regiment (The Buffs), was killed in action on 18 September 1918, aged 27. His DCM was posthumously gazetted on 30 October 1918 and was awarded for conspicuous gallantry and devotion to duty during a raid in which he demonstrated great courage and dash. Being the first over the parapet, he made his way directly to the objective, where he assisted his officer in getting five of the enemy out of a dug-out, killing one of them and capturing the rest. All this was done before the rest of his platoon reached the position. The citation concludes that throughout the entire operation he set a splendid example to those around him.

His battalion's advance on 18 September depended on the capture of Fresnoy-le-Petit. Once the 2nd York & Lancaster Regiment had captured the village, the 1st East Kent Regiment (The Buffs) and the 1st King's (Shropshire Light Infantry) were to continue the advance and take their objectives south of Gricourt, a village north-north-west of Saint-Quentin. Although parts of Fresnoy-le-Petit were captured, the 2nd York & Lancaster Regiment had not captured the entire village. Consequently, the advance by the 1st East Kent Regiment (The Buffs) was held up by machine-gun fire from those parts of the village still in German hands. Some casualties had also occurred from shell fire before the advance began. The battalion's casualties that day came to six officers and around 150 other ranks.

Private Frederick BUTCHER, 7th East Kent Regiment (The Buffs), was executed on 27 August 1918, the day on which the villages of Vis-en-Artois and Haucourt were captured by the Canadian Corps. He had enlisted in 1915 and had been a good soldier, but after three years' service he went absent from his unit, no doubt under stress, and was eventually shot by men of his own battalion. His grave, which was presumably marked and recorded, was inexplicably lost and has never been identified. He would have been executed some distance from the front line, and with the Allied forces continually moving forwards, the chances of his grave being destroyed by shell fire seem fairly remote, but not impossible. It may be that the map reference for the grave was noted down incorrectly.

Private Rudolf Charles Kasper OLESEN, 7th East Kent Regiment (The Buffs), was killed in action on 8 August 1918, aged 23. He fell in action north of the River Somme on the opening day of the Allied offensive. His parents lived in Copenhagen, Denmark, and he was one of a number of Danes who fought with British and Canadian units during the war. OLESEN happened to be living in Bermondsey when the war broke out and his motives for enlisting are not clear. He did, however, enlist with another Dane, Carl Olaf Groesmayer, who appears to have survived the war. In March 1917 representations were made through diplomatic channels by the King of Denmark to the German military authorities with regard to members of the East Kent Regiment who were being held as prisoners of war. Consequently, a number of officers of the East Kent Regiment were transferred from captivity in Germany to neutral countries. The National Army Museum in London now holds the regimental archives for the Buffs, including a number of documents relating to Danes who served in the regiment.

The King's Own (Royal Lancaster Regiment)
Company Serjeant Major Francis (Frank) LAVERY DCM, 8th King's Own (Royal Lancaster Regiment) was killed in action on 23 August 1918 near Gommecourt. He had served for eight years with the King's (Liverpool Regiment) and

had won his DCM with the regiment's 1st Battalion. He was one of seven men killed during a well executed night attack that saw 76 Brigade capture around 300 prisoners, three field guns, two 5.9 guns, two trench mortars and seventy machine guns. By hugging the creeping barrage that accompanied the attack, the 8th Battalion suffered relatively few casualties and the attack was entirely successful.

His DCM was gazetted on 13 August 1915, though it is shown in error under the name of 'A. Lavery'. It was awarded for his actions at the Battle of Festubert on 16 May 1915 after the officer commanding his company had been shot. He then took command in a very exposed and difficult situation showing great skill and gallantry. During that time he shot several of the enemy himself. The citation adds that his cheerfulness and bravery under very trying conditions set a splendid example to the men under his command.

The Northumberland Fusiliers
Private Lewis Edward DUCROQ, 1/5th Northumberland Fusiliers, though posted to the 1st Battalion, was killed in action on 23 October 1918, aged 19. In 1915 he had enlisted in the Royal Field Artillery at the age of 15, but was discharged on 27 October the same year. He subsequently re-enlisted in the Welsh Regiment, but at some stage he was transferred to the Northumberland Fusiliers. His parents lived in Cardiff. There appears to be no trace of this man in any of the sections of *Soldiers Died in the Great War* covering the regiments in which he served.

Private Joseph MOORE, 12/13th Northumberland Fusiliers, was killed in action on 8 September 1918, aged 27. The register notes that he was one of three brothers who fell, but the CWGC records are inconclusive with regard to the identity of the other two.

The Royal Warwickshire Regiment
Company Serjeant Major Ernest Robert FREEMAN DCM, 10th Royal Warwickshire Regiment, was killed in action on 23 October 1918, aged 28. His DCM was gazetted on 26 September 1916 and was awarded for conspicuous gallantry in action. When all his company officers had become casualties, he led the company with great coolness and ability for many hours whilst it was heavily engaged with the enemy at close quarters. The citation concludes that he had done fine and gallant work. Sadly, *Soldiers Died in the Great War* makes no reference to his DCM. He was also awarded the *Croix de Guerre* (Belgium).

Private Stanley Frederick SMITH, 14th Royal Warwickshire Regiment, formerly Welsh Regiment, was killed in action on 27 September 1918, aged 19. His battalion was engaged in the first stage of operations against the Hindenburg defences when he was killed. Having passed through the 1st Queen's Own (Royal West Kent Regiment), the 14th Royal Warwickshire Regiment was heavily counter-attacked and its positions temporarily lost. He was the son of Lieutenant Colonel F.W. Smith of Gorwydd Lodge, Gowerton, near Swansea.

The Royal Fusiliers (City of London Regiment)

Second Lieutenant Frederick Charles Leonard HARRUP MC, 9th Royal Fusiliers, was killed in action on 21 September 1918. He was one of three officers from the battalion killed that day. Two days earlier his battalion had pushed on between Epéhy and Ronssoy, but on reaching its objective had found its flanks in the air owing to heavy resistance around Epéhy itself. The battalion then dug in and used its Lewis guns to protect its flanks. In doing so, it sustained 113 casualties, including two officers. When the attack was renewed on 21 September, the battalion was still unable to make much headway and further casualties that day had a significant effect in weakening the battalion.

HARRUP had originally served as a private in the Army Service Corps. His MC was gazetted on 13 January 1919 and was awarded after leading his platoon in an attack with great gallantry and skill. On capturing his objective he found his flank was uncovered, but he immediately took excellent tactical measures to defend it and subsequently repelled two strong counter-attacks. The actions described in the citation refer quite possibly to the events that took place on 19 September, two days before his death.

Second Lieutenant William Henry MEASURES MC, 5th Royal Fusiliers, attached 11th Battalion, was killed in action on 22 August 1918, aged 34. Prior to enlisting he was a minister at Brentford Congregational Church. His MC was won shortly before his death during an action to restore part of the British line that had been captured in a surprise attack early on the morning of 6 August. The 27th Würtemberg Division, which had recently been brought to the Somme from Lille in order to strengthen the line and bolster morale, broke through to a depth of nearly half a mile, severely disrupting the preparations being made by III Corps for its part in the offensive due to be delivered two days hence in front of Amiens. The 11th Royal Fusiliers took part in a counter-attack in the early hours of 7 August to recapture the lost ground. Some partial gains were made, but the Germans responded with a number of counter-attacks of their own. By the end of the day, having run out of bombs and ammunition and, in spite of gallant efforts to withstand these assaults, the battalion had been driven back to its original positions.

On the day that Second Lieutenant MEASURES was killed, his battalion had to cross the River Ancre in order to capture ground between Méaulte and Albert. The Germans, however, soon became aware of the advance and put down heavy machine-gun fire. Casualties were incurred in the marshy terrain on either side of the river, where many of the men had to wade through waterlogged ground up to their hips in order to advance.

Private Frederick LEDIARD, 13th Royal Fusiliers, was killed in action on 28 August 1918, aged 31. He had enlisted in August 1914 and, according to the CWGC register, he was the youngest of six brothers, all of whom served during the war. He is shown living in Bow in east London, but his mother resided in the

Hanwell district of Birmingham. There are three more casualties in the CWGC records with the same surname, but their parental details are different, although all three men came from families in the Birmingham area.

Private William MACNAY, 'C' Company, 11th Royal Fusiliers, was killed in action on 18 August 1918, aged 34. He had previously been mentioned in despatches. An adopted son, he had worked in Calcutta before the war, but for some reason in August 1914 he volunteered for military service with the French army. In March 1915 he joined the British Army and served in East Africa with the 25th Royal Fusiliers (Frontiersmen) before being transferred to the 11th Battalion.

Private Frederick Wallace RUSSELL, 9th Royal Fusiliers, was killed in action on 24 September 1918, aged 18. His father, Frederick, also fell during the war whilst serving with the Royal Field Artillery. Frederick senior, who had served during the South African campaign, died of wounds on 28 May 1918, aged 40. He is buried at Saint-Sever Cemetery, Rouen.

The King's (Liverpool Regiment)

Serjeant Percy CAMPBELL DCM MM, 1st King's (Liverpool Regiment), was killed in action on 29 September 1918. He had previously served with the Lancashire Fusiliers. His DCM was gazetted on 15 November 1918 and was awarded for conspicuous gallantry and fine leadership in attack and during patrol work under heavy machine-gun fire. The citation notes that throughout two days' operations he set a splendid example and showed skill and sound military knowledge in all his work.

Serjeant William George GRIFFITHS DCM MM and Bar, 9th King's (Liverpool Regiment), was killed in action on 28 August 1918, aged 34. His DCM was gazetted on 6 February 1918 and was awarded for conspicuous gallantry and devotion to duty when acting as company serjeant major during an attack. Realizing that the attack was held up, he led a party of twelve men in a flank attack on the enemy's position. With great skill, and in the face of heavy machine-gun fire, he advanced his men to within assaulting distance and timed his attack to coincide with other attacks being made on the position. He was responsible for the capture and consolidation of the strongpoint. The citation concludes that his courage and contempt for danger had a marked influence on his men.

Serjeant Thomas JONES DCM MM, 1st King's (Liverpool Regiment), was killed in action on 25 August 1918, aged 23. His DCM was gazetted on 15 November 1918 and was awarded for conspicuous gallantry and fine leadership in attack and patrolling whilst under heavy machine-gun fire. Throughout the two days' operations he displayed a strong offensive spirit in attack and his coolness and determination had a marked effect in maintaining the momentum of those operations. He had previously served with the South Lancashire Regiment. Unfortunately, *Soldiers Died in the Great War* makes no reference to his DCM.

Private Stanley MORGAN, 13th King's (Liverpool Regiment), was killed in action on 21 August 1918, aged 20. His brother, George Morgan, also served in the King's (Liverpool Regiment), but with the 12th Battalion, and was killed in action on 9 May 1917, aged 34. He is commemorated on the Thiepval Memorial.

Private Walter RUST, 1st King's (Liverpool Regiment), was killed in action on 25 August 1918, aged 19. He had previously served with the Sherwood Foresters. According to the CWGC register, he held a Royal Humane Society Certificate for saving someone from drowning in the River Ouse on 13 August 1913.

Private Gordon Frank Sterio SERGIADI, 1st King's (Liverpool Regiment), formerly Army Cyclist Corps, was killed in action on 25 August 1918, aged 26. He was born in Finsbury, London, but his parents lived at Courbevoie, Seine, France. Presumably, he was also living in France when the war broke out, as according to *Soldiers Died in the Great War* he enlisted in Paris.

The Norfolk Regiment
Private Samuel GILL, 1st Norfolk Regiment, was killed in action on 22 August 1918, aged 19. His elder brother, Private John William Gill, also fell in action serving with the 12th Northumberland Fusiliers. He was killed on 4 October 1917, aged 28, and is commemorated on the Tyne Cot Memorial.

The Lincolnshire Regiment
Private Frank Douglas Jenner SUTHERLAND, 1/5th Lincolnshire Regiment, who had previously served with the regiment's 2nd Battalion, was killed in action on 29 September 1918, aged 26, and had originally gone to France in November 1914. The CWGC register notes that his father, Fred Sutherland, lived at the Royal Hospital, Chelsea, as a Chelsea Pensioner. Frank was born just down the road from the Royal Hospital in Fulham. Curiously, I could find no trace of Frank's father in the Royal Hospital Book of Remembrance.

The Devonshire Regiment
Serjeant William Giles Woolway COLE DCM, 16th (Royal 1st Devon & Royal North Devon Yeomanry) Devonshire Regiment, was killed in action on 2 September 1918. His DCM was gazetted on 27 September 1901 whilst serving as a trooper with the 27th Company, 7th Battalion, Imperial Yeomanry. During the South African campaign he saw action at Diamond Hill, Cape Colony and in Orange Free State, and was also mentioned in despatches on 10 September 1901. He came from the village of South Molton in Devon and began his journey through the Great War by enlisting in Barnstaple. He is also commemorated on the Boer War Memorial Tablet in the Town Hall at South Molton.

Private William Henry Douglas CROMBIE DCM, 9th Devonshire Regiment, was killed in action on 4 October 1918, aged 27. His DCM was gazetted on

20 October 1916 whilst serving in the Army Ordnance Corps and was awarded for conspicuous gallantry after a shell had fallen from a box. He carried it some thirty feet away to a place of safety while the fuse was still burning.

Serjeant James Norman WILLIAMS DCM MM, 9th Devonshire Regiment, was killed in action on 5 October 1918. His DCM was gazetted on 3 October 1918 and was awarded for conspicuous gallantry and devotion to duty in carrying out a reconnaissance for a raid in which he later took part. The raid took place in daylight and in full view of the enemy's lines. Towards the end of it, he held back an enemy party by skilful bombing until his own men had got clear. His MM had been gazetted earlier that year on 28 January.

Prince Albert's (Somerset Light Infantry)

Lance Serjeant Phillip Frederick CORNISH, 1st Somerset Light Infantry, was killed in action on 2 September 1918, aged 25. He enlisted on 2 September 1914 and had therefore served for exactly four years to the day when he died. He was killed during operations against the Drocourt–Quéant Line. A number of casualties within the battalion were caused by shelling before operations began and during the initial stages. Later on, machine-gun fire from the direction of Prospect Farm caused further casualties and delays to the advance.

Private Charles STRADLING, 12th (West Somerset Yeomanry) Somerset Light Infantry, was killed in action on 2 September 1918, aged 25. He had previously served in Gallipoli and Palestine. The 12th Battalion was formed in Egypt in early January 1917, largely around the dismounted members of the North Somerset Yeomanry. The battalion was part of the 74th (Yeomanry) Division, which began its move from Egypt to France at the end of April 1918. After a period of training and familiarization on the Western Front, it took part in the Second Battle of Bapaume, the Battle of Epéhy and the final advances through northern France and Flanders during October and early November.

The East Yorkshire Regiment

Lance Corporal Austin ELLIS DCM, 1st East Yorkshire Regiment, was killed in action on 18 September 1918, aged 35. His DCM was gazetted on 3 October 1918 where he is shown as serving with the Northumberland Fusiliers. *Soldiers Died in the Great War* shows him as serving with the 1st East Yorkshire Regiment at the time of his death, but it also refers to his previous service with the Northumberland Fusiliers. The DCM was awarded for conspicuous gallantry and devotion to duty during a massed attack by the enemy in which he kept on firing his Lewis gun under intense bombardment until it was put out of action. He then went through a very heavy bombardment to obtain a fresh gun and kept it firing until he was ordered to withdraw. He showed tremendous pluck and endurance throughout, firing his guns continuously for several hours, inflicting heavy casualties on the enemy.

The Bedfordshire Regiment

Captain Harold Charles LOE MC, 1st Bedfordshire Regiment, was killed in action on 27 September 1918, aged 27. That morning, the 1st Bedfordshire Regiment had captured part of the village of Beaucamp, near the Canal du Nord, but during the afternoon the Germans made a strong bombing attack and forced the battalion to withdraw from the village into a sunken road outside it. It was during this fighting that LOE was killed. The Germans pulled out of Beaucamp the following day and the village was then re-occupied.

His MC was gazetted on 23 April 1918 and was awarded for conspicuous gallantry and devotion to duty as a second lieutenant commanding one of the front line companies during five days of operations. Although the part of the line that he had taken over was in a precarious state, he threw out a defensive flank and then oversaw the construction of a further system of trenches. During this time he was buried on three occasions by exploding shells. On another occasion during these five days, he crawled out and dressed a wounded man who could not be brought in owing to the presence of enemy snipers.

Second Lieutenant Walter WHITBOURN MC, 6th Bedfordshire Regiment, attached 2nd Battalion, was killed in action near the Albert–Bapaume road, just west of Tara Hill, on 22 August 1918. He was one of three officers and eighty-nine other ranks who had joined the 2nd Battalion from the 8th Battalion on 8 February 1918. His MC was gazetted on 26 July 1918 and was awarded for conspicuous gallantry and devotion to duty whilst carrying out several excellent reconnaissance patrols to the front and flanks of his unit's position and bringing back useful information as to the enemy's dispositions. On one occasion that information helped to frustrate an enveloping movement by the enemy.

Company Serjeant Major Percy COMPTON DCM, 2nd Bedfordshire Regiment, was killed in action on 21 September 1918, near Ronssoy. His DCM, which he won as a serjeant, was gazetted on 6 February 1918. It was awarded for conspicuous gallantry and devotion to duty when he and a party of men were ordered to raid some concrete enemy posts. On reaching their objective, they were held up by wire and also came under heavy fire from two machine guns and snipers from a range of about twenty yards. During the attack he tried to put one of the machine guns out of action by firing a rifle grenade through the slit in the concrete post. When ordered to withdraw, he brought back wounded men and placed them in shell holes. He then returned to the enemy's wire and helped more wounded men to reach cover. After that, he crossed no man's land under heavy fire in broad daylight to get stretchers for them.

Serjeant Reuben JEFFRIES DCM, 1st Bedfordshire Regiment, was killed in action on 23 October 1918 during operations to capture the village of Beaurain, about five miles north of Le Cateau. The battalion reported fourteen men killed that day, but a further 105 were wounded and five were recorded as missing in action. His DCM was gazetted on 18 July 1917 and was awarded for conspicuous gallantry and devotion to duty during an attack after his battalion had become held up by a machine gun. Realizing this, he crawled across the open under fire and rushed the gun single-handed, shooting one of its crew and bayoneting two of the gunners, thus enabling the advance to continue.

Private Sydney Robert JARY DCM, 2nd Bedfordshire Regiment, was killed in action on 18 September 1918, aged 19. His DCM was gazetted on 2 December 1919 and was awarded for most conspicuous gallantry and initiative on the morning of 18 September 1918 during his battalion's attack on Ronssoy, where he showed great courage and dash when his platoon was held up by a machine gun. He picked up a Lewis gun from a wounded man, and rushing to a suitable position on the flank, he opened fire with deadly accuracy. After killing most of the machine gun's team, he rushed the three remaining members of its crew single-handed and captured them. The citation concludes that it was his splendid conduct that undoubtedly saved many casualties and allowed the advance to continue. Unfortunately, he was killed later that same day.

The Royal Irish Regiment
Private John WHITE, 'A' Company, 2nd Royal Irish Regiment, was killed in action on 21 August 1918, aged 27. The family lived at Queen Street in Dublin where he had worked as a cooper at the Guinness Brewery. He was born in Limerick and had previously served in the Royal Dublin Fusiliers and the Army Service Corps.

The Lancashire Fusiliers
Captain Sydney VASEY MC, 9th Lancashire Fusiliers, attached 16th Battalion, was killed in action on 10 August 1918 near Damery, aged 27. His MC, gazetted on 26 July 1918, was awarded for conspicuous gallantry and devotion to duty as a second lieutenant when in charge of two sections that had been ordered to clear a sunken road near Ayette on 3 April 1918. In spite of heavy machine-gun and rifle fire, he drove the enemy out of the road and captured two machine guns. He subsequently helped to consolidate a new line by pushing out 300 yards beyond the objective, thereby greatly assisting those working behind him on the consolidation. The citation concludes that throughout this operation he handled his men with great skill and determination.

Serjeant Jonathan Adam SMITH DCM, 1/7th Lancashire Fusiliers, was killed in action on 27 September 1918 near Trescault during operations on the approach to the Hindenburg Line. His DCM was awarded for his part in a successful attack carried out by his company during which he led his platoon forward with conspicuous courage and skill under heavy machine-gun fire, capturing two machine-gun posts. Although the enemy outnumbered his party three to one, he showed so much dash and leadership that it led to the capture of the position with very few casualties.

The Royal Scots Fusiliers

Second Lieutenant Neil Wallace ROBERTSON MC and Bar, 1st Royal Scots Fusiliers, was killed in action on 2 September 1918, aged 20. He was the son of the late Major M.W. Robertson CMG, Cape Mounted Rifles, whose family lived in Cape Province, South Africa. His MC was gazetted posthumously on 15 October 1918 and was awarded for conspicuous gallantry and devotion to duty whilst on his way to attack an enemy machine-gun position with three other men. Before reaching it, he encountered a large party of the enemy well inside their own wire. He called on them to surrender, but when they showed willingness to fight he shot two of their officers, whilst a third was shot by one of the men in his patrol. He and his men then returned to their lines. During the incident he showed fine courage and initiative, typical of the previous work he had carried out.

The bar to his MC was gazetted on 2 December 1918 and was awarded for conspicuous gallantry in an attack during which he led his men to their objective through thick fog against strong opposition where he reorganized them. The citation notes that throughout the ensuing thirty-six hours, his cheerfulness and coolness inspired his men, adding that his fine example was instrumental in causing the company's position to be maintained during these operations.

Serjeant Ernest LAMB, 1/4th Royal Scots Fusiliers, attached 155 Brigade, Light Trench Mortar Battery, was killed in action on 1 September 1918, aged 32. He enlisted in September 1914 and was gassed in May 1916. He was also torpedoed on board the SS *Arcadian* en route to Egypt in 1917 when 277 lives were lost, including nineteen officers and 214 other ranks. Thirty-four of the crew and ten naval personnel were also drowned, but over 1,000 men were saved, many of them by the destroyer that was accompanying the troop ship.

The Cheshire Regiment

Corporal F. Ernest WALKER DCM, 1st Cheshire Regiment, was killed in action on 2 September 1918 during operations to capture the village of Beugny. His DCM was gazetted on 18 November 1918 and was awarded for conspicuous gallantry and devotion to duty during an advance when the line was twice held up by enemy machine-gun fire. On each occasion, he went out alone and bombed the positions, accounting for both crews and capturing the guns. Thanks to his courage and determination his company was able to advance and reach its objectives. The citation notes that throughout the entire operation he showed great coolness and leadership.

Private John James SUFFLER, 1st Cheshire Regiment, was killed in action on 2 September 1918, aged 19, during the same operations as Corporal WALKER. His father, Serjeant John Suffler, 4th King's (Liverpool Regiment), died at home on 21 March 1917 as a result of wounds and is burried in Liverpool (Ford) Roman Catholic Cemetery.

The Royal Welsh Fusiliers

Serjeant Harry McHALE DCM, 14th Royal Welsh Fusiliers, was killed in action near Gouzeaucourt on 18 September 1918. His DCM was awarded for conspicuous gallantry as an acting serjeant during a raid on the enemy's trenches. He and his officer were the first to enter the trenches where they accounted for several of the enemy. Later, at the conclusion of the raid, he showed great determination by covering the withdrawal and also assisted in bringing in two wounded men. The award was gazetted on 27 July 1916.

Private Michael CONDON DCM MM, 25th (Montgomeryshire and Welsh Horse Yeomanry) Royal Welsh Fusiliers, was killed in action on 21 September 1918 when his battalion took part in an attack on a system of trenches known as the Quadrilateral, east of Ronssoy. The battalion's left flank became exposed after the 24th Welsh Regiment had lost its bearings. This gave the Germans the opportunity to reoccupy the Quadrilateral, attacking the battalion frontally and from behind, as well as on the exposed flank. His DCM was gazetted earlier in the year on 4 March 1918. It was awarded for conspicuous gallantry and devotion to duty during an attack in which he rallied small parties of men, reorganizing them and gallantly leading them to the assault. The citation concludes that he showed splendid leadership and resource.

Private Cecil Thomas EVANS, 16th Royal Welsh Fusiliers, was killed in action at La Boisselle on 24 August 1918, aged 20. The village of La Boisselle earned its place in history on 1 July 1916, but it was also recaptured by the 38th (Welsh) Division on 24 August 1918. Although the advance went well, heavy resistance was encountered at two locations: firstly at Bécourt Wood, which was strongly held, and secondly around the Lochnagar mine crater. The crater was only captured around 8.00pm after a separate attack was made with the assistance of Stokes mortars. When the crater and the surrounding area were finally cleared, 200 prisoners were also captured. Regrettably, this part of the story of La Boisselle is rarely told.

The South Wales Borderers

Private James ARMITAGE, 10th South Wales Borderers, was killed in action on 2 September 1918, aged 19. His father, Corporal Henry Armitage, also fell in action whilst serving with the 2nd Battalion, Army Cyclist Corps, on 2 August 1917, aged 39; he had previously served in the Cheshire Regiment. He is buried in Dickebusch New Military Cemetery Extension.

The King's Own Scottish Borderers

Second Lieutenant Henry Alder COMMON, 1/2nd King's Own Scottish Borderers, attached 1/4th Battalion, died on 4 October 1918 from wounds received at Cambrai, aged 30. He was a regular soldier who had only joined the battalion in Egypt in April 1918. He was killed commanding 'B' Company, which was part of the leading wave of an attack to clear the Faubourg de Paris, a suburb of Cambrai on the road leading from Masnières. The attack, which began at 11.50pm, was not successful and failed to clear the suburb. A few days later the Germans abandoned Cambrai in favour of a defensive line along the River Selle. His original battalion, as shown in the CWGC register, makes no sense. The regiment's two regular battalions were separate entities throughout the war.

Lance Serjeant John Martin ROONEY DCM MM, 2nd King's Own Scottish Borderers, was killed in action on 26 August 1918. His DCM was gazetted on 30 October 1918 and was awarded for conspicuous gallantry and devotion to duty on 28 June 1918. After his platoon commander had become a casualty, he went forward and led the way. At one point he was attacked by an enemy officer who lamed him severely by a blow to the leg with the butt of a rifle. Corporal Rooney, having bayoneted the officer, continued to limp on ahead until he reached the enemy's support line where he captured a machine gun single handed, killing the gunner and taking three other men prisoners. In spite of his injured leg, he dispatched nine of the enemy and worked with tireless energy. He was of the greatest assistance to his company commander, encouraging the men by his example of gallantry and unflinching endurance.

This action took place during fighting at the end of June 1918 near Arrewage, where in the words of the regimental history, '*the Germans stood to the bayonet, and died by it*'. ROONEY was heavily involved in the hand-to-hand fighting that day. The battalion, which entered the fight with around 500 other ranks, sustained just over 200 casualties, including nine officers wounded.

Private Peter CARMICHAEL, 1/5th King's Own Scottish Borderers, was killed in action on 31 October 1918. He was awarded the *Croix de Guerre* (France) and had previously served with the Highland Light Infantry.

The Worcestershire Regiment
Lieutenant Hillgrove CROYDON-FOWLER, 2nd Worcestershire Regiment, attached from the 1st (Garrison) Battalion, was killed in action on 12 October 1918. He was one of a large draft of 330 men who joined the battalion between 21 and 23 April 1918 while it was out of the line at Noordpeene.

On the night of 11 October, two companies from the 2nd Worcestershire Regiment provided a covering party for sappers placing light footbridges across the River Selle south-east of Neuvilly, to the north of Le Cateau. The 16th King's Royal Rifle Corps and the 9th Highland Light Infantry then attacked the German positions along the railway embankment that runs roughly parallel to the river on the far side. The 16th King's Royal Rifle Corps managed to gain the crest of the rise, but the units from the 17th (Northern) Division on its left were unable to do likewise. With the left flank exposed, some of the covering party went forward to assist, but their advance was met by a strong counter-attack. Thanks to the assistance provided by the Worcestershire men, the enemy's move was temporarily checked, but our line was eventually forced back to the river bank. Although a line of outposts was then established on the east bank, the decision was taken to halt any further attacks until the operation could be properly supported. The German counter-attack was accompanied by artillery fire and this caused many casualties, including Lieutenant CROYDON-FOWLER. He was one of four officer casualties within the battalion that day along with forty-five NCOs and men.

The East Surrey Regiment
Private Humphrey John GILBERT, 8th East Surrey Regiment, was killed in action on 1 September 1918, aged 43. The CWGC register notes that he was wounded on three previous occasions and that he had enlisted in September 1914.

Private Alfred KING DCM, 8th East Surrey Regiment, died of wounds on 2 September 1918, aged 35. He was severely wounded during the fighting around Le Priez Farm, near Combles and the approaches to Rancourt, where further strong resistance was met. His DCM was gazetted posthumously on 16 January 1919 and refers to conspicuous gallantry and devotion to duty on 22 August 1918 during mopping up operations in Albert as the Allies advanced across the old Somme battlefields. When a group of men in the town became isolated by a combination of heavy shell fire and bombing from a large party of the enemy, he rushed forward with a Lewis gun and brought concentrated return fire to bear from close range forcing the enemy to surrender. Later, he assisted the advance of his platoon by pushing well forward on one of the flanks from where he was able to enfilade the enemy.

The Duke of Cornwall's Light Infantry
Private Thomas FARADAY, 1st Duke of Cornwall's Light Infantry, was killed in action on 23 August 1918, aged 36. He held the *Croix de Guerre* (Belgium). He is one of eleven men from the regiment awarded this decoration, but is the only private, all the others being NCOs or officers.

The Border Regiment
Captain William CONSTANTINE MC, 7th (Westmorland and Cumberland Yeomanry) Border Regiment, was killed in action at Gauche Wood on 18 September 1918, aged 23. He had been wounded at Messines Ridge the previous year. He was one of six officers from the 6th Lincolnshire Regiment who joined the 7th Border Regiment in October 1916. Although *Officers Died in the Great War* refers to his MC, I can find no reference to it in any of the gazettes. His file at the National Archives acknowledges his MC, but it makes no mention of the date on which it was gazetted or the circumstances in which it was awarded.

Second Lieutenant David James CLOW DCM, 4th Border Regiment, attached 15th Durham Light Infantry, was killed in action on 24 August 1918, aged 28. His DCM was gazetted on 21 June 1916 and was won whilst serving as a serjeant with the 1/2nd Scottish Horse. It was awarded for conspicuous gallantry, standing by his wounded officer under heavy fire when his party had been ordered to seek cover. He later assisted both the wounded officer and another wounded man to safety. His brother, Private Thomas Howie Clow, was killed in action on 28 June 1915 whilst serving with the 6th Royal Scots in Gallipoli. He is commemorated on the Helles Memorial.

Private Robert CASSON DCM, 5th Border Regiment, was killed in action on 10 August 1918. He had served with the battalion continuously since 1914 and for a long time was one of his company's runners. His DCM was gazetted on 21 October 1918. The citation goes on to say that in the many engagements in which he was involved, his conduct had at all times been an example to those around him and that he had never failed to deliver a message entrusted to him.

Private Donald Edgar TINKLER, 7th (Westmorland and Cumberland Yeomanry) Border Regiment, was killed in action on 18 September 1918, aged 20. His brothers, Tom and Fred, also died whilst serving with different branches of the Royal Engineers. Sapper Fred Tinkler was 23 years old when he died of wounds on 4 February 1916. He served with the Third Army Signal Section, Royal Engineers, and is buried at St Sever Cemetery, Rouen. Tom Tinkler died after the war, on 13 February 1919, aged 28, whilst serving with the 212th Field Company, Royal Engineers. He is buried at Sainte-Marie Cemetery, Le Havre.

The Royal Sussex Regiment
Lieutenant Basil Charles WRIGHT MC and Bar, 2nd Royal Sussex Regiment, was killed in action on 24 September 1918. His MC was gazetted on 20 October 1916 and was awarded for conspicuous gallantry in action. After taking part in a successful assault, he showed great coolness and courage in beating back a counter-attack, having previously done much fine work. The bar to his MC was gazetted on 15 February 1919 and its citation appeared later that year on 30 July. It was awarded in connection with operations on 18 September 1918 near Pontruet where he commanded a platoon with great gallantry. On one occasion, when the enemy was forming up for a counter-attack, he charged with what few men he could gather together and successfully dispersed the attack. Throughout the battle he showed bold leadership and resourcefulness and, by keeping close control of his platoon and using it with skill, he materially assisted in the capture of the enemy's positions and in doing so incurred very few casualties.

Officers Died in the Great War only shows the MC against his name and makes no reference to the bar. Even the village memorial at High Halden, where he is also commemorated, fails to acknowledge the second award. The CWGC has since been notified of the omission.

Private Frederick Ernest BARKER, 9th Royal Sussex Regiment, was killed in action on 4 November, exactly one week before the end of the war. Unknown to him at the time, his wife back home in Bexhill-on-Sea was gravely ill. She never recovered and died on 3 November, the day before her husband. The family tragedy was compounded by the death, that same month, of their youngest child who was around three months old. Three other children, aged seven, five, and three, were left orphaned as a result of their parents' death.

The Dorsetshire Regiment

Second Lieutenant Herbert Alfred FORD MC, 1st Dorsetshire Regiment, was killed in action near Damery on 11 August 1918, aged 23. His MC was gazetted on 13 May 1918 and was awarded for conspicuous gallantry and devotion to duty after he had been sent out to locate some advanced posts held by a neighbouring unit, the position of which was in some doubt. As he did this, he came under fire and when both of the men accompanying him were wounded by machine-gun fire he bandaged one of them and carried the other man 250 yards back to the nearest post. He then went out and completed his reconnaissance. After that, despite increasing daylight, he made his way back to the other wounded man and, with the help of his orderly, carried him in under machine-gun fire. Throughout the operation he set a splendid example of courage and resource.

Private Leslie William BLATCHFORD, 6th Dorsetshire Regiment, was killed in action on 27 August 1918, aged 19. His death occurred during fighting near the village of Flers on the old Somme battlefield. According to the CWGC register, his father, the late William Henry Blatchford, fell whilst serving with the Australian Imperial Force. However, out of twenty-seven 'Blatchfords' listed as having died whilst serving with British and Commonwealth forces during the Great War, there is no obvious match. There are only two shown serving with Australian units, one of whom cannot have been his father by virtue of age; besides, both men have different first names. Several of the twenty-seven 'Blatchfords' do, however, come from the area of south Devon where his family lived. William Henry Blatchford is shown on the Crediton war memorial and local records note that he died at home in England in September 1921. His rank is listed as 'driver' and he is shown as serving with the 2nd Pioneer Battalion, Australian Infantry.

The Welsh Regiment

Private James SWINDLEHURST, 24th (Pembroke and Glamorgan Yeomanry) Welsh Regiment, was killed in action on 21 September 1918, aged 18. His father, Private John Swindlehurst, fell whilst serving with the 1/4th Loyal North Lancashire Regiment. He was killed in action on 28 September 1916 and is commemorated on the Thiepval Memorial.

Private Robert Frederick TATE, 2nd Welch Regiment, was killed in action on 23 October 1918, aged 19. Despite his age, he had previously served in Gallipoli and Mesopotamia with the regiment's 8th Battalion. He was therefore quite an experienced soldier.

The Black Watch (Royal Highlanders)

Serjeant Duncan WATTERS DCM, 6th Black Watch, was killed in action on 27 August 1918, aged 33. The battalion formed the left flank of an operation aimed at regaining the line originally held in March 1918. It began on 26 August and extended over two days. The third phase of the operation took place the following morning at 10.00am. His battalion successfully captured some trenches to the north-west of Greenland Hill and, although casualties were not heavy, WATTERS was one of five men from the battalion who were killed that day. His DCM, gazetted on 30 October 1918, was awarded for conspicuous gallantry after his party had become held up by an enemy machine gun. Crawling out to a flank, he shot several members of the crew, capturing the gun single-handed. The citation adds that his was a magnificent act of courage and prompt initiative, and that he had set a splendid example of coolness and determination throughout the operation. He came from the village of Auchterarder in Perthshire.

The Oxfordshire & Buckinghamshire Light Infantry

Lance Corporal Joseph Henry VALE DCM MSM, 2nd Oxfordshire & Buckinghamshire Light Infantry, was killed in action on 12 September 1918. His DCM was gazetted on 10 January 1920 and was won on 11 and 12 September near Hermies whilst under shell fire. Although exhausted from re-laying lines over a period of two days, he went out again on four separate occasions under a very heavy barrage to mend lines whose preservation was of the utmost importance. On the third occasion he also brought in a wounded man. The citation rightly points out that he showed the greatest courage and devotion to duty.

The Essex Regiment

Company Serjeant Major George COCKS DCM, 10th Essex Regiment, was killed in action on 8 August 1918. He had formerly served with the Lancashire Fusiliers and had won his DCM with that regiment. His DCM was gazetted on 21 October 1918 and was awarded for conspicuous gallantry and devotion to duty. The citation states that his work had consistently been '*all that could be desired*', and that whilst acting as regimental serjeant major, he had rendered valuable service prior to, and during an attack, guiding and supervising the ration and ammunition parties.

Private Walter William AGER DCM, 2nd Essex Regiment, was killed in action on 27 October 1918, aged 33. He had previously served with the Suffolk Regiment. His DCM was gazetted on 16 January 1919 and was awarded for conspicuous gallantry and devotion to duty. On 2 September 1918, north of Dury, he and another man were the only two left with a Lewis gun after all the rest had been killed or wounded and much of the ammunition had been lost. Collecting drums from abandoned guns, they worked their way round to a flank of their company's front and brought enfilade fire to bear on the enemy's position, materially assisting the rest of the infantry in its advance. Whilst others consolidated the new position, they pushed on ahead and kept down hostile fire, one working the gun, the other collecting ammunition.

The Sherwood Foresters (Nottinghamshire & Derbyshire Regiment)

Captain Cyril Ward BARTLETT MC, 11th Sherwood Foresters, was killed in action on 9 October 1918, aged 26. Although his MC is acknowledged in *Officers Died in the Great War*, there appears to be no reference to it in any of the gazettes. His file at the National Archives contains a note with regard to his MC, but does not give any reference to the date on which it was gazetted or the reason for the award.

Captain Herbert Henry TYLER MC, 6th Sherwood Foresters, attached 2nd Battalion, was killed in action between 17 and 19 September 1918. His MC was gazetted on 11 May 1917 and was awarded for conspicuous gallantry and devotion to duty whilst in charge of a Bangalore torpedo party. Although wounded, he remained with the party until the torpedoes were fired. In preparation for this operation, and during its execution, he carried out splendid reconnaissance work.

Serjeant Jack BROWN DCM MM, 1/5th Sherwood Foresters, was killed in action on 3 October 1918 during operations near Montbrehain and Ramicourt. His DCM, gazetted on 2 December 1919, was won on 29 September 1918 at Le Haucourt, just north of the Saint-Quentin Canal, where he showed great gallantry and coolness in charge of his platoon. When the left flank became held up, he pushed his platoon forward on the right, gaining his objective and capturing three 5.9 guns, three machine guns and an anti-tank gun, along with numerous prisoners, thus enabling the left flank to gain its objective. His gallantry throughout the day was described as splendid.

Serjeant James LIEVESLEY DCM, 1/6th Sherwood Foresters, was killed in action on 3 October 1918. His DCM was gazetted on 5 December 1918 and awarded for conspicuous gallantry and devotion to duty. Whilst commanding his platoon, he passed through another battalion in order to attack two posts that were holding up the advance. He succeeded in working around the first one causing the enemy to retire. He then rushed the second, killing six of the enemy and securing two prisoners and a machine gun. After reorganizing his men, he charged a third post, driving the enemy out, but shooting four before they could retire. The citation states that he showed great qualities of leadership and disregard for danger during this operation.

Serjeant Louis WILKINS, 2nd Sherwood Foresters, was killed in action on 19 September 1918, aged 38. He had previously served in the South African campaign and was an experienced soldier of considerable value to his battalion at a time when there were relatively few men left with his skills and leadership abilities.

The Loyal North Lancashire Regiment

Serjeant William GLOVER DCM, 2/4th Loyal North Lancashire Regiment, was killed in action on 12 September 1918. His DCM was gazetted on 18 November 1918 and was awarded for conspicuous gallantry and good leadership when in command of his platoon during an attack, leading it to its final objective with great skill. He cleared several dug-outs and inflicted heavy casualties on the enemy. Later, when counter-attacked on four separate occasions by two enemy companies, he held his ground with splendid determination.

The Northamptonshire Regiment

Corporal Allan Leonard LEWIS VC, 6th Northamptonshire Regiment, was killed in action on 21 September 1918, aged 23. His VC was awarded for most conspicuous bravery at Ronssoy on 18 September 1918 when in command of a section on the right of an attacking line that was held up by intense machine-gun fire. Realizing that two enemy machine guns were enfilading the line, he crawled forward alone and successfully bombed them, and then by rifle fire caused both teams to surrender.

On 21 September he again displayed great powers of command, but after rushing his company through the enemy's barrage, he was killed getting his men under cover from heavy machine-gun fire. Throughout this period he showed a splendid disregard for danger and his leadership at a critical time was beyond all praise. He came from Whitney-on-Wye.

Princess Charlotte of Wales's (Royal Berkshire Regiment)

Private John James PHIPPS, 5th Royal Berkshire Regiment, was killed in action at Carnoy on the old Somme battlefield on 26 August 1918, aged 19. His battalion's attack left forty-three dead, many of whom were killed by machine-gun fire. The majority are now buried at Péronne Road Cemetery; Private PHIPPS happens to be the only one with no known grave. His father, John James Phipps, died on 23 September 1918 whilst serving as an Air Mechanic 3rd Class based at 1st Aeroplane Supply Depot Repair Park. He is buried at Terlincthun British Cemetery, Wimille.

The Queen's Own (Royal West Kent Regiment)

Captain Harold Robert SMITH MC, 8th Queen's Own (Royal West Kent Regiment), was killed in action on 7 November 1918, aged 26. He was one of two officers from the battalion killed that day. His death occurred about a mile and a half east of Bavai when his battalion's advance became checked by heavy machine-gun fire. Although it dug in there, the battalion continued to push out patrols during the night to deal with these machine-gun posts. His MC was gazetted on 16 September 1918 and was awarded for conspicuous gallantry and devotion to duty as a temporary lieutenant after his company was held up by heavy and continuous machine-gun fire from an enemy post. With a party of Lewis gunners, he worked his way around the flank of the post and brought heavy fire to bear on it, enabling the rest of his company to advance. He personally led the assault on the post and captured it in a splendid display of dash and leadership.

The King's Own (Yorkshire Light Infantry)
Second Lieutenant Merfyn Harman SALUSBURY-JONES, 8th King's Own (Yorkshire Light Infantry), was killed in action on 11 August 1918, aged 22. His brother, Lieutenant Ivor Cynric Salusbury-Jones, also served with the King's Own (Yorkshire Light Infantry), but fell in action with the 5th Battalion on 21 September 1916, aged 22. He is buried at Puchevillers British Cemetery.

Private Henry Thomas SMITH, 5th King's Own (Yorkshire Light Infantry), was killed in action on 29 September 1918, aged 23. The CWGC register notes that he had been awarded the *Croix de Guerre* (Belgium). The award was gazetted on 12 July 1918 and was one of many conferred on that date.

The King's (Shropshire Light Infantry)
Second Lieutenant Robert Guy SHACKLES MC, 10th (Shropshire and Cheshire Yeomanry) King's (Shropshire Light Infantry), was killed in action on 19 September 1918, near Epéhy. He had only been with his battalion for a short time, having come out from England on 12 July. His MC, gazetted on 15 October 1918, was awarded for his leadership during a successful daylight raid on 27 July against an enemy post, which he managed to locate after two days' careful reconnaissance in no man's land. In the hand-to-hand fighting that took place all the enemy were accounted for, although his party, which consisted of two NCOs and eleven men, suffered no casualties. The citation notes that during the raid he handled his men with great skill, displaying great gallantry and energy. Two of the enemy were killed and four more were captured along with their machine gun. He clearly wasted no time before becoming actively involved with his new battalion.

Private Edward ROBERTS, 10th (Shropshire and Cheshire Yeomanry) King's (Shropshire Light Infantry), was killed in action on 19 September 1918, aged 26. He had previously served in Palestine and Egypt. The 1/1st Shropshire Yeomanry went to Egypt in March 1916, but a year later it merged with the 1/1st Cheshire Yeomanry to form the 10th Battalion (Shropshire and Cheshire Yeomanry), King's (Shropshire Light Infantry). The battalion went to France in May 1918 as part of the 74th (Yeomanry) Division.

The Duke of Cambridge's Own (Middlesex Regiment)
Major Richard Francis Montague BULLER, 7th Middlesex Regiment, attached 8th Battalion, was killed in action on 24 August 1918, aged 24, north-west of Croisilles during the attack on Summit Trench.

Second Lieutenant William Edward SMITH MC, Middlesex Regiment, attached 1/13th Battalion, London Regiment (Kensingtons), was killed in action south-west of Bullecourt on 29 August 1918 along with forty-two other men from his battalion. Their division, the 56th (London) Division, had captured the village of Croisilles the previous day and was continuing its advance when the men were killed.

His MC was gazetted on 16 September 1918 and awarded for conspicuous gallantry and devotion to duty whilst in command of a raiding party on 9 March. He was initially responsible for working out the details of the raid which he did with great thoroughness. During the raid itself he showed the greatest courage and powers of leadership, particularly during the withdrawal phase when he made successful use of his Lewis guns to keep down hostile fire. The raid resulted in the capture of four prisoners and the citation attributes the operation's success to his careful organization and fine example. SMITH was also involved in a more recent raid on 1 June after the officer in charge of its preparation had been wounded by shell fragments on 26 May. That raid was also considered a success. All the wounded were brought in, although one man was killed during the raid, and a further three subsequently died of wounds.

Private Sidney Malcolm Langholt MARSTON, Middlesex Regiment, attached 19th Battalion, London Regiment (St Pancras Rifles), was another man who had been posted elsewhere. He was killed in action on 5 September 1918, aged 21. According to the CWGC register, he was one of two brothers who fell in action during the war, although there appears to be no exact match to any other soldier in its records. Sidney's battalion was part of the 47th (London) Division. He had previously served with the East Surrey Regiment.

The King's Royal Rifle Corps

Second Lieutenant Douglas Russell WILSON MC, 6th King's Royal Rifle Corps, attached 16th Battalion, was killed in action near Englefontaine on 25 October 1918, aged 21. His MC was gazetted on 1 February 1919 and was awarded for conspicuous gallantry and devotion to duty near Ossus between 29 September and 2 October 1918. During part of those operations, when in charge of the leading wave of his company, the enemy put down a smoke screen after which he was heavily involved in the fighting that ensued. Although surrounded, he fought on, collecting remnants of other platoons, and eventually extricated his men, enabling them to rejoin their battalion. Later, he was in command of a daylight reconnaissance patrol on the Canal de l'Escaut and brought back valuable information after spending two hours under machine-gun fire.

Serjeant John WALLACE DCM, 'B' Company, 4th King's Royal Rifle Corps, was killed in action on 18 October 1918, aged 32, during operations near the River Selle to assist the American 27th Division in the capture of La Roue Farm. His DCM was gazetted on 2 December 1919 and was awarded for actions on 3 October 1918 at Le Catelet when acting as company serjeant major. After the leading waves had passed through the village, he and a small party of men mopped up some machine-gun nests in a quarry under heavy fire. Later, when all the officers in charge of platoons had become casualties and his company commander was away making a reconnaissance for a flanking attack, he led the remainder of the company to its objective in the face of heavy machine-gun fire. When he attempted to consolidate the new position he found himself completely isolated, and so withdrew his party with considerable skill, bringing back all the wounded with him. He then set up a new defensive position, showing marked gallantry and an ability to command.

Rifleman Gwilym Mansel Pritchard DAVIES, King's Royal Rifle Corps, attached 12th Battalion, London Regiment (The Rangers), died of wounds on 24 August 1918, aged 29. He was an only son who was educated at Bristol and Aberystwyth universities before going on to teach.

The Manchester Regiment
Captain John Cottier RICHARDSON DCM, 2nd Manchester Regiment, was killed in action on 4 October 1918, aged 37. His promotion within the regiment from colour serjeant to second lieutenant was gazetted on 17 November 1914, the same date on which he was seconded to the West African Regiment. His DCM, which he won whilst serving as a corporal with the Manchester Regiment during the South African War, was gazetted on 23 April 1901 and awarded for distinguished conduct in the field. That same year on 10 September he was also mentioned in despatches. His brother, Private Sydney Cottier Richardson, 1/6th Manchester Regiment, fell in action on 27 March 1918 and is commemorated on the Arras Memorial.

Company Serjeant Major John William NEWMAN DCM, 2nd Manchester Regiment, was killed in action on 1 October 1918, aged 31. His DCM was gazetted on 3 September 1919 for gallant and consistent good work and devotion to duty. The citation goes on to state that he had always shown remarkable efficiency in carrying out his duties, frequently under heavy shell and machine-gun fire, adding that it was mainly due to his remarkable coolness and discipline, both in and out of the line, that his company was maintained to a high standard of smartness and efficiency at all times. It concludes by stating that he had never spared himself and that he was of enormous value to his commanding officer, particularly during the fighting between 25 February and 16/17 September 1918.

Private Lawrence William PAYNE, 12th (Duke of Lancaster's Own Yeomanry) Manchester Regiment, was killed in action on 9 September 1918, aged 20. His brother, Robert, also fell, but there appears to be no exact match for him in CWGC records.

Private Edgar WAREHAM, 'C' Company, 1/8th Manchester Regiment, was killed in action on 30 August 1918, aged 31. He was another experienced soldier and had previously served in Gallipoli and Egypt.

The York & Lancaster Regiment
Lieutenant Gilbert Clare FITZHERBERT MC, 2nd York & Lancaster Regiment, was killed in action on 18 September 1918. Before the war he was a student at Sidney Sussex College, Cambridge. His MC was gazetted on 10 January 1917 and awarded for conspicuous gallantry in action after he and three other men had taken a Bangalore torpedo across no man's land and successfully fired it under the enemy's wire. The citation concludes by stating that throughout the operation he set a particularly fine example of courage and coolness.

Serjeant Frederick Charles RIGGS VC MM, 6th York & Lancaster Regiment, was killed in action on 1 October 1918, aged 29. His MM was won on the Somme in 1916 where he was wounded. His VC was gazetted posthumously on 6 January 1919 and was awarded for conspicuous bravery and self-sacrifice on the morning of 1 October 1918 near Épinoy. Having led his platoon through strong uncut wire whilst under heavy fire, he continued to advance and, although losing heavily from flanking fire, he and his remaining men reached their final objective where he captured an enemy machine gun. Later on, he handled two captured guns with great effect causing around fifty of the enemy to surrender. Subsequently, when the enemy again advanced in force, he cheerfully encouraged his men insisting they stand to the last man, but was killed in action whilst doing so. Riggs had served in Gallipoli and Egypt before coming to France.

The Durham Light Infantry
Captain Sidney Edward YOUDEN, 1st Durham Light Infantry, attached 7th Highland Light Infantry, was a veteran of the campaigns in Gallipoli, Egypt and Palestine. He was killed on 27 August 1918, aged 27, and was another soldier with a wealth of experience behind him. He died fighting with the 52nd (Lowland) Division, which played a significant part during the Advance to Victory.

Lieutenant Hugo Burr Craig WATT MC, 8th Durham Light Infantry, was killed in action on 24 August 1918 whilst attached to the regiment's 15th Battalion. Although his mother still lived at Portrush, County Antrim, he happened to be working for the Hudson's Bay Company when war broke out. He left Fort Norman in Canada in order to return home and enlist. His MC was gazetted in the New Year's Honours List on 1 January 1918.

The Highland Light Infantry
Lieutenant Francis LEGATE, 5th Highland Light Infantry, was also killed in action on 27 August 1918, aged 35. He fell during operations to capture Fontaine-lès-Croisilles and Riencourt, even though his battalion was in reserve that day.

Second Lieutenant William Hay McCALLUM, 7th Highland Light Infantry, was killed in action on the same day as Lieutenant LEGATE. His battalion and the regiment's 6th Battalion took a leading part that day when both units advanced on the villages of Fontaine-lès-Croisilles and Riencourt.

Second Lieutenant Thomas Hope PULLAR, 8th Highland Light Infantry, attached 7th Battalion, was killed in action near Hénin on 24 August 1918 when the village fell to his division, the 52nd (Lowland) Division.

Lance Corporal James McARTHUR MM and Bar, 9th (Glasgow Highlanders) Highland Light Infantry, was killed in action on 12 October 1918. His MM was gazetted on 18 July 1917 and the bar on 13 September the following year. He was killed in action during operations around the River Selle; he came from Airdrie in Scotland.

Private Alexander C. COOPER, 15th Highland Light Infantry, was killed in action on 11 August 1918, aged 20. Before the war he was a medical student at Glasgow University and lived there with his family in the city's Bishopbriggs district.

Private John DEMPSEY, 6th Highland Light Infantry, was killed in action on 24 August 1918, aged 26. He went to France in September 1914 and had also served in Palestine. He was wounded in 1916.

The Gordon Highlanders
Amongst the ninety men from this regiment recorded on the memorial, there is only one officer, Second Lieutenant John Grant WATT, 7th Gordon High-landers, who was killed in action on 27 August 1918. There is also just one gal-lantry award holder, Private James MAIR MM, who served with the regiment's 4th Battalion and was killed in action on 31 August 1918.

Serjeant Thomas McLEOD, 7th Gordon Highlanders, was killed in action on 28 August 1918, aged 32. He returned from South America in 1915 in order to enlist.

The Connaught Rangers
Lieutenant Thomas Francis GILMORE MC, 4th Connaught Rangers, attached 5th Battalion, was killed in action on 8 November 1918, aged 24. His MC was gazetted on 4 October 1919 and was awarded for marked courage and able leadership during the attack on the village of Serain on 8 October 1918. When confronted by an enemy strongpoint that was threatening the advance, he led the assault on it with his platoon. By a brilliant manoeuvre, he overwhelmed the position capturing sixty-seven prisoners and three field guns. He again led his platoon with great gallantry during the attack on Le Cateau on the night of 10 and 11 October 1918.

Second Lieutenant John COADY, Connaught Rangers, attached 2nd Royal Irish Regiment, was killed in action on 21 August 1918, aged 37. He died during operations referred to collectively as the Second Battle of the Somme, in the

Battle of Albert. When his battalion was heavily counter-attacked by units from a Bavarian regiment, he and his men succeeded in defeating the enemy, though at a cost of 329 casualties. Second Lieutenant COADY also held the *Croix de Guerre* (Belgium).

Princess Louise's (Argyll & Sutherland Highlanders)
Lieutenant Joseph Macintyre TAYLOR, 2nd Argyll & Sutherland Highlanders, was killed in action on 24 October 1918, aged 21. According to the CWGC register, he was wounded on four previous occasions and had been on active service from December 1914 until his death. He had previously served in Salonika. He was an only son and came from Shandon, Dumbartonshire.

Lance Corporal James MILROY DCM, 2nd Argyll & Sutherland Highlanders, was killed in action on 23 October 1918. His DCM was gazetted on 10 January 1920 and was won as a private for conspicuous gallantry and good work. On the night of 10 October 1918, near Neuvilly, he was sent forward as part of a patrol with orders to find crossings over the River Selle for his company. He found a footbridge that was heavily wired, but very close to the enemy's positions. Under heavy rifle and machine-gun fire he cut the wire, thus making the bridge passable for his company. When his company did eventually cross the river it was able to do so without incurring serious losses.

Private Charles CANT DCM, 2nd Argyll & Sutherland Highlanders, was killed in action on 24 September 1918. His DCM was gazetted on 3 September 1918 and awarded for conspicuous gallantry and devotion to duty as a company stretcher-bearer during no fewer than seven operations when he organized many parties to bring in the wounded under heavy fire. On one occasion when the enemy was pressing forward in large numbers, he rushed out under intense rifle and machine-gun fire, picked up a wounded man and carried him back to the company lines, where he was able to dress his wounds.

Private William CAVIN, 2nd Argyll & Sutherland Highlanders, was killed in action on 24 September 1918, aged 24. He was one of five brothers who served during the war, two of whom also fell. The family came from the Shawlands area of Glasgow. His brother, James Cavin, died on 29 June 1916, aged 28. He is buried at Ismailia War Memorial Cemetery in Egypt. He was serving in the Royal Engineers, but was attached to the Royal Field Artillery as a driver when he apparently died from illness. The other brother, John, died at home in Glasgow on 19 October 1918, aged 26. He is now buried in the city's Eastwood Cemetery and was serving with the 2nd Highland Light Infantry. Curiously, there is no trace of John serving with any of the Highland Light Infantry battalions in *Soldiers Died in the Great War*.

The Royal Munster Fusiliers
Private Thomas FLYNN DCM MM, 2nd Royal Munster Fusiliers, formerly Connaught Rangers, was killed in action on 12 October 1918, aged 29. His DCM

was gazetted on 11 March 1916 whilst serving with the Connaught Rangers and was awarded for conspicuous bravery when scouting at night under heavy fire. The citation also states that he had frequently come to notice for great bravery and gathering intelligence and acknowledges that his devotion to duty had always been most marked. The battalion war diary shows just one man killed during the early morning of 12 October near Saint-Bénin, noting that the line was heavily shelled at around 5.00am. FLYNN had also been awarded the *Médaille Militaire* (France).

The Royal Dublin Fusiliers

Regimental Serjeant Major Herbert KNIGHT DCM, 2nd Royal Dublin Fusiliers, attached to Anson Battalion, Royal Naval Volunteer Reserve, was killed in action on 8 October 1918. His DCM was gazetted after the war on 3 September 1919. The citation states that whilst acting as regimental serjeant major he had done excellent work with the battalion. When in the line, his gallantry and devotion to duty were very marked and served as an excellent example to all junior officers and men in the battalion. It goes on to say that during the heavy fighting in March and April 1918 he showed great courage and determination in organizing ammunition parties, so that at all times and under the most trying conditions the firing line was supplied continuously with ammunition.

The London Regiment

Second Lieutenant Herbert Quey HOWARD DCM, 2nd (City of London) Battalion, London Regiment (Royal Fusiliers), was killed in action on 8 August 1918, aged 21. His DCM was awarded for actions near Saint-Pierre-Divion on 13 November 1916 at the Battle of the Ancre. It was gazetted under the name of 'H. HOWARD' on 26 January 1917 and was won whilst serving as a private in the Cambridgeshire Regiment, which was part of the 39th Division. It was awarded for conspicuous gallantry in action when, with just a few men, he rushed a German machine-gun post, capturing the gun and its crew in a fine display of coolness and courage.

Company Serjeant Major Charles Christopher George CLARK, 'B' Company, 2/2nd (City of London) Battalion, London Regiment (Royal Fusiliers), was killed in action near Epéhy on 10 September 1918, aged 21.

Captain Arthur CURTIS MC, 3rd (City of London) Battalion, London Regiment (Royal Fusiliers), was killed in action on 27 August 1918, aged 33. His MC was awarded whilst serving as a second lieutenant and was gazetted on 18 March 1918. It was awarded for conspicuous gallantry and devotion to duty, going out on several occasions with patrols in front of our advanced posts and obtaining valuable information as to the enemy's dispositions. During an attack he did excellent work, organizing parties of men and bringing in the wounded and, although blown up by a shell, he remained on duty, showing great courage and determination.

Second Lieutenant Victor Charles PRINCE, MC, 4th (City of London) Battalion, London Regiment (Royal Fusiliers), was killed in action on 1 September 1918, aged 20. His MC was gazetted on 1 January 1919 and was awarded for conspicuous gallantry and able leadership. When his company was held up by heavy machine-gun fire 400 yards from its objective, he went forward to the front line and personally led a platoon against the position with great dash causing heavy casualties to the enemy. The citation notes that his example at this critical moment earned him the highest praise.

Lance Corporal Ernest David OVER, 5th (City of London) Battalion, London Regiment (London Rifle Brigade), attached 2 Rifle Brigade, was killed in action on 29 August 1918, aged 40. He was formerly with the Royal Army Medical Corps and was the eldest of six brothers who served.

Private Charles Henry STARK, 7th (City of London) Battalion, London Regiment, was killed in action on 22 August 1918, aged 34. When the war broke out he was still a reservist. He re-enlisted in the 2nd Dragoon Guards (Queen's Bays) in August 1914, although at the time of his death he was posted to the 19th (County of London) Battalion, London Regiment (St Pancras Rifles).

Captain Edwin Charles Kaye CLARKE MC, Inns of Court OTC, attached 8th (City of London) Battalion, London Regiment (Post Office Rifles), was killed in action near Howitzer Wood, about three miles south of Combles, on 31 August 1918, aged 27. His MC was awarded for his part during a raid on German trenches in June 1918. He and his party succeeded in killing ten of the enemy and capturing fourteen prisoners, as well as two machine guns. Having dealt with their objective, they were then able to assist the companies on either flank.

Second Lieutenant Edward Charles KNELL MC, 8th (City of London) Battalion, London Regiment (Post Office Rifles), was killed in action on 9 August 1918, aged 25. His battalion was part of the 58th (2/1st London) Division, which the previous day had attacked astride the River Somme. His MC was gazetted on 7 November 1918 and was awarded for conspicuous gallantry and devotion to duty as the battalion's intelligence officer. Whilst performing that role he carried out several reconnaissance patrols of great value, on one occasion capturing six machine guns and many prisoners. Another time, when his battalion had lost its direction, he went forward to locate the correct position and, although wounded, he managed to get an important message back to his battalion commander. The citation acknowledges that throughout all of these operations he showed marked zeal and great courage.

Rifleman Frank Mason SHARPIN, 2/9th (County of London) Battalion, London Regiment (Queen Victoria's Rifles), attached 15th Battalion, London Regiment (Prince of Wales's Own Civil Service Rifles), was killed in action on 2 September 1918, aged 25. He was educated at the Royal Masonic School, Bushey, in Hertfordshire.

Serjeant John Edward Stanley POOLE DCM, 1/13th (County of London) Battalion, London Regiment (Kensingtons), was killed in action on 1 September 1918. His DCM was won as a lance corporal with the 5th Battalion, London Regiment (London Rifle Brigade), The citation states that during an attack he showed conspicuous gallantry as he tried to get in touch with the battalion on the left. As he did so, he came under very heavy machine-gun fire. He immediately rushed the gun single-handed, killing three of the crew and dispersing the rest. Later he returned with a party of men, capturing the gun and three prisoners; he then brought in wounded men under machine-gun fire. The citation also states that throughout the action he did splendid work and showed great courage and initiative when scouting. The award was gazetted on 5 December 1918. He was 24 years old when he was killed.

Private Cedric Seymour BREWER, 1/14th (County of London) Battalion, London Regiment (London Scottish), was killed in action at Bullecourt on 29 August 1918, aged 28. He was born at Niagara Falls, Ontario, and his parents lived in New York. The CWGC register tells us that he volunteered twice. He initially enlisted in Montreal in May 1915 with the 42nd Battalion, Canadian Infantry (Cameron Highlanders of Canada). He served with that unit until he was wounded and discharged from military service. However, after convalescence in the United States, he re-enlisted in the London Regiment and was posted to the 14th Battalion (London Scottish). Whilst recovering from his wounds in the United States he spent much of his time making public speeches and writing articles on behalf of the Allied cause.

Private John Roderick MACLEOD DCM, 1/14th (County of London) Battalion, London Regiment (London Scottish), was killed in action at Bullecourt on 29 August 1918. His DCM was gazetted on 23 October 1918 and was awarded for conspicuous gallantry and devotion to duty over a period of six months during which he consistently carried out good work as a stretcher-bearer. At all times, but especially during periods of heavy fighting, he rendered prompt assistance to the wounded and undoubtedly saved numerous lives.

Staff Serjeant Harold BACON MSM, GHQ 1st Echelon, Army Service Corps, attached 1/15th (County of London) Battalion, London Regiment (Prince of Wales's Own Civil Service Rifles), was killed in action on 2 September 1918, aged 24. He fell during operations to capture the village of Nurlu. The 140 Brigade was placed in support of the 74th (Yeomanry) Division for this task, but when the division's attack failed, the units of 140 Brigade, including the 15th Battalion, found themselves isolated to the west of Moislaines, near Moislaines Trench. The Germans then launched a strong counter-attack and fierce fighting took place. The position held by the battalion was a precarious one and, although it held on for some time, it was eventually forced to retire.

Rifleman Arthur RICHARDSON, 1/16th (County of London) Battalion, London Regiment (Queen's Westminster Rifles), was killed in action on 28 September 1918, aged 35. He had previously served in Salonika, Egypt and Palestine.

Lieutenant Robert Charles Rudolph Busby BENNETT MC, 20th (County of London) Battalion, London Regiment (Blackheath and Woolwich), was killed in action south-east of Albert on 24 August 1918, aged 31. He had served with the 20th Battalion, London Regiment, since enlisting as a private in 1915 and initially saw action at Festubert and Givenchy. He was wounded at Loos and subsequently spent time in England recovering from his injuries. Whilst doing so, he joined the Inns of Court OTC and from there he was commissioned in the 20th Battalion in December 1916.

His MC was gazetted for conspicuous gallantry and devotion to duty, leading his company with remarkable courage and ability under heavy artillery and machine-gun fire, during which he maintained the spirit of his men under very trying circumstances by his fine personal example. After the war, one of the houses at St Dunstan's College, Catford, was named after him. As a former pupil, a prize bearing his name was inaugurated as a further tribute to his memory, awarded annually for an outstanding contribution to the house. The CWGC register omits 'Busby' from his list of first names and there are also several variations on his first name, some records showing him as 'Robertio' or 'Robertis'.

Second Lieutenant Duncan Francis Charles ADAMSON, 20th (County of London) Battalion, London Regiment (Blackheath and Woolwich), attached 9th Battalion (Queen Victoria's Rifles), was killed in action on 12 September 1918, aged 21. His father, Francis Richard Duncan Adamson, served as a company quartermaster serjeant with the same battalion and died of wounds on 25 May 1915 in hospital near Boulogne, aged 41. He is buried at Boulogne East Cemetery. The family came from Catford in south-east London.

Lance Corporal Arthur Sydney COOPER, 'A' Company, 21st (County of London) Battalion, London Regiment (First Surrey Rifles), was killed in action on 24 August 1918, aged 23. He was an only son; his family lived at Forest Hill in south London. He was a member of Toc H in Poperinghe, Belgium.

Serjeant William PARTRIDGE DCM, 1/23rd (County of London) Battalion, London Regiment, was killed in action on 1 September 1918. His DCM, gazetted on 14 November 1916, was won when he was serving as a lance corporal in the South Staffordshire Regiment. It was awarded for conspicuous gallantry in action during operations when he and others were sent out on patrol to locate gaps in the enemy's wire. In the assault that followed, he was the first man through the gap, rushing to the parapet and bombing the enemy back. Though wounded in the attack, he refused to retire. The citation ends with the acknowledgement that his bravery and devotion to duty set a fine example to all ranks.

Lieutenant Robert Victor TODD DCM, 1/24th (County of London) Battalion, London Regiment (The Queen's), attached 7th (City of London) Battalion, London Regiment, was killed in action on 9 August 1918. His DCM was won as a serjeant with the 5th Battalion, London Regiment (London Rifle Brigade), and the action that led to the award took place on 13 May 1915 after neighbouring troops had evacuated their trenches. On his own initiative and under heavy shell fire without the benefit of any cover, he mounted a machine gun out in the open on the Wieltje road. Later, after hearing that a machine gun team in the front trench had suffered several casualties, he volunteered to take a fresh team across 800–900 yards of ground in order to take over the gun. The fire was so heavy that he reached the post with only two of the men, both of whom were severely wounded during the journey. The citation ends by noting that throughout the day he was conspicuous in his gallantry and service. The award was gazetted on 13 August 1915.

Corporal Charles THEIS DCM, 1/24th (County of London) Battalion, London Regiment (The Queen's), was killed in action south-east of Albert on 22 August 1918, aged 32. His DCM was won as an acting lance corporal during a raid in which he bayoneted, shot and bombed, in rapid succession, nine of the enemy who were putting up resistance. The award was gazetted on 4 March 1918. THEIS came from Bermondsey in south London.

The Hertfordshire Regiment
Second Lieutenant Henry John HENSMAN MC, 1/1st Hertfordshire Regiment, was killed in action on 18 September 1918 during a German counter-attack near Havrincourt. His MC was gazetted on 16 September 1918, two days before his death. It was awarded for conspicuous gallantry and devotion to duty at a time when his brigade was being hard pressed during a retirement. He organized a detachment gathered up from the brigade's HQ and led it forward, delivering a successful counter-attack and causing delay to the enemy. The citation concludes that the success of the attack was entirely due to his energy and determination and goes on to state that throughout operations during this period he was untiring in his efforts, setting a fine example to all.

The Army Cyclist Corps
Lance Corporal Charles William COLLINS MM, IX Corps Cyclist Battalion, Army Cyclist Corps, was killed in action on 5 October 1918, aged 20. He had enlisted in August 1914 and held the *Croix de Guerre* with Palm (France). He previously served with the East Kent Regiment (The Buffs).

The Machine Gun Corps (Infantry)
Serjeant Phillips COLLINGWOOD DCM, 18th Battalion, Machine Gun Corps, died of wounds on 2 September 1918. His DCM was gazetted on 26 January 1918 and was won as an acting corporal. It was awarded for conspicuous gallantry and devotion to duty during an action in which he carried his gun and belt box a distance of 2,500 yards to his objective from where he opened fire. When his gun was put out of action and he was the only surviving member of his team, he fought his way back with a revolver, assisting a wounded NCO to safety on the way. Picking up a rifle, he then joined another infantry unit and later, with

assistance from one of its officers, he got a captured machine gun into action and forced the enemy to retire. Throughout the day he set a magnificent example of courage and devotion to duty.

Private Richard Thomas PARKINSON, 62nd Company, Machine Gun Corps, formerly King's Royal Rifle Corps, was killed in action on 23 October 1918, aged 32. His brother, Joseph, also fell whilst serving with the 7th Battalion, South Lancashire Regiment, on 18 December 1917, aged 25. Joseph won the MM, which was gazetted on 16 August 1917, although this is not acknowledged in *Soldiers Died in the Great War*. He is commemorated on the Thiepval Memorial.

The Tank Corps

Captain Percival Baron BAYLISS, Tank Corps, was killed in action on 3 October 1918, aged 21, and had previously been mentioned in despatches. It was on 3 October when an infantry assault made a six-mile breach in the final part of the Beaurevoir Line with the aid of forty tanks. The village strongholds of Mont-brehain and Beaurevoir were not captured that day, but on 5 October the former was finally taken by Australian troops with the aid of eleven tanks of the 16th Battalion, Tank Corps. Five tanks from the 4th Battalion, Tank Corps, made a triumphal procession into Beaurevoir the same day, but troops from the 25th Division failed to follow up and take the village, even though the tanks made a second sweep through its streets. It was, however, captured and occupied later that evening with very little opposition.

Captain Austen BRADBURY MC, 5th Battalion, Tank Corps, was killed in action on 8 August 1918. His MC was gazetted on 26 July 1918 and was awarded for conspicuous gallantry and devotion to duty whilst in command of nine Lewis guns and their teams. When the infantry was compelled to withdraw following a heavy hostile attack, he remained with his guns and covered the withdrawal, firing on the enemy until his ammunition was exhausted and inflicting many casualties. When he rejoined the infantry, he collected a party of stragglers and held a trench for twenty-four hours until ordered to withdraw.

Second Lieutenant William Robert HEDGES MC, 2nd Battalion, Tank Corps, was killed in action on 18 September 1918, aged 21. His MC was gazetted on 5 February 1919 and was awarded for great gallantry near Villers-Bretonneux on 8 August 1918 when he led his tank forward through fog to within 100 yards of the barrage. The next day, near Vauvillers, his tank became ditched within 500 yards of some enemy machine-gun positions. Instructing two of his crew to keep up harassing fire in front, he and the rest of his men got out and succeeded in unditching their machine under heavy fire and aerial bombardment. No sooner had they re-entered the tank than it burst into flames. Ordering his crew to evacuate it, he was the last man to leave and was badly burnt. Throughout the two days he set a splendid example to his men.

Serjeant Percy Edwin HATTON DCM, 11th Battalion, Tank Corps, formerly King Edward's Horse, was killed in action on 29 September 1918, aged 42. His award was gazetted on 15 November 1918 and won after he had destroyed a number of strongpoints. In doing so, his tank became ditched at such an angle as to make its guns useless. He then evacuated it and formed a strongpoint around it well in advance of the infantry. When the enemy counter-attacked they got as far as his tank, but he and his crew charged them and forced them back. He remained in his strongpoint for twenty-four hours, fighting almost the whole time. He set a fine example to his crew, cheering and encouraging them, even though they were weary and exhausted by their long and arduous fight.

Private John Archibald LIND, 15th Battalion, Tank Corps, formerly King's Royal Rifle Corps, was killed in action on 27 September 1918, aged 20. His brother, Private Albert James Lind, died on 5 October 1916 when serving with the 2nd Queen's Own (Royal West Kent Regiment). He is buried in Baghdad (North Gate) War Cemetery.

Private R. MATHIESON, 5th Battalion, Tank Corps, was killed in action on 3 October 1918, aged 21. Although his parents lived in Surrey, he was studying at the Stevens Institute of Technology in Hoboken, New Jersey, when war broke out. He therefore joined the British Army as a volunteer in New York and went on to serve with the Royal Engineers before joining the Tank Corps.

Appendix

British Aircraft Identification Numbers Displayed as Trophies by Manfred von Richthofen (See Photograph 11 – Arras Memorials)

Aircraft No.	Victory	Name(s)	Unit	Date	Aircraft	Outcome
6618	4th	Second Lieutenant W.C. FENWICK	21 Sqn, RFC	7 Oct 1916	BE12	Commemorated Flying Services Memorial, Arras.
6580	5th	Second Lieutenant J. THOMPSON DCM MiD	19 Sqn, RFC	16 Oct 1916	BE12	Buried Lebucquière Communal Cemetery Extension.
2506	8th	Second Lieutenant I.G. CAMERON	12 Sqn, RFC	9 Nov 1916	BE2c	Buried Achiet-le-Grand Communal Cemetery Extension.
A5446	14th	Lieutenant L.G. D'ARCY and Sub-Lieutenant R.C. WHITESIDE	18 Sqn, RFC	20 Dec 1916	FE2b	Both commemorated Flying Services Memorial, Arras.
N5193	16th	Flight Lieutenant A.S. TODD	8 Sqn, RNAS	4 Jan 1917	Sopwith Pup	Commemorated Flying Services Memorial, Arras.
6997	18th	Lieutenant J.E. MacLENNAN	25 Sqn, RFC	24 Jan 1917	FE2b	PoW and survived.
A1108	23rd	Second Lieutenant H.J. GREEN and Second Lieutenant A.W. REID	43 Sqn, RFC	4 Mar 1917	Sopwith 1½ Strutter	Both buried Cabaret Rouge British Cemetery.
6232	26th	Second Lieutenant J. SMYTH and Second Lieutenant E. BYRNE	2 Sqn, RFC	11 Mar 1917	BE2d	Both buried Cabaret Rouge British Cemetery.
5841	32nd	Lieutenant P.J.G. POWELL and Air Mechanic 1st Class P. BONNER	13 Sqn, RFC	2 Apr 1917	BE2d	Both commemorated Flying Services Memorial, Arras.
A2401	33rd	Second Lieutenant A.P. WARREN and Serjeant R. DUNN	43 Sqn, RFC	2 Apr 1917	Sopwith 1½ Strutter	WARREN, PoW and survived; DUNN, buried Cabaret Rouge British Cemetery.

A6382	34th	Second Lieutenant D.P. McDONALD and Second Lieutenant J.I.M. O'BEIRNE	25 Sqn, RFC	3 Apr 1917	FE2d	McDONALD, PoW and survived; O'BEIRNE, commemorated Flying Services Memorial, Arras.
A3340	35th	Second Lieutenant A.N. LECHLER and Second Lieutenant H.D.K. GEORGE	48 Sqn, RFC	5 Apr 1917	BF2a	LECHLER, PoW and survived; GEORGE, buried Douai Communal Cemetery.
4997	43rd	Second Lieutenant A.H. BATES and Serjeant W.A BARNES MSM	25 Sqn, RFC	13 Apr 1917	FE2b	Both buried Noyelles-Godault Communal Cemetery.

A67?? – The last two numbers are not shown in the photograph. There are two possible candidates:

A6706	30th	Lieutenant R.P. BAKER	19 Sqn, RFC	24 Mar 1917	Spad S.VII	PoW and survived.
A6796	44th	Lieutenant W.O. RUSSELL	60 Sqn, RFC	14 Apr 1917	Nieuport XVII	POW and survived.

59?? – The last two numbers are not shown in the photograph. There are three possible candidates:

5964	11th	Major L.G. HAWKER VC DSO	24 Sqn, RFC	23 Nov 1916	DH2	Commemorated Flying Services Memorial, Arras.
5986	12th	Lieutenant B.P.G. HUNT	32 Sqn, RFC	11 Dec 1916	DH2	POW and survived.

Addenda *Visiting the Fallen: Arras North*

Within a few days of publication, I found myself needing to refer to *Arras North* with regard to Zouave Valley Cemetery. When I turned to the index at the back of the book the cemetery was not there, and neither was Zivy Crater. I was able to draw some comfort from the fact that I had covered both sites within the book itself (pp. 178–185). I was also aware that I had not covered Bailleul-Sir Berthoult Communal Cemetery, but I was prepared to live with that in the knowledge that I could always include it in a short piece on my website (www.visitingthefallen. co.uk).

I do not really understand how it occurred, but I also failed to include Thélus Military Cemetery, this time not just from the index, but from the main body of the text. Not only had I researched it thoroughly, I had prepared several pages on it in my initial draft and had visited the cemetery on at least two occasions. Fortunately, *Arras Memorials* now presents me with an opportunity to apologise and rectify this by way of a short appendix.

Thélus Military Cemetery

The cemetery is situated in open fields to the north-west of Thélus, not far from the Canadian Artillery Memorial that stands at the junction of Rue des Artilleurs Canadiens and the D.49. It is very easy to find. If coming from Bois Carré British Cemetery along the D.49, continue through the village of Thélus and turn right at the main crossroads by the memorial. If coming from the direction of Roclincourt, continue over the A.26 Autoroute, picking up the D.49 as it passes through Thélus. Follow it as if heading towards Neuville-Saint-Vaast, as far as the above-mentioned crossroads, then turn right as above. The cemetery has to be reached via a footpath, but the trees in the cemetery are visible from the road.

Of the 262 identified burials here, fifty-two are noted as being from British rather than Canadian units, though the village of Thélus was captured on the opening day of the Battle of Arras by the Canadian 2nd Division. A main German second line trench ran about a hundred yards west of the cemetery in a north – south direction. After the 24th and 26th battalions, Canadian Infantry, had reached this position on the morning of 9 April 1917, the 25th Battalion passed through it and on to the German third line trenches just east of today's cemetery.

The original battlefield cemetery, which now forms Plot II, was made soon after this part of the ridge had been secured. The site was enlarged after the war when a cemetery containing men from the Canadian 3rd Division was cleared. Today, there are ninety Canadian dead from 9 April 1917, which equates to just under a third of the total identified casualties buried here. The 24th and 25th battalions, Canadian Infantry, are well represented, as are men from the 4th and 2nd Canadian Mounted Rifles, who attacked across the fields to the north of the cemetery. A further seventy-four Canadians who fell the following year can also be found here, along with a number of men from British units, notably the 2nd Middlesex Regiment, part of the 8th Division, and several from Scottish battalions belonging to the 52nd (Lowland) Division.

Although the CWGC records show three 1916 casualties buried here, in each case the year of death is incorrect. Plots I and III, according to the cemetery register, were made between June 1917 and September 1918, whilst Plots IV and V were made after the Armistice. Around thirty graves remain unidentified.

Lieutenant John Angus CAMERON DSO, 31st Battalion, Canadian Infantry, was killed in action on 17 February 1918. His DSO, awarded for conspicuous gallantry and devotion to duty, was gazetted on 18 January 1918. When the attack was held up by a strong enemy bombing post, he rushed forward ahead of his platoon and charged the post single handed, bayoneting one of the enemy and compelling the other twelve to surrender. Although wounded, he remained with his men, setting a fine example of leadership until he was again wounded, this time so seriously that he had to be evacuated. The citation was gazetted on 25 April 1918. (Plot I.A.7)

Serjeant Alexander Lewis ROBINSON MM, 20th Battalion, Canadian Infantry, was killed in action on 26 January 1918, aged 21. He had enlisted in Toronto in November 1914. His death occurred in trenches near Avion when an aerial torpedo, described as a 'fishtail' bomb, landed next to him and Private Ernest Albert FRYERS, aged 19. The men are now buried next to each other. (Plot I.B.2 and 3)

Private Hector Norman MacLEAN, 85th Battalion, Canadian Infantry, was killed in action on 12 January 1918, aged 23 (Plot I.B.7). His two brothers also fell during the war. James MacGlashen MacLean served as a private in the same battalion as his brother and died of wounds on 21 June 1917, aged 25. He is buried at Barlin Communal Cemetery Extension. Lance Corporal Neil Archibald MacLean, 25th Battalion, Canadian Infantry, was killed in action on 16 September 1916, aged 27. He has no known grave and is commemorated on the Vimy Memorial.

The same plot also contains two brothers buried side by side. Private Henri DENIS, aged 22, and Signaller Albert DENIS, aged 27, both served with the 22nd Battalion, Canadian Infantry, and were killed in action on the same day, 24 September 1917. Henri was also serving as a signaller when he died. Both men came from Montreal. (Plot I.E.4 and 5)

Lieutenant Osbert Richmond KNIGHT MC, Royal Flying Corps, was killed in action on 6 April 1917, aged 27 (Plot II.B.2). Buried next to him is Second Lieutenant Ubalde Hormisdas SEGUIN, aged 24 (Plot II.B.3). Both men were killed in action while serving with 16 Squadron, Royal Flying Corps. KNIGHT had originally arrived in England with the First Canadian Contingent, serving with the 5th Battalion, Canadian Infantry, and crossing to France with it in February 1915. For nine months he served as a private, during which time he was wounded at Festubert. In November 1915 he received his commission and joined the Queen's (Royal West Surrey Regiment), but in June the following year he transferred to the Royal Flying Corps. He qualified as a pilot two months later, after which he spent a period as a flying instructor based near Salisbury Plain. However, in February 1917, he returned to France where he was again wounded. On Good Friday he and SEGUIN were reported missing in action after their machine crashed near Thélus behind enemy lines.

His MC was awarded for gallantry and devotion to duty after carrying out work of outstanding quality on several occasions, but especially on 6 March 1917 whilst engaged on artillery observation. On that occasion he was attacked simultaneously by two hostile machines above Neuville-Saint-Vaast. Although slightly wounded in the arm during the initial attack, he managed to drive both machines away, enabling him to continue observing for the batteries below. An hour later he was attacked at close quarters by a hostile scout, but managed to engage with it and drove it away, by which time his own aircraft had been damaged. However, despite the risk of further attacks, he remained airborne and carried on observing. The award was gazetted on 17 April that year, soon after his death.

Lieutenant Robert HENDERSON, 21st Battalion, Canadian Infantry, was killed by enemy shell fire, aged 42, whilst leading his men across no man's land on 9 April 1917. He was originally reported as having been wounded and missing in action, but his body was later recovered from the battlefield once the ridge was secure (Plot II.E.4). He is not the oldest casualty in this cemetery, though he was known affectionately among his fellow officers as 'Old Pop'. Before the war he had been a member of the Hastings Rifles, a militia unit in Canada, though he was Scottish by birth. He sailed for England in May 1916 arriving in Liverpool at the end of the month. He served briefly with the 51st Battalion, Canadian Infantry, but then transferred to the 75th Battalion. He eventually reached the Western Front on 7 October 1916, and was involved in the fighting for, and around, Regina Trench on the Somme.

His last letter home, written the night before the opening of the Battle of Arras, bears testimony not only to his coolness and quiet determination, but also reveals him to be the 'gallant, old gentleman', which was how one of his fellow officers described him. We know from the memoirs of Captain Robert James Manion MC, the battalion's medical officer, that HENDERSON was a well respected figure within his unit. Described as having a friendly smile, but fearless eyes, he was also a man with a sense of humour. On one occasion, during a conversation, Manion recalls him saying: '*You know, Doc, the main objection I have to death is that it's so damned permanent.*' Manion, whose memoir, *A Surgeon in Arms*, was published in 1918, went on to lead the Conservative Party in Canada between 1938 and 1940, but died soon after in 1943.

Lieutenant Francis McKider SHIRRIFF, 25th Battalion, Canadian Infantry, was killed in action on 9 April 1917, aged 23 (Plot II.E.16). Some records show his middle name as McNider. He was mentioned in despatches. His brother, Private Alexander Fraser Shirriff, served with Princess Patricia's Canadian Light Infantry and survived the war, though he was wounded on 4 May 1915, just four days into active service with his battalion. Another man, Private Francis Shirriff, is shown in CWGC records as killed in action on 8 May 1917, though I have been unable to establish whether he was related to the other two. He is commemorated on the Vimy Memorial.

The most senior officer buried here is Major Thomas D'Arcy SNEATH MC, 5th Canadian Mounted Rifles, who was killed in action, aged 29, during a raid carried out by his battalion on 15 March 1918 (Plot III.A.2). The battalion's war diary praises his role during the affair, including the organization and preparations for it. The raid consisted of three parties, including covering parties on either flank, as well as a detachment of stretcher-bearers. He was standing on the enemy's parapet directing operations when he was killed by shell fire. Total casualties for the raid amounted to two officers and twenty other ranks, but the raiders returned with fourteen prisoners and estimated that they had left around twenty of the enemy dead.

SNEATH was one of five men killed during the raid, which took place near Méricourt on the outskirts of Lens. Their funeral, which took place at Thélus on 17 March, was attended by the GOC, Canadian 3rd Division, Major General Lipsett CB CMG, Brigadier General Percy Pollexfen de Blaquière Radcliffe KCB KCMG DSO, Brigadier General James Harold Elmsley CB CMG DSO, 8 Canadian Infantry Brigade, as well as many officers from their own and other battalions of the brigade. SNEATH had previously served with the militia and with the Royal North-West Mounted Police, and was highly regarded for his coolness, courage and leadership qualities. His MC was awarded for his role in operations on 15 September 1916 near Courcelette. He was in charge of his company's attack that day, during which he and his men overcame all opposition, capturing three machine guns and a number of prisoners. The citation also notes that, owing to his courage and skilful handling of the situation, his company incurred minimal losses and succeeded in holding the captured position. The citation was gazetted on 25 November 1916.

The other men killed with him are: Private Wilfred Holman DAVY (Plot III.A.3); Private Joseph MERIK (Plot III.A.4); Private James Arch STEWART (Plot III.B.10) and Corporal Edward MILLAR (Plot III.A.10).

Another man, Lieutenant Kenneth Ian SOMERVILLE, who died of wounds early the following day, is buried next to SNEATH (Plot III.A.1). SOMERVILLE was 22 years old when he died and had enlisted straight from Toronto University in October 1915, aged 19. He went overseas the following April and served on the Western Front from June 1916 until his death. During that time he saw a considerable amount of action, firstly at Ypres, then on the Somme, followed by operations at Vimy Ridge during the Battle of Arras. When the 60th Battalion was disbanded he transferred to the 5th Canadian Mounted Rifles and took part in the fighting at Hill 70 in August 1917, then at Passchendaele. He spent a brief period during the winter of 1917–1918 attached to brigade HQ before returning to his battalion. During the raid on 15 March he was wounded in the face and blinded. As he was being brought back to our lines he was wounded for a second time by an enemy shell. Despite receiving prompt medical attention and undergoing an operation, he succumbed to his injuries the next day.

Although Private Thomas Alfred Jaynes THOMPSON, 8th Canadian Light Trench Mortar Battery, is shown in the CWGC register as having been killed in action on 10 March 1916, the year of death is incorrect and should read 1918. The register notes that he was born in New Zealand and that his parents lived in Victoria, British Columbia, which is where he had originally enlisted in March 1915. Canadian records also show that he had previously served with the 80th Battalion and the 88th Battalion, Canadian Infantry, before transferring to trench mortar duties. He was 20 years old when he died. (Plot III.B.3)

Captain St Clair DUNN, Canadian Army Medical Corps, was killed in action on 18 March 1918, aged 37. He graduated from the University of Manitoba in 1902 with a degree in Pharmacy followed by a degree in Medicine six years later. His practice was in Manitoba. In April 1916 he joined the 108th Battalion, Canadian Infantry. He went to France in September 1916 where he was attached to the 8th Canadian Field Ambulance. (Plot III.C.6)

Lieutenant Roy Warren BIGGAR, 116th Battalion, Canadian Infantry, was killed in action on 3 March 1918, aged 21. After graduating from high school in 1914, he went on to study law between 1914 and 1917, but the war cut short his promising legal career. His father, Sanford Dennis Biggar KC, was a prominent lawyer who served as mayor of Hamilton, Ontario, between 1905 and 1906. (Plot III.E.6)

Regimental Sergeant Major Frank William HINCHCLIFFE MC, 25th Battalion, Canadian Infantry, was killed in action on 9 April 1917. He had reached the enemy's first line of trenches when he was mortally wounded by a gunshot wound to the chest. As he lay dying he is reported to have said to his commanding officer: '*I played the game, Sir, didn't I?*' The citation for his MC, which was gazetted on 18 August 1916, is fairly short and simply notes that it was awarded for conspicuous and consistent gallantry in the presence of the enemy, as well as for good work and setting a fine example. He had enlisted in November 1914 and came from Nova Scotia. (Plot IV.A.10)

Lieutenant Lyell Corson JOHNSTON, 4th Canadian Mounted Rifles, was killed in action on 11 April 1917 when the enemy put down a bombardment on the newly captured positions occupied by his battalion. Seven others were killed with him and twenty other ranks were also wounded by the shelling. That night, in a snow storm, the battalion was relieved after sixty-five hours in action. The battalion's war diary comments on the atrocious conditions after a combination of weather and fighting had made the ground extremely difficult to negotiate. (Plot IV.E.2)

Lieutenant Edwin Austin ABBEY, 4th Canadian Mounted Rifles, was killed by a sniper near Cable House on Vimy Ridge on 10 April 1917 and was originally reported missing. The CWGC register notes that his family lived in Philadelphia. His letters home were published in 1918 under the title *An American Soldier*. His family had lived in Scotland, but subsequently moved to the United States where Edwin trained as a civil engineer. He was working on a project in Canada for the first year of the war, but enlisted in October 1915. In April 1916, while serving as a lance corporal, he was wounded by an enemy shell, but returned to the front in December that year after a period of convalescence in England, gazetted as a lieutenant. He was named after his uncle, an established artist, who had exhibited work at the Royal Academy in London. (Plot IV. E.9)

Lieutenant Charles Milton STEWART, 1st Canadian Mounted Rifles, was one of three officers from his battalion killed in action on Vimy Ridge on 9 April 1917. The total battalion casualties for that day were around 250. (Plot V.B.5)

Another Canadian soldier whose date of death is incorrectly recorded in the CWGC register is Private Hugh GRAHAM, 25th Battalion, Canadian Infantry (Plot V.B.3). The register notes that he was killed on 9 April 1916, whereas the year of death should read 1917. According to the unit's war diary, his battalion was behind the lines near Ypres on 9 April 1916 where the men attended church parade and were later paid. He originally came from Sutherland in the north of Scotland. Similarly, Gunner William TILDESLEY, 280th Siege Battery, Royal Garrison Artillery, was killed in action on 13 May 1918, not 1916. He is buried next to another man from that unit killed in action on the same day. (Plot V.E.5 and 6)

Lieutenant Albert Cecil Cutting BLOOMFIELD, 1st Canadian Mounted Rifles, was killed in action on 8 April 1918, aged 19. He had previously served as Trumpet Sergeant Major with Lord Strathcona's Horse and had joined up in December 1914, well under the age for enlistment. (Plot V.F.5)

Finally, listed below, are the three remaining holders of gallantry awards that are buried here. Private Elie POMART MM, 22nd Battalion, Canadian Infantry, was killed in action on 24 September 1917. He was one of six other ranks killed that day by heavy shelling after his battalion had been required to supply working parties of around 300 men to dig trenches in the Méricourt sector (Plot I.E.7). Private George STYLES MM, 43rd Battalion, Canadian Infantry, was killed in action on 6 March 1918, aged 24. During the early hours of the morning the battalion trenches were subjected to heavy shelling, including gas projectiles, which killed eleven men and wounded eighty others (Plot III.D.7). Sergeant Alexander

BUCHAN MM, 43rd Battalion, Canadian Infantry, was killed in action on 13 April 1917, aged 25. His MM was gazetted just two weeks before his death. His family came from Huntly, in Aberdeenshire, Scotland. He was one of two other ranks killed that day from this battalion (Plot IV.F.5).

Thélus Communal Cemetery
The cemetery is a triangular plot of land lying on the northern outskirts of the village. There are just three war graves here, two of which are unidentified. They are situated in the north-east section of the cemetery. The one casualty whose identity is known is Corporal Charles Edward BOWEN, 5th Divisional Signals, Royal Corps of Signals, who died on 22 May 1940, aged 37. (Grave 3)

Bailleul-Sir-Berthoult Communal Cemetery
The cemetery lies on the eastern side of the village along the D.49 and is situated on the right hand side of the road when heading towards Gavrelle. It contains just nine identified casualties from the Second World War, including one officer, Second Lieutenant Alexander Christopher KING, 4th Green Howards (Yorkshire Regiment), whose date of death is shown as 24 May 1940. The remaining eight casualties all died during that last week in May, some of whom also belonged to his battalion. The others served with the 1st East Yorkshire Regiment, the 4th East Yorkshire Regiment, the 2nd Middlesex Regiment, the 5th Green Howards and the 50th Division Signals. The 50th (Northumbrian) Division was heavily involved in the retreat to Dunkirk.

Bibliography

In addition to the works referred to below, I have made extensive use of battalion war diaries held at the National Archives, Kew, and elsewhere. Similarly, I have referred to numerous Rolls of Honour, mainly those relating to schools, colleges, and universities but also those held by professional and commercial bodies, as well as other organizations throughout Britain and various parts of the world. Another key source of reference was the collection of battalion war diaries that forms part of the Canadian Great War Project.

It will also become evident to the reader that I have consulted just about every divisional and regimental history relevant to this work, whether from my own collection, through the British Library or the reference section of the Imperial War Museum, London. The works listed below do not include those specifically mentioned within the text. The following titles are merely the works to which frequent reference was made; it is by no means exhaustive.

Military Operations in France & Belgium 1914 (2 Volumes); 1915 (2 Volumes); 1916 (2 Volumes); 1917 (3 Volumes); 1918 (5 Volumes) (All Appendices and Maps). Brig. General Sir James E. Edmonds, CB, CMG. IWM & Battery Press, 1995.

Military Operations: Gallipoli (2 Volumes). Brig. General Aspinall-Oglander CB CMG DSO. IWM & Battery Press.

Military Operations: Italy 1915–1919. Brigadier General Sir James Edmonds CB CMG D. Litt and Major General H.R. Davies, CB. IWM & Battery Press.

Military Operations Macedonia (2 Volumes). Captain Cyril Falls. IWM & Battery Press.

Military Operations Mesopotamia (4 Volumes). Brigadier General F.J. Moberly CB CSI DSO. IWM & Battery Press.

Military Operations Egypt & Palestine (3 Volumes). Lieutenant General Sir George Macmunn KCB KCSI DSO & Captain Cyril Falls. IWM & Battery Press.

Military Operations Togoland and the Cameroons. Brigadier General F.J. Moberly CB CSI DSO. IWM & Battery Press.

Military Operations East Africa. Lieutenant Colonel Charles Hordern. IWM & Battery Press.

The Register of the Victoria Cross. Compiled by Nora Buzzell. This England Books, 1988.

VCs of the First World War: Arras & Messines 1917. Gerald Gliddon. Sutton, Stroud, 1998.

VCs of the First World War: The Spring Offensive 1918. Gerald Gliddon. Stroud History, 2013.

VCs of the First World War: The Final Days 1918. Gerald Gliddon. Sutton, Stroud, 2000.

The Distinguished Service Order 1886–1923, Parts I & II. Sir O'Moore Creagh VC GCB GCSI and E.M. Humphris. J.B. Hayward & Son, 1978.

Citations of the Distinguished Conduct Medal in the Great War 1914–1920, Section One; Section Two (Part One); Section Two (Part Two); Section Three; Section Four. Naval & Military Press, 2007.

Recipients of the Distinguished Conduct Medal 1914–1920. R.W. Walker. Military Medals, Birmingham, 1981.

Recipients of the Distinguished Conduct Medal 1855–1909. P.E. Abbott. J.B. Hayward & Son, 1975.

The Distinguished Conduct Medal to the Canadian Expeditionary Force 1914–1920. David K. Riddle and Donald G. Mitchell. Kirkby Marlton Press, 1991.

Recipients of Bars to the Military Cross 1916–1920: To which is added MCs to Warrant Officers 1915–1919. J.V. Webb, 1988.

The Distinguished Flying Cross and how it was won 1918–1995. Nick Carter. Savannah, London, 1998.

The Distinguished Flying Medal: A Record of Courage 1918–1982. I.T.Tavender. J.B. Hayward, 1990.

For Gallantry in the Performance of Military Duty: An Account of the Use of the Army Meritorious Service Medal to Recognize Non-Combatant Gallantry 1916–1928. J.D. Sainsbury. Samson Books, London, 1980.

Soldiers Died in the Great War 1914–1919: Parts 1 to 80. J.B. Hayward & Sons, 1989.

Officers Died in the Great War 1914–1919: Parts I & II (3rd Edition). HMSO. Samson Books Ltd, 1979.

The House of Commons Book of Remembrance 1914–1918. Edward Whitaker Moss Blundell. Elkin Mathews & Marrot, London, 1931.

Officers of the Canadian Expeditionary Force who died Overseas 1914–1919. N.M. Christie. Eugene G. Ursual, 1989 (Canada).

Airmen Died in the Great War 1914–1918: The Roll of Honour of the British and Commonwealth Air Services of the First World War. Chris Hobson. Hayward, 1995.

Royal Flying Corps (Military Wing) Casualties and Honours during the War of 1914–1917. Captain G.L. Campbell RFA and R.H. Blinkhorn. Picton Publishing, 1987.

British Regiments 1914–1918. Brigadier E.A. James OBE TD. Samson Books Ltd, London, 1978.

The Bond of Sacrifice Volumes I & II. Naval & Military Press Ltd, 1992.

De Ruvigny's Roll of Honour: A Biographical Record of Members of His Majesty's Naval and Military Forces Who Fell in the Great War 1914–1918. Marquis de Ruvigny, London Stamp Exchange, 1987.

British Battalions in France & Belgium 1914. Ray Westlake. Leo Cooper, London, 1997.

British Battalions on the Western Front: January to June 1915. Ray Westlake. Leo Cooper, London, 2001.

British Battalions on the Somme. Ray Westlake. Leo Cooper, London, 1994.

British Regiments at Gallipoli. Ray Westlake. Leo Cooper, London, 1996.

Above the Lines. Norman L.R. Franks, Frank W. Bailey and Russell Guest. Grub Street, London, 1993.

Above the War Fronts. Norman L.R. Franks, Russell Guest and Gregory Alegi. Grub Street, 1997.

Royal Flying Corps Communiqués 1915–1916. Edited by Christopher Cole. Tom Donovan, London, 1990.

Royal Flying Corps Communiqués 1917–1918. Edited by Chaz Bowyer. Grub Street, London, 1998.

Royal Air Force Communiqués 1918. Edited by Christopher Cole. Tom Donovan, London, 1990.

Under the Guns of the Red Baron. Norman Franks, Hal Giblin and Nigel McCrery. Grub Street, London, 1995.

The Royal Flying Corps in France: From Mons to the Somme. Ralph Barker. Constable & Co. Ltd, London, 1994.

The Royal Flying Corps in France: From Bloody April 1917 to Final Victory. Ralph Barker. Constable & Co. Ltd, London, 1995.

The Underground War – Vimy Ridge to Arras. Phillip Robinson and Nigel Cave. Pen & Sword Military, Barnsley, 2011.

The Student Soldiers. John McConachie. Moravian Press, Elgin, 1995.

The Sword of the North: Highland Memories of the Great War. Dugald Macechern. R. Carruthers & Sons, Inverness, 1993.

A Medico's Luck in the Great War: Royal Army Medical Corps Work with the 51st (Highland) Division. David Rorie. Milne & Hutchinson, 1929.

Warriors of the King: Prairie Indians in World War I. Lloyd James Dempsey. Association of Canadian Archivists, 1999.

Native Soldiers – Foreign Battlefields. Janice Summerby. Veterans Affairs Canada, Communications Division, 1993.

With the Royal Army Medical Corps at the Front. Evelyn Charles Vivian, 1914.

A Stretcher Bearer's Diary: Three Years in France with the 21st Division. J.H. Newton. A.H. Stockwell, London, 1932.

A Lack of Offensive Spirit? – The 46th (North Midland) Division at Gommecourt, 1st July 1916. Alan MacDonald. Iona Books, 2008.

Orange, Green & Khaki: The Story of Irish Regiments in the Great War 1914–1918. Tom Johnstone. Gill & Macmillan & Co., Dublin, 1992.

'Come On, Highlanders': Glasgow Territorials in the Great War. Alec Weir. Sutton Publishing Limited, Stroud, 2005.

The Letters of Agar Adamson. Edited N.M. Christie. CEF Books (Canada), 1997.

In Good Company: The First World War Letters & Diaries of the Hon. William Fraser, Gordon Highlanders. Edited by David Fraser. Michael Russell (Publishing) Ltd, Salisbury, 1990.

Shot at Dawn. Julian Putkowski & Julian Sykes. Wharncliffe Publishing Ltd, Barnsley, 1989.

With Rifle & Pick. Janet Dixon and John Dixon. Cwm Publications, Cardiff, 1991.

Prelude to Victory. Brigadier General E.L. Spears CB CBE MC. Jonathan Cape, London, 1939.

Surrender Be Damned: A History of the 1/1st Battalion, The Monmouthshire Regiment, 1914–1918. Les Hughes & John Dixon. Cwm Press, Caerphilly, 1995.

Brigadier General R.B. Bradford VC MC and his Brothers. Privately Printed, Eden Fisher & Co. Ltd, London. Copy signed & dated 1928.

Campaign in South-West Africa 1914–1915. Brigadier General J.J. Collyer. Pretoria, Government Print, 1937.

University of London OTC: Roll of Honour 1914–1919. Military Education Committee, University of London, 1921.

Etonians Who Fought in the Great War 1914–1919. (No Author or Publisher Shown)

Record of Service of Solicitors & Articled Clerks in HM Forces 1914–1918. Spottiswoode, Ballantyne & Co. Ltd, 1920.

Tanks in the Great War. J.F.C. Fuller DSO. John Murray, London, 1920.

The New Zealand Division 1916–1919 – Colonel H. Stewart CMG DSO MC. Whitcombe & Tombs Ltd, 1921.

The South African Forces in France. John Buchan. IWM & Battery Press, 1992.

The A.I.F. in France Volumes III, IV, V, VI. C.E.W. Bean. University of Queensland Press, 1982–1983.

Tyneside Scottish: (20th, 21st, 22nd & 23rd (Service) Battalions, Northumberland Fusiliers). Graham Stewart and John Sheen. Leo Cooper, London, 1999.

Tyneside Irish: (24th, 25th, 26th & 27th (Service) Battalions, Northumberland Fusiliers). John Sheen. Pen & Sword, Barnsley, 1998.

The First Birmingham Battalion in the Great War 1914–1919: Being a History of the 14th (Service) Battalion of the Royal Warwickshire Regiment. J.E.B. Fairclough. Cornish Brothers Ltd, Birmingham, 1933.

Birmingham Pals: (The 14th, 15th & 16th (Service) Battalions, Royal Warwickshire Regiment). Terry Carter. Pen & Sword, Barnsley, 1997.

Liverpool Pals: (The 17th, 18th, 19th & 20th (Service) Battalions, King's Liverpool Regiment). Graham Maddocks. Leo Cooper, London, 1991.

Bradford Pals: (The 16th (Service) Battalion, West Yorkshire Regiment). Ralph N. Hudson. Bradford Libraries, 2000.

Leeds Pals: (The 15th (Service) Battalion, West Yorkshire Regiment). Laurie Milner. Pen & Sword Books, Barnsley, 1998.

Hull Pals: (The 10th, 11th 12th & 13th (Service) Battalions, East Yorkshire Regiment). David Bilton. Leo Cooper, Barnsley, 2002.

The Tigers: (The 6th, 7th, 8th & 9th (Service) Battalions, Leicestershire Regiment). Matthew Richardson. Leo Cooper, London, 2000.

Salford Pals: (The 15th, 16th, 19th & 20th (Service) Battalions, Lancashire Fusiliers). Michael Stedman. Leo Cooper, London, 1993.

Accrington Pals: 11th (Service) Battalion, East Lancashire Regiment. William Turner. Leo Cooper, London, 1998.

The Blast of War: A History of Nottingham's Bantams: The 15th (Service) Battalion, Sherwood Foresters, 1915–1919. Maurice Bacon and David E. Langley. Sherwood Press, Nottingham, 1986.

Kitchener's Pioneers: The 5th (Service) Battalion, Northamptonshire Regiment. Geoffrey Moore, 1978.

On the Somme: The Kitchener Battalions of the Royal Berkshire Regiment 1916. Colin Fox & Others. University of Reading, 1996.

Arras To Cambrai: The Kitchener Battalions of the Royal Berkshire Regiment 1917. Colin Fox & Others. University of Reading, 1997.

Their Duty Done: The Kitchener Battalions of the Royal Berkshire Regiment. Colin Fox & Others. University of Reading, 1998.

Manchester Pals: The 16th, 17th, 18th, 19th, 20th, 21st, 22nd & 23rd (Service) Battalions, Manchester Regiment). Michael Stedman. Leo Cooper, Barnsley, 2004.

Cotton Town Comrades: The Story of the Oldham Pals Battalion. K.W. Mitchinson and I. McInnes. Bayonet Publications, 1993.

Sheffield City Battalion: (The 12th York & Lancaster Regiment). Ralph Gibson and Paul Oldfield. Barnsley Chronicle, 1988.

Barnsley Pals: (The 13th & 14th York & Lancaster Regiment). Jon Cooksey. Leo Cooper, London, 1996.

Campaign Reminiscences: The 6th Seaforth Highlanders. R.T. Peel and Captain A.H. Macdonald. W.R. Walker, Elgin, 1923.

List of Officers and Other Ranks of the Rifle Brigade Awarded Decorations, or Mentioned in Despatches for Services during the Great War (Published as Appendix to Above Work). Lieutenant Colonel T.R. Eastwood and Major H.G. Parkyn. The Rifle Brigade Club.

List of Officers and Other Ranks of the Rifle Brigade Awarded Decorations, or Mentioned in Despatches for Services during the Great War (Published as Appendix to Above Work). Lieutenant Colonel T.R. Eastwood and Major H.G. Parkyn. The Rifle Brigade Club.

The Bomber Command Diaries 1939–1945. Martin Middlebrook and Chris Everitt. Viking, Harmondsworth, 1985.

The History of the Northamptonshire Regiment 1934–1948. Brigadier General W.J. Jervois. Printed for the Regimental History Committee, 1953.

Index to Regiments –
Arras Memorial

Index to Regiments – Vis-en-Artois Memorial